PRAISE FOR
RICH CHRISTIANS IN AN AGE OF HUNGER

Rich Christians in an Age of Hunger brought the world a challenging book that has inspired many of us to do more than talk about loving our neighbor. Ron Sider is a rare package of depth and meekness who minces no words regarding the truth about God's call to believers: live at the need level rather than the greed level.

— GLENN KAISER

JPUSA, Cornerstone Festival, Rez Band

America is about to have a great debate on the nature of democratic capitalism. Christians will find no better companion than this revised edition of *Rich Christians in an Age of Hunger.*

— BILL MOYERS

Public Affairs Television

This was one of the first books I bought as a new Christian and it has impacted me deeply. I am delighted to see this new release, and applaud the author once again for delivering such a potent message. We as Christians need to balance our moral stand as believers with a social commitment to aid those in need. This book is a voice for our time.

— T. DAVIS BUNN

Bestselling Author

Rich Christians in an Age of Hunger came to me at a time when my approach to spirituality was becoming hyper-intellectualized, arid, and academic. *Rich Christians* was where dirty-fingernails theology and the profound simplicity of Love God / Love neighbor met in a harmony that was both concrete and connected to the earth . . . nay, connected to the things of God's kingdom! Thank you, Dr. Sider!

— BILL MALLONEE

"Vigilantes of Love"

Ron Sider invites us to act on the responsibility and possibility of expanding the circles of productivity and exchange that produce prosperity. We should accept the invitation.

— RICHARD JOHN NEUHAUS

Editor, *First Things*

Probably no book has had a greater impact on more Christians about the Bible's unequivocal demand of justice for poor people.

— JIM WALLIS
Covener, Call to Renewal
Editor-in-Chief, *Sojourners*

We must look beyond ourselves to the world God so loves, and especially to the poor and marginalized. Ron Sider has been a strong influence on my thinking in this direction, and this new *Rich Christians* edition will, I hope, extend and deepen his good influence.

— BRIAN MCCLAREN
Author of *A New Kind of Christian*

Ron Sider is one of the most penetrating and relevant Christian thinkers of our age.

— MILLARD FULLER
Founder, Habitat for Humanity
International

The publication in 1977 of *Rich Christians in an Age of Hunger* was something of a sensation. His critics need to read him again, and all of us need to face his challenge.

— REV. DR. JOHN R. W. STOTT

Rich Christians

_in an_

AGE OF HUNGER

OTHER BOOKS BY RONALD J. SIDER

Andreas Bodenstein Von Karlstadt

Karlstadt's Battle with Luther: Documents
in a Liberal-Radical Debate (Ed.)

Christ and Violence

Completely Pro-Life

Good News and Good Works: A Theology for the Whole Gospel

Cup of Water, Bread of Life: Inspiring Stories
About Overcoming Lopsided Christianity

Living Like Jesus: Eleven Essentials for Growing a Genuine Faith

Just Generosity: A New Vision for Overcoming Poverty in America

Churches That Make a Difference: Reaching Your
Community with Good News and Good Works

Doing Evangelism Jesus' Way: How Christians
Demonstrate the Good News

Toward an Evangelical Public Policy: Political
Strategies for the Health of the Nations (Ed.)

The Scandal of the Evangelical Conscience: Why Are
Christians Living Just Like the Rest of the World?

Nonviolent Action: What Christian Ethics Demands
But Most Christians Have Never Really Tried

Fixing the Moral Deficit: A Balanced Way to Balance the Budget

The Early Church on Killing: A Comprehensive Sourcebook
on War, Abortion, and Capital Punishment

Just Politics: A Guide for Christian Engagement

Rich
Christians
in an
AGE OF
HUNGER

Moving From Affluence to Generosity

RONALD J. SIDER

Sixth Edition

W PUBLISHING GROUP

AN IMPRINT OF THOMAS NELSON

To Ted, Michael, and Sonya

CONTENTS

PREFACE TO THE SIXTH EDITION

The world has changed, and so have I. In the almost forty years since I wrote *Rich Christians in an Age of Hunger*, amazing changes have occurred in the world.

Communism has collapsed. Expanding market economies, increasing global trade, and new technologies have dramatically reduced poverty. As we moved into the twenty-first century, it was clear that "democratic capitalism" won the major economic/political debate of the last one hundred years. Communism's state ownership and central planning had proved not to work; they were inefficient and totalitarian. Market economies, on the other hand, have produced enormous wealth. And not only in Western nations. Most countries have adopted market economies. The result has been a dramatic drop in poverty. Between 1990 and 2014, the number of people living below the international poverty level ($1.25 per day per person) plunged by more than 50 percent!

My thinking has also changed. I've learned more about economics. And I have continued to study the Scriptures.

When the choice is communism or democratic capitalism, I support democratic government and market economies. That does not mean, however, that the Bible prescribes either democracy or markets. Nor does it mean ignoring the problems and injustices of today's market-oriented economies.

The collapse of communism is not the only dramatic change that has occurred since I originally wrote this book. Tragically, many of the other changes are bad rather than good. The dread disease of AIDS has exploded in poor nations. Islamic terrorists have changed world politics. Environmental decay—especially in the developing world—has grown dangerously. Expanding economies have dramatically increased the production of greenhouse gases and the result is a dangerous global warming that threatens the future. Materialism and consumerism, the collapse of biblical ethical standards, and the breakdown of the family have increased at a galloping pace. Frequent headlines about corporate mergers underline the fact that global economic power has become much more centralized. Anyone who honestly evaluates the way today's market economies function cannot ignore these growing dangers. Nor dare we forget that in most nations, there is a large minority (sometimes a majority) who have virtually no capital and, therefore, almost no ability to enjoy the benefits of today's market economies. I believe that a market-oriented economy is clearly better than any alternative framework we now know. I also believe that private property is so good that everybody ought to have some. Precisely if we think that market economies offer a good framework, we should be eager to correct their weaknesses.

My biblical analysis has also changed at one substantial point. I have thought a lot about what the Bible has to say concerning equality and equity. I never thought that biblical revelation demanded absolute equality of income and wealth. But I used to be more concerned than I am today with the proportion of income and wealth that different groups possess.

I feel absolutely confident, however, that the biblical understanding of "economic equality," or equity, demands at least this: *God wants every person and family to have equality of economic opportunity, at least to the point of having access to the resources necessary (land, money, education), so that by working responsibly they can earn a decent living and participate as dignified members of their community.* This kind of equality of economic opportunity is, as chapter 4 argues, a clear, powerful biblical demand—which, if implemented in our world, would help correct terrible evil that still persists.

We still live with more than a billion desperately poor neighbors. Another 1.2 billion struggle in near poverty with very little hope for a decent life. Nor has God's special concern for the poor changed. Hundreds of biblical texts tell us that God still measures our societies by what we do to the poorest. Jesus' words still say to those with abundance that if they do not feed the hungry and clothe the naked, they go to hell.

What has changed is our knowledge of how to empower the poor. Many Asian countries have successfully combined substantial government programs designed to lift the poorest within a basic market framework. The result? Hundreds of millions have escaped poverty.

One of the success stories of the last forty years is the explosion of micro-loans. Millions of desperately poor people have received tiny loans of $75, $200, or $500 so they could start small businesses and thus provide a better living for their families.

I'll never forget Mrs. Kumar's joyous, confident smile. When I visited her, she lived in a tiny one-room house in a poor village in South India near Bangalore. The Bridge Foundation (a Christian micro-loan organization founded by Indian evangelical leaders Vinay and Colleen Samuel) had given her and her husband, Vijay, a small loan of $219. They had purchased a small, inexpensive sound system and a bicycle. With this equipment, the Kumars were able to provide the sound for weddings, funerals, and other celebrations in poor villages of several surrounding communities. By the time I visited, they owned three sound systems and had hired a couple of employees.

Mrs. Kumar proudly showed me the new lighting equipment and the bicycle loaded down with their third sound system. Their little one-room cement house with a thatched roof had no indoor plumbing, but I could see many improvements. Family income had grown significantly. Most important, the Kumars had new dignity, hope, and confidence.

Most of the poor want to earn their own way. They have enormous social capital: intact families, a desire to work, pride, and integrity. But they need some help. That is exactly what more and more Christian organizations are doing.

By themselves, of course, Christian development agencies cannot end all poverty. As chapter 7 demonstrates, some people are poor because of misguided personal choices and others because of unfair systems. Coming to a living, personal faith in Christ reduces poverty. So does wise political activity that creates more just legal and economic structures.

We have the money. And we know what to do. Are we generous enough to do it? In 1960, the 20 percent of the world's people living in the richest nations had thirty times more than the poorest 20 percent. By 2005, the richest had fifty times as much. But the percentage of their giving had dropped dramatically.

It is tragic that so many rich Christians are missing Jesus' path to joy and self-fulfillment. We are neglecting the fact that genuine joy and enduring happiness flow from practicing Jesus' paradoxical teaching that it is better to give than to receive.

Millions of North Americans, Western Europeans, and increasingly rich people everywhere are in despair as they seek in vain for happiness through ever-greater material abundance. The idolatrous materialism of the economic rat race creates alcoholics, ruined marriages, and heart attacks.

Jesus, on the other hand, offers true joy—not through getting, but through giving. We cannot gain happiness by seeking it directly. It comes as a by-product as we give ourselves to others. I can personally witness to this truth. Many suppose that the lifestyle I have written about and sought to live is hard and painful. In truth, my life overflows with happiness. This book is truly a guide to joy and self-fulfillment.

Millions of people die unnecessarily every year because rich folk like you and me have ignored the Bible's clear teaching that God measures the integrity of our faith by how we respond to the poor. So I report the tragic facts of hunger and starvation (Part One), explain the biblical teaching about God's special compassion for the poor and weak (Part Two), and show what causes poverty (Part Three).

But this book also shares exciting news (Part Four) about how you and I can assist the poor to help themselves—and in the process, also help ourselves. Joy and happiness do come from giving. By spending less on ourselves, we can transform the lives of neighbors who will die unless we care.

We live in an age of both enormous wealth and great poverty. We know what to do to empower the poor. Will we do it? Will rich Christians (which describes virtually all readers of this book) also be generous? Will we share the capital that the poor need to earn a decent living? Rich, generous Christians could, in the next twenty years, dramatically reduce poverty in our world if we would become partners with God's poor. This sixth edition invites us to that exhilarating, transforming journey.

ACKNOWLEDGMENTS

Note to the first edition:

I have benefited from the critical comments of many good friends who read parts of the first draft: Judy and John F. Alexander, Arthur Simon, Edgar Stoesz, Richard Taylor, Carol and Merold Westphal. Since I am not an economist, I particularly appreciate the extensive help of two friends who are: Carl Gambs and John Mason. I stubbornly rejected their advice on occasion. Hence they cannot be faulted for the results. But their help and friendship are deeply appreciated.

To Debbie Reumann and Titus Peachey I give special thanks for long hours spent at the typewriter. To Mrs. Anne Allen, who typed some of the early chapters, I want to express deep appreciation for her superb secretarial and administrative assistance over several years.

Finally, I want to thank *HIS* magazine for publishing an early version of chapter 7, and Ashland Theological Seminary and Emmanuel School of Religion for the opportunity to present parts of this material as public lectures.

Perhaps all books must be lived before they are written. That is certainly true of books like this one. I make no claim to be living out the full implications of this book. But I have begun the pilgrimage. The most important reason I am even a little way down the path is my wife, Arbutus Lichti Sider. Always enthusiastic about a simpler living standard, spontaneously generous, and eager to experiment, she has slowly tugged me along. For her critical reading of the manuscript, for our life together—without which this book would never have been possible—and for her love, I express my deepest appreciation.

Note to the second edition:

In revising chapters 1, 2, 6, and 9, I benefited greatly from the extensive assistance of Roland Hoksbergen, now assistant professor of economics at Calvin College. His help and patience are deeply appreciated. In addition, a number of friends who are economists provided critical reaction either to the first edition or to a preliminary draft of the second: Robert Chase, Carl Gambs, Donald Hay, Carl Kreider, John Mason, George Monsma, Henry Rempel, and John P. Tiemstra. None of them, I am sure, will be fully satisfied with all my final decisions. Their much appreciated counsel, however, has significantly improved the text.

Helping on this revised edition, Robin Songer was her usual efficient, precise self as she worked with my short deadlines.

Note to the third edition:

I am grateful to many people who provided critical suggestions and data for the third edition: John Mason, Nancy Alexander, Stephen L. S. Smith, Tom Sine, Calvin DeWitt, Roland Hoksbergen, Linwood Geiger, Joe Sheldon, Michael Trueblood, Larry Hollar, Bill Ray, Don Reeves, Gil Heebner, Grant Power, and Philip Shea helped with research. My colleague, Tom McDaniel, provided invaluable help to enable different computers to communicate. Ketly Pierre worked overtime at the typewriter. My administrative secretary, Naomi Miller, helped with the manuscript in addition to providing her usual superb support as a partner in my diverse ministries. And Mary Beekley-Peacock did a fantastic job supervising the total revision, doing much of the necessary updating and retyping several chapters. To all these friends, I say thanks.

Note to the fourth edition:

Special thanks to a number of people who contributed to the twentieth-anniversary edition. Ron Sage provided superb help as my primary research assistant, and economists Linwood Geiger and George Monsma devoted many hours of precious time to offer detailed suggestions. David Moberg at W Publishing Group demonstrated unusual commitment to this project as he made time in his hectic schedule to oversee the numerous, critical aspects of publishing a book. Julie Link at Blue Water Ink became a friend as she carefully edited the manuscript. Many friends offered important suggestions and/or found time for a critical reading of parts of the manuscript: Vinay Samuel, Chris Sugden, David Beckman, Marc Cohen, Dick Hoehn, Don Reeves, Andrew Steer, Tim Dearborn, Jim Wallis, Norman Ewert, Rob Van Drimmelen, Arthur Simon, Robert Hadley, Wesley Balda, Janis Balda, Barbara Bouder, Patricia Boyland, Carol Cool, Catherine Kroeger, Arthur Scotchmer, Sheila Scotchmer, Richard Wright, and Daniel Schwartz. Graduate assistants David Kuguru and Chris and Joan Hoppe-Spink tracked down materials, and many of my colleagues at Evangelicals for Social Action—Cliff Benzel, Fred Clark, Dwight Ozard, Heidi Rolland-Unruh, Terry Cooper, Keith Pavlischek, Fred Krueger, and Stan LeQuire—offered valued insight. My gifted administrative assistant, Naomi Miller, handled numerous, diverse tasks with her usual grace and skill. To our three children, who continue to make us proud, I express special appreciation for carrying the burdens that go with having this kind of book dedicated to them. To my wife, Arbutus, who has lived this book with me for thirty-six years of marriage, I feel a depth of gratitude that words can hardly begin to communicate.

Note to the fifth edition:

Robin Weinstein oversaw detailed revisions on chapters 1 and 2, and Helen Orombi did the same on chapters 8 and 11. Jim Ball revised the sections on the environment. Chris Klopp and Jokotáde Agunloye provided important help in the later stages. Lin Geiger and George Monsma (my longtime friends and advisers on economics for several revisions of this book) and a new friend, Sabina Alkire, all made very helpful suggestions for this edition. Several people at Bread for the World provided important help. As usual, Naomi Miller, my administrative assistant for more than twenty-one years, not only helped with these revisions but also kept the rest of my professional life functioning smoothly. To all, I say thanks without blaming them for remaining mistakes.

Note to the sixth edition:

Again, I am indebted to many people for their help and advice. Three economists—Roland Hoksbergen, Van Weigel, and Bruce Wydick—spent a great deal of time reviewing chapters 8 and 11, providing invaluable help and answering further queries. Derek Schwabe at Bread for the World replied to repeated questions about Bread for the World's data and recommendations. Many others graciously responded to my questions: Jim Ball, JoAnn Flett, Paul Niehaus, Stephen Smith, and Adam Taylor. My gifted graduate assistant David Fuller did a great deal of research and typed several drafts of the manuscript. Palmer Seminary at Eastern University, where I have taught for thirty-seven years, continues to provide a supportive context for my work. Finally, celebrating fifty-three years of marriage to Arbutus Lichti Sider as I complete this sixth edition reminds me of what an incredible gift she has been to me. Her wisdom, support, and love have been God's best gift to me after his son. To all these, I extend my thanks while accepting full responsibility for continuing weaknesses and mistakes.

Poor Lazarus
and Rich Christians

We usually compare our budgets and lifestyles with those of our affluent neighbors. Part One invites you to compare yourself with the poorest one-third of the world's people.

Poor Lazarus
and Rich Christians

1

A BILLION HUNGRY NEIGHBORS

Sometimes I think, "If I die, I won't have to see my children
suffering as they are." Sometimes I even think of killing
myself. So often I see them crying, hungry; and there I am,
without a cent to buy them some bread. I think, "My God, I
can't face it! I'll end my life. I don't want to look anymore!"[1]

—IRACEMA DA SILVA
RESIDENT OF A SLUM IN BRAZIL

Can an overfed, comfortably clothed, and luxuriously housed persons understand poverty? Can we truly feel what it is like to be a nine-year-old boy playing outside a village school he cannot attend because his father is unable to afford the books? (Which, incidentally, would cost less than my wife and I spent on entertainment one evening during the writing of this book.) Can we comprehend what it means for poverty-stricken parents to watch with helpless grief as their baby daughter dies of a common childhood disease because they lack access to elementary health services? Can we grasp the awful truth that eighteen thousand children die every day, most of hunger and preventable diseases?[2]

To help us imagine what poverty means, a prominent economist itemized the "luxuries" we would have to abandon if we were to adopt the lifestyle of our 1.2 billion neighbors who live in desperate poverty trying to survive on $1.25 per day:

3

We begin by invading the house of our imaginary American family to strip it of its furniture. Everything goes: beds, chairs, tables, television set, lamps. We will leave the family with a few old blankets, a kitchen table, a wooden chair. Along with the bureaus go the clothes. Each member of the family may keep in his "wardrobe" his oldest suit or dress, a shirt or blouse. We will permit a pair of shoes for the head of the family, but none for the wife or children.

We move to the kitchen. The appliances have already been taken out, so we turn to the cupboards . . . The box of matches may stay, a small bag of flour, some sugar, and salt. A few moldy potatoes, already in the garbage can, must be hastily rescued, for they will provide much of tonight's meal. We will leave a handful of onions, and a dish of dried beans. All the rest we take away: the meat, the fresh vegetables, the canned goods, the crackers, the candy.

Now we have stripped the house: the bathroom has been dismantled, the running water shut off, the electric wires taken out. Next we take away the house. The family can move to the toolshed . . .

Communications must go next. No more newspapers, magazines, books—not that they are missed, since we must take away our family's literacy as well. Instead, in our shantytown we will allow one radio . . .

Now government services must go. No more postman, no more firemen. There is a school, but it is three miles away and consists of two classrooms . . . There are, of course, no hospitals or doctors nearby. The nearest clinic is ten miles away and is tended by a midwife. It can be reached by bicycle, provided that the family has a bicycle, which is unlikely . . .

Finally, money. We will allow our family a cash hoard of $5.00. This will prevent our breadwinner from experiencing the tragedy of an Iranian peasant who went blind because he could not raise the $3.94, which he mistakenly thought he needed to receive admission to a hospital where he could have been cured.[3]

It is difficult to obtain precise statistics, but the World Bank estimates that 1.2 billion people live in that kind of grinding poverty—trying to survive on $1.25 a day.[4] In addition to these 1.2 billion who live in almost absolute poverty, another 1.2 billion are very poor, living on two dollars or less a day. That means almost one-third of the world's people (2.4 billion) struggle to exist on two dollars a day or less.[5]

Hunger and starvation stalk our world. Famine and disease are alive and well on planet Earth. Those suffering in grinding poverty are at greatest risk. Eighteen thousand children under five die every day, most from hunger and preventable diseases. A third of those deaths result from pneumonia, diarrhea, and malaria—which are easily treated or prevented.[6] In 2010–2012, 870 million people were chronically undernourished.[7]

In a book published in 2013, prominent development economists Abhijit V. Banerjee and Esther Duflo help us understand the dire situation of more than 800 million of the world's poorest. When we take into account the differing costs in various countries, their situation is like trying to live in Miami, Florida on 99 American cents per day![8]

The news, however, is not all bad. In fact, there is very good news. More people escaped poverty in the first decade of the twenty-first century than in any decade in human history! Globally, the percentage of people living below the international poverty level ($1.25 per person per day) has plunged by more than 50 percent since 1990![9] (see chart 1 on page 6)

In 2010, the millennium development goal to cut in half the percentage of people living in poverty was met, five years ahead of schedule.[10] The Global Hunger Index (GHI) dropped 34 percent from 1990 to 2013. The GHI measures hunger through three factors: undernourishment, underweight children, and child mortality. The Human Development Index (HDI) is another important measure of poverty. The HDI is a composite index that takes into account life expectancy, educational attainment, and command over resources for a decent living—to measure progress in reducing poverty and improving well-being. The number of countries in the bottom quarter of the HDI dropped from 33 in 1990 to 15 in 2012.[11] For the world as a whole, the global average HDI improved 41 percent between 1970 and 2010.[12]

The main reason for this improvement has been the dramatic growth of some Global South economies, where many of the poor live. Between 1990 and 2008, China lifted an astonishing "510 million people

Chart 1

Proportion of people living on less than $1.25 a day, 1990 and 2010 (Percentage)

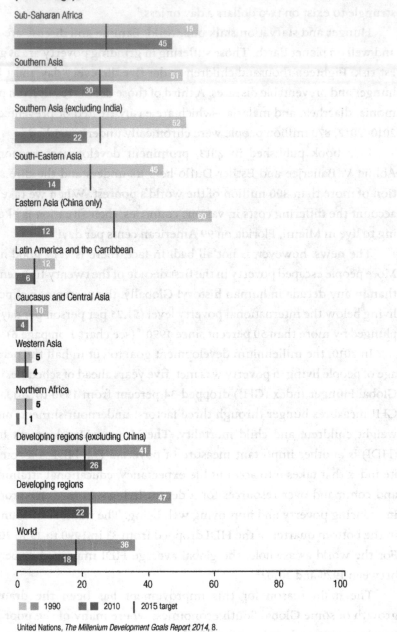

Sub-Saharan Africa
15
45

Southern Asia
51
30

Southern Asia (excluding India)
52
22

South-Eastern Asia
45
14

Eastern Asia (China only)
60
12

Latin America and the Carribbean
12
6

Caucasus and Central Asia
10
4

Western Asia
5
4

Northern Africa
5
1

Developing regions (excluding China)
41
26

Developing regions
47
22

World
36
18

0   20   40   60   80   100

■ 1990   ■ 2010 | 2015 target

United Nations, *The Millenium Development Goals Report 2014*, 8.

6

out of poverty."[13] "China's per capita income grew an astounding 1,200 percent" between 1970 and 2010.[14] India's poor decreased from half the population in 1990 to less than one-third in 2012. And in Brazil, the percentage of those living on $1.25 a day went from 17 percent to just 6 percent.[15]

The Global South in general has seen tremendous and unprecedented economic growth. In 1990, the South produced only about a third of global economic output, but in 2013 the South accounted for half.[16] Trade has increased among countries of the South, tripling in the period from 1980 to 2011.[17]

Between 1968 and 2012, Indonesia's economy grew at a rate of 6.2 percent per year.[18]

Unfortunately, the picture is not nearly so bright for many. Countries in South Asia reduced those living in extreme poverty from 61 percent in 1981 to 36 percent in 2008, but over half a billion people are still mired in extreme poverty.[19] In spite of major growth in total GDP in India, there has been no drop in the number of hungry people ("those who regularly lack enough calories for an active, healthy life"[20]) in India over the last decade. There were 214 million in 2001 and 217 million in 2011.[21]

In sub-Saharan Africa, nearly 70 percent of the population lived on $2 a day or less in the years 2007–2010. Both the number and percentage of hungry people have increased. In 1970, the figure was 103 million (38 percent of the region's population). By 1980, the number had grown to 125.4 million. By 2001, it was 198.4 million.[22] A decade later, there were 234 million hungry people in sub-Saharan Africa.[23]

In dozens of poor nations, a child has a smaller chance of living to age 5 than an American child has of living to age 65. And in a number of poor nations, one out of every 25 women die from complications in pregnancy and childbirth.[24] In fact, in sub-Saharan Africa, women in childbirth have a one-in-thirty chance of dying. In the developed world, the figure is one in 5600![25]

We cannot know the exact number of people lacking minimally adequate diets, clothing, and shelter. And this number varies depending on harvests, war, and natural disasters. Even though we have seen significant improvement, the overall picture is still tragic. More than a billion desperate neighbors live in wrenching poverty—and another 1.2 billion struggle to make ends meet on $2 a day.

New Economic Divisions in the World

Almost all of the 1.2 billion desperately poor people live in what used to be called the Third World. For many years, all countries that were not part of the developed world (whether capitalist or communist) were lumped together as "Third World" nations. But changes in the last forty years have necessitated a new division. The World Bank divides countries into four categories: low income, lower-middle income, upper-middle income, and high income. According to the World Bank, "Economies are divided according to 2012 GNI [Gross National Income] per capita, calculated using the World Bank Atlas method. The four groups are: low income ($1,035 or less); lower middle income ($1,036–$4,085); upper middle income ($4,086–$12,615); and high income ($12,616 or more)."[26]

Low-income countries (847 million people).[27] Nepal, Cambodia, Bangladesh, North Korea, Afghanistan, and many African countries, including Ethiopia, Burundi, Chad, Tanzania, Rwanda, and Malawi belong to the low-income countries.[28] The per capita GNI in low-income countries is $1,035 or less. According to the World Bank's World Development Indicators, in 2012 the infant mortality rate in low-income countries was 56 per 1,000 live births, compared to 6 per 1,000 live births in the United States.[29]

According to the World Development Indicators database, in 2011 39 percent of the people in low-income countries over the age of fifteen could not read. But illiteracy in some low-income countries was much worse. In Guinea, 75 percent were illiterate.[30]

Hundreds of millions of people in low-income countries still live—unnecessarily!—in appalling conditions.

Lower-middle-income countries (2.5 billion people).[31] This category includes many Latin American countries, such as Bolivia ($2,200); a few African nations like Nigeria ($1,440); states that were once part of the former Soviet bloc, such as Ukraine ($3,500) and Georgia ($3,290); and

Asian nations like Vietnam ($1,550) and Laos ($1,270) at the bottom of the scale, and Indonesia ($3,420) at the top. The annual per capita GNI in these countries ranges from $1,036–$4,085.[32] These countries have a somewhat brighter future, although they still have large numbers of very poor people.

Upper-middle-income countries (2.4 billion people).[33] Included in this category are the richest Latin American nations (e.g., Brazil and Venezuela). China ($5,720) has moved up from the low income classification in just the past two decades. Per capita GNI ranges from Albania's $4,030 to Venezuela's $12,460.[34]

High-income countries (1.3 billion people).[35] Per capita GNI in these developed countries ranges from Poland's $12,660 to Norway's $98,780 and Switzerland's $80,780. For the U.S., it is $52,340, the U.K., $38,500, and Japan, $47,870.[36]

Uneven Distribution

Over the past half-century, economic growth in the developing countries has differed by region (see Table 1). We see healthy growth in most areas during 1965–73. However, beginning in the 1970s, the regions begin to diverge. The annual growth of the Gross Domestic Product (GDP) in sub-Saharan Africa was actually 1 percent during the 1980s. But the population was growing so fast that the per capita GDP actually declined an average of .8 percent per year from 1980 to 1990.[37] The average per capita GDP growth rate of the region since 1961 has been a mere .8 percent. Modest growth occurred between 2002–09 (2.7 percent), but that has cooled in recent years to 1.5 percent. Latin America's per capita growth was substantial through about 1980, then declined significantly during the 1980s and 1990s, and then improved somewhat in the last decade (except for the Great Recession in 2009). This is in stark contrast to the situation in East and South Asia. East Asia (including China, South Korea, and Taiwan) has experienced per capita growth of 5.6 percent per year for more than five decades. South Asia, including India and Pakistan, experienced an annual 3 percent per capita growth during the same period.[38]

Table 1—Annual GDP per capita growth by region 1965–2002

Regions	1965-73	1973-80	1980-93	1993-02	2002-09	2009	2011	2012
Sub-Saharan Africa	2.2%	0.7%	-1.5%	.27%	2.7%	-.6%	1.6%	1.5%
East Asia and the Pacific	4.5%	4.9%	6.4%	6.7%	8.4%	6.7%	7.6%	6.7%
South Asia	.5%	1.5%	2.9%	3.4%	5.5%	6.2%	4.7%	2.3%
Mid East, N. Africa	5.2%	1.3%	-.2%	1.5%	2.7%	1.6%	--	--
Latin America and Caribbean	3.7%	3.5%	0.2%	.88%	1.9%	-2.9%	2.7%	1.8

Source: World Bank's World Development Indicators 2014[39]

Economic growth by itself, however, is not enough. Everyone in a country, especially the poorest, should benefit. Too often, however, overall economic growth primarily benefits the already rich. In Brazil a military dictatorship strongly supported by the United States fostered GDP growth at the rate of about 10 percent per year from 1968 to 1976. Growth of nearly 7 percent per year continued through 1980, but slowed to 2.2 percent from 1980 through 1993.[40]

Who profited? Even Brazil's own minister of finance admitted in 1972 that only 5 percent of the people had benefited from the fantastic growth of the Brazilian economy. The Brazilian government did not challenge a 1974 study showing that the real purchasing power of the poorest two-thirds of the people had declined by more than one-half in the preceding ten years. In 1989, two-thirds of Brazilian families tried to survive on less than $500 a month.[41]

But things began to change substantially in 2003 with the election of President Luis Lula da Silva. He adopted the goal of "Zero hunger" in Brazil and began major new government programs to improve education, health care, and nutrition among poor Brazilians. Extreme poverty in Brazil fell from 10 percent in 2004 to 2 percent in 2009. The income of poor families jumped seven times as fast as the income of the richest. Although income inequality in Brazil is still very high, by 2009, it had dropped to the lowest level in fifty years.[42] Government policies play a significant role in whether economic growth improves or bypasses the lot of the poor.

The story of Indonesia further illustrates this truth. Indonesia, a large, densely populated country with vast natural resources like Brazil, experienced an impressive annual economic growth of 7.2 percent for three decades from 1968 to 1998.[43] Because of Indonesian government policies designed to improve the lot of the poor, their situation steadily improved over this whole period. From 1987 to 2011, the proportion of the population living on less than $1.25 a day declined from 68 percent to 16 percent—reflecting the government's strong commitment to poverty reduction.[44] In 2011, the share of national income enjoyed by Indonesia's poorest fifth of the population was 7.3 percent. In Brazil it was still a mere 2.9 percent in spite of the successful anti-poverty measures by the Brazilian government starting in 2003.[45]

There is a striking new development that has resulted from the fact that the rich too often benefit much more than the poor when a country experiences economic growth. In 1990, 90 percent of all the world's poor people lived in low-income countries.[46] Today, 72 percent of the world's poor live in middle income countries![47] Countries like China, India, and Brazil have experienced rapid economic growth. But in spite of some major programs to assist the poorest, this great economic growth has left hundreds of millions mired in desperate poverty.

The story of the Alarins—a poor Filipino family—conveys their agony. Mr. Alarin made 70 cents on good days as an ice vendor. Several nights a month Mrs. Alarin stayed up all night to make a coconut sweet that she sold on the street. Total income for her midnight toil was 40 cents. Cooking utensils were their only furniture. The family had not tasted meat for a month when the president of World Vision visited them and wrote this account:

> Tears washed her dark, sunken eye-sockets as she spoke: "I feel so sad
> when my children cry at night because they have no food. I know my
> life will never change. What can I do to solve my problems? I am so
> worried about the future of my children. I want them to go to school,
> but how can we afford it? I am sick most of the time, but I can't go to the
> doctor because each visit costs two pesos [28 cents] and the medicine
> is extra. What can I do?" She broke down into quiet sobbing. I admit
> without shame that I wept with her.[48]

The tears and agony of the world's poor are captured in the words of Mrs. Alarin. World poverty is a hundred million mothers like Mrs. Alarin, weeping because they cannot feed their children.

Famine Redefined

The rich today can ignore famine because it manifests itself differently from earlier times: "In earlier historical periods, . . . whole nations . . . experienced widespread starvation and death. Today the advancement in both national and international distribution systems has concentrated the effects of food scarcity among the world's poor, wherever they are."[49]

People with money can always buy food; famine affects only the poor. When food scarcity triples the price of grain imports, as it did from 1972 to 1974, middle- and upper-income persons in developing countries continue to eat. But people already devoting 60 to 80 percent of their income to food simply eat less and die sooner. Death usually results from diseases that underfed bodies cannot resist.[50]

Children are the first victims. In 2012, low-income countries had a child mortality rate thirteen times higher than in high-income countries.[51] Of the 6.6 million kids under 5 who die every year, half is due to under-nutrition.[52] It is estimated that in 2011, there were 165 million children under five years of age who were stunted due to lack of food.[53]

There is hope, however. Since 1990, Vietnam "reduced the proportion of undernourished from 47 percent to only 9 percent, lowered under-weight in children from more than 40 percent around 1990 to 12 percent in 2011, and more than halved the under-five mortality rate."[54] With vaccines that already exist, we could prevent the deaths of over 2 million young children each year.[55]

Are rich Christians generous enough to save these lives?

Carolina Maria de Jesus helps us feel the terror and anguish endured by the poor in a land where they could have enough food. This uneducated but brilliant woman struggling to survive in the slums of Brazil's largest city, São Paulo, kept a daily record of her feelings on scraps of paper. Later they were published in a gripping diary called *Child of the Dark*.

Today I'm sad. I'm nervous. I don't know if I should start crying or start running until I fall unconscious. At dawn it was raining. I couldn't go out to get any money [she gathered junk each day to earn money for food] . . . I have a few tin cans and a little scrap that I'm going to sell to Senhor Manuel. When Joao came home from school, I sent him to sell the scrap. He got 13 cruzeiros. He bought a glass of mineral water: two cruzeiros. I was furious with him . . .

The children eat a lot of bread. They like soft bread but when they don't have it, they eat hard bread . . .

Oh Sao Paulo! A queen that vainly shows her skyscrapers that are her crown of gold. All dressed up in velvet and silk but with cheap stockings underneath—the favela [the slum].

The money didn't stretch far enough to buy meat, so I cooked macaroni with a carrot. I didn't have any grease, it was horrible. Vera was the only one who complained yet asked for more.

"Mama, sell me to Dona Julita, because she has delicious food."[56]

A former president of World Vision visited the home of Sebastian and Maria Nascimento, a poor Brazilian couple whose home was a one-room, thatched lean-to with a sand floor. Inside, one stool, a charcoal hibachi, and four cots covered with sacks partly filled with straw were the only furniture. He wrote this heartrending account about his visit:

My emotions could scarcely take in what I saw and heard. The three-year-old twins, lying naked and unmoving on a small cot, were in the last act of their personal drama. Mercifully, the curtain was coming down on their brief appearance. Malnutrition was the villain. The two-year-old played a silent role, his brain already vegetating from marasmus, a severe form of malnutrition.

The father is without work. Both he and Maria are anguished over their existence, but they are too proud to beg. He tries to shine shoes. Maria cannot talk about their condition. She tries, but the words just will not come. Her mother's love is deep and tender, and the daily deterioration of her children is more than she can bear. Tears must be the vocabulary of the anguished soul.[57]

Carolina's little girl need not have begged to be sold to a rich neighbor. And while Sebastian and Maria's twins lay dying, there was an abundance of food in the world. But it was not divided fairly. The well-to-do in Brazil had plenty to eat. More than two hundred million U.S. citizens were consuming enough food (partly because of high consumption of grain-fed livestock) to feed more than one billion people in the poor countries. Oxford economist Donald Hay has pointed out that a mere 2 percent of the world's grain harvest would be enough, if shared, to erase the problem of hunger and malnutrition around the world![58]

This is how famine has been redefined, or rather, redistributed! It no longer inconveniences the rich and powerful. It strikes only the poor and powerless. Since the poor usually die quietly in relative obscurity, the rich of all nations comfortably ignore this kind of famine. But famine—redefined and redistributed—is alive and well. Even in good times, millions and millions of persons go to bed hungry, and children's brains vegetate and their bodies succumb prematurely to disease.

Poverty's Children

Poverty means illiteracy, inadequate medical care, disease, and stunting.

Illiteracy

Only 63 percent of India's population of 1.2 billion people could read in 2006. From 1990 to 2006, the percentage of Indians who could read improved from 48 to 63 percent. But that still leaves about 444 million illiterates. For Pakistan's 170 million, the proportion of illiterates is 55 percent.[59]

We can be grateful for the progress that has been made. In 1990, only 51 percent of the people in low-income countries could read, but that increased to 61 percent by 2012.[60] Youth literacy increased in Southern Asia from 60 percent in 1990 to 81 percent in 2011 and in northern Africa from 68 percent to 89 percent over the same time period. In northern Africa female literacy improved 28 percentage points![61]

Unfortunately, there were still 824 million people in the world over the age of fifteen who could not read in 2012.[62]

Inadequate Medical Care and Disease

Most people in the industrialized North have enjoyed the security of modern medicine for so long that we assume it is now available for all. Indeed, things have gotten better. We now deal successfully with treatable illnesses throughout the developing world. 1.1 million lives were saved between 2000–2010 from successful treatment of malaria. Between 1995–2010 over 20 million lives were saved from tuberculosis.[63] In 1960, life expectancy in the low and middle-income countries was 46 years. In 1990, it had improved to 63 years. In 2012, it was 69 years. People living in high-income countries can expect to live a decade longer.[64]

Similarly, the number of children under age five who died was 220 out of 1,000 in 1960, but had declined to 99 out of 1,000 by 1990 and is 53 out of 1,000 in 2012.[65] But inadequate food and medicine in poor nations means they have much higher infant mortality rates than the developed world.

Table 2—Infant Mortality Per 1000 Live Births (2012)

Japan	2
Finland	2
Germany	3
U.K.	4
Australia	4
Cuba	4
U.S.	6
Chile	8
Ukraine	9
Russia	9
China	12
Egypt	18
Guatemala	27
Malawi	46
Niger	63
Angola	100
Sierra Leone	117

Source: World Bank's World Development Indicators 2014[66]

In spite of the improvements that have been made, the World Bank reports that 752 million people do not have access to safe water, and 2.5 billion do not have access to improved sanitation.[67] In 2012, over eleven thousand children under five died every day from the following: HIV/AIDS, diarrheal diseases, measles, malaria, acute lower respiratory infections, prematurity, and birth complications.[68] Six thousand kids died every day from three very preventable causes: pneumonia, diarrhea, and malaria.[69] In high income countries, less than six kids died every day of child death due to HIV/Aids, diarrhea, measles, or malaria.[70]

Providing cleaner water and better sanitation would bring huge economic benefits. The World Health Organization estimated in 2004 that each dollar invested would return economic benefit of no less than $3 and as much as $60 in the major regions of the developing world. If the world committed to invest $11.3 billion towards improving water and sanitation, the annual economic return would reach $85 billion. Most of this benefit would be in developing regions in Africa and Asia—places that need it most.[71] Surely the people in wealthy nations can find $11.3 billion to transform the lives of hundreds of millions of people. People in the United States spend around $60 billion each year trying to lose weight because they eat more food than they need.[72]

Stunting

In 2011, there were 165 million stunted children in the world under the age of five because of chronic malnutrition. Stunting simply means that a child is too short for his or her age, but it has dire consequences including brain damage.[73] No one knows how many poor children have suffered irreversible brain damage due to chronic malnutrition during childhood, but there are millions of such children.

> Marli, a happy six-year-old girl from Rio de Janeiro[,] is just one of these. Marli looks normal in every way. Healthy. Happy. There is just one thing wrong with her. She can't learn. At first the teachers thought perhaps her difficulty was psychological, the result of neglect in a family of eleven children. Her younger sister had the same problem. But after careful observation and testing, it became evident that Marli, a child of Brazil's poor and wretched favelas [slums], was unable to learn because as an infant her malnourished body could not produce a healthy brain.[74]

Permanent brain damage caused by protein deficiency is one of the most devastating aspects of world poverty. Eighty percent of total brain development takes place between conception and age two. Adequate protein intake—precisely what over one-fourth of all children under five in

developing countries do not have—is necessary for proper brain development.[75] A study in the early 1980s in Mexico found that a group of severely
malnourished children under five had an IQ thirteen points lower than a
scientifically selected, adequately fed control group.[76] Medical science has
demonstrated that severe malnutrition produces irreversible brain damage.

When a poor family runs out of food, the children suffer most. For
people eking out a day-to-day existence, an inactive child is not as serious
a problem as an inactive wage earner. But malnutrition produces millions
of retarded children that become a serious problem in the future.

AIDS

AIDS is one of the most deadly killers of the poor, especially in Africa.
Globally, about 35 million are infected with the virus. 24 million of those
are in Africa.[77]

In wealthy nations today, people who get AIDS receive expensive
(antiretroviral) drugs that prolong life for many years and enable people
to live a largely normal life. Only 1 percent of AIDS-related deaths now
occur in wealthy countries. Despite improvements in treatment, people in
poor countries continue to die at alarming rates.

We now know a lot about combating AIDS, but in poor countries
there are many obstacles. The World Health Organization has outlined an
HIV treatment cascade that outlines the steps to successful treatment of
HIV. As the chart below shows, with each step more and more people fall
through the cracks. After diagnosis, a patient must be linked to care, initiated onto ARVs, and retained on the drug before the virus is suppressed.

Chart 2[78] shows how radically different is the treatment of AIDS in the
U.S. and Africa.

Every day in sub-Saharan Africa, 3,300 people die of AIDS.[79] Twenty-
seven million have already died, leaving families destitute and alone;[80] 16
million African children have lost one or both parents.[81] Parents, farmers,
teachers, and leaders are gone. Whole communities are devastated.

The personal stories are wrenching. Before he got AIDS, a hardworking father sold milk from his goats to provide for his wife and family.
When he fell ill, he used the children's school fee money to pay for traditional medicine. Finally, he sold two goats so he could visit a clinic—only

Chart 2

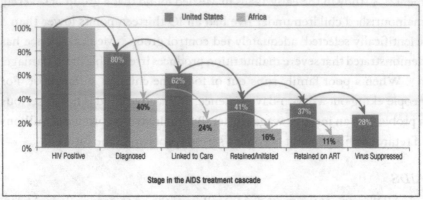

Source: US data is from CDC's June 2013 "Today's HIV/AIDS epidemic". Africa estimates are derived by the authors from Elvin Geng's PEPFAR SAR presentation (October 2012) which credits Rosen S, Fox MP (2011) Retention in HIV Care between Testing and Treatment in sub-Saharan Africa: A Systematic Review. PLoS Med 8(7): e1001056., Fox MP, Rosen S (2010) Patient retention in antiretroviral therapy programs up to three years on treatment in sub-Saharan Africa, 2007–2009: systemic review. Trop Med Int Health 2010-Jun:15 Suppli 1:1-15.

to discover that it was AIDS that was devastating not only him, but his wife and their toddler. His wife sold another goat to pay for his funeral. All the goats were gone by the time the wife died.

Two daughters, nine and ten, were left to take care of their dying brother. When they visited their grandmother, she told them they must take care of themselves, because she was already caring for five grandchildren orphaned by AIDS. All she could give them was a cardboard box—a coffin to bury their dying brother.[82]

Millions of African children face that kind of terrifying future.

The 2011 UN Political Declaration made a target of spending $24 billion annually to combat AIDS. In 2012, the world devoted $18.9 billion to this fight. This was a 10 percent increase over the year before, but only 78 percent of what was needed.[83]

From 1996 to 2013, the price of drugs for AIDS sufferers in poor nations has dropped from $10,000 per person annually to around $100.[84] In 2012, 9.7 million people in poor countries received these live-saving drugs. But that is only 34 percent of those eligible under World Health Organization guidelines.[85]

Hunger, illiteracy, disease, brain damage, death. That's what grinding poverty means. About one billion impoverished people of the world experience this anguish regularly. A little more help from rich nations would save many lives.

Developing nations must also change their priorities. Many developing nations are not meeting their own health spending commitments. "For instance, if Nigeria were to meet its health spending commitment each year from 2013 to 2015, the total projected additional resources ($22.5 billion), if invested in effective health programs, could provide anti-malarial bednets to every single citizen, fully vaccinate every young child against deadly childhood diseases (such as pneumonia, rotavirus, diphtheria, and whooping cough) and provide antiretroviral treatment to every single person who is HIV-positive in Nigeria. The malaria intervention alone could save the lives of almost half a million children over time."[86] If sub-Saharan African countries met their own spending commitments for health, education, and agriculture, there would be an additional $243 billion available between 2013–2015 to combat poverty.[87]

Making Progress

The results of modest efforts can be dramatic. During the 1980s and 1990s, a few inexpensive actions saved the lives of millions of children. During that time, the immunization levels in the developing world rose from 20 percent to about 80 percent.[88] In the early 1980s, about 75 million children contracted measles each year and more than 2.5 million died. By 2011 only 350,000 measles cases were reported worldwide.[89] Vaccines now save the lives of at least 2.5 million annually. By expanding coverage for all the basic vaccines, an additional 2 million lives could be saved.[90]

Even though the cost of vaccines has risen somewhat, it is estimated to cost on average only $65 per child from 2006–2015 to provide comprehensive childhood vaccines to all children who do not now receive them in poorer countries.[91] "By 2015, more than 70 million children in the world's 72 poorest countries can be protected annually against 14 major childhood diseases if an additional U.S. $1 billion per year can be invested towards immunization."[92] Surely we can find another $1 billion annually to protect 70 million children.

The success story on river blindness shows how much can be done at a modest cost. A cooperative effort among several international organizations, including the World Bank and the World Health Organization (WHO), set out in 1974 to combat river blindness in eleven African countries. Spread by a tiny black fly and caused by a microscopic parasite, this disease causes intense itching, debilitation, and eventually blindness. The initial effort involved spraying biodegradable insecticides (which are harmless to the environment). The program was a glowing success and allowed farmers to return to about sixty million acres of prime farmland;[93] and the costs of the program were only $570 million, or roughly $1 per person protected from blindness per year.[94]

More recently, Mectizan, a drug donated by Merck, has been used in a number of additional countries in Africa. Through the Mectizan Control Program at the Carter Presidential Center, over one billion treatment doses have been distributed to communities in need. This agent has both treatment and control benefits and may eventually lead to the elimination of river blindness as a public health problem. Colombia became the first country to apply for WHO certification for the elimination of river blindness.[95]

Iodine deficiency is another terrible problem that could be easily solved. Nearly two billion people suffer from insufficient iodine intake. Two-hundred sixty-six million of them are school-age children.[96] Children born to iodine-deficient mothers are at risk of goiter (the swelling of the thyroid gland), speech defects, deafness, and cretinism (people with stunted, deformed bodies and brains). The solution? Iodize each country's salt supply, which costs only 5 cents per person per year.[97] The total cost of such a program would be around $100 million—half the cost of just one Raptor F-22 fighter plane.[98]

The good news is that we have made major progress since 1990. Some countries have seen dramatic success. China's iodization rate went from 39 percent to 95 percent in just ten years. Likewise, Jordan increased from 5 percent to 90 percent. Globally, approximately 70 percent of the population has iodized household salt, up from 20 percent in 1990. It could easily be 100 percent![99]

Oral rehydration therapy (ORT) is an inexpensive health procedure that prevents children from dehydrating from diarrhea. In 1980, 10,000 children died every day from diarrheal dehydration. In 1999, it was lower at 4,100 deaths per day globally.[100] Today the number is at 1,600; that's about 600,000 unnecessary deaths each year from diarrhea.[101] Bags of oral rehydration salts cost just 10 cents each.[102] They can be used by parents themselves.[103] With a little more help, millions more would live.

Since 1988, "the Global Polio Eradication Initiative (GPEI) has reduced the global incidence of polio by more than 99% and the number of countries with endemic polio from 125 to 3."[104] Over 10 million people have avoided polio and its debilitating effects. Only 223 cases were reported at the end of 2012. Never before has the goal of eliminating polio been so close. GPEI hopes to certify all regions of the world as polio free by 2018.[105]

The fight against HIV/AIDS has seen tremendous success. Globally, there has been a 33 percent decrease in new HIV cases since 2001. Fewer people who have HIV are dying; 2.3 million died in 2005, 1.6 million died in 2012.[106] There has been an "805 percent increase in the number of people receiving treatment in Africa from 2005 to 2012."[107] Treatment and preventative measures have reduced the number of people dying in sub-Saharan Africa by 50 percent from 2004 to 2012.[108] "From 1995 to 2012, antiretroviral therapy averted 6.6 million AIDS-related deaths worldwide, including 5.5 million in low- and middle-income countries."[109]

We are making progress. Increased expenditures have reduced malnutrition and greatly increased immunization levels. UNICEF estimates that the total cost of providing basic social services in the 50 poorest developing countries (with 85 million people), including health, education, family planning, and clean water, would only cost $2.2 billion per year.[110] That is less than what the U.S. Department of Defense spends on just one nuclear submarine.[111]

Progress in reducing poverty, of course, does not flow only from improved health care for the poor. Expanding market economies have significantly reduced poverty in Asia (see chapter 8). And there is a wide range of changes—both personal and structural—that you and I can make to reduce the agony of poor people (see chapters 9–11).

Population

The population explosion is another fundamental problem. Not until around 1800 did the world have one billion people. It took only one hundred-thirty years more to add another billion. Within a mere thirty years another billion human beings appeared. The fourth billion arrived in only fourteen years, by 1975. Now we are adding a billion every twelve years. In 2011, the world reached seven billion human inhabitants.[112] This number could rise to more than 10.9 billion in the next forty years (see Chart 3).[113]

There is good news here, too, however. Total fertility rates (the average number of children each woman will bear) have declined from 5.2 births per woman in the 1970s to 2.4 in the 2000s.[114] In 44 developing countries in Africa, Asia, and Oceana, fertility rates are still over four children per woman; in Guinea-Bissau and Niger the rates are 7.4 and 7.0, respectively.[115] But we are getting closer globally to the fertility rate of 2.1 children per couple, which is the rate at which the population remains the same; 80 countries are at or below this level.[116] Still today, however, many young people are entering their reproductive years. Even if most couples today have fewer children than previous generations (which they are doing), the total population will still grow.[117]

A population of 100 million people growing at 1.5 percent per year expands to 145 million in 25 years, and 443 million in 100 years. And a population of 100 million growing at 2.7 percent (which is the rate for sub-Saharan Africa, which has about 912 million people[118]) expands to 379 million in 50 years and 1,436 million in 100 years.

It is impossible to predict exactly how many people will be alive in 2050 or 2100. The United Nations projects three scenarios (see Chart 3).

Table 3—Future of World Population Growth, Three Scenarios, 2000 to 2050

Figure 1. Population of the world, 1950–2100, according to different projections and variants

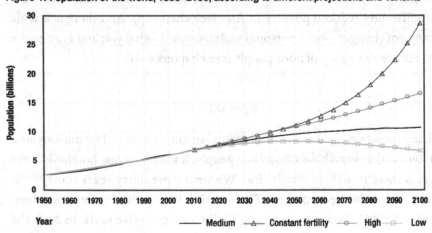

Source: United Nations, World Population Prospects 2012[119]

The median projection indicates that total population would increase to 8.1 billion by 2025, and reach 9.6 billion by 2050. As the century progresses, the growth rate will fall and total population will reach 10.9 billion by 2100.[120]

Much depends on what we do. Table 3 indicates the current growth rates in different regions.

Table 4—Projected 2050 Population Size for Major Regions, Three Scenarios

		2050		
	2010	High	Medium	Low
Region/country		Population in millions		
World	6,916	10,868	9,551	8,342
More Developed	1,241	1,470	1,303	1,149
Less Developed	5,675	9,398	8,248	7,193
Africa	1,031	2,686	2,393	2,119
Sub-Saharan Africa	831	2,322	2,074	1,842
Asia	4,165	5,912	5,164	4,482
China	1,360	1,580	1,384	1,209
Japan	127	121	108	96
Latin America/ Caribbean	596	902	782	674
North America	347	500	446	395
Europe	740	804	709	622
Oceania	37	64	57	50

Source: UN Population Division, *World Population Prospects: The 2012 Revision* (2013).[121]

The population explosion prompts some people to apocalyptic hysteria. One group ran an advertisement in 1976 in many newspapers, including *The New York Times* and *The Wall Street Journal*. Drafted by prominent scholars William Paddock and Garrett Hardin, among others, the statement read, in part, "The world as we know it will likely be ruined before the year 2000 . . . The momentum toward tragedy is at this moment so great that there is probably no way of halting it."[122]

Such views were alarmist, pessimistic, and obviously untrue (from the perspective of 2014!).[123] Population trends in the last forty years offer some hope. Whereas the overall annual population growth rate in the world was about 2.1 percent in 1963, the World Development Indicators report that it had dropped to 1.1 percent by 2012.[124] We can be grateful for the improvement, but the present rate of population growth is still too high. At this rate, the population will exceed ten billion people by 2048.[125] We are already damaging the environment to feed today's seven billion—and not all of those receive sufficient food.

In considering the issue of population growth, it is important to remember that although Northern developed nations now have much lower population growth rates than developing nations (see Table 3), the number of children per family in Western Europe and North America was much higher in the latter half of the nineteenth century than the two children or less per family common now. Infant mortality rates, of course, were also higher. Despite this, family size and population growth in the industrializing nations at that time were quite close to the size and growth rates in many developing countries since World War II. Affluence and decline in population growth seem to go together, in the long term anyway.

Fortunately, empowering the poor is an effective way to reduce the population explosion (see chapters 2 and 11). When poor people receive adequate food, health care, and education (especially women), population growth drops dramatically.

Environmental Degradation

Our survival depends on agriculture. We need food to live. Yet, agricultural lands are threatened by desertification, land degradation, and drought. 12 million hectares (the size of Mississippi) of agricultural land are lost each year. Globally, half of all agricultural land is moderately or severely degraded.[126] The poorest are most vulnerable with 74 percent suffering from land degradation.[127] In chapter 8, we will explore further how environmental decay and global warming increase the problem of global poverty.

The Future and Our Response

We live at a time of swelling affluence combined with persistent poverty. How will we as Christians respond? Will we dare to remember that the God we worship tells us that "whoever is kind to the poor lends to the Lord" (Prov. 19:17 NRSV)? Will Christians have the courage to seek justice for the poor, even if that means disapproval from affluent neighbors?

Where will you and I stand? With the starving or the overfed? With poor Lazarus or the rich man? Most of the rich countries are at least nominally Christian. What an ironic tragedy that an affluent, "Christian" minority in the world continues to hoard its wealth while hundreds of millions of people hover on the edge of starvation!

One popular fundamentalist newsletter has called on Christians to stockpile new dried foods. In a most ingenious combination of apocalyptic piety and slick salesmanship, the newsletter quoted several "Bible scholars" to prove that some Christians will live through the tribulation. And the conclusion? Since we cannot be absolutely certain where we will be during the tribulation, we ought to purchase a seven-year supply of reserve foods for a couple thousand dollars![128]

In an age of affluence and poverty, most Christians, regardless of theological labels, are tempted to succumb to the heresy of following society's materialistic values rather than biblical truth. Advertisements offer demonically convincing justifications for enjoying our affluence while neglecting billions of poor neighbors.

Imagine what one quarter of the world's Christians could do if they became truly generous. A few of us could move to desperately poor areas to help combat poverty. The rest of us could defy surrounding materialism. We could refuse to let our affluent world squeeze us into its consumeristic mold. Instead, we could become generous nonconformists who love Jesus more than wealth. In obedience to our Lord, we could empower the poor through generous giving, community development, and better societal systems. And in the process, we would learn again His paradoxical truth that true happiness flows from generosity.

Study Questions

1. What are your strongest feelings as you read this chapter?
2. What facts were most surprising to you? Most disturbing?

3. How has famine been redefined?
4. What concretely does poverty mean in day-to-day life?
5. How do you think most Christians you know would respond if they truly understood the problem of world hunger?

2

THE AFFLUENT MINORITY

*I used to think when I was a child, that Christ might have
been exaggerating when he warned about the dangers of
wealth. Today I know better. I know how very hard it is to be
rich and still keep the milk of human kindness. Money has
a dangerous way of putting scales on one's eyes, a dangerous
way of freezing people's hands, eyes, lips and hearts.[1]*

—DOM HÉLDER CÂMARA

Create more desire" shrieked an inch-high headline for an unusually honest ad in *The New York Times*. It continued: "Now, as always, profit and growth stem directly from the ability of salesmanship to create more desire."[2]

Costly, manipulative advertising bombards us at every turn, and its primary purpose is not to inform; it is to create desire. Luxurious houses in *Better Homes and Gardens* make our perfectly adequate houses shrink by comparison into dilapidated, tiny cottages in need of immediate renovation. The advertisements for the new fall fashions make our almost-new dresses and suits from previous years look shabby and old-fashioned.

We in the U.S. spend more money on advertising than on all our public institutions of higher education. In 2002, we spent $237 billion on advertising but only $223 billion on higher education.[3] Advertising expenses are expected to soar to $390 billion in 2014.[4] Worldwide expenditures for advertising are expected to be $505.4 billion.[5] Tragically, a lot of advertising is used "to convince us that Jesus was wrong about the abundance of possessions."[6]

One of the most astounding things about the affluent minority is that we honestly think we have barely enough to survive in modest comfort. Constant, seductive advertising helps to create this destructive delusion. Advertisers regularly deceive us into thinking that we genuinely need one luxury after another. We are convinced that we are in competition with our neighbors. So we buy another dress, sports jacket, or sports car, and thereby force up the standard of living.

The increasingly affluent standard of living is the god of twenty-first-century North America, and the adman is its prophet.

Advertising reclassifies luxuries as necessities. Our postman once delivered an elegant brochure complete with glossy photographs of exceedingly expensive homes. The brochure announced the seductive lie that *Architectural Digest* would help quench "man's passionate *need* for beauty and *luxury*" (my emphasis). How much luxury do we *need*?

New technology has greatly increased how much advertising we see. The average American child (8+) sees 7 hours of "screen time" a day—viewing television, computer, video game, and hand held devices. Kids aged 2–8 watch about 2 hours per day.[7] Adults spend about 4.5 hours watching T.V. a day, and nearly another hour on programs recorded on their DVRs.[8] Quantifying the advertising we see each day is nearly impossible. In addition to the traditional T.V. commercial, advertisers now use "product placements, immersive websites, advergaming, viral marketing, mobile ads, social-media marketing, and precise behavioral and location targeting. More than ever before, advertising and entertainment are inextricably linked. In many cases, the content is the ad."[9]

Sometimes advertising overkill is hilarious. An evangelical book discount house once created this promotional gem: "Your mouth is going to water, and your soul is going to glow, when you feast your eyes on the bargains which have been providentially provided for your benefit this month." (I promptly ordered books worth twenty-four dollars.)

Promises, Promises

Perhaps the most demonic part of advertising is that it attempts to persuade us that material possessions will bring joy and fulfillment. "That happiness is to be attained through limitless material acquisition is denied by every religion and philosophy known to man, but is preached incessantly by every American television set."[10]

Advertisers promise that their products will satisfy our deepest needs and inner longings for love, acceptance, security, and sexual fulfillment. The right deodorant will bring acceptance and friendship. The newest toothpaste or shampoo will make us irresistible. A comment by New York jewelry designer Barry Kieselstein shows how people search for meaning and friendship in things: "A nice piece of *jewelry you can relate to is like having a friend* who's always there" (emphasis mine).[11]

A bank in Washington, D.C., advertised for new savings accounts with the question "Who's gonna love you when you're old and gray?"

For a decade, my own savings bank used a particularly enticing ad: "Put a little love away. Everybody needs a penny for a rainy day. Put a little love away." Responsible saving is good stewardship. But promising that a bank account guarantees love is unbiblical, heretical, and demonic. This ad teaches the big lie of our secular, materialistic society. But the words and music were so seductive that they danced through my head hundreds of times.

If no one paid any attention to these lies, they would be harmless. But advertising has a powerful effect on all of us, and it shapes the values of our children.

In a sense we pay too little attention to advertisements. Most of us think we ignore them, but in fact they seep into the subconscious. We experience them instead of analyze them. John V. Taylor suggested that Christian families ought to adopt the slogan "Who are you kidding?" and shout it in unison every time a commercial appears on the television screen.[12]

Where Did It All Begin?

Theologian Patrick Kerans has argued that commitment to unlimited growth and an ever-increasing materialistic "standard of living" is really a sellout to the Enlightenment. During the eighteenth century, many Western thinkers decided that science was the only way to find knowledge. This thinking elevated all things quantitative and devalued all things nonquantitative. Thus, intangible values such as community, trust, friendship, and the beauty of creation became less important. It is hard to measure the value of friendship, unspoiled nature, and justice. But Gross National Income (GNI) is easy to measure. The result is our competitive growth economy where economic success and material things are all-important to many people.[13]

If Christianity is true and Kerans is correct, our society will eventually collapse. A social structure built on the heretical ideas that the scientific method is the only way to reach truth and value and that material things are all-important will eventually self-destruct.

Much (but not all) advertising contains a fundamental inner contradiction.[14] Advertisers know that we all long for the qualities of life that will satisfy our deepest needs; we long for significance, love, and joy. Marketing recognizes these needs and hooks into them. But then, in order to sell us more gadgets, it promotes the big lie. It says that love and fulfillment come from more and more material abundance.

Christians, of course, know that affluence does not guarantee love, beauty, acceptance, and joy. Our deepest joy comes from right relationships—with God, neighbor, and the earth. But our inherent bent toward idolatry gives advertisers the power to convince us that more gadgets and bigger bank accounts are an easy way to meet our needs. As a result, people persist in the fruitless effort to quench their thirst for meaning and fulfillment with an ever-rising river of possessions.

The personal result is agonizing distress and undefined dissatisfaction. The social result is environmental pollution and neglected poor people. Affluence fails to satisfy our restless hearts. It also keeps us from sharing food and assistance with our more than one billion hungry neighbors. Will we affluent Christians have the generosity and faithfulness to refuse to conform to society's seductive advertising?

How Affluent Are We?

By any objective criterion, the 4.5 percent of the world's people who live in the United States are an incredibly rich aristocracy living on the same little planet with billions of very poor neighbors. Combined with the rest of North America, Europe, and Japan, we comprise an affluent northern aristocracy.

30

Our standard of living, compared with that of more than 2.4 billion very poor neighbors living on two dollars or less per day, is at least as luxurious as was the lifestyle of the medieval aristocracy compared with their serfs.

Though this trend is beginning to diminish, the rich countries are in the Northern Hemisphere. The poor countries are more to the south. The north-south division is one of the most dangerous fault lines in the world today.

In 1960, the one-fifth of the world's people living in the richest nations enjoyed an income 30 times that of the poorest one-fifth. In 2005, the richest one-fifth of the world enjoyed an income 50 times greater than the poorest fifth.[15] In 1999–2008, the top 10 percent earned 50 percent of global income, while the bottom 50 percent earned just over 9 percent.[16]

According to a 2014 Oxfam report, the richest 1 percent have 65 times more wealth than the bottom half of the world. In fact, the richest 85 individuals in the world have more wealth than 3.5 billion people![17]

The Gross National Income (GNI)—or Gross Domestic Product (GDP), which is similar—provides one standard of comparison between rich and poor countries.[18] (These measures, however, say nothing about income equality within a country.) By dividing a country's GNI by its population, you arrive at a per capita GNI. As Table 5 shows, the annual per capita GNI in the United States was $52,340 in 2012. In India it was $1,550.[19]

Table 5—Per Capita GNI in 2012 (U.S. Dollars/Atlas Method)

Switzerland	80,970
United States	52,340
Japan	47,870
United Kingdom	38,620
Mexico	9,640
Egypt	2,980
India	1,550
Kenya	860
Bangladesh	840
Ethiopia	380

Source: World Bank, World Development Indicators 2014[20]

Merely comparing per capita GNI, however, is misleading. In 1996, haircuts cost $25 in New York and only 65 cents in Bangladesh, but the

New York haircut was not worth 38 times more![21] Development specialists have tried to improve on the GNI comparisons.

One way is to measure GNI using Purchasing Power Parity (PPP). To understand how this is better, you need to understand how the GNI is usually figured. GNI (and also GDP and GNP)[22] per capita is usually expressed in terms of U.S. dollars. Economists calculate a country's Gross National Income (GNI) per capita and then convert it to U.S. dollars using the market rate for foreign exchange. For example, in 2012 the GNI per capita in Bangladesh was 65,104 taka (the local currency), which could buy U.S. $840. But 65,104 taka will purchase far more in Bangladesh than $840 will purchase in the United States, partly because wages are lower.[23]

Using the PPP helps to reduce this distortion. A similar bundle of goods in both countries is priced to see how much each currency can actually purchase. Then GNI per capita is adjusted into PPP dollars that are equal and comparable among countries. Table 6 shows that Bangladesh's GNI per capita in PPP dollars is actually $2,030. This means that the Bangladeshi, with 65,104 taka, can only get $840 U.S. in the foreign currency market, but can purchase goods in Bangladesh that would cost $2,030 to purchase in the United States. Poor countries do not appear to be as poor when measured in PPP dollars.

Does that mean people in poor countries are really not so poor after all? Yes, but only slightly. They are still very poor. Table 6 shows that the average person in Bangladesh (where more than 155 million people live) has an annual income of $2,030 in PPP. That would be like trying to live in the U.S. on about $170 per person per month! Imagine a family of four trying to survive in the U.S. or Canada on $680 a month. That would not even pay the rent for an apartment in most places.

Another measure of countries' well-being is the Human Development Index (HDI). Created in 1990 by the United Nations Development Programme, it attempts to measure well-being more broadly than simply by how much money people have. It uses three measures—life expectancy, education (adult literacy and mean years of schooling combined), and income (purchasing power parity dollars per capita). Each of the three figures is weighted equally to produce the HDI. The HDI is rated from zero to one—higher numbers mean the country is better off in those three areas. The HDI measures human well-being in terms of persons' ability to enjoy a long life and basic education as well as income. A country's standing changes when the availability of education and health care, not just purchasing power, is taken into account.

Table 6—Comparison of Different Measures of Wealth (2012)

Country	GNI/Capita	PPP/Capita	HDI
U.S.	$52,340	$52,610	.937
Switzerland	$80,970	$55,000	.913
Japan	$47,870	$36,750	.912
U.K.	$38,500	$35,620	.875
Canada	$51,570	$42,270	.911
Saudi Arabia	$24,310	$30,160	.782
Ecuador	$5,170	$9,490	.724
India	$1,550	$3,820	.554
Pakistan	$1,260	$2,880	.515
Kenya	$860	$1,730	.519
Bangladesh	$840	$2,030	.515

Source: World Bank, World Development Indicators (2012); United Nations Development Programme, Human Development Report 2013[24]

The story of money spent on health research underlines our affluence. Rich countries "of course" have almost all the available money for medical research to solve medical problems. "Naturally," they spend it on health problems in rich nations even though health problems are much worse in poor nations. Ninety percent of all spending on health research is invested in rich countries and only a small percentage is devoted to research diseases affecting the poor.[25]

The percentage of personal expenses spent on food in different countries provides another stark comparison (see Table 7). In the United States, it is a mere 6.6 percent. In France, it is 13.2 percent. In the Philippines, it is 42.8 percent.[26]

Agony and anguish are concealed in the simple statistics of Table 7. For persons in the U.S. spending 6.6 percent of their consumer expenditures on food, a 50 percent increase in food costs is troubling but not disastrous. But for persons already spending nearly 50 percent on food, a 50 percent increase means hunger, malnutrition, and perhaps starvation.

Table 7—Expenditures for Food (2012) (as percent of consumer expenditures)

United States	6.6%
United Kingdom	9.1%
Canada	9.6%
Australia	10.2%
France	13.2%
Italy	14.2%
Ecuador	21.9%
Thailand	32.0%
Philippines	42.8%
Sri Lanka	47.7%

Source: USDA, Economic Research Service[27]

Calorie consumption tells the same story. People in many poor nations consume fewer than the daily minimal calorie requirements while people in the developed world have more than they need. While lack of food destroys millions in poor lands, too much food is devastating millions in affluent countries. According to the U.S. Centers for Disease Control and Prevention, 69.2 percent of all American adults were overweight or obese in 2009–2010.[28]

Table 8—Daily per Capita Calorie Consumption by Region

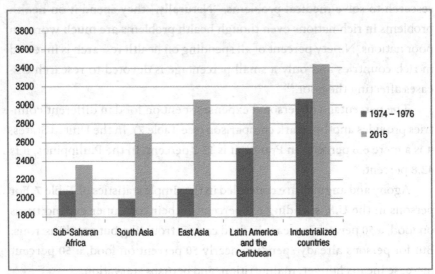

Source: World Health Organization[29]

The facts are clear. Whether measured in terms of Gross National Income, Purchasing Power Parity, The Human Development Index, or the percent spent on food, North Americans, Europeans, and Japanese are many, many times more affluent than the poorest one third of our sisters and brothers.

Poverty at $72,000 a Year?

It was late 1974. Millions were dying from starvation. But that was not the concern of Judd Arnett, a syndicated columnist with Knight Newspapers. In a column read (and probably believed) by millions of North Americans, Arnett lamented the fact that people earning $15,000 ($72,000 in 2014 dollars) a year were on the edge of poverty.[30] "One of the great mysteries of life to me," Arnett wrote, "is how a family in the [$72,000] bracket, before taxes, or even [$86,000], can meet all its obligations and still educate its children."[31]

A few years later *Newsweek* did a story titled "The Middle Class Poor," calmly reporting that U.S. citizens earning $58,700, $70,400, or even $90,800 a year felt they were at the edge of poverty.[32] One resident of New York City grumbled that "you just can't live in this city" on $180,000 a year.[33] A presidential candidate said in 2012 that Americans making $200,000 to $250,000 were middle class.[34]

To the vast majority of the world's people, such statements would be unintelligible—or dishonest. To be sure, we do need $70,000, $86,000, or even much more each year if we insist on having two cars, an expensively furnished, sprawling suburban home, a million-dollar life insurance policy, new clothes every time fashions change, the most recent "laborsaving devices" for home and garden, an annual three-week vacation, and so on. Many North Americans have come to expect precisely that. But that is hardly life at the edge of poverty.

How Generous Are We?

The United States has the largest economy in the world. The U.S. also gives more money in foreign aid than any other nation—$31 billion in 2013. That is almost double the second-highest giver. But as a percent of our national income, the U.S. is almost at the bottom—i.e., one of the least generous donors. As Table 9 shows, the U.S. government's generosity (as a percentage of GNI) is very low, just above that of Italy! The U.S. gives just .19 percent (i.e., less than one-fifth of 1 percent!) of GNI in foreign aid.

Table 9—Estimated Official Development Assistance from Industrialized Countries as Percentage of GNI (2013/2003/1993)

Country	2013	2003	1993
Norway	1.07	0.92	1.01
Sweden	1.02	0.7	0.98
Denmark	0.85	0.84	1.03
U.K.	0.72	0.34	0.31
Netherlands	0.67	0.81	0.82
Finland	0.55	0.34	0.46
Switzerland	0.47	0.38	0.33
Belgium	0.45	0.61	0.39
Ireland	0.45	0.41	0.2
France	0.41	0.41	0.63
Germany	0.38	0.28	0.37
Australia	0.34	0.25	0.35
Austria	0.28	0.2	0.3
Canada	0.27	0.26	0.45
New Zealand	0.26	0.23	0.25
Japan	0.23	0.2	0.26
United States	0.19	0.14	0.15
Italy	0.16	0.16	0.31

Source: Organization for Co-operation and Development[65]

Popular opinion suggests we are far more generous. Polls over several decades have shown that the average American thinks the U.S. government's spending on foreign aid is twenty to fifty times as much as it is in reality.[36] When asked in the same polls how much foreign aid the U.S. should give, people regularly cite a figure that is ten times as much as it is in reality.[37]

The United States did display much greater national generosity at the end of World War II. At the height of the Marshall Plan (begun in 1947 to rebuild war-torn Europe) we annually gave 2.79 percent of our total GNI.[38] But by 1960 the figure for foreign aid had dropped to .54 percent of GNI, and by 2003 it had plummeted to a mere .14 percent (see Table 9). Fortunately, the trend has reversed over the past decade, but only slightly; the U.S. now only gives .19 percent. The richer we become, the less we share with others.

The same pattern holds for many rich nations. Since 1970, rich nations have agreed (and reaffirmed since then) a goal of increasing foreign aid to .7 percent of total GNI.[39] In 1961, rich countries were close to meeting this goal. As a whole they gave .54 percent of their total GNP in foreign aid. But by 1970 it had declined to .33 percent and by 1993 the figure had fallen to a mere .29 percent. In 2003, it dipped to .24 percent before returning to .30 percent in 2013.[40] Ironically, between 1965 and 1980 the economies of rich countries grew at an annual rate of 4.11 percent, between 1980 and 1993 at an annual rate of 2.69 percent, between 1993 and 2003 at an annual rate of 2.59 percent, and between 2003–2012 at an annual rate of 1.53 percent.[41] Not only have we failed to meet our commitments, as we grew richer and richer, we shared a smaller percentage.

A comparison of Western expenditures on foreign aid and the military is startling. In 1991, major aid donors spent 3.55 percent of their GNP on military expenditures but gave only .34 percent of their GNP for economic foreign aid.[42] The level of global military spending in 2003 was fourteen times more than aid given to developing countries.[43] In 2011, world military spending was $1.8 trillion dollars ($1,800,000,000,000), which exceeds the combined income of 2.4 billion of the world's poorest![44]

Is that the way we want to use our abundance?

For a time after the collapse of the Soviet Union, global military expenditures fell. Between 1987 and 1994, global military spending declined at an estimated annual rate of 3.6 percent. That yielded a cumulative peace dividend of $935 billion—$810 billion in industrialized countries and $125 billion in developing countries.[45] Tragically, we were not willing to spend the peace dividend on increasing foreign aid for the poor. And in more recent years, especially since September 11, 2001, military expenditures, especially in the U.S., have rapidly increased. The U.S. has increased military expenditures by 236 percent between 2000 and 2011 in absolute dollars and increased 156 percent as percentage of total GDP.[46] Globally, the UN peacekeeping budget equals less than two days of world military spending.[47]

Rationalizing Our Affluence

It would be impossible for us as a rich minority to live with ourselves if we did not invent plausible justifications. These rationalizations take many forms. Analyzing a few of the most common may help us spot each year's new models.

Lifeboat Ethics

Garrett Hardin, for many years a distinguished biologist at the University of California at Santa Barbara, popularized the term lifeboat ethics. He provoked impassioned, widespread debate with his provocative articles on the subject.[48] He argued that we should not help the poor with food or aid. According to his theory, each rich country is a lifeboat that will survive only if it refuses to waste its limited resources on the hungry masses swimming in the water around it. If we eat together today, we will all starve together tomorrow. Furthermore, since poor countries "irresponsibly" permit unrestrained population growth, starvation is the only way to check the ever-growing number of hungry mouths. The poor will always reproduce like rabbits until starvation reduces their number. Hence, increased aid merely postpones the day of reckoning. Aid simply preserves more persons for ultimate starvation. Therefore, it is ethically correct to help them learn the hard way—by letting them starve now.

Hardin ignored data showing that poor countries can (and have) cut population growth fairly rapidly when they concentrate on improving the lot of the poor. If the poor have a secure food supply, access to some (relatively in-expensive) health services, and modest educational opportunities, population growth tends to decline quickly. Lester Brown summarized these findings:

> There is striking evidence that in an increasing number of poor countries . . . birth rates have dropped sharply despite relatively low per capita

income . . . Examination of societies as different as China, Barbados, Sri Lanka, Uruguay, Taiwan, The Indian Punjab, Cuba and South Korea suggests a common factor. In all these countries, a large portion of the population has gained access to modern social and economic services—such as education, employment, and credit systems . . . There is increasing evidence that the very strategies which cause the greatest improvement in the welfare of the entire population also have the greatest effect on reducing population growth.[49]

Harvard economist Amartya Sen made the same point in his important 1994 essay on population.[50]

Education for women is especially important. Bread for the World reports that "education, especially of girls, is . . . strongly correlated with lower birthrates . . . In Bangladesh, a midday meal program designed to increase the enrollment of girls in school resulted in a 25 percent decline in birthrates over six years."[51] Education delays the time when women marry and begin having children. It also gives them more self-confidence in making reproductive decisions with their husbands.

The right kind of aid—focused especially on empowering the poorest and educating women—will help check population growth.[52] Hardin suggested doing nothing at a time when the right kind of action could produce dramatic improvement.

Another omission in Hardin's thesis is even more astonishing. He totally ignored the fact that there is more than enough food to feed everyone if it is shared fairly.[53] The boat in which the rich sail is not an austerely equipped lifeboat. It is a lavishly stocked luxury liner.

To Evangelize the Rich

A second rationalization has a pious ring to it. Some evangelical Christians argue that they must live in affluence to evangelize the wealthy. Rationalization is dreadfully easy. Garden Grove Community Church in California for many years had a lavish, multimillion-dollar plant complete with a series of water fountains that began spraying when the minister touched a button in the pulpit. The pastor, Robert Schuller, defended his luxurious facilities:

We are trying to make a big, beautiful impression upon the affluent non-religious American who is riding by on this busy freeway. It's obvious that we are not trying to impress the Christians! . . . Nor are we trying to impress the social workers in the County Welfare Department. They would tell us that we ought to be content to remain in the Orange Drive-In Theater and give the money to feed the poor. But suppose we had given this money to feed the poor? What would we have today? We would still have hungry, poor people and God would not have this tremendous base of operations which He is using to inspire people to become more successful, more affluent, more generous, more genuinely unselfish in their giving of themselves.[54]

Beautiful church construction is sometimes appropriate. But how many more glass cathedrals would we build if we first examined the needs of the billion-plus people who live on one dollar a day?

Trickle-Down Wealth

A lively conversation that I had some years ago with a wealthy friend illustrates a third widespread rationalization. This prominent business leader insisted that the best thing he could do for the poor was to buy more things for himself. If he purchased more Jaguars, he argued, then the economy would grow and the poor would have more jobs. This is a dangerous half-truth. Fortunately, some of the benefits of a growing economy do trickle down to the poor—at least to a degree. My response to my friend, however, was that if he spent $100,000 less on Jaguars and used that $100,000 for direct economic empowerment of the poor (via effective economic development programs—see chapter 9), the poor would benefit far more quickly and substantially. That way, the $100,000 would offer the same stimulus to the economy and immediately reduce poverty. My friend insisted that buying Jaguars would work just as well.

Where does valid justification end and rationalization begin?

We must, of course, avoid simplistic legalism. Christians certainly ought to live in the suburbs as well as the inner city. But those who defend an affluent lifestyle on the basis of their call to witness to the rich must ask themselves hard questions:

- How much of my affluent lifestyle is directly related to my witnessing to rich neighbors?
- How much of it could I abandon for the sake of Christ's poor and still be able to witness effectively?
- Indeed how much of it must I abandon in order to faithfully proclaim the biblical Christ who taught that failure to feed the poor leads to eternal damnation (Matt. 25:45–46)?

In the coming decades rationalizations for affluence will abound. They will be popular and persuasive. "Truly I tell you, it will be hard for a rich person to enter the kingdom of heaven" (Matt. 19:23 NRSV). But all things are possible with God—if we will hear and obey his Word. We can move toward a more hopeful future for our world and more genuine joy and fulfillment in our personal lives if we affluent Christians will dare to allow the Bible to shape our relationship to a billion sons and daughters of poor Lazarus. Will rich Christians also be generous?

Study Questions

1. How is the gap between rich and poor different from what you had thought?
2. What are some of the best measures of that gap?
3. How does advertising contribute to our problem? What are some of the theological questions raised by advertising?
4. How does solving poverty help reduce overpopulation?
5. What rationalizations of affluence are most convincing? For yourself? Your friends?
6. Is there any sense in which this book is about joy and self-fulfillment? Explain.

PART TWO

A Biblical Perspective on the Poor and Possessions

If you preach the gospel in all aspects with the exception of the issues which deal specifically with your time you are not preaching the gospel at all.[1]

—MARTIN LUTHER

Social scientists who examined the factors that shape American attitudes on matters related to the development of the poorest nations discovered that religion plays no significant role at all! Those with deep religious beliefs are no more concerned about assistance and development for the poor than are persons with little or no religious commitment.[2]

Most wealthy Christians have failed to seek God's perspective on the plight of our billion plus desperately poor neighbors—surely one of the most pressing issues of our time.

Bur I refuse to believe that this failure must inevitably continue. I believe there are millions of affluent Christians who care more about Jesus than anything else in the world. There are millions of Christians who will take any risk, make any sacrifice, forsake any treasure, if they see clearly that God's Word demands it. That is why Part Two—A Biblical Perspective on the Poor and Possessions—is the most important section of this book.

Part Two is full of Scripture. But even so it is only a small selection of the vast volume of biblical material. My book *For They Shall Be Fed* contains almost two hundred pages of biblical texts that relate directly to the four chapters in this section.[3]

3

GOD AND THE POOR

He who is kind to the poor lends to the LORD.

—PROVERBS 19:17

I know that the LORD maintains the cause of the
afflicted, and executes justice for the needy.

—PSALM 140:12

Is God biased in favor of the poor? Is he on their side in a way that he is not on the side of the rich? Some theologians say yes.[1] But until we clarify the meaning of the question, we cannot answer it correctly. Does it mean that God desires the salvation of poor people more than that of the rich? Does it mean that God and his people treat the poor so much differently from the way the ungodly treat them that God seems to have a special concern for the poor and oppressed? Furthermore, just who are "the poor" in the Bible?

The Hebrew words for the poor are *ani, anaw, ebyon, dal,* and *ras. Ani* (and *anaw*, which originally had approximately the same meaning) denotes one who is "wrongfully impoverished or dispossessed."[2] *Ebyon* refers to a beggar imploring charity. *Dal* connotes a thin, weakly person such as an impoverished, deprived peasant.[3] Unlike the others, *ras* is an essentially neutral term. In their persistent polemic against the oppression of the poor, the prophets used the terms *ebyon, ani,* and *dal*. In the New Testament, the primary word for the poor is *ptochos*, which refers to

45

someone, like a beggar, who is completely destitute and must seek help from others. It is the Greek equivalent of *ani* and *dal.*[4] Thus the primary connotation of "the poor" in Scripture has to do with low economic status usually due to calamity or some form of oppression.

The Scriptures also teach that some folk are poor because they are lazy and slothful (e.g., Prov. 6:6–11; 19:15; 20:13; 21:25; 24:30–34). And, of course, the Bible speaks of voluntary poverty for the sake of the kingdom.

The most common biblical connotation of "the poor," however, relates to those who are economically impoverished due to calamity or exploitation.[5] This chapter deals with this last category.

We can answer the questions about God's alleged bias toward the poor only after finding biblical answers to five related questions: (1) What concern for the poor did God disclose at pivotal points in history when he revealed himself (especially the Exodus, the destruction of Israel and Judah, and the Incarnation)? (2) In what sense does God identify with the poor? (3) Of what significance is the fact that God frequently chooses to work through the poor and oppressed? (4) What does the Bible mean by the recurring teaching that God frequently destroys the rich and exalts the poor? (5) Does God command his people to have a special concern for the poor?

Pivotal Points of Revelation History

The Bible clearly and repeatedly teaches a fundamental point that we often overlook. At the crucial moments when God displayed his mighty acts to reveal his nature and will, God also intervened to liberate the poor and oppressed.

The Exodus

God displayed his power at the Exodus in part to free oppressed slaves. When he called Moses at the burning bush, part of God's intent was to end suffering and injustice: "I have observed the misery of my people who are in Egypt; I have heard their cry on account of their taskmasters. Indeed I know their sufferings, and I have come down to deliver them from the Egyptians" (Ex. 3:7–8 NRSV).

This text does not reflect an isolated perspective on the great event of the Exodus. Each year at the harvest festival the Israelites repeated a liturgical confession celebrating the way God had acted to free their poor, oppressed nation.

> A wandering Aramean was my ancestor; he went down into Egypt and
> lived there. . . . When the Egyptians treated us harshly and afflicted
> us, by imposing hard labor on us, we cried to the LORD, the God of our
> ancestors; the LORD heard our voice and saw our affliction, our toil, and
> our oppression. The LORD brought us out of Egypt with a mighty hand.
> (Deut. 26:5–8 NRSV)

The God of the Bible cares when people enslave and oppress others. At the Exodus, God acted to end economic oppression and bring freedom to slaves.

The liberation of slaves was not, of course, God's only purpose in the Exodus. He also acted because of his covenant with Abraham, Isaac, and Jacob. In addition, God wanted to create a special people to whom he could reveal himself.[6] Both of these concerns were central to God's activity at the Exodus. The liberation of a poor, oppressed people, however, was also at the heart of God's design. The following passage discloses God's multifaceted purpose in the Exodus:

> I have also heard the groaning of the Israelites whom the Egyptians are
> holding as slaves, and I have remembered my covenant [with Abraham,
> Isaac, and Jacob] . . . I will free you from the burdens of the Egyptians and
> deliver you from slavery to them. I will redeem you with an outstretched
> arm and with mighty acts of judgment. I will take you as my people, and
> I will be your God. You shall know that I am the LORD your God, who
> has freed you from the burdens of the Egyptians. (Ex. 6:5–7 NRSV)

Yahweh wanted his people to know him as the One who freed them from slavery and oppression.

The preamble to the Ten Commandments, probably the most important portion of the entire law for Israel, begins with this same revolutionary truth. Before he gives the two tables of the law, Yahweh identifies himself: "I am the Lord your God, who brought you out of the land of Egypt, out of the house of slavery" (Deut. 5:6; Ex. 20:2 NRSV). Yahweh is the one who frees from bondage. The God of the Bible wants to be known as the liberator of the oppressed.

The Exodus was the decisive event in the creation of the chosen people. We distort the biblical interpretation of this momentous occasion if we fail to see that the Lord of the universe was at work correcting oppression and liberating the poor.

Destruction and Captivity

Soon after the Israelites settled in the Promised Land, they discovered that Yahweh's passion for justice was a two-edged sword. When they were oppressed, it led to their freedom. But when they became the oppressors, it led to their destruction.

When God called Israel out of Egypt and made his covenant with them, God gave them his law so that they could live together in peace and justice. But Israel failed to obey the law of the covenant. As a result, God destroyed Israel and sent his chosen people back into captivity.

Why?

The explosive message of the prophets is that God destroyed Israel because of their mistreatment of the poor. Idolatry was an equally prominent reason, but too often we remember only Israel's "spiritual" problem of idolatry and overlook the startling biblical teaching that economic exploitation also sent the chosen people into captivity.

The middle of the eighth century BC was a time of political success and economic prosperity unknown since the days of Solomon.[7] But it was precisely at this moment that God sent his prophet Amos to announce the unwelcome news that the northern kingdom of Israel would be destroyed. Behind the facade of prosperity and fantastic economic growth, Amos saw oppression of the poor. He saw the rich "trample the head of the poor into the dust of the earth" (2:7). He saw that the lifestyle of the rich was built on oppression of the poor (6:1–7). Even in the courts the poor had no hope because the rich bribed the judges (5:10–15).

Archaeologists have confirmed Amos's picture of shocking extremes of wealth and poverty.[8] In the early days of settlement in Canaan, the land was distributed more or less equally among the families and tribes. Most Israelites enjoyed a similar standard of living. In fact, archaeologists have found that houses as late as the tenth century BC were all approximately the same size. But by Amos's day, two centuries later, everything had changed. Bigger, better built houses were found in one area and poorer houses were huddled together in another section.[9] No wonder Amos warned the rich, "You have built houses of hewn stone, but you shall not live in them" (5:11 NRSV)!

God's word through Amos was that the northern kingdom would be destroyed and the people taken into exile (7:11, 17): "Alas for those who lie on beds of ivory, and lounge on their couches, and eat lambs from the flock, and calves from the stall . . . Therefore they shall now be the first to go into exile, and the revelry of the loungers shall pass away" (6:4, 7 NRSV).

A few years after Amos spoke, it happened just as God had said. The Assyrians conquered the northern kingdom and took thousands into captivity. Because of their mistreatment of the poor, God destroyed the northern kingdom—forever.

As in the case of Exodus, we dare not ignore another important factor. The nation's idolatry was also a central cause of their destruction. Because they had forsaken Yahweh for idols, the nation was destroyed (Hosea 8:1–6; 9:1–3).[10] According to the prophets, then, the northern kingdom fell because of both idolatry and economic exploitation of the poor.

God sent other prophets to announce the same fate for the southern kingdom of Judah. Isaiah warned that destruction from afar would befall Judah because of its mistreatment of the poor: "Woe to those who decree iniquitous decrees . . . to turn aside the needy from justice and to rob the poor of my people of their right . . . What will you do on the day of punishment, in the calamity that will come from far away?" (Isa. 10:1–3 NRSV).

Micah denounced those in Judah who "covet fields, and seize them; houses, and take them away; they oppress householder and house, people and their inheritance" (2:2). As a result, he warned, Jerusalem would one day become "a heap of ruins" (3:12) (NRSV, both).

Fortunately, Judah was more open to the prophetic word, and the nation was spared for a time. But oppression of the poor continued. A hundred years after Isaiah, the prophet Jeremiah again condemned the wealthy who had amassed riches by oppressing the poor:

"Wicked men are found among my people; they lurk like fowlers lying in wait. They set a trap; they catch men. Like a basket full of birds, their houses are full of treachery; therefore they have become great and rich, they have grown fat and sleek. They know no bounds in deeds of wickedness; they judge not with justice the cause of the fatherless, to make it prosper, and they do not defend the rights of the needy. Shall I not punish them for these things? says the LORD, and shall I not avenge myself on a nation such as this?" (Jer. 5:26–29)

Even at that late date Jeremiah offered hope if the people would forsake injustice and idolatry. "If you truly act justly one with another, if you do not oppress the alien, the orphan, and the widow . . . then I will dwell with you in this place, in the land that I gave of old to your ancestors forever" (Jer. 7:5–7 NRSV).

But they continued to oppress the poor and helpless (Jer. 34:3–17). As a result, Jeremiah persisted in warning that God would use the Babylonians to destroy Judah. In 587 BC Jerusalem fell, and the Babylonian captivity began.

The destruction of Israel and Judah was not mere punishment. God used the Assyrians and Babylonians to purge his people of oppression and injustice. In a remarkable passage, Isaiah showed how God would attack his foes and enemies (that is, his chosen people!) in order to purify them and restore justice.

How the faithful city [Jerusalem] has become a harlot, she that was full of justice! Righteousness lodged in her, but now murderers. Your silver has become dross, your wine mixed with water . . . Every one loves a bribe and runs after gifts. They do not defend the fatherless, and the widow's cause does not come to them. Therefore the Lord says, the LORD of hosts, the Mighty One of Israel: "Ah, I will vent my wrath on my enemies, and avenge myself on my foes. I will turn my hand against you and will smelt away your dross as with lye and remove all your alloy. And I will restore your judges as at the first, and your counselors as at the beginning. Afterward you shall be called the city of righteousness, the faithful city." (1:21–26)

The catastrophe of national destruction and captivity reveals the God of the Exodus still at work correcting the oppression of the poor.

The Incarnation

Christians believe that God revealed himself most completely in Jesus of Nazareth, so to understand God's work in the world it is important to understand how the Incarnate One defined his mission.

Jesus' words in the synagogue at Nazareth, spoken near the beginning of his public ministry, throb with hope for the poor. He read from the prophet Isaiah: "The Spirit of the Lord is upon me, because he has anointed me to preach good news to the poor. He has sent me to proclaim release to the captives and recovering of sight to the blind, to set at liberty those who are oppressed, to proclaim the acceptable year of the Lord" (Luke 4:18–19).

After reading these words, Jesus informed his audience that this Scripture was now fulfilled in himself. The mission of the Incarnate One included freeing the oppressed and healing the blind. (It was also to preach the gospel, which is equally important, but the focus of this book precludes further discussion of it.)[11] The poor are the only group specifically singled out as recipients of Jesus' gospel. Certainly the gospel he proclaimed was for all, but he was particularly concerned that the poor realize that his good news was for them.

Some try to avoid the clear meaning of Jesus' statement by spiritualizing his words. Certainly, as other texts show, he came to open our blinded hearts, to die for our sins, and to free us from the oppression of guilt. But that is not what he means here. The words about releasing captives and liberating the oppressed are from Isaiah. In their original Old Testament setting they unquestionably referred to physical oppression and captivity. In Luke 7:18–23, which contains a list similar to the one in Luke 4:18–19, it is clear that Jesus is referring to material, physical problems.[12]

Jesus' actual ministry corresponded precisely to the words of Luke 4.

He spent considerable time ministering to lepers, despised women, and other marginalized folk. He healed the sick and blind. He fed the hungry. And he warned his followers in the strongest possible words that those who do not feed the hungry, clothe the naked, and visit the prisoners will experience eternal damnation (Matt. 25:31–46).

At the supreme moment of history, when God took on human flesh, the God of Israel was still liberating the poor and oppressed and summoning his people to do the same. That is the central reason for Christian concern for the poor.

It is not just at the Exodus, captivity, and Incarnation, however, that we learn of God's concern for the poor, the weak, and the oppressed. The Bible is full of passages that speak of this. Two illustrations from the Psalms are typical of a host of other texts.

Psalm 10 begins with despair. God seems to have hidden himself far away while the wicked prosper by oppressing the poor (vv. 2, 9). But the psalmist concludes with hope: "The hapless commits himself to thee; thou hast been the helper of the fatherless . . . O Lord, thou wilt hear the desire of the meek . . . thou wilt incline thy ear to do justice to the fatherless and the oppressed" (vv. 14, 17–18).

Psalm 146 is a ringing declaration that to care for the poor is central to the very nature of God. The psalmist exults in the God of Jacob because he is both the creator of the universe and the defender of the oppressed.

> Praise the Lord! Praise the Lord, O my soul . . . Happy is he whose help is
> the God of Jacob, whose hope is in the Lord his God, who made heaven
> and earth, the sea, and all that is in them; who keeps faith for ever; who
> executes justice for the oppressed; who gives food to the hungry. The
> Lord sets the prisoners free; the Lord opens the eyes of the blind. The
> Lord lifts up those who are bowed down; the Lord loves the righteous.
> The Lord watches over the sojourners, he upholds the widow and the
> fatherless; but the way of the wicked he brings to ruin. (vv. 1, 5–9)

According to Scripture, defending the weak, the stranger, and the oppressed is as much an expression of God's essence as creating the universe. Because of who he is, Yahweh lifts up the mistreated.[13] The foundation of Christian concern for the hungry and oppressed is that God cares especially for them.

God Identifies with the Poor

God not only acts in history to liberate the poor, but in a mysterious way that we can only partly fathom, the Sovereign of the universe identifies with the weak and destitute. Two proverbs state this beautiful truth. Proverbs 14:31 puts it negatively: "Those who oppress the poor insult their Maker" (NRSV). Even more moving is the positive formulation: "He who is kind to the poor lends to the Lord" (19:17). What a statement! Assisting a poor person is like helping the Creator of all things with a loan.

Only in the Incarnation can we begin to perceive what God's identification with the weak, oppressed, and poor really means. "Though he was rich," Paul says of our Lord Jesus, "yet for your sake he became poor" (2 Cor. 8:9).

Jesus was born in a small, insignificant province of the Roman Empire. His first visitors, the shepherds, were viewed by Jewish society as thieves. His parents were too poor to bring the normal offering for purification. Instead of a lamb, they brought two pigeons to the Temple (Luke 2:24; cf. Lev. 12:6–8). Jesus was a refugee (Matt. 2:13–15). Since Jewish rabbis received no fees for their teaching, Jesus had no regular income during his public ministry.[14] (Scholars belonged to the poorer classes in Judaism.) Nor did he have a home of his own. Jesus warned an eager follower who promised to follow him everywhere, "Foxes have holes, and birds of the air have nests; but the Son of man has nowhere to lay his head" (Matt. 8:20). He sent out disciples with very little to sustain them (Luke 9:3; 10:4).

God did not become flesh as a wealthy aristocrat. However, it is also true that Jesus' family probably was not from the poorest class. At Jesus' birth, Joseph and Mary must have been fairly poor—as their sacrifice shows. And as refugees in Egypt they probably had very little. But Jesus lived much of his life in a carpenter's family in Nazareth, and Galilean carpenters in Jesus' day normally earned a reasonable income. So we should not think of the family in which Jesus grew up as living in poverty.[15]

Jesus, however, identified with the poor in important ways. He insisted that his preaching to the poor was a sign that he was the Messiah. When John the Baptist sent messengers to ask him if he were the long expected Messiah, Jesus simply pointed to his deeds: he was healing the sick and preaching to the poor (Matt. 11:2–6). Jesus also preached to the rich. But apparently it was his particular concern to preach to the poor that validated his claim to messiahship. His extensive engagement with the poor and disadvantaged contrasted sharply with the style of his contemporaries. Was that part of the reason he added a final word to take back to John: "Blessed is he who takes no offense at me" (Matt. 11:6)?

The clearest statement about Jesus' identification with the poor is in Matthew 25: "I was hungry and you gave me food, I was thirsty and you gave me something to drink. . . . I was naked and you gave me clothing. . . . Truly, I tell you, just as you did it to one of the least of these who are members of my family, you did it to me" (vv. 35–36, 40 NRSV).

What does it mean to feed and clothe the Creator of all things? We cannot know. We can only look on the poor and oppressed with new eyes and resolve to heal their hurts and help end their oppression.

If Jesus' teaching in Matthew 25:40 is startling, its parallel is terrifying: "Truly, I say to you, as you did it not to one of the least of these, you did it not to me" (v. 45). What does that mean in a world where millions die each year of starvation while rich Christians live in escalating affluence?

What does it mean to see the Lord of the universe lying by the roadside starving and walk by on the other side? We cannot know. We can only pledge, in fear and trembling, not to kill him again.

God's Special Instruments

When God selected a chosen people, he picked poor slaves in Egypt. When God called the early church, many of the members were poor. When God became flesh, he chose, for our sakes, to become poor (2 Cor. 8:9). Are these facts isolated phenomena or part of an important pattern?

God could have selected a rich, powerful nation as his chosen people. Instead he chose impoverished, oppressed slaves to be his special instrument of revelation and salvation for all people. (See also the story of Gideon in Judges 6:15–16; 7:2.)

In the early church, many members were poor. In a book sketching the social history of early Christianity, Martin Hengel points out that the early Gentile Christian communities "were predominantly poor."[16] The apostle Paul marveled at the kind of people God called into the church:

> Not many of you were wise according to worldly standards, not many were powerful, not many were of noble birth; but God chose what is foolish in the world to shame the wise, God chose what is weak in the world to shame the strong, God chose what is low and despised in the world, even things that are not, to bring to nothing things that are, so that no human being might boast in the presence of God. (1 Cor. 1:26–29)

Likewise James:

> My brothers and sisters, do you with your acts of favoritism really believe in our glorious Lord Jesus Christ? For if a person with gold rings and in fine clothes comes into your assembly, and if a poor person in dirty clothes also comes in, and if you take notice of the one wearing the fine clothes and say, "Have a seat here, please," while to the one who is poor you say, "Stand there," or, "Sit at my feet," have you not made distinctions among yourselves, and become judges with evil thoughts? Listen, my beloved brothers and sisters. *Has not God chosen the poor in the world to be rich in faith and to be heirs of the kingdom that he has promised to those who love him?* But you have dishonored the poor. Is it not the rich who oppress you? Is it not they who drag you into court? Is it not they who blaspheme the excellent name that was invoked over you? (James 2:1–7 NRSV, italics added)

The rhetorical question in verse 5 (in italics) indicates that the Jerusalem church was far from rich. But the passage illustrates how the church so often forsakes God's way and opts instead for the way of the world. At both the Exodus and the emergence of the early church, God chose poor folk as his special instruments.

We must, however, beware of overstating the case. Abraham seems to have been well off. Moses lived at Pharaoh's court for forty years. Not all the early Christians were poor. Paul and Luke were educated and at least reasonably well-to-do. God does not work exclusively through impover-ished, oppressed people. There is, nonetheless, a sharp contrast between God's procedure and ours. When we want to effect change, we almost always contact people with influence, prestige, and power. When God wants to save the world, he often selects slaves, prostitutes, and sundry other disadvantaged folk. He sees potential that we do not. And when the task is done, the poor and weak are less likely to boast that they deserve the credit. God's frequent selection of the lowly to be his special messengers of salvation to the world is striking evidence of his special concern for them.

Again, the Incarnation is important. God might have entered history as a powerful Roman emperor living in luxurious power at the center of the greatest empire of the time. Or he could have appeared at least as an influential Sadducee with a prominent place in the Sanhedrin in the holy city of Jerusalem. Instead he came and lived as a carpenter in the small town of Nazareth—a place too insignificant to be mentioned either in the Old Testament or the writings of Josephus, the first-century Jewish histo-rian.[17] Yet this is how God chose to effect our salvation.

Why Does God Cast Down the Rich?

Jesus' story of the rich man and Lazarus illustrates a fourth teaching prominent throughout Scripture. God actually works in history to cast down some rich, powerful people. Does that sound too strong? Listen to the biblical texts.

Mary's Magnificat puts it simply and bluntly: "My soul magnifies the Lord . . . He has put down the mighty from their thrones, and exalted those of low degree; he has filled the hungry with good things, and the rich he has sent empty away" (Luke 1:46, 52–53). Centuries earlier, Hannah's song proclaimed the same truth:

> There is none holy like the Lord, there is none besides thee . . . Talk no more so very proudly, let not arrogance come from your mouth . . . The bows of the mighty are broken, but the feeble gird on strength. Those who were full have hired themselves out for bread, but those who were

hungry have ceased to hunger . . . The Lord makes poor and makes rich . . . He raises up the poor from the dust; he lifts the needy from the ash heap. (1 Sam. 2:2–8)

Jesus pronounced a blessing on the poor and a curse on the rich: "Blessed are you poor, for yours is the kingdom of God. Blessed are you that hunger now, for you shall be satisfied . . . Woe to you that are rich, for you have received your consolation. Woe to you that are full now, for you shall hunger" (Luke 6:20–25).[18]

"Come now, you rich, weep and howl for the miseries that are coming upon you" (James 5:1) is a frequent theme of biblical revelation.

Why does Scripture declare that God sometimes reverses the good fortunes of the rich? Is it because creating wealth is bad? No. The Bible says exactly the opposite. Is God engaged in class warfare? Not at all. Scripture never says that God loves the poor more than the rich. But it does regularly assert that God lifts up the poor and disadvantaged. And it frequently teaches that God casts down the wealthy and powerful in two specific situations: (1) when they become wealthy by oppressing the poor; or (2) when they fail to share with the needy.

Casting Down Rich Oppressors

Why did James warn some rich folk he knew to weep and howl because of impending misery? Because they had cheated their workers: "You have laid up treasure for the last days. Behold, the wages of the laborers who mowed your fields, which you kept back by fraud, cry out; and the cries of the harvesters have reached the ears of the Lord of hosts. You have lived on the earth in luxury and in pleasure; you have fattened your hearts in a day of slaughter" (James 5:3–5).

God does not have class enemies. But he hates and punishes both oppression and neglect of the poor. And the rich, if we accept the repeated warnings of Scripture, are frequently guilty of one or both.[19]

Long before the days of James, the psalmist knew that the rich were often rich because of oppression. He took comfort in the assurance that God would punish such evildoers:

In arrogance the wicked hotly pursue the poor . . . His ways prosper at all times . . . He thinks in his heart, "I shall not be moved; throughout all generations I shall not meet adversity." . . . He lurks in secret like a lion in his covert; he lurks that he may seize the poor, he seizes the poor when he draws him into his net . . . Arise, O Lord; O God, lift up thy hand; forget not the afflicted . . . Break thou the arm of the wicked and evildoer . . . O Lord, thou wilt hear the desire of the meek; thou wilt strengthen their heart, thou wilt incline thy ear to do justice to the fatherless and the oppressed. (Ps. 10:2–18)

God announced the same message through the prophet Jeremiah:

Wicked men are found among my people; they lurk like fowlers lying in wait. They set a trap; they catch men. Like a basket full of birds their houses are full of treachery; therefore they have become great and rich, they have grown fat and sleek. They know no bounds in deeds of wickedness; they judge not with justice the cause of the fatherless, to make it prosper, and they do not defend the rights of the needy. Shall I not punish them for these things? says the Lord. (Jer. 5:26–29)

Nor was the faith of Jeremiah and the psalmist mere wishful thinking. Through the prophets, God announced devastation and destruction for both rich individuals and rich nations who oppressed the poor. And it happened as they predicted.

Jeremiah pronounced one of the most biting, satirical diatribes in all of Scripture against the unjust King Jehoiakim of Judah:

"Woe to him who builds his house by unrighteousness, and his upper rooms by injustice; who makes his neighbor serve him for nothing, and does not give him his wages; who says, 'I will build myself a great house with spacious upper rooms,' and cuts out windows for it, paneling it with cedar, and painting it with vermilion. Do you think you are a king because you compete in cedar? Did not your father eat and drink and do justice and righteousness? Then it was well with him. He judged the cause of the poor and needy; then it was well. Is not this to know me?

says the LORD. But you have eyes and heart only for your dishonest gain, for shedding innocent blood, and for practicing oppression and vio- lence." Therefore thus says the LORD concerning Jehoiakim . . . "With the burial of an ass he shall be buried, dragged and cast forth beyond the gates of Jerusalem." (Jer. 22:13–19)

Jehoiakim, historians think, was assassinated.[20]

God destroys whole nations as well as rich individuals because of their oppression of the poor. We have already examined a few of the pertinent texts.[21] One more is important. Through Isaiah, God declared that the rul- ers of Judah were rich because they had cheated the poor. Surfeited with affluence, the wealthy women had indulged in self-centered wantonness, oblivious to the suffering of the oppressed. The result, God said, would be destruction.

The LORD enters into judgment with the elders and princes of his people: "It is you who have devoured the vineyard, the spoil of the poor is in your houses. What do you mean by crushing my people, by grinding the face of the poor?" says the Lord GOD of hosts. The LORD said: Because the daughters of Zion are haughty and walk with outstretched necks, glancing wantonly with their eyes, mincing along as they go, tinkling with their feet; the Lord will smite with a scab the heads of the daughters of Zion . . . In that day the Lord will take away the finery of the anklets, the head- bands, and the crescents . . . Instead of perfume there will be rottenness; and instead of a girdle, a rope; and instead of well-set hair, baldness; and instead of a rich robe, a girding of sackcloth; instead of beauty, shame. Your men shall fall by the sword and your mighty men in battle. (Isa. 3:14–25)

When the rich oppress the poor and weak, the Lord of history is at work pulling down their houses and kingdoms.

Neglecting the Poor

Sometimes Scripture simply accuses the rich of failure to share with the needy and does not suggest that their wealth was acquired in unjust ways. But the result is the same.

In the story of the rich man and Lazarus, Jesus does not say that the rich man exploited Lazarus (Luke 16). He merely shows his lack of concern for the sick beggar lying outside his gate. "Clothed in purple and fine linen [the rich man] feasted sumptuously every day" (Luke 16:19). Lazarus, on the other hand, "desired to be fed with what fell from the rich man's table" (v. 21). Did the rich man deny hungry Lazarus even the scraps? Perhaps not. But obviously he had no real concern for him.

Such sinful neglect of the needy infuriates the God of the poor. When Lazarus died, God comforted him in Abraham's bosom. When the rich man died, torment confronted him.[22] The meaning of the name Lazarus, "one whom God has helped," underlines the basic point.[23] God aids the poor, but the rich who neglect poor neighbors go to hell.

Clark Pinnock is surely correct when he notes that the story of the rich man and Lazarus "ought to explode in our hands when we read it sitting at our well-covered tables while the third world stands outside."[24] It is not merely the Law and the Prophets but also Jesus our Lord who declares the terrifying word that God destroys the rich when they fail to assist the poor.

The biblical explanation of Sodom's destruction provides another illustration of this fearsome truth. If asked why Sodom was destroyed, most Christians would point to the city's sexual perversity. But that is a one-sided view of what Scripture teaches. Ezekiel says that one important reason God destroyed Sodom was that it stubbornly refused to share with the poor: "Behold, this was the guilt of your sister Sodom: she and her daughters had pride, surfeit of food, and prosperous ease, but did not aid the poor and needy. They were haughty, and did abominable things before me; therefore I removed them, when I saw it (Ezek. 16:49–50; see also Isa. 1:10–17).

The text does not say that they oppressed the poor, although they may have. It simply accuses them of failing to assist the needy.

Affluent Christians remember Sodom's sexual misconduct and forget its sinful unconcern for the poor. Is it because the former is less upsetting? Have we allowed our economic self-interest to distort our interpretation of Scripture? Undoubtedly we have. But to the extent that our affirmation of scriptural authority is sincere, we will permit painful texts to correct our thinking. As we do, we will acknowledge in fear and trembling that the God of the Bible wreaks horrendous havoc on some kinds of rich people—not because he does not love those who are rich (God loves everyone equally), but because the rich sometimes oppress the poor or neglect the needy.

God's Concern and Ours

Since God cares so much for the poor, it is hardly surprising that God wants his people to do the same.

Equal justice for the poor in court is a constant concern of Scripture. The law commanded it (Ex. 23:6). The psalmist invoked divine assistance for the king so that he could provide it (Ps. 72:1–4). And the prophets announced destruction because the rulers stubbornly subverted it (Amos 5:10–15).

Widows, orphans, and strangers also receive frequent attention: "You shall not wrong a stranger or oppress him, for you were strangers in the land of Egypt. You shall not afflict any widow or orphan. If you do afflict them, and they cry out to me, I will surely hear their cry; and my wrath will burn, and I will kill you with the sword, and your wives shall become widows and your children fatherless" (Ex. 22:21–24).

"The fatherless, widows, and foreigners," John F. Alexander has observed, "each have about forty verses that command justice for them. God wants to make it very clear that in a special sense he is the protector of these weak ones. Strangers are to be treated nearly the same as Jews, and woe to people who take advantage of orphans or widows."[25]

Rare indeed are Christians who pay any attention to Jesus' command to show bias toward the poor in their dinner invitations: "When you give a dinner or a banquet, do not invite your friends or your brothers or your kinsmen or rich neighbors . . . But when you give a feast, invite the poor, the maimed, the lame, the blind, and you will be blessed, because they cannot repay you" (Luke 14:12–14; see also Heb. 13:1–3).

Jesus was using hyperbole, a typical technique of Hebrew literature to emphasize his point. He did not mean to forbid parties with friends and relatives. But he did mean that we ought to entertain the poor and disadvantaged (who cannot reciprocate) at least as often—and perhaps a lot more often—than we entertain friends, relatives, and "successful" folk. Have you ever known a Christian who took Jesus that seriously?

The Bible specifically commands believers to imitate God's special concern for the poor and oppressed. In the Old Testament, Yahweh frequently reminded the Israelites of their former oppression in Egypt when he commanded them to care for the poor. God's unmerited concern for the Hebrew slaves in Egyptian bondage is the model to imitate (Ex. 22:21–24; Deut. 15:13–15).

Jesus taught his followers to imitate God's mercy in their lending as well.

> If you do good to those who do good to you, what credit is that to you? . . . If you lend to those from whom you hope to receive, what credit is that to you? . . . Lend, expecting nothing in return. Your reward will be great, and you will be children of the Most High; for he is kind to the ungrateful and the wicked. Be merciful, just as your Father is merciful. (Luke 6:33–36 NRSV)

Why lend without expecting return? Because that is the way our Father acts. Jesus' followers are to reverse normal human patterns precisely because they are sons and daughters of God and want to reflect his nature.

When Paul took up the collection for the poor in Jerusalem, he pointedly reminded the Corinthians that the Lord Jesus became poor so that they might become rich (2 Cor. 8:9). When John called on Christians to share with the needy, he first mentioned the example of Christ: "We know love by this, that he laid down his life for us—and we ought to lay down our lives for one another" (1 John 3:16 NRSV). Then, in the very next verse, he urged Christians to give generously to the needy. It is the amazing self-sacrifice of Christ that Christians are to imitate as they relate to the poor and oppressed.

We have seen that God's Word commands believers to care for the poor. In fact the Bible underlines the command by teaching that when God's people care for the poor, they imitate God himself. But that is not all.

God's Word teaches a very hard, disturbing truth. Those who neglect the poor and oppressed are really not God's people at all—no matter how frequent their religious rituals or how orthodox their creeds and confessions.

God thundered again and again through the prophets that worship in the context of mistreatment of the poor and disadvantaged is an outrage. Isaiah denounced Israel (he called it Sodom and Gomorrah!) because it tried to worship Yahweh and oppress the weak at the same time:

> Hear the word of the Lord, you rulers of Sodom! Give ear to the teach-
> ing of our God, you people of Gomorrah! "What to me is the multitude
> of your sacrifices? . . . Bring no more vain offerings; incense is an abomi-
> nation to me. New moon and sabbath and the calling of assemblies—I
> cannot endure iniquity and solemn assembly. Your new moons and your
> appointed feasts my soul hates; . . . even though you make many prayers,
> I will not listen; your hands are full of blood." (Isa. 1:10–15)

What does God want? The very next verses tell us. "Cease to do evil, learn to do good; seek justice, correct oppression; defend the fatherless, plead for the widow" (vv. 16–17).

Equally powerful are Isaiah's words against mixing fasting and injustice:

> "Why have we fasted, and thou seest it not? Why have we humbled our-
> selves, and thou takest no knowledge of it?" Behold, in the day of your
> fast you seek your own pleasure, and oppress all your workers . . . Is not
> this the fast that I choose: to loose the bonds of wickedness, to undo the
> thongs of the yoke, to let the oppressed go free, and to break every yoke?
> Is it not to share your bread with the hungry, and bring the homeless
> poor into your house? (58:3–7)

God's words through the prophet Amos are also harsh: "I hate, I despise your feasts, and I take no delight in your solemn assemblies. Even though you offer me your burnt offerings and cereal offerings, I will not accept them . . . But let justice roll down like waters, and righteousness like an everflowing stream" (5:21–24).[26]

Earlier, the prophet had condemned the rich and powerful for oppress-ing the poor. They even bribed judges to prevent redress in the courts.

Their worship was a mockery and an abomination to the God of the poor, who wants justice, not mere religious rituals.[27]

God has not changed. Jesus repeated the same theme. He warned the people about the scribes "who devour widows' houses and for a pretense make long prayers" (Mark 12:40). Their pious-looking garments and frequent visits to the synagogue were a sham. Jesus was a Hebrew prophet in the tradition of Amos and Isaiah. Like them he announced God's outrage against those who try to mix pious practices and mistreatment of the poor.

The prophetic word against religious hypocrites raises a difficult question. Are the people who call themselves by Christ's name truly God's people if they neglect the poor? Is the church really the church if it does not work to free the oppressed?

We have seen how God declared that the people of Israel were really Sodom and Gomorrah rather than the people of God (Is. 1:10). God could not tolerate their exploitation of the poor and disadvantaged any longer. Hosea solemnly announced that, because of their sins, Israel was no longer God's people and he was no longer their God (1:8–9). In fact, God destroyed them.

Jesus expressed it even more pointedly. To those who do not feed the hungry, clothe the naked, and visit the prisoners, he will speak a terrifying word at the final judgment: "Depart from me, you cursed, into the eternal fire prepared for the devil and his angels" (Matt. 25:41). The meaning is clear. Jesus intends that his disciples imitate his own concern for the poor and needy. Those who disobey will experience eternal damnation.

But perhaps we have misinterpreted Matthew 25. Some people think that "the least of these" (v. 45) and "the least of these who are members of my family" (v. 40 NRSV) refer only to Christians.[28] This exegesis is not certain. But even if the primary reference of these words is to poor believers, other aspects of Jesus' teaching not only permit but require us to extend the meaning of Matthew 25 to both believers and unbelievers who are poor and oppressed. The story of the good Samaritan teaches that anybody in need is our neighbor (Luke 10:29–37). Matthew 5:43–45 (NRSV) is even more explicit: "You have heard that it was said, 'You shall love your neighbor and hate your enemy.' But I say to you, Love your enemies and pray for those who persecute you, so that you may be children of your

Father in heaven; for he makes his sun rise on the evil and on the good, and sends rain on the righteous and on the unrighteous."

The ideal in the Qumran community (known to us as the place where the Dead Sea Scrolls were found) was indeed to "love all the sons of light" and "hate all the sons of darkness" (1 QS 1:9–10, the Essenes' Community Rule). Even in the Old Testament, Israelites were commanded to love the neighbor who was the child of their own people and ordered not to seek the prosperity of Ammonites and Moabites (Lev. 19:17–18; Deut. 23:36). But Jesus forbids his followers to limit their concern to the neighbors who are members of their own ethnic or religious group. On the other hand, he commands his followers to imitate God, who does good for all people everywhere.

As evangelical New Testament scholar George Ladd said, "Jesus redefines the meaning of love for neighbor; it means love for any man in need."[29] In light of the Parable of the Good Samaritan and the clear teaching of Matthew 5:43–48, one is compelled to say that part of the teaching of Matthew 25 is that those who fail to aid the poor and oppressed (whether they are believers or not) are simply not the people of God.

We find the same message in 1 John 3:17–18 (NRSV): "How does God's love abide in anyone who has the world's goods and sees a brother or sister in need and yet refuses help? Little children, let us love, not in word or speech, but in truth and action." (See also James 2:14–17.)

Again the words are plain. What do they mean for rich Christians who demand increasing affluence while poor Christians in developing nations suffer from malnutrition, deformed bodies and brains, even starvation? The text says that if we fail to aid the needy, we do not have God's love—no matter what we may say. It is deeds that count, not pious phrases and saintly speeches. Regardless of what we do or say at 11:00 a.m. on Sunday morning, rich Christians who neglect the poor are not the people of God.

But still the question persists. Does continuing sin mean that professing believers are really not Christians? Obviously not. The Christian knows that sinful selfishness continues to plague even the most saintly. Salvation is by grace alone, not works of righteousness. We are members of the people of God not because of our own righteousness but solely because of Christ's death for us.

That response is true—but inadequate by itself. Matthew 25 and 1 John 3 surely mean more than that the people of God are disobedient (but still justified all the same) when they persistently neglect the poor. These verses pointedly assert that some people so disobey God that they are not his people at all in spite of their pious profession. Neglect of the poor is one of the oft-repeated biblical signs of such disobedience. Certainly none of us would claim that we fulfill Matthew 25 perfectly. And we cling to the hope of forgiveness. But there comes a point (and, thank God, he alone knows where!) when neglect of the poor is not forgiven. It is punished. Eternally.

Is it not possible that many rich "Christians" have reached that point? Christians in North America and Western Europe earn $15 trillion (more than the GDP of low and lower-middle income countries combined), but give only a tiny faction (.7 percent) of our affluence to the church.[30] Most churches spend much of that pittance on themselves. Can we claim we are obeying the biblical command to have a special concern for the poor? Can we honestly say we are imitating God's concern for the poor and oppressed? If the Bible is true, can we seriously hope to experience eternal love rather than eternal separation from the God of the poor?

The biblical teaching that Yahweh has a special concern for the poor and oppressed is without ambiguity. But that does not mean, as some assert today, that God is biased in favor of the poor. In fact, Scripture explicitly forbids partiality. "You shall do no injustice in judgment; you shall not be partial to the poor or defer to the great, but in righteousness shall you judge your neighbor" (Lev. 19:15; also Deut. 1:11). Exodus 23:3 contains the same injunction: "Nor shall you be partial to a poor man in his suit."

The most crucial point for us, however, is not God's impartiality, but rather the result of his freedom from bias. The text declares Yahweh's impartiality and then immediately portrays God's tender care for the weak and disadvantaged. "For the Lord your God is God of gods and Lord of lords, the great, the mighty, and the terrible God, who is not partial and takes no bribe. He executes justice for the fatherless and the widow, and loves the sojourner, giving him food and clothing" (Deut. 10:17–18).

God is not partial. He has the same loving concern for each person he has created.[31] Precisely for that reason he cares as much for the weak and disadvantaged as he does for the strong and fortunate. By contrast with the way you and I, as well as the comfortable and powerful of every age and society, normally act toward the poor, God seems to have an overwhelming bias in favor of the poor. But he is biased only in contrast with our sinful unconcern. It is only when we take our sinful preoccupation with the successful and wealthy as natural and normative that God's equal concern for all looks like a bias for the poor.

Is God on the Side of the Poor?

Before we can answer whether or not God is on the side of the poor, we need to remember some things God is not. First, as mentioned above, God is not biased. Second, material poverty is not a biblical ideal. Third, being poor and oppressed does not make people members of the church. (The poor disobey God just as much as the rich and middle class; they, too, need to repent and be saved by God's justifying grace.) Fourth, God does not care more about the salvation of the poor than of the rich. Fifth, we dare not start with some ideologically interpreted context of oppression (for example, Marxist analysis) and then reinterpret Scripture from that ideological bias. Sixth, God does not overlook the sin of those who are poor due to sloth or alcoholism. God punishes such sinners.

God, however, is not neutral. His freedom from bias does not mean that he maintains neutrality in the struggle for justice. The Bible clearly and repeatedly teaches that God is at work in history exalting the poor and casting down the rich who got that way by oppressing or neglecting the poor. In that sense, God is on the side of the poor. He has a special concern for them because of their vulnerability.

God demands that all people have the opportunity to earn a reasonable living. For that reason, he works to empower the poor. The God of the Bible is, in the sense just indicated, on the side of the poor precisely because he is not biased, precisely because he is a God of impartial justice who cares equally about everyone.

The rich often neglect or oppose justice because it demands that they end their oppression and share with the poor. God actively opposes that kind of rich person and society, but that does not mean God loves the rich any less than the poor. God longs for the salvation of both and desires fulfillment, joy, and happiness for all his creatures. He knows that neither those who are oppressed nor those who do the oppressing find those things.

God's equal concern for everyone, however, does not mean that God is neutral in contexts of neglect and oppression. Genuine biblical repentance and conversion lead people to turn away from all sin—including economic oppression.[32] Salvation for the rich includes freedom from the sin of being unjust. Thus God's desire for the salvation and fulfillment of the rich is in complete harmony with the scriptural teaching that God is on the side of the poor in the specific sense that God actively seeks justice for those who are oppressed and neglected. (In fact, by pulling down oppressors and lifting up the oppressed, God does what is good for both groups.)

In light of this biblical teaching, how biblical is our theology? I think we must confess that rich Christians are largely on the side of the rich rather than the poor. But imagine what would happen if all our church institutions—our youth organizations, our publications, our colleges and seminaries, our congregations and denominational headquarters—would all dare to undertake a comprehensive two-year examination of their programs and activities to answer this question: Is there the same balance and emphasis on justice for the poor and oppressed in our programs as there is in Scripture? If we were to do this with an unconditional readiness to change whatever did not correspond with the scriptural revelation of God's special concern for the poor and oppressed, I predict that we would unleash a new movement of biblical social concern that would transform the world.

I hope and believe that in the next decades millions of Christians will allow this important biblical truth to fundamentally reshape our culturally conditioned theology and our unbiblically one-sided programs and institutions. If that happens, we will forge a new, truly biblical theology of liberation that will change the course of modern history.[33]

Study Questions

1. Review the five major foundations for the thesis that God has a special concern for the poor. Which do you find most convincing? Least convincing? Why?

2. Why does it seem that God is biased toward the poor? In what ways is he always unbiased?

3. Does the preaching and teaching you hear place as much emphasis on the welfare of the poor as does the Bible? If not, how do you explain the difference?

4. If we ignore the poor, what are we saying about our belief in God?

5. What does Matthew 25:31–46 really mean?

4

ECONOMIC FELLOWSHIP AND ECONOMIC JUSTICE

I do not mean that others should be eased and you burdened, but that as a matter of equality your abundance at the present time should supply their want, so that their abundance may supply your want, that there may be equality. As it is written, "He who gathered much had nothing over, and he who gathered little had no lack."

—2 CORINTHIANS 8:13–15

God requires radically transformed economic relationships among his people because sin has alienated us from God and from each other. The result is personal selfishness, structural injustice, and economic oppression. Among the people of God, however, the power of sin is broken. The community of the redeemed is to display a dramatically new set of personal, social, and economic relationships. The quality of life among the people of God is to be a sign of the coming perfection and justice that will be revealed when the kingdoms of this world finally and completely become the kingdom of our Lord at his Second Coming.

God wants structures where those who can work have the productive resources to earn their own way, and those who cannot work are adequately cared for. Economic relationships that are redeemed within the body of Christ will point convincingly to the coming kingdom. And—as if that were

71

not enough—the loving oneness among Christians is to become so visible that it convinces the world that Jesus came from the Father (John 17:20–23).

Does this mean this chapter applies only to the church? Not at all.

There is, of course, a difference between theocratic Israel or a voluntary community of Christian believers on the one hand and a modern, secular, pluralistic society on the other. I believe that the first application of the biblical teaching on economic relations is to the church, and I expect the church to be well ahead of the rest of society in implementing God's will. But I also believe there is a secondary application of the biblical social vision to secular society. God's revelation to Israel about how to structure society for the sake of wholeness and justice was not arbitrary. Rather, it is the Creator's communication about how people live together in social harmony. To the extent that a modern society approximates the biblical ideal in any area (say, economic justice), to that extent it will experience wholeness. This chapter therefore also provides important clues about a biblical perspective on economic justice for the whole society.

Central to the discussion is the biblical material on Israel and the land.[1]

Capital in an Agricultural Society

The contrast between early Israel and surrounding societies was striking.[2] In Egypt, most of the land belonged to Pharaoh or the temples. In most other near-Eastern contexts a feudal system of landholding prevailed. The king granted large tracts of land, worked by landless laborers, to a small number of elite royal vassals. Only at the theological level did this feudal system exist in early Israel. Yahweh the King owned all the land and made important demands on those to whom he gave it to use. Under Yahweh, however, each family had their own land. Israel's ideal was decentralized, and family "ownership" understood as stewardship under Yahweh's absolute ownership. In the period of the Judges, the pattern in Israel was, according to one scholar, "free peasants on small land holdings of equal size and apportioned by the clans."[3]

Land was the basic capital in early Israel's agricultural economy, and the land seems to have been divided in such a way that each extended family had the resources to produce the things needed for a decent life.

Joshua 18 and Numbers 26 contain accounts of the division of the land. They represent Israel's social ideal with regard to the land. In Joshua 18:1–10, the people came before God in an act of worship and then proceeded to measure the land and share it (by casting lots) among the various tribes. Numbers 26:52–56 states that the land was allocated according to the size of each tribe. Some approximation of equality of land ownership is implied. Albrecht Alt, a prominent Old Testament scholar, goes so far as to say that the prophets understood Yahweh's ancient regulation on property to be "one man-one house-one allotment of land."[4] Decentralized land ownership by extended families was the economic base for a relatively egalitarian society of small landowners and vinedressers in the time of the Judges.[5]

The story of Naboth's vineyard (1 Kings 21) demonstrates the importance of each family's ancestral land. Frequent Old Testament references about not moving ancient boundary markers (e.g., Deut. 19:14; 27:17; Job 24:2; Prov. 22:28; Hosea 5:10) support the concept that Israel's social ideal called for each family to have available to them the land needed to supply life's necessities.

"Necessities" is not meant to be understood as the minimum necessary to keep from starving. In the nonhierarchical, relatively egalitarian society of small farmers depicted above, families possessed resources to earn a living that would have been considered reasonable and acceptable, not embarrassingly minimal. That is not to suggest that every family had exactly the same income. It does mean, however, that every family had an equality of economic opportunity up to the point that they had the resources to earn a living that would enable them not only to meet minimal needs of food, clothing, and housing but also to be respected participants in the community. Possessing their own land enabled each extended family to acquire the necessities for a decent life through responsible work.

The Year of Jubilee

Two astonishing biblical texts—Leviticus 25 and Deuteronomy 15—show how important this basic equality of opportunity was to God. The jubilee text in Leviticus demanded that the land return to the original owners

73

every fifty years. And Deuteronomy 15 called for the release of debts every seven years.

Leviticus 25 is one of the most radical texts in all of Scripture;[6] at least it seems that way to people committed either to communism or to unrestricted capitalism. Every fifty years, God said, the land was to return to the original owners! Physical handicaps, death of a breadwinner, or lack of natural ability may lead some families to become poorer than others. But God does not want such disadvantages to lead to ever-increasing extremes of wealth and poverty with the result that the poor eventually lack the basic resources to earn a decent livelihood. God therefore gave his people a law to guarantee that no family would permanently lose its land. Every fifty years, the land returned to the original owners so that every family had enough productive resources to function as dignified, participating members of the community (vv. 10–24).

In an agricultural society, land is capital, so land was the basic means of producing wealth in Israel. At the beginning, as we have seen, the land was divided more or less equally among the tribes and families.[7] Apparently God wanted that basic equality of economic opportunity to continue. Hence his command to return all land to the original owners every fifty years. Private property was not abolished. Regularly, however, the means of producing wealth was to be equalized—up to the point of every family having the resources to earn a decent living.

What is the theological basis for this startling command? Yahweh's ownership of everything is the presupposition. The land cannot be sold permanently because Yahweh owns it: "The land shall not be sold in perpetuity, for the land is mine; for you are strangers and sojourners with me" (Lev. 25:23).

God, the landowner, permits his people to sojourn on his good earth, cultivate it, eat its produce, and enjoy its beauty. But we are only stewards. Stewardship is one of the central theological categories of any biblical understanding of our relationship to the land and economic resources.[8]

Before and after the year of jubilee, land could be "bought" or "sold." Actually, the buyer purchased a specific number of harvests, not the land itself (Lev. 25:16). And woe to the person who tried to get more than a just price for the intervening harvests from the date of purchase to the next jubilee! "If the years are many you shall increase the price, and if the years are few you shall diminish the price, for it is the number of the crops that he is selling to you. You shall not wrong one another, but you shall fear your God; for I am the Lord your God" (vv. 16–17).

Yahweh is Lord of all, even of economics. There is no hint here of a sacred law of supply and demand that operates independently of biblical ethics and the Lordship of Yahweh. The people of God should submit to God, and God demands economic justice among his people.

The assumption in this text that people must suffer the consequences of wrong choices is also striking. A whole generation or more could suffer the loss of ancestral land, but every fifty years the basic source of wealth would be returned so that each family had the opportunity to provide for its basic needs.

Verses 25–28 imply that this equality of opportunity is a higher value than that of absolute property rights. If a person became poor and sold his land to a more prosperous neighbor but then recovered enough to buy back his land before the jubilee, the new owner was obligated to return it. The original owner's right to have his ancestral land to earn his own way is a higher right than that of the second owner to maximize profits.

This passage prescribes justice in a way that haphazard handouts by wealthy philanthropists never will. The year of jubilee was an institutionalized structure that affected all Israelites automatically. It was the poor family's right to recover their inherited land at the jubilee. Returning the land was not a charitable courtesy that the wealthy might extend if they pleased.[9]

Interestingly, the principles of jubilee challenge both unrestricted capitalism and communism in a fundamental way. Only God is an absolute owner. And the right of each family to have the means to earn a living takes priority over a purchaser's "property rights" or a totally free market economy. At the same time, jubilee affirms not only the right but the importance of private property managed by families who understand that they are stewards responsible to God. This text does not point us in the direction of the communist model where the state owns all the land. God wants each family to have the resources to produce its own livelihood. Why? To strengthen the family (This is a very important "pro-family" text!). To give people the freedom to participate in shaping history. And to prevent the centralization of power, injustice and totalitarianism, which almost always accompanies centralized ownership of land or capital by either the state or small elites.

One final aspect of Leviticus 25 is striking. I believe it is more than coincidental that the trumpet blast announcing the jubilee sounded on the Day of Atonement (v. 9). Reconciliation with God is the precondition for reconciliation with brothers and sisters.[10] Conversely, genuine reconciliation with God leads inevitably to a transformation of all other relationships. Reconciled with God by the sacrifice on the Day of Atonement, the more prosperous Israelites were summoned to liberate the poor by freeing Hebrew slaves and by returning all land to the original owners.[11]

Unfortunately, we do not know whether the people of Israel ever practiced the year of jubilee. The absence of references to it in the historical books suggests that it may never have been implemented.[12] Regardless of its antiquity or possible lack of implementation, however, Leviticus 25 remains a part of God's authoritative Word.

The teaching of the prophets about the land underlines the principles of Leviticus 25.

In the tenth to the eighth centuries BC, a major centralization of landholding occurred. Poorer farmers lost their land, becoming landless laborers or slaves. The prophets regularly denounced the bribery, political assassination, and economic oppression that destroyed the earlier decentralized economy described above. Elijah condemned Ahab's seizure of Naboth's vineyard (1 Kings 21). Isaiah attacked rich landowners for adding field to field until they dwelt alone in the countryside, because the smaller farmers had been destroyed (Isa. 15:5–8).

The prophets, however, did not merely condemn. They also expressed a powerful eschatological hope for a future Messianic time of justice when all would have their own land again. In the "latter days," the future Messianic time of justice and wholeness, "they shall sit every man under his vine and under his fig tree" (Mic. 4:4; cf. Zech. 3:10). No longer will the leaders oppress the people; instead they will guarantee that all people again enjoy their ancestral land (Ezek. 45:1–9, esp. vv. 8–9).

In the giving of the land, the denunciation of oppressors who seized the land of the poor, and the Messianic vision of a new day when once again all will delight in the fruits of their own land and labor, we see a social ideal being depicted in which families are to have the economic means to earn their own way. A basic equality of economic opportunity up to the point that all can at least provide for their own basic needs through responsible work is the norm. Failure to act responsibly has economic consequences, so there is no assumption of equality. Hints of economic incentive for extra effort also are present. Central, however, is the demand that each family have the necessary capital (land) so that responsible stewardship will result in an economically decent life.[13]

The Sabbatical Year

God's law also provides for liberation of soil, slaves, and debtors every seven years. Again the concern is justice for the poor and disadvantaged as well as the well-being of the land.

Every seven years the land is to lie fallow (Ex. 23:10–11; Lev. 25:2–7).[14] The purpose, apparently, is both ecological and humanitarian. Not planting any crops every seventh year helps preserve the fertility of the soil. It also was God's way of showing his concern for the poor: "For six years you shall sow your land and gather in its yield; but the seventh year you shall let it rest and lie fallow, that the poor of your people may eat" (Ex. 23:10–11). In the seventh year the poor were free to gather for themselves whatever grew spontaneously in the fields and vineyards.

Hebrew slaves also received their freedom in the sabbatical year (Deut. 15:12–18). Poverty sometimes forced Israelites to sell themselves as slaves to more prosperous neighbors (Lev. 25:39–40).[15] But this inequality and lack of property, God decrees, is not to be permanent. At the end of six years Hebrew slaves are to be set free. And masters are to share the proceeds of their joint labors with departing male slaves: "And when you let him go free from you, you shall not let him go empty-handed; you shall furnish him liberally out of your flock, out of your threshing floor, and out of your wine press; as the Lord your God has blessed you, you shall give to him" (Deut. 15:13–14; also Ex. 21:2–6).

The freed slave would thereby have the means to earn his own way.[16]

The sabbatical provision on loans is even more surprising (Deut. 15:1–6) if, as some scholars think, the text calls for cancellation of debts every seventh year.[17] Yahweh even adds a footnote for those with a sharp eye for loopholes: it is sinful to refuse a loan to a poor man just because it is the sixth year and financial loss might occur in twelve months.

> Be careful that you do not entertain a mean thought, thinking, "The seventh year, the year of remission, is near," and therefore view your needy neighbor with hostility and give nothing; your neighbor might cry to the Lord against you, and you would incur guilt. Give liberally and be ungrudging when you do so, for on this account the Lord your God will bless you in all your work and in all that you undertake. (vv. 9–10 NRSV)

As in the case of the year of jubilee, this passage involves structured justice rather than mere charity. The sabbatical release of debts was an institutionalized mechanism to prevent the kind of economic divisions where a few people would possess all the capital while others had no productive resources.

Deuteronomy 15 is both an idealistic statement of God's demand and also a realistic reference to Israel's sinful performance. Verse 4 promises that there will be no poor in Israel—if they obey all of God's commands! But God knew they would not attain that standard. Hence the recognition that poor people will always exist (v. 11). The conclusion, however, is not permission to ignore the needy because hordes of paupers will always exceed available resources. God commands precisely the opposite: "Since there will never cease to be some in need on the earth, I therefore command you, 'Open your hand to the poor and needy neighbor, in your land'" (v. 11).

Jesus knew, and Deuteronomy implies, that sinful persons and societies will always produce poor people (Matt. 26:11). Rather than justifying neglect, however, God intends that this knowledge will be used by his people as a reminder to show generosity and to create structural mechanisms that promote justice.

The sabbatical year, unfortunately, was practiced only sporadically.

Some texts suggest that failure to obey this law was one reason for the Babylonian exile (2 Chron. 36:20–21; Lev. 26:34–36).[18] Disobedience, however, does not negate God's demand. Institutionalized structures to reduce poverty are central to God's will for his people.

Laws on Tithing and Gleaning

Israel's laws on tithing and gleaning are part of God's provision for those who temporarily lack productive capital. The law calls for one tenth of all farm produce to be set aside as a tithe: "At the end of every three years you shall bring forth all the tithe of your produce in the same year; . . . and the Levite . . . and the sojourner, the fatherless, and the widow, who are within your towns, shall come and eat and be filled; that the Lord your God may bless you" (Deut. 14:28–29; also Lev. 27:30–32; Deut. 26:12–15; Num. 18:21–32).[19]

The poor widow Ruth was able to survive because of this law. When she and Naomi returned to Bethlehem penniless, Ruth went into the fields at harvest time and gathered the stalks of grain dropped by the gleaners (Ruth 2). God's law that farmers should leave for the poor some of the harvest, including the corners of grain fields, made it possible for Ruth to do this. Grapes that had been dropped accidentally also were to be left. "You shall leave them for the poor and for the sojourner: I am the Lord your God" (Lev. 19:10).

The memory of their own poverty and oppression in Egypt was to prompt them to leave generous gleanings for the poor, the sojourner, the widow, and the fatherless. "You shall remember that you were a slave in the land of Egypt; therefore I command you to do this" (Deut. 24:22).

The laws on gleaning did not guarantee handouts; Ruth had to work hard for the grain she received. But they did guarantee poor people the opportunity to acquire basic necessities.[20]

Models to Follow and Avoid

How do we apply biblical revelation concerning the year of jubilee, the sabbatical year, tithes, and gleaning to today's situation? Should we try to incorporate these mechanisms into modern society? Are these laws, or the basic principles behind them, applicable to the church at all?

God gave Israel the law so that they would know how to live together in peace and justice. The church is now the new people of God (Gal. 3:6–9; 6:16; 1 Pet. 2:9–10). As Paul and other New Testament writers indicate, parts of the Mosaic law (the ceremonial law, for instance) do not apply to New Testament believers (i.e., the church). But there is no indication that God's moral law has ceased to apply (Matt. 5:17–20, Rom. 8:4).[21] And embedded in the civil law of the Old Testament are principles that both guide the church and inform our understanding of economic justice for society.

How then do we apply the laws we have discussed? Should we try to revive the detailed specifics in Leviticus 25 and Deuteronomy 15?

Certainly not. The specific provisions of the year of jubilee are not binding today. Modern technological society is vastly different from rural Palestine. If Kansas farmers left grain standing in the corners of their fields, it would not help the hungry in inner-city New York or rural India. We need methods appropriate to our own civilization. It is the principles, not the details, that are important today.

The history of the prohibition against charging interest illustrates this. The annual rate of interest in the ancient Near East was incredibly high—often 25 percent or more.[22] It is not hard, therefore, to understand the reason for a law that prohibits charging interest to fellow Israelites (Ex. 22:25; Deut. 23:19–20; Lev. 25:35–38).[23] According to *The International Critical Commentary*, this legislation reflects a time when most loans were not commercial but charitable. Commercial loans to establish or extend a business were not common. Most loans were needed by a poor person or by someone in an emergency.[24] The texts on interest make it clear that the well-being of the poor is a central concern: "If you lend money to my people, to the poor among you, you shall not deal with them as a creditor; you shall not exact interest from them" (Ex. 22:25 NRSV). The legislation on interest is part of an extensive set of laws designed to protect the poor and to prevent the creation of a class of desperately poor folk with no productive resources.

Failing to understand this, the Christian church attempted to apply these texts in a legalistic way. Several church councils wrestled with the question. Eventually, in 1179 at the Third Lateran Council, all interest on loans was prohibited. But the results were tragic. Medieval monarchs invited Jews, who were not bound by the church's teaching, to be money lenders. This practice resulted in intense anti-Semitism and in casuistic schemes developed by theologians to circumvent the prohibition.[25]

This misguided preoccupation with the letter of the law and the resulting adoption of an unworkable, legalistic application helped discredit, or at least obscure, the important biblical teaching that the God of the poor is Lord of economics—Lord even of interest rates. It also contributed to the modern mentality that views loans and banking—indeed the whole field of economics—as independent and autonomous. From the standpoint of revealed faith, of course, such a view is heretical. It stems from modern secularism, not from the Bible.[26]

This history warns us against wooden application of God's living Word. But we dare not let past mistakes end in timid silence. These biblical texts demand that Christian lenders count the borrower's need more important than their own maximization of profit.

In applying the biblical teachings on the year of jubilee, the sabbatical year, gleaning, and tithing, then, we must discover the underlying principles. Then we can search for contemporary strategies to give flesh to these basic principles.

The texts we have examined show that God wills justice, not mere charity. Therefore, Christians should work to eliminate poverty among believers. At the same time, Christians informed by the biblical understanding of economic justice will search for effective structures in the larger society that enable every family to have the basic capital needed to earn a living. There is an implication here that private property is so good that God wants everybody to have some!

Jesus' New Community

First-century Christians reaffirmed the Old Testament teaching. Jesus walked the roads of Galilee announcing the startling news that the Messianic kingdom of peace and righteousness was at hand. Economic relationships in the new community of his followers were a powerful sign confirming this awesome announcement.

The Hebrew prophets had not only predicted that Israel would be destroyed because of her idolatry and oppression of the poor; they had also proclaimed a message of hope—the hope of a future messianic kingdom. The days are coming, they promised, when God will raise up a righteous branch from the Davidic line. Peace, righteousness, and justice will then abound in a new, redeemed society. When the shoot comes from the stump of Jesse, Isaiah predicted, the poor and meek will finally receive their due: "With righteousness he shall judge the poor, and decide with equity for the meek of the earth" (Isa. 11:4; see also Isaiah 9:6–7; 61:1; Jeremiah 23:5; Hosea 2:18–20).

The essence of the good news that Jesus proclaimed was that the expected messianic kingdom had come.[27] Certainly the kingdom Jesus announced disappointed popular Jewish expectations. He did not recruit an army to drive out the Romans. He did not establish a free Jewish state. But neither did he remain alone as an isolated, individualistic prophet. He called and trained disciples. He established a visible community of disciples joined together by their submission to him as Lord. His new community began to live the values of the promised kingdom. As a result, all relationships, even economic ones, were transformed in the community of Jesus' followers.

They shared a common purse (John 12:6).[28] Judas administered the common fund, buying provisions or giving to the poor at Jesus' direction (John 13:29). The new community of sharing extended beyond Jesus and the Twelve. It included a number of women whom Jesus had healed. The women traveled with Jesus and the disciples, sharing their financial resources with them (Luke 8:1–3; see also Mark 15:40–41).[29]

Starting with this understanding, some of Jesus' words gain new meaning and power. Consider his advice to the rich young man.

When Jesus asked the rich young man to sell his goods and give to the poor, he did not say, "Become destitute and friendless." Rather, he said, "Come, follow me" (Matt. 19:21). In other words, he invited him to join a community of sharing and love, where his security would not be based on individual property holdings, but on openness to the Spirit and on the loving care of new-found brothers and sisters.[30]

Jesus invited the rich young man to share the joyful common life of his new kingdom.

Jesus' words in Mark 10:29–30 used to puzzle me: "Truly, I say to you, there is no one who has left house or brothers or sisters or mother or father or children or lands, for my sake and for the gospel, who will not receive a hundredfold now in this time, houses and brothers and sisters and mothers and children and lands, with persecutions, and in the age to come eternal life." Why, I used to wonder, did he end his advice with a promise that seems too good to be true: "But seek first his kingdom and his righteousness, and all these things [i.e., food, clothing, and so on] shall be yours as well." I didn't know how to make sense out of this seemingly naive statement.

But the words came alive with meaning when I read them in the context of what was happening among his followers. Jesus had begun a new community, a new social order, a new kingdom of faithful followers who were experiencing redeemed economic relationships.

The common purse of Jesus' disciples symbolized their amazing availability to each other. In that kind of community, there would be genuine economic security. Each person would indeed have many more loving brothers and sisters than before. The economic resources available in difficult times would in fact be compounded a hundredfold and more. The resources of the entire community of obedient disciples would be available to anyone in need. Such unprecedented unselfishness would certainly challenge surrounding society so pointedly that many would want to join while others, out of jealousy, would want to destroy through persecution. But even in the most desperate days, the promise would not be empty. Even if persecution led to death, children of martyred parents would receive new mothers and fathers in the community of believers.

In the community of the redeemed, all relationships are being transformed. Jesus and his first followers vividly demonstrated that the old covenant's pattern of economic relationships among God's people is not only to be continued but also deepened.

The Jerusalem Model

The massive economic sharing of the earliest Christian church is indisputable. "Now the company of those who believed were of one heart and soul, and no one said that any of the things which he possessed was his own, but they had everything in common" (Acts 4:32).

The evidence in the early chapters of Acts is abundant and unambiguous (Acts 2:43–47; 4:32–37; 5:1–11; 6:1–7). The early church continued the pattern of economic sharing practiced by Jesus. Immediately after reporting the three thousand conversions at Pentecost, Acts notes that "all who believed were together and had all things in common" (2:44). Whenever anyone was in need, they shared. Giving surplus to needy brothers and sisters was not enough. They regularly dipped into capital reserves and sold property to aid the needy. Barnabas sold a field he owned (4:36–37). Ananias and Sapphira sold property, but then lied about the price (5:3–4).

Long ago, God promised Israel that obedience would eliminate poverty among his people (Deut. 15:4). That promise came true in the earliest church. "There was not a needy person among them, for as many as were possessors of lands or houses sold them; . . . and distribution was made to each as any had need" (Acts 4:34–35).

Two millennia later the texts still throb with the joy and excitement of the first community. They ate meals together "with glad and generous hearts" (Acts 2:46). They experienced an exciting unity as all sensed they "were of one heart and soul" (4:32). They were not isolated individuals, struggling alone to follow Jesus. A new community, in which all areas of life (including economics) were being transformed, became a joyful reality.

The evangelistic impact of their demonstration of oneness is striking. The texts repeatedly relate the transformed economic relationships in the Jerusalem church to their phenomenal evangelistic outreach: "And day by day, attending the temple together and breaking bread in their homes, they partook of food with glad and generous hearts, praising God and having favor with all the people. And the Lord added to their number day by day" (Acts 2:46–47). The joy and love expressed in their common life was contagious.

Acts 4 underlines the evangelistic impact of their transformed economic relationships. Verse 32 describes their sweeping economic sharing, and the very next verse adds, "And with great power the apostles gave their testimony to the resurrection of the Lord Jesus" (v. 33). Jesus' prayer that the loving unity of his followers would be so striking that it would convince the world that he had come from the Father has been answered—at least once! It happened in the Jerusalem church. The unusual quality of their economic life together gave power to the apostolic preaching.

Acts 6 gives a striking example of how the new system worked. Apparently the Jerusalem church included a significant minority of Hellenists (Greek-speaking Jews, perhaps even Greeks that had converted to Judaism). Somehow, the Jewish-speaking majority had overlooked the needs of the Hellenist widows. When the injustice was pointed out, the church's response was startling. The seven men chosen to look after the matter were all from the minority group! Every one of their names is Greek.[31] The church turned over its funds for needy widows to the minority group that had been discriminated against. What was the result of this new kind of financial fellowship? "And the word of God increased; and the number of disciples multiplied greatly in Jerusalem" (Acts 6:7).

Redeemed economic relationships in the early church resulted in the spread of the Gospel. What a sobering thought! Could the same thing happen today? Would similar economic changes produce a dramatic increase of believers? Probably. Are those who talk about the importance of evangelism prepared to pay that price?

The earliest church did not insist on absolute economic equality. Nor did they abolish private property. Peter reminded Ananias that he had been under no obligation either to sell his property or to donate the proceeds to the church (Acts 5:4). Sharing was voluntary, not compulsory.[32] But love for brothers and sisters was so overwhelming that many freely abandoned legitimate claims to private possessions. That does not mean that everyone donated everything. Later in Acts we read that John Mark's mother, Mary, still owned her own house (12:12). Additional passages indicate that others retained some private property.

The tense of the Greek words confirms this interpretation. In both Acts 2:45 and 4:34, the verbs denote continued, repeated action over an extended period of time. Thus the meaning is, "they often sold possessions," or, "they were in the habit of regularly bringing the proceeds of what was being sold."[33] The text does not suggest that the community abolished all private property or that everyone immediately sold everything. It suggests instead that over a period of time, whenever there was need, believers sold lands and houses to aid the needy.

What then was the essence of the transformed economic relationships in the Jerusalem church? The best way to describe their practice is to speak of sweeping liability for and availability to each other. Their sharing was not superficial or occasional. Regularly and repeatedly, "they sold their possessions and goods and distributed them to all, as any had need" (2:45). If the need was greater than current cash reserves, they sold property. They simply gave until the needs were met. The needs of the sister and brother, not legal property rights or future financial security, were the deciding factors. For the earliest Christians, oneness in Christ meant sweeping liability for and availability to the other members of Christ's body.

Unfortunately most Christians ignore the example of the Jerusalem church. Perhaps it is because of the economic self-interest of affluent Christians. We have developed convenient rationales for relegating the pattern of the Jerusalem church to the archivists' attic of irrelevant historical trivia. Why did Paul have to take a collection for the Jerusalem church a few decades later? A modern book offers the familiar response:

> The trouble in Jerusalem was that they turned their capital into income, and had no cushion for hard times, and the Gentile Christians had to come to their rescue. It is possible not to live for bread alone, not to be overcome by materialist values, and at the same time to act responsibly; and this is why the Church may be grateful for the protest of the commune movement, but still consider that it has no answer.[34]

But were the Jerusalem Christians really irresponsible, naive communal-types whom we should respect but certainly not imitate? It is essential to insist that the Jerusalem principle of sweeping financial availability does not require communal living. It did not in Jerusalem. The Christian commune is only one of many faithful models. We dare not let the communal hobgoblin distort our discussion of the Jerusalem model.

But why did the Jerusalem church run into financial difficulty? It is unlikely that economic sharing was to blame. More likely the need was due to a unique set of historical circumstances. Jerusalem attracted an unusually large number of poor people. Since Jews considered alms given in Jerusalem to be particularly meritorious, the many pilgrims to the city were especially generous. As a result, crowds of impoverished beggars flocked to the city. In addition, a disproportionately large number of the elderly gravitated to the Holy City to die or wait for the Messiah (see Luke 2:25, 36). Also, because Jerusalem was the center of Jewish faith, it attracted a large number of rabbis, who depended on charity because they were not paid for teaching. Their students likewise often were poor. Hence the large number of religious scholars in Jerusalem swelled the ranks of the destitute.[35]

And that was not all. Natural disasters struck at midcentury. The Roman historians Suetonius and Tacitus report recurring food shortages and famines during the reign of the Emperor Claudius (AD 41–54). Josephus dates such shortages in Palestine around AD 44 to 48.[36] At one point, famine was so severe that the Antioch church quickly sent assistance (Acts 11:27–30).

Special circumstances within the first church also caused unusual poverty. Jesus' particular concern for the poor and oppressed probably attracted a disproportionately large number of impoverished persons. Acts records considerable persecution (8:1–3; 9:29; 12:1–5; 23:12–15), so Christians probably experienced discrimination in employment, which wreaked havoc with their normal income.[37] Finally, the original Twelve seem to have given up their means of livelihood when they moved from Galilee to Jerusalem, so their need for support would have increased the demand on the church's resources.

These are some of the many reasons why the first community of Christians faced financial difficulty at midcentury. Misguided generosity was not likely a significant factor. In fact, the unusually large number of poor in their midst is probably what made dramatic sharing such an obvious necessity. That the rich among them gave with overflowing generosity to meet a desperate need indicates unconditional discipleship, not naive idealism.

The costly generosity of the first church stands as a challenge to Christians of all ages. They gave visible expression to the oneness of believers. In the new messianic community of Jesus' first followers, God was redeeming all relationships.

Was the beauty of this example a vision that quickly faded? Many believe it was. But the actual practice of the early church proves the contrary.

Economic Koinonia

Paul broadened the vision of economic sharing in a dramatic way by devoting a great deal of time to raising money for Jewish Christians in Jerusalem among Gentile congregations in Greece. In the process he developed intrachurch assistance (within one local church) into interchurch sharing among the scattered congregations of believers. Since Jerusalem is in Asia and Greece belongs to Europe, Paul pioneered intercontinental economic sharing in the church.

From the time of the Exodus, God had taught his chosen people to exhibit transformed economic relations among themselves. With Peter and Paul, however, biblical religion moved beyond one ethnic group and became a universal, multiethnic faith. Paul's collection demonstrated that the oneness of believers entails economic sharing across ethnic and geographic lines.

Paul's concern for economic sharing in the body of Christ began early. Famine struck Palestine in AD 46. In response, the believers at Antioch gave *"every one according to his ability,* to send relief to the brethren who lived in Judea"* (Acts 11:29, italics mine). Paul helped Barnabas take this economic assistance from Antioch to Jerusalem.[38]

That trip was just the beginning of Paul's concern for economic sharing. For several years he devoted much time and energy to his great collection. He discusses his concern in several letters. In Galatians he expresses eagerness to assist the poor Jerusalem Christians (Gal. 2:10). He mentions it also in the letter to Rome (Rom. 15:22–28) and notes it briefly in 1 Corinthians 16:1–4. The collection is a major preoccupation in 2 Corinthians 8–9. He also arranged for the collection in the churches of Macedonia, Galatia, Corinth, Ephesus, and probably elsewhere.[39]

Knowing he faced certain danger and possible death from angry Jews in Jerusalem, Paul nevertheless insisted on accompanying the offering. While delivering this financial assistance, he was arrested for the last time. His letter to the Romans shows that he was not blind to the danger (Rom. 15:31). Friends and prophets repeatedly warned Paul as he and the representatives of the contributing churches journeyed toward Jerusalem (Acts 21:4, 10–14). But Paul had a deep conviction that this financial symbol of Christian unity mattered far more even than his own life. "What are you doing, weeping and breaking my heart?" he chided friends imploring him not to accompany the others to Jerusalem. "For I am ready not only to be imprisoned but even to die at Jerusalem for the name of the Lord Jesus" (Acts 21:13). So he continued the journey. His passionate commitment to economic sharing with brothers and sisters led to his final arrest and martyrdom (Acts 24:17). This is not to suggest that some economic ideal had replaced Paul's central commitment to Christ. But it does mean that Paul understood that embracing Christ means embracing Christ's body and that living out the oneness of Christ's body demands economic sharing.

Why was Paul so concerned with the financial problems of the Jerusalem church? Because of his understanding of Christian fellowship. The word *koinonia* plays an important role in Paul's theology, and it is central in his discussion of the collection.

Koinonia means fellowship with someone or participation in something. Believers enjoy fellowship with the Lord Jesus (1 Cor. 1:9).[40] Experiencing the *koinonia* of Jesus means having his righteousness imputed to us. It also entails sharing in the self-sacrificing, cross-bearing life he lived (Phil. 3:8–10). Nowhere is the Christian's fellowship with Christ experienced more powerfully than in the Eucharist. Sharing in the Lord's Supper draws the believer into a participation (*koinonia*) in the mystery of the cross: "The cup of blessing which we bless, is it not a participation [*koinonia*] in the blood of Christ? The bread which we break, is it not a participation [*koinonia*] in the body of Christ?" (1 Cor. 10:16).

Paul's inference is that *koinonia* with Christ involves *koinonia* with all the members of the body of Christ. "Because there is one bread, we who are many are one body, for we all partake of the one bread" (1 Cor. 10:17; see also 1 John 1:3–4).

As Ephesians 2 teaches, Christ's death for Jew and Gentile, male and female, has broken down all ethnic, gender, and cultural dividing walls. In Christ there is one new person, one new body of believers. When the brothers and sisters share the one bread and the common cup in the Lord's Supper, they symbolize their participation in the one body of Christ.

That is why the class divisions at Corinth so horrified Paul. Apparently, wealthy Christians were feasting at the Eucharistic celebration while poor believers were going hungry. Paul angrily denied that they were eating the Lord's Supper at all (1 Cor. 11:20–22). In fact, they were profaning the Lord's body and blood because they did not discern his body (vv. 27–29). "All who eat and drink without discerning the body, eat and drink judgment against themselves" (v. 29 NRSV).

But what did Paul mean when he charged that they did not discern the Lord's body? To discern the Lord's body is to understand and live the truth that fellowship with Christ is inseparable from membership in his body, where our oneness in Christ far transcends differences of race or class. Discernment of that one body of believers leads to sweeping availability to and responsibility for the other sisters and brothers. Discernment of that one body prompts us to weep with those who weep and rejoice with those who rejoice. Discernment of that one body is totally incompatible with feasting without sharing in costly ways with other members of the body who are hungry. Those who live a practical denial of their unity and fellowship in Christ, Paul insists, drink judgment on themselves when they go to the Lord's table. In fact, they do not really partake of the Lord's Supper at all.

Once we understand the implication of Paul's teaching on discerning the body in the Lord's Supper, we dare not rest until the scandal of starving Christians is removed. As long as any Christian anywhere in the world is hungry, the Eucharistic celebration of all Christians everywhere in the world is imperfect.

For Paul, intimate fellowship in the body of Christ has economic implications, for he uses the same word, *koinonia*, to designate financial sharing among believers. Early in Paul's ministry, after a dramatic debate, the Jerusalem leaders endorsed his mission to the Gentiles. When they extended the "right hand of fellowship" (*koinonia*), they stipulated a single tangible expression of that fellowship, and Paul promised financial assistance for his fellow Christians in Jerusalem (Gal. 2:9–10).[41]

Paul frequently used the word *koinonia* as a synonym for "collection." He speaks of the "liberality of the fellowship" (*koinonia*) that the Corinthians' generous offering would demonstrate (2 Cor. 9:13, my translation; see also 8:4).[42] He used the same language to report the Macedonian

Christians' offering for Jerusalem. It seemed good to the Macedonians "to make fellowship [*koinonia*] with the poor among the saints at Jerusalem" (Rom. 15:26, my translation). Indeed, this financial sharing was just one part of a total fellowship. The Gentile Christians had come to share in (he uses the verb form of *koinonia*) the spiritual blessings of the Jews. Therefore it was fitting for the Gentiles to share their material resources. Economic sharing was an obvious and crucial part of Christian fellowship for Paul.[43]

Paul's first guideline for sharing was general: give all you can. Each person should give "as he may prosper" (1 Cor. 16:2). But that does not mean a small donation that costs nothing. Paul praised the Macedonians who "gave according to their means . . . and beyond their means" (2 Cor. 8:3). The Macedonians were extremely poor. Apparently they faced particularly severe financial difficulties at the time when Paul asked for a generous offering (v. 2). But still they were generous. No hint here of a mechanical 10 percent for pauper and millionaire. Giving as much as you can is the Pauline pattern.

Second, giving was voluntary (2 Cor. 8:3). Paul specifically noted that he was not issuing a command to the Corinthians (v. 8). Legalism is not the answer.

Paul's third guideline is the most startling. In advising the Corinthians how to share, Paul used the word *equality*: "I do not mean that others should be eased and you burdened, but that as a matter of equality your abundance at the present time should supply their want, so that their abundance may supply your want, that there may be equality." To support his principle, Paul alludes to the biblical story of the manna. "As it is written, 'He who gathered much had nothing over, and he who gathered little had no lack'" (2 Cor. 8:13–15).

According to the Exodus account, Moses commanded the people to gather only as much manna as they needed for one day (16:13–21). One omer (about four pints) per person would be enough, Moses said. Some greedy souls, however, apparently tried to gather more than they could use. But when they measured what they had, they had just one omer per person. "He that gathered much had nothing over, and he that gathered little had no lack" (16:18).

Paul quotes from the biblical account of the manna to support his guideline for economic sharing. In the wilderness, God provided equal portions of manna for all his people. Now the Corinthians were to give "that there may be equality" in the body of Christ.

Does this mean that God's standard for economic relations—whether in the church or society—is absolute equality of economic resources and consumption? I doubt it. Other biblical texts presuppose different economic outcomes based on individuals' choices.[44]

At a minimum, however, it summons us to share economically so that those who cannot provide for their own basic necessities are cared for. The text at least demands an equality of outcome up to the point that those who cannot provide for their own basic necessities receive a generous supply from others.

It is exciting to see how the biblical teaching on transformed economic relationships among God's people created in the early church a concern for the poor that was unique. Writing about AD 125, the Christian philosopher Aristides painted the following picture of economic sharing in the church:

They walk in all humility and kindness, and falsehood is not found among them, and they love one another. They despise not the widow, and grieve not the orphan. He that hath, distributeth liberally to him that hath not. If they see a stranger, they bring him under their roof, and rejoice over him, as it were their own brother: for they call themselves brethren, not after the flesh, but after the spirit and in God; but when one of their poor passes away from the world, and any of them see him, then he provides for his burial according to his ability; and if they hear that any of their number is imprisoned or oppressed for the name of their Messiah, all of them provide for his needs, and if it is possible that he may be delivered, they deliver him. And if there is among them a man that is poor and needy, and they have not an abundance of necessaries, they fast two or three days that they may supply the needy with their necessary food.[45]

By AD 250 the church at Rome supported fifteen hundred needy persons. According to the German scholar Martin Hengel, this kind of economic sharing was unique in the late Roman Empire.[46]

That this transformed lifestyle made a powerful impression on outsiders is clear from a grudging comment by a pagan emperor. During his short reign (AD 361–63), Julian the Apostate tried to stamp out Christianity. But he was forced to admit to a fellow pagan "that the godless Galileans [Christians] feed not only their poor but ours also." With chagrin he acknowledged that the pagan cult which he had tried to revive had failed miserably in the task of aiding the poor.[47]

Over and over God commanded his people to live together in community in such a way that all families would have the resources to earn a decent livelihood and that those who could not care for themselves would be generously taken care of. This principle is at the heart of the Old Testament legislation on the jubilee, the sabbatical year, tithing, gleaning, and loans. Again and again, Jesus instructed his followers to share with those in need. When some Christians became so poor that they lacked basic necessities, others generously shared.

The powerful evangelistic impact of economic sharing indicates that God approved and blessed the practice of the Jerusalem church. When in some places Scripture commands transformed economic relationships among God's people and in other places describes God's blessing on his people as they implement these commands, we can be sure that we have discovered a normative pattern for the church today.

The continuity of biblical teaching and practice on this point is striking. The Bible repeatedly and pointedly reveals that God wills transformed economic relationships among his people. Paul's collection was a simple application of this principle. Paul's method was different from that of Leviticus 25 (the people of God in Paul's time were a multiethnic body living in different lands), but the principle was the same. Since the Greeks at Corinth were now part of the people of God, they were to share with the poor Jewish Christians at Jerusalem—that there might be redeemed economic relationships among God's people.

How Then Shall We Live?

Certainly the church today need not slavishly imitate every detail of the life of the early church depicted in Acts. It is scriptural teaching, not the action of the Jerusalem church, that is normative. But that does not mean that we can dismiss the economic principles described in Acts and the Pauline letters.

Scripture offers two crucial clues about the nature of economic justice that God demands. First, God wants all people to have the productive resources to be able to earn a decent living and be dignified members of their community. We should work to structure society so that all people who can work have access to the resources to earn a decent living in today's global economy. Second, God wants the rest of us to provide a generous share of the necessities of life to those who cannot work.

The first application of the biblical teaching is to the church. Present economic relationships in the worldwide body of Christ are unbiblical and sinful; they hinder evangelism and desecrate the body and blood of Jesus Christ. The dollar value of the food Americans throw away each year is more than one-quarter of the total annual income of all the Christians in Africa.[48] It is a sinful abomination for one part of the world's Christians to grow richer year by year while our brothers and sisters ache and suffer for lack of minimal health care, minimal education, and even—in some cases—enough food to escape starvation.

Like the rich Corinthian Christians who feasted without sharing with the hungry members of the church (1 Cor. 11:20–29), we have failed to comprehend the concept that the church worldwide is one body. The tragic consequence is that we profane the body and blood of the Lord Jesus we worship. Christian churches and other Christian religious organizations in the United States spent more than $650 billion on building construction between 2003 and 2013.[49] Would we go on building lavishly furnished expensive church buildings if members of our own congregations were starving? Do we not flatly contradict Paul if we live as if African or Latin American Christians are not also part of Christ's one body along with those in our home congregation?[50]

The division between the *haves* and *have nots* in the body of Christ is a major hindrance to world evangelism. Hungry people in the developing world have difficulty accepting a Christ preached by people who symbolize (and often defend the materialism of) the richest societies on earth.

Lost opportunities and past and present sin, however, must not blind us to potential progress. We live in a world dangerously divided between rich and poor. If a mere fraction of rich Christians would begin to apply biblical principles of economic sharing, the world would be astounded. Few other steps would have such a powerful evangelistic impact today. The mutual love and unity within Christ's body would convince many that Jesus indeed came from the Father (John 17:20–23).

The church is the most universal body in the world today. It has the opportunity to live a new model of sharing at a crucial moment in world history. Because of its concern for the poor, the church in the past pioneered the development of schools and hospitals. Later, secular governments institutionalized the new models. In the early twenty-first century, a dangerously divided world awaits a new model of economic sharing. Will there be enough rich Christians who are also generous?

Study Questions

1. Do most Christians you know think that their faith in Christ has anything to do with their economic relationships with others in the worldwide body of Christ? How does the Bible challenge their assumptions?
2. What are the basic implications of the jubilee and the sabbatical release of debts for today?
3. What would be the best words to describe the economic sharing occurring in the earliest church at Jerusalem?
4. What are the implications of Paul's intercontinental offering for the global church today?
5. What does the Bible tell us about economic justice in society?

5

THINKING BIBLICALLY ABOUT PROPERTY AND POSSESSIONS

In the house of the righteous there is much treasure.

—PROVERBS 15:6

*Do not wear yourself out to get rich; have
the wisdom to show restraint.*

—PROVERBS 23:4 NIV

"Tell me what you think about money," Billy Graham says, "and I can tell you what you think about God."[1] What is our attitude about money telling the world about our belief in God? Are we in agreement with God on the subject? Do we even know what God says about it? What does God say about real estate? The poor? The rich? Does money matter to God?

Private Property

The Ten Commandments sanction private property implicitly and explicitly.[2] God forbids stealing, indeed even coveting the house, land, or animals of one's neighbors (Ex. 20:15, 17; Deut. 5:19, 21; also Deut. 27:17; Prov. 22:28). Jesus commanded his followers to give to the poor and to loan money even when there was no reasonable hope of repayment (Matt. 6:2–4; 5:42; Luke 6:34–35). The ability to make loans depends on the

97

possession of property and money, so Jesus must have assumed such were legitimate. His disciple Simon Peter owned a house that Jesus visited frequently (Mark 1:29); in fact, those who owned houses had an opportunity to provide hospitality to God's servants (Luke 10:5–7).

Not even the dramatic economic sharing in the first Jerusalem church led to a rejection of private ownership (see chapter 4). Throughout biblical revelation the legitimacy of private property is constantly affirmed.[3]

Absolute Rights

But the right of private property is not absolute. From the perspective of biblical revelation, property owners are not free to seek their own profit without regard for the needs of their neighbors.

Some modern folk disagree. They think that the right of private ownership is absolute, and they argue that Adam Smith proves them right.

Smith published a book in 1776 that has profoundly shaped Western society in the past two centuries.[4] Smith argued that an invisible hand would guarantee the good of all if each person would pursue his or her own economic self-interest in the context of a competitive society. Supply and demand for goods and services were to be the sole, or at least primary, determinants of prices and wages. If the law of supply and demand reigns, and if all seek their own advantage within a competitive, nonmonopolistic economy, the good of society will be served. Adam Smith might not agree fully, but modern advocates of pure laissez-faire economics conclude that owners of land and capital therefore have not only the right but also the obligation to seek as much profit as possible, and they reject virtually all government intervention in the economy as a violation of the absolute right of private property.

Such a viewpoint may be attractive to the economically successful. Indeed, laissez-faire economics has been espoused by some as the Christian economics.[5] In reality, however, it is, to a substantial degree, a product of the Enlightenment.[6] It reflects a modern, secularized perspective rather than the biblical truth that God is Lord even of economics. That is not to say that socialist economies are better than market economies. A basic market framework plus the right kind of private and governmental activity to empower the poor is the best alternative known today (see chapters 8 and 11). But that is very different from a pure laissez-faire or libertarian approach that rejects almost all government intervention in the economy.

The pure laissez-faire and the pagan Roman attitude toward private property parallel each other. Carl F. H. Henry, former editor of *Christianity Today*, has contrasted the biblical and Roman understandings: "The Roman or Justinian view derives ownership from natural right; it defines ownership as the individual's unconditional and exclusive power over property. It implies an owner's right to use property as he pleases . . . irrespective of the will of others." Henry admits that this pagan view "still remains the silent presupposition of much of the free world's common practice today."[7]

Absolute Owner

According to biblical faith, Yahweh is Lord of all things. He is the sovereign Lord of history. Economics is not a neutral, secular sphere independent of his Lordship. Economic activity, like every other area of life, is to be subject to God's will and revelation.

How does the biblical view that Yahweh is Lord of all of life require a modification of the common belief that the right of private property is absolute and inviolable? The Bible insists that God alone has an absolute right to property. Furthermore, it teaches that this Absolute Owner places significant limitations on how his people are to acquire and use his property.

The psalmist summarized the biblical view of Yahweh's absolute ownership: "The earth is the Lord's and the fulness thereof, the world and those who dwell therein" (Ps. 24:1). "Whatever is under the whole heaven is mine," God informed Job (Job 41:11; see also Ps. 50:12; Deut. 26:10; Ex. 19:5). It is precisely because absolute ownership of the land rested with Yahweh rather than the Israelite farmers that God could command the return of the land every fiftieth year: "The land shall not be sold in perpetuity, for the land is mine; for you are strangers and sojourners with me" (Lev. 25:23).

People Principle

As absolute owner, God places limitations on the acquisition and use of property. According to the Old Testament, "the right to property was in principle subordinated to the obligation to care for the weaker members of society."[8] That is the clear implication of the legislation on the jubilee, the sabbatical year, gleaning, and interest (as discussed in chapter 4). Property owners did not have the right to harvest everything in their fields. They were to leave some for the poor. When an Israelite farmer purchased land, he really only bought the use of the land until the year of jubilee (Lev. 25:15–17). Indeed, even the right to use the land for the intervening years was not absolute. If a relative of the seller appeared, the purchaser had to sell the land back promptly. Or if the seller recovered financial solvency, he had the right to buy back his land immediately (vv. 25–28). The purchaser's right of ownership was subordinate to the original owner's right to possess his ancestral land.

God wants all people to have access to the productive resources to be able to earn a living. Justice for everyone, particularly the disadvantaged, takes precedence over the rights of the person able to pay the market price for land. Thus, the rights of the poor and disadvantaged to possess the means to earn a decent living take precedence over the rights of the more prosperous to make a profit.

At the same time, biblical principles by no means support a communist economic system. Biblical principles point in the direction of decentralized private ownership that allows families to control their economic destinies. As stewards of the land and other economic resources that belong ultimately to God, they have the responsibility and privilege of earning their own way and sharing generously with others. This kind of decentralized economic system empowers all people to be coworkers with God. It also protects everyone against centralized economic power that might threaten freedom, foster injustice, and promote totalitarianism (as when the state owns the means of production or when small groups of elites control huge multinational corporations).

The Old Testament attitude toward property stems from the high view of persons held in Israel. Old Testament scholars have pointed out that Israel, unlike other ancient civilizations such as Babylon, Assyria, and Egypt, considered all citizens equal before the law. In other societies, social status (royal official, poor man, priest) determined how a person's offense was judged and punished. In Israel all citizens were equal before the law. This high view of persons made property less important.

Whereas in neighboring states property offenses such as theft or robbery were frequently punished with death, this was not the case under

God's law. The life of even the most degraded person is worth more than the most valuable possession.[9]

The case of slaves illustrates the respect for persons. All other ancient civilizations viewed slaves as mere property. Owners were free to treat slaves according to their whims. But in Israel the slave was a person, not a piece of property. Specific laws guaranteed certain rights to slaves (Ex. 21:20, 26–28; Deut. 23:15–16). Walter Eichrodt says, "The fact that, in accordance with God's order, the life of every individual, even of the poorest, is of greater value than all material things—this fact represents an insurmountable stumbling block to all economic developments which make profits for the few out of human misery."[10]

The Danger of Riches

An abundance of possessions can easily lead us to forget that God is the source of all good. We trust in ourselves and our wealth rather than in the Almighty. When we focus on ourselves, we forget not only God but also the people he created. In our self-absorption, we are fooled by the pleasure of possessing.

Most rich Christians (and that includes most of us in the Northern Hemisphere) simply do not believe Jesus' teaching about the deadly danger of possessions. Jesus warned that possessions are highly dangerous—so dangerous, in fact, that it is extremely difficult for a rich person to be a Christian at all: "It is easier for a camel to go through the eye of a needle than for someone who is rich to enter the kingdom of God" (Luke 18:25 NRSV). Christians in the United States live in one of the richest societies in the history of the world, surrounded by a billion desperately needy neighbors and another two billion who are poor. We are far more interested in whether the economy grows than in whether the lot of the poor improves. We insist on more and more, and reason that if Jesus was so un-American that he considered riches dangerous, then we must ignore or reinterpret his message.

Forgetting God

But he said it all the same. Matthew, Mark, and Luke all record the terrible warning: "How hard it is for those who have riches to enter the kingdom of God!" (Luke 18:24; Matt. 19:23; Mark 10:23). The context of this saying shows why possessions are dangerous. Jesus spoke these troubling words to his disciples immediately after the rich young man had decided to cling to his wealth rather than follow Jesus (Luke 18:18–23). Riches are dangerous because their seductive power frequently persuades us to reject Jesus and his kingdom.

The sixth chapter of 1 Timothy reinforces Jesus' teaching. Christians should be content with the necessities of food and clothing (v. 8). Why? "Those who want to be rich fall into temptation and are trapped by many senseless and harmful desires that plunge people into ruin and destruction. For the love of money is a root of all kinds of evil, and in their eagerness to be rich some have wandered away from the faith and pierced themselves with many pains" (vv. 9–10 NRSV).

A desire for riches prompts some people to do almost anything for the sake of economic success. The result, Scripture warns, is anguish now and damnation later.

That economic success tempts people to forget God was already a biblical theme in the Old Testament. Before the Israelites entered the Promised Land, God warned them about the danger of riches.

> Take heed lest you forget the Lord your God . . . lest, when you have
> eaten and are full, and have built goodly houses and live in them, and
> when your herds and flocks multiply, and your silver and gold is multi-
> plied, and all that you have is multiplied, then your heart be lifted up,
> and you forget the Lord your God . . . Beware lest you say in your heart,
> "My power and the might of my hand have gotten me this wealth."
> (Deut. 8:11–14, 17)

Fighting Wars

Not only do possessions tempt us to forsake God, but the pursuit of wealth often results in war and neglect of the poor. "What causes wars, and what causes fightings among you? . . . You desire and do not have; so you kill. And you covet and cannot obtain; so you fight and wage war" (James 4:1–2). A quick glance through world history confirms this tragic truth.

Forgetting the Poor

Instead of fostering more compassion toward the poor, riches often harden the hearts of the wealthy. Scripture is full of instances in which rich persons are unconcerned about the poor at their doorstep (Isa. 5:8–10; Amos 6:4–7; Luke 16:19–31; James 5:1–5). Dom Hélder Câmara, a Brazilian archbishop, who devoted his life to seeking justice for the poor, makes the point forcefully: "I used to think, when I was a child, that Christ might have been exaggerating when he warned about the dangers of wealth. Today I know better. I know how very hard it is to be rich and still keep the milk of human kindness. Money has a dangerous way of putting scales on one's eyes, a dangerous way of freezing people's hands, eyes, lips, and hearts."[11]

Possessions are dangerous because they often encourage unconcern for the poor, because they lead to strife and war, and because they seduce people into forsaking God. Even more, they put people in the never-ending loop of covetousness.

Coveting Without End

The use of the word *covetousness* (which occurs nineteen times in the New Testament) reflects the biblical understanding of the dangers of riches. The Greek word *pleonexia* (translated "covetousness" or "greed") means "striving for material possessions."[12]

Jesus' Parable of the Rich Fool vividly portrays the nature of covetousness. When a man came running to Jesus for help in obtaining his share of a family inheritance, Jesus refused to consider the case. Perceiving the real problem, Jesus instead warned of the danger of covetousness. "Take care! Be on your guard against all kinds of greed [*pleonexia*]; for one's life does not consist in the abundance of possessions" (Luke 12:15 NRSV). Knowing that the man was obsessed with material things, Jesus told him a story about a rich fool.

> The land of a rich man produced abundantly. And he thought to himself, "What should I do, for I have no place to store my crops?" Then he said, "I will do this: I will pull down my barns and build larger ones, and there I will store all my grain and my goods. And I will say to my soul,

'Soul, you have ample goods laid up for many years; relax, eat, drink, be merry.'" But God said to him, "You fool! This very night your life is being demanded of you. And the things you have prepared, whose will they be?" So it is with those who store up treasures for themselves but are not rich toward God. (Luke 12:16–21 NRSV)

The rich fool is the epitome of the covetous person. He has a greedy compulsion to acquire more and more possessions, even though he does not need them. And his phenomenal success at piling up more and more property and wealth leads to the blasphemous conclusion that material possessions can satisfy all his needs. From the divine perspective, this attitude is sheer madness. He is a raving fool.

One cannot read the Parable of the Rich Fool without thinking of our own society. We madly multiply sophisticated gadgets, bigger houses, fancier cars, and fashionable clothes—not because such things truly enrich our lives but because we are driven by an obsession for more and more. Covetousness, a striving for more and more material possessions, has become a cardinal vice of modern civilization.

The New Testament has a great deal to say about covetousness. In its essence, it is idolatry. Scripture teaches that greedy persons must be expelled from the church. Certainly no covetous person will inherit the kingdom. Giving people over to their covetousness is divine punishment for sin. In Romans 1, Paul indicates that God sometimes punishes sin by letting sinners experience the ever more destructive consequences of their continuing rebellion against God. "And since they did not see fit to acknowledge God, God gave them up to a base mind and to improper conduct. They were filled with all manner of wickedness, evil, covetousness, . . . murder, strife, deceit" (Rom. 1:28–29). Covetousness is one of the sins with which God punishes our rebellion. The Parable of the Rich Fool suggests how the punishment works. Since we are made for communion with the Creator, we cannot obtain genuine fulfillment when we seek it primarily in material possessions. Hence we seek ever more frantically and desperately for more houses and bigger barns. Eventually we worship our possessions. As Paul indicates, covetousness becomes idolatry (Eph. 5:5; Col. 3:5).

Christians today are not at all surprised that Paul urged the Corinthians to excommunicate a church member living with his father's wife (1 Cor. 5:1–5). But we quietly overlook the fact that Paul, in the same paragraph, also urged them not to associate or even eat meals with those who claim to be Christians but are guilty of greed.

Are we not guilty of greed when we demand an ever-higher standard of living while neglecting millions of children who are starving to death each year? Is it not time for the church to begin applying church discipline to those guilty of this sin?[13] Would it not be more biblical to apply church discipline to people whose greedy acquisitiveness has led to "financial success" than to elect them to the board of elders?

Such action may be the last means we have of communicating the biblical warning that greedy persons will not inherit the kingdom. "Do you not know that the wicked will not inherit the kingdom of God? Do not be deceived; neither the sexually immoral, nor idolators, nor adulterers, nor male prostitutes, nor homosexual offenders, nor thieves, *nor the greedy* [the covetous], nor drunkards, nor slanderers, nor swindlers will inherit the kingdom of God" (1 Cor. 6:9–10 NIV). Covetousness is just as sinful as idolatry and adultery.

Another unambiguous statement about covetousness, or greed, appears in Ephesians: "Be sure of this, that no fornicator or impure person, or one who is greedy (that is, an idolater), has any inheritance in the kingdom of Christ" (5:5 NRSV). These biblical passages should drive us all to our knees. I am afraid that I have been repeatedly and sinfully covetous. The same is true of the vast majority of the Christians who read this book.

Possessions lead to a multitude of sins, including idolatry. Christians today desperately need to turn away from their covetous civilization's grasping materialism.

The Ring and the Beloved

Yes, possessions are dangerous. But they are not innately evil.[14] Biblical revelation begins with creation. And created things, God said, are good (Gen. 1).

Biblical faith knows nothing of the ascetic notion that forsaking food, possessions, or sex is inherently virtuous. To be sure, these created goods are, as St. Augustine said, only rings from our Beloved. They are not the Beloved himself. Sometimes particular circumstances—such as an urgent mission or the needs of the poor—may require their renunciation. But these things are part of God's good creation. Like the ring given by the beloved, they are signs of God's love. If we treasure them as good tokens of his affection, instead of mistaking them for the Beloved himself, they are marvelous gifts that enrich our lives.

God's provision for Israel's use of the tithe symbolizes the scriptural perspective (Deut. 14:22–27). Every third year the tithe was given to the poor. In the other years, however, the people were to go to the place of worship and have a fantastic feast. They were to have a great big, joyful celebration! "Before the Lord your God, in the place which he will choose, to make his name dwell there, you shall eat the tithe of your grain, of your wine, and of your oil, and the firstlings of your herd and flock" (v. 23). Those who lived far from the place of worship could sell the tithe of their produce and take the money with them. Listen to God's directions for the party: "Spend the money for whatever you desire, oxen, or sheep, or wine or strong drink, whatever your appetite craves; and you shall eat there before the Lord your God and rejoice" (v. 26). God wants his people to celebrate the glorious goodness of creation.

Jesus' example fits in perfectly with the Old Testament view. Certainly he said a great deal about the danger of possessions. But he was not an ascetic. He was happy to join in marriage celebrations and even contribute the beverage (John 2:1–11). He dined with the prosperous. Apparently he was sufficiently fond of feasts and celebrations that his enemies could spread the false rumor that he was a glutton and a drunkard (Matt. 11:19). Christian asceticism has a long history, but Jesus' life undermines its basic assumptions.

A short passage in 1 Timothy succinctly summarizes the biblical view: "In the latter days people will forbid marriage and advocate abstinence from foods. But this is misguided, 'for everything created by God is good, and nothing is to be rejected if it is received with thanksgiving'" (4:4).

The biblical teaching on the goodness of creation does not contradict the other biblical themes. God's people must practice self-denial to aid the poor and share the gospel. But we must maintain a biblical balance. It is not because food, clothes, wealth, and property are inherently evil that Christians today must lower their standard of living. It is because others are starving. Creation is good. But the one who gave us this gorgeous token of affection has asked us to share it with our sisters and brothers.

Righteousness and Riches

If we respect God and people, understand the dangers of riches, and delight in the goodness of creation, will prosperity follow? Does our obedience guarantee it? Is it true that "in the house of the righteous there is much treasure" (Prov. 15:6)? Is the reverse also true? Are riches a sure sign of righteousness?

Biblical Balance

The Bible certainly does not romanticize poverty. It is a curse (2 Sam. 3:29; Ps. 109:8–11). Sometimes it is the result of sin, but not always. A fundamental point of the book of Job is that poverty and suffering are not always due to disobedience. In fact, they can be redemptive (Isa. 53). Even so, poverty and suffering are not inherently good. They are tragic distortions of God's good creation.

Prosperity and wealth, on the other hand, are good and desirable. God repeatedly promised his people Israel that obedience would bring abundant prosperity in a land flowing with milk and honey (Deut. 6:1–3). "All these blessings shall come upon you . . . if you obey the voice of the Lord your God . . . And the Lord will make you abound in prosperity, in the fruit of your body, and in the fruit of your cattle, and in the fruit of your ground" (Deut. 28:2, 11; see also 7:12–15). That God frequently rewards obedience with material abundance is a clear teaching of Scripture.

But the threat of a curse always accompanied the promise of blessing (Deut. 6:14–15; 8:11–20; 28:15–68). One of God's most frequent commands to his people was to feed the hungry and to seek justice for the poor (see chapters 3–4). For repeatedly ignoring this command, Israel experienced God's curse. Many rich people in the days of Amos and Isaiah were rich, not because of divine blessing, but because of sinful oppression of the poor. God consequently destroyed the nation.

More biblical texts warn of God's punishment of those who neglect or oppress the poor than tell us that material abundance results from obedience.[15] The two statements, however, are not contradictory. Both are true. It is the biblical balance that we need.

The Bible does teach that God rewards obedience with prosperity. But it denies the converse. It is a heresy, particularly common in rich nations, to think that wealth and prosperity are always a sure sign of righteousness. They may be the result of sin and oppression, as in the case of Israel (see chapter 3). The crucial test is whether the prosperous are obeying God's command to bring justice to the oppressed.[16] If they are not, they are living in damnable disobedience to God. On biblical grounds, therefore, one can be sure that prosperity in the context of injustice results from oppression rather than obedience and that it is not a sign of righteousness.

The connection between righteousness, prosperity, and concern for the poor is explicitly taught in Scripture. The picture of the good wife in Proverbs 31 provides one beautiful illustration. This woman is a diligent businessperson who buys fields and engages in trade (vv. 14, 16, 18). She is a righteous woman who fears the Lord (v. 30). Her obedience and diligence clearly bring prosperity. But material possessions do not harden her heart against the poor: "She opens her hand to the poor, and reaches out her hands to the needy" (v. 20). Psalm 112 is equally explicit: "Happy are those who fear the Lord, who greatly delight in his commandments. . . . Wealth and riches are in their houses, . . . they are gracious, merciful, and righteous. It is well with those who deal generously and lend, who conduct their affairs with justice. . . . They have distributed freely, they have given to the poor" (vv. 1, 3–5, 9 NRSV).

The righteous person shares generously with the poor. She works to establish justice for the oppressed. That kind of life is a sign that one's prosperity results from obedience rather than oppression.

God wills prosperity with justice. As John V. Taylor has pointed out so beautifully, the biblical norm for material possessions is "sufficiency."[17] Proverbs 30:8–9 is a marvelous summary: "Give me neither poverty nor riches; feed me with the food that is needful for me, lest I be full, and deny thee, and say, 'Who is the Lord?' or lest I be poor, and steal, and profane the name of my God."

Rich Christians must be careful not to distort the biblical teaching that God sometimes rewards obedience with material abundance. Wealthy persons who make Christmas baskets and give them to relief agencies have not satisfied God's demand. God wills justice for the poor, not occasional charity. And justice means things like the jubilee and the sabbatical remission of debts. It means economic structures that guarantee all people access to the productive resources needed to earn a decent living. Prosperity without that kind of biblical concern for justice unambiguously signifies disobedience.

Pious Poor

The Old Testament teaches that material possessions sometimes result from divine blessing. But is this view compatible with Jesus' saying: "Blessed are you poor, for yours is the kingdom of God" (Luke 6:20)? Does Jesus consider poverty itself a virtue? Furthermore, how can one reconcile the Lucan version of this beatitude with Matthew's version: "Blessed are the poor in spirit" (Matt. 5:3)?

The development of the idea of the "pious poor" in the centuries just prior to Christ helps answer these questions. Already in the Psalms the poor were often identified as the special objects of God's favor and protection precisely because they were oppressed by the wicked rich (9:18; 10:1–2).[18] When Greece and then Rome conquered Palestine, they forced Hellenistic culture and values on the Jews. Those who remained faithful to Yahweh often suffered financially. Thus the term poor came to be used to describe faithful Jews.

It was virtually equivalent to pious, God fearing, and godly, and reflects a situation where the rich were mainly those who had sold out to the incoming culture and had allowed their religious devotion to become corrupted by the new ways. If the poor were the pious, the faithful, and largely oppressed, the rich were the powerful, ungodly, worldly, even apostate.[19]

In such a setting the righteous are often poor and hungry, not just "in spirit" but materially. Matthew has not "spiritualized" Jesus' words. He has simply captured another aspect of Jesus' original meaning. Jesus was talking about those faithful persons who so hungered for righteousness that they sacrificed even their material prosperity when that became

109

necessary. Jesus did not mean that poverty and hunger are desirable in themselves. But in a sinful world where, frequently, success and prosperity are possible only if one transgresses God's law, poverty and hunger are indeed a blessing. The kingdom is for precisely such people.

Jesus' comment in Mark 10:29–30 adds further clarification. He promised that those who forsake all for the kingdom will receive a hundredfold even in this life. He even included houses and lands, part of the good creation intended for our enjoyment. In the same sentence, however, he also promised persecution. Sometimes—perhaps most of the time—the wicked, powerful, and rich will persecute those who dare to follow Jesus' teaching without compromise. Hunger and poverty sometimes result. In such a time poor and hungry disciples are indeed blessed.

In our day some who have dared to preach and live what the Bible teaches about the poor and possessions have experienced terrible persecution. Christians in Latin America have experienced torture, some even death, because they identified with the poor.

Carefree Living

Most of us, however, face far more subtle pressures. Society's prevailing materialism mocks those who try to follow Jesus' carefree attitude toward possessions. Imagine the social disapproval that would descend upon anyone who suggested that Jesus' words should guide the advertising business or even church construction.

> Therefore I tell you, do not worry about your life, what you will eat, or about your body, what you will wear. For life is more than food, and the body more than clothing. Consider the ravens: they neither sow nor reap, they have neither storehouse nor barn, and yet God feeds them. Of how much more value are you than the birds! And can any of you by worrying add a single hour to your span of life? If then you are not able to do so small a thing as that, why do you worry about the rest? Consider the lilies, how they grow: they neither toil nor spin; yet I tell you, even Solomon in all his glory was not clothed like one of these. But if God so clothes the grass of the field, which is alive today and tomorrow is

thrown into the oven, how much more will he clothe you—you of little faith! And do not keep striving for what you are to eat and what you are to drink, and do not keep worrying. For it is the nations of the world that strive after all these things and your Father knows that you need them. Instead, strive for his kingdom, and these things will be given to you as well. (Luke 12:22–31 NRSV; see also 2 Cor. 9:8–11)

Jesus' words are anathema both to Marxists and to certain kinds of capitalists: to Marxists because they worship mammon by claiming that economic forces are the ultimate causal factors in history; to some capitalists because they worship mammon by idolizing economic efficiency and success as the highest goods.[20] Indeed, at another level, Jesus' words are anathema to the ordinary, comfortable Christian. In fact, I must confess that I cannot read them without an underlying sense of uneasiness. The beauty and appeal of Luke 12:22–31 always overwhelm me. But the passage also reminds me that I have not, in spite of continuing struggle and effort, attained the kind of carefree attitude Jesus depicts.

The Secret

What is the secret of such carefree living? First, many people cling to their possessions instead of sharing them because they are worried about the future. But is not such an attitude finally unbelief? If we really believe that God is who Jesus said he is, then we can begin to live without anxiety for the future. Jesus taught us that God is our loving Father. That is why we can call him *abba*, a tender, intimate word like *papa* (Mark 14:36). If we really believe that the almighty Creator and Sustainer of the cosmos is our loving papa, then we can begin to cast aside anxiety about earthly possessions.

Second, such carefree living presupposes an unconditional commitment to Jesus as Lord. We must genuinely want to seek first the kingdom of heaven. Jesus was blunt. We cannot serve God and possessions. "No one can serve two masters; for either he will hate the one and love the other, or he will be devoted to the one and despise the other. You cannot serve God and mammon" (Matt. 6:24). Mammon is not some mysterious pagan God. The word *mammon* is simply the Aramaic word for wealth or property.[21] Like the rich young ruler and Zacchaeus, we must decide between Jesus and riches. Like the merchant in Jesus' parable, we must decide between the kingdom of heaven and our affluent life: "The kingdom of heaven is like a merchant in search of fine pearls, who, on finding one pearl of great value, went and sold all that he had and bought it" (Matthew 13:45–46; see also v. 44). Either Jesus and his kingdom matter so much that we are ready to sacrifice everything else, including our possessions, or we are not serious about Jesus.

Will We Sacrifice?

If Jesus is truly Lord and if we trust in a loving heavenly Father, then we can courageously live without anxiety about possessions. That kind of carefree unconcern for possessions, however, is not merely an inner spiritual attitude. It involves action. Immediately following the moving statement about the carefree life of the ravens and lilies, Jesus says, "Sell your possessions, and give alms; provide yourselves with purses that do not grow old, with a treasure in the heavens that does not fail . . . For where your treasure is, there will your heart be also" (Luke 12:33–34).

If there are poor people who need assistance, Jesus' carefree disciple will help—even if that means selling possessions. People are vastly more important than property. The "laying up [of] treasure in heaven" is accomplished by helping others. "In Jewish literature, the good deeds of a religious person are often described as treasures stored up in heaven."[22] One stores up treasure in heaven by doing righteousness on earth. And aiding the poor is one of the most basic acts of righteousness. Jesus does not mean that we earn salvation by assisting the needy. But he does mean to urge his followers—out of gratitude for God's forgiving grace—to be so unconcerned with property that they gladly sell it to aid the poor and oppressed. Such activity is an integral part of living with joyful unconcern for possessions.

But a difficult question remains. Did Jesus mean that we should sell all our possessions? How literally should we understand what he said in Luke 6:30: "Give to every one who begs from you; and of him who takes away your goods do not ask them again"?

Jesus sometimes engaged in typical Jewish hyperbole to make a point. He hardly meant in Luke 14:26 that one must actively hate father and mother in order to be his disciple. But we have become so familiar with Jesus' words, so accustomed to compromising their call to unconditional commitment and radical discipleship, that we weaken his real intent. What 99 percent of North Americans need to hear 99 percent of the time is this: "Give to everyone who begs from you," and "sell your possessions." It is certainly true that Jesus' followers continued to own some private property. But Jesus clearly taught that the kind of substantial sharing he desired would involve selling possessions. His first followers at Jerusalem took him seriously. If rich Christians today want to experience Jesus' carefree outlook on property and possessions, they will need to do the same.

Other parts of the New Testament continue the same theme. Bishops must not be lovers of money (1 Tim. 3:3; Titus 1:7). Deacons likewise dare not be "greedy for gain" (1 Tim. 3:8). In many churches today, "success" in business is one of the chief criteria for selection to the church board. Is that not a blatant reversal of biblical teaching on the importance of possessions? Even those who are rich should be careful not to set their hope in "uncertain riches." Instead, they should trust in God and share generously (1 Tim. 6:17–18). "Keep your life free from love of money, and be content with what you have; for he has said, 'I will never fail you nor forsake you'" (Heb. 13:5). Our future is secure not because of our possessions but because it rests in the hands of a loving, omnipotent Father. If we truly trust in him and are unconditionally submitted to his Lordship, we can confidently imitate Jesus' carefree unconcern for property and possessions.

In a consumer society that increasingly measures a person's worth and importance by the amount of his or her material possessions, biblical Christians will reject materialism without falling into asceticism. They will delight in the splendor of the material world but not forget that things cannot ultimately satisfy. They will enjoy the good earth and celebrate its abundance without neglecting sacrificial sharing with the needy. They will distinguish between necessities and luxuries. They will enjoy possessions while recognizing their seductive danger. When forced to choose between Jesus and possessions, they will gladly forsake the ring for the Beloved.

Study Questions

1. How does the biblical perspective on private property challenge modern ideas?
2. What are the dangers of possessions? Why is this part of biblical truth especially difficult for modern folk to grasp?
3. What is the biblical connection between righteousness and riches? How is this truth perverted today?
4. How would you change your life if you were truly to implement Jesus' teaching about carefree living?
5. How does St. Augustine's image of the ring and the Beloved summarize the proper attitude toward possessions?

6

SOCIAL EVIL: SIN EMBEDDED IN SOCIETAL SYSTEMS

You yourself were not anti-Semitic. . . . You had your Jewish
neighbors in to dinner. . . . But if you did not protest against
[Hitler's] public policy which made them wear armbands,
defrauded them of property, and shipped them off to death,
your little kindnesses were of no importance whatever.[1]

—RICHARD G. WATTS

ortheast High School in Philadelphia was famous for its superb academic standards and its brilliant, long-standing athletic triumphs. The second oldest school in the city, Northeast had excellent teachers and a great tradition. And it was almost entirely white. Then in the mid-fifties, the neighborhood began to change. Black people moved in. Whites began to flee to the Greater Northeast, a new, all-white section of Philadelphia. A new high school soon became a necessity in this developing, overwhelmingly white area.

When the excellent new school was completed in 1957, it took the name of the old one, and with the name went the memories and traditions as well as the school's history of academic excellence and athletic triumph. The new school also took all the academic and athletic trophies and awards, school colors, songs, as well as the powerful alumni and their treasury. Worst of all, the teachers were given the option of transferring to the new Northeast High. Two-thirds of them did.[2]

The inner-city school was renamed Edison High, and the black students attending it had nothing but an old, rapidly deteriorating building, frequent substitute teachers, and no traditions. Nor did the next several decades bring better teachers or adequate teaching materials. The academic record after 1957 was terrible. But Edison High has one national record. More students from Edison died in the U.S. Army in Vietnam than from any other high school in the United States.

Who was responsible for this terrible evil? Local, state, and federal politicians who for decades had promoted de facto housing segregation? The school board? Parents who had, at best, only a partial picture of what was going on? Christian community leaders? White students at the new Northeast High, whose excellent education and job prospects have been possible, in part, because of the poor facilities and bad teachers left behind for the black students at Edison?

Many would deny any personal responsibility. "That's just the way things are!" And they would be quite right. Long-standing patterns in jobs and housing created a system that automatically produced Edison High. But that hardly silences the query about responsibility. Do we sin when we participate in evil social systems and societal structures that unfairly benefit some and harm others?

Neglect of the biblical teaching on structural injustice or institutionalized evil is one of the most deadly omissions in many parts of the church today. Christians frequently restrict ethics to a narrow class of "personal" sins. In a study of over fifteen hundred ministers, researchers discovered that theologically conservative pastors spoke out on sins such as drug abuse and sexual misconduct,[3] but failed to preach about the sins of institutionalized racism and unjust economic structures that destroy just as many people.

There is an important difference between consciously willed, individual acts (like lying to a friend or committing an act of adultery) and participation in evil social structures. Slavery is an example of the latter. So is the Victorian factory system that had ten-year-old children working twelve to sixteen hours a day. Both slavery and child labor were legal, but they destroyed people by the millions. They were institutionalized, or structural, evils.

In the twentieth century, evangelicals have become imbalanced in their stand against sin, expressing concern and moral outrage about individual sinful acts while ignoring, perhaps even participating in, evil social structures.[4] But the Bible condemns both.

The Old Testament

Speaking through his prophet Amos, the Lord declared, "For three transgressions of Israel, and for four, I will not revoke the punishment; because they sell the righteous for silver, and the needy for a pair of shoes—they that trample the head of the poor into the dust of the earth, and turn aside the way of the afflicted; a man and his father go in to the same maiden, so that my holy name is profaned" (Amos 2:6–7).

Biblical scholars have shown that some kind of legal fiction or technicality underlies the phrase "selling the needy for a pair of shoes."[5] This mistreatment of the poor was legal! In one breath God condemned two detestable practices: sexual misconduct and the legalized oppression of the poor. Sexual sins and economic injustice are equally displeasing to God.

The prophet Isaiah also condemned both personal and social sin:

> Woe to those who join house to house, who add field to field, until there is no more room, and you are made to dwell alone in the midst of the land. The Lord of hosts has sworn in my hearing: "Surely many houses shall be desolate, large and beautiful houses, without inhabitant . . . Woe to those who rise early in the morning, that they may run after strong drink, who tarry late into the evening till wine inflames them!" (Isa. 5:8–9, 11)

Equally powerful is the succinct, satirical summary in verses 22 and 23 of the same chapter: "Woe to those who are heroes at drinking wine, and valiant men in mixing strong drink, who acquit the guilty for a bribe, and deprive the innocent of his right!" Here, in one brief denunciation, God condemns both those who amass large landholdings at the expense of the poor and those who are drunkards. Economic injustice is just as abominable to our God as drunkenness.

117

Some young activists suppose that as long as they fight for the rights of minorities and oppose militarism they are morally righteous, regardless of how often they shack up for the night with a man or woman involved with them in the fight for social justice and peace.

Some of their elders, on the other hand, suppose that because they do not sleep around they are morally upright even though they live in seg- regated communities and own stock in companies that exploit the poor. From a biblical perspective, however, robbing your workers of a fair wage and robbing a bank are both sinful. Voting for a racist because he is a racist and sleeping with your neighbor's wife are both sinful. Silent participation in a company that carelessly pollutes the environment and thus imposes heavy costs on others and destroying your own lungs with tobacco are both sinful.

In the first edition of this book, I said that social evil hurts more people than personal evil. That may be true in the developing world, but I no longer believe that it is true in North America and Western Europe. Within the industrialized nations, the agony caused by broken homes, sexual promiscuity, marital breakdown, domestic violence, and divorce probably equals the pain caused by structural injustice. That is not to deny or deemphasize the latter. It is merely to underline the fact that both kinds of evil devastate societies today.

God clearly reveals his displeasure at evil institutions through the prophet Amos (to understand the meaning of this passage, keep in mind that Israel's court sessions were held at the city gate): "They hate him who reproves in the gate . . . I know how many are your transgressions, and how great are your sins—you who . . . take a bribe, and turn aside the needy in the gate . . . Hate evil, and love good, and establish justice in the gate" (5:10–15).

"Let justice roll down like waters" (v. 24) is not abstract verbalization. The prophet is calling for justice in the legal system. He means, get rid of the corrupt legal system that allows the wealthy to buy their way out of trouble but gives the poor long prison terms.

The dishonest and corrupt individuals in the legal system are not the only ones who stand condemned. Laws themselves are sometimes an abomination to God:

Can wicked rulers be allied with thee, who frame mischief by statute? They band together against the life of the righteous, and condemn the innocent to death. But the Lord has become my stronghold, and my God the rock of my refuge. He will bring back on them their iniquity and wipe them out for their wickedness; the Lord our God will wipe them out. (Ps. 94:20–23)

The Jerusalem Bible has an excellent rendition of verse 20: "You never consent to that corrupt tribunal that imposes disorder as law." God wants his people to know that wicked governments "frame mischief by statute." Or, as the New English Bible puts it, they contrive evil "under cover of law."

God proclaims the same word through the prophet Isaiah:

Woe to those who decree iniquitous decrees, and the writers who keep writing oppression, to turn aside the needy from justice and to rob the poor of my people of their right . . . What will you do on the day of punishment, in the storm which will come from afar? To whom will you flee for help, and where will you leave your wealth? Nothing remains but to crouch among the prisoners or fall among the slain. For all this [God's] anger is not turned away and his hand is stretched out still. (Isa. 10:1–4)

It is possible to make oppression legal. Now, as then, legislators devise unjust laws, and bureaucrats implement the injustice. But God shouts a divine woe against rulers who use their official position to write unjust laws and unfair legal decisions. Legalized oppression is an abomination to our God. Therefore, God calls his people to oppose political structures that frame mischief by statute.

God hates evil economic structures and unjust legal systems because they destroy people by the hundreds and thousands and millions. We can be sure that the just Lord of the universe will destroy wicked rulers and unjust social institutions (see 1 Kings 21).

Another side to institutionalized evil makes it especially pernicious. Structural evil is so subtle that we become ensnared without fully realizing it. God inspired his prophet Amos to utter some of the harshest words in Scripture against the cultured upper-class women of his day: "Hear this word, you cows of Bashan . . . who oppress the poor, who crush the needy, who say to [your] husbands, 'Bring, that we may drink!' The Lord God has sworn by his holiness that, behold, the days are coming upon you, when they shall take you away with hooks, even the last of you with fishhooks" (4:1–2).

The women involved may have had little direct contact with the impoverished peasants. They may never have fully realized that their gorgeous clothes and spirited parties were possible partly because of the sweat and tears of the poor. In fact, they may even have been kind on occasion to individual peasants. (Perhaps they gave them "Christmas baskets" once a year.) But God called these privileged women "cows" because they participated in social evil. Before God they were personally and individually guilty.[6]

If we are members of a privileged group that profits from structural evil, and if we have at least some understanding of the evil yet fail to do what God wants us to do to change things, we stand guilty before God. Social evil is just as displeasing to God as personal evil. And it is more subtle.

Some people disagree. John Schneider has sharply criticized my views on social sin. First, he says that I argue that structural evil is "morally indistinguishable from personal evil."[7] Actually, however, I do not say or believe that. Structures do not have minds and wills in the way individuals do. Evil systems cannot repent of their sins, receive forgiveness through Christ's atonement, receive baptism, and be on their way to eternal life, the way sinful persons can. Responsibility is not the same thing as guilt. Every individual in a society has some responsibility to correct the evil around them, whether the evil is individual or corporate, but that does not mean each person is guilty of every sin in their society.

Years ago, I rejected the notion that "a person is guilty in the same sense and to the same degree as his grandfather or fellow citizen for a wrong done by the grandfather or fellow citizen."[8] There are clear biblical examples of persons confessing the sins of their ancestors and relatives (Dan. 9:4–20; Neh. 1:4–5; Isa. 6:1–5). But Ezekiel 18:1–20 explicitly teaches that the individual who sins, not relatives or neighbors, is the one God considers guilty.

But do we sin personally when we participate in an evil system? That depends on our knowledge and our response. If we have absolutely no understanding of the evil, then our participating does not involve personal sin. If we do understand something of the evil and do all God wants us to do to correct the injustice, then again, we do not sin. Persons sin by participating in evil systems when they understand, at least to some degree, that the system displeases God but fail to act responsibly to change things.

Schneider, however, argues secondly that we often do not know about our involvement in sinful social structures. "Usually, we have no way to know about them."[9] Therefore we are not guilty even though we participate in them. Schneider is partly right here. If we know absolutely nothing about the evil of some system we participate in, then, as I just argued, we do not personally sin by our participation.

Three additional points, however, are crucial. First, the fact that I have no knowledge of a system's evil and am not personally guilty before God for participating in that system does not change the fact that the system is nonetheless wicked and evil and stands under God's condemnation. God always hates structural evils and works to end their injustice. Whether or not I have any understanding of a system's oppression does not change the objective fact that it is an abomination to our holy God.

Furthermore, most of the time, people living in and benefiting from unjust structures know something—albeit not everything—about their evil. In fact, very often we know enough to choose not to learn more lest we feel guilty. Mafia wives know enough about their husband's activity to decide not to ask many questions. Rich Christians know enough about the ravages of poverty that we turn off the TV special on poverty in the developing world or inner city. We rush past the bookstore's section on economic justice. Why? Because we know that knowing more will make us morally obligated to change. Are we not guilty, to some extent, for choosing not to know about evils that benefit us and injure others? "All who do evil hate the light and do not come to the light, so that their deeds may not be exposed" (John 3:20 NRSV).

Finally, different levels of understanding and conscious choice also correspond to different levels of responsibility and guilt. The mafia wife who tries not to know very much is not guilty in the same way as the mafia leader who personally orders executions. But surely she has some understanding, some guilt, and some responsibility.

Schneider has a third, fascinating argument. Jesus lived and worked as a carpenter in an empire full of all kinds of structural injustices. Therefore "it was simply impossible that he not profit from very great structural evils. And so far as we know he did nothing directly to change them."[10] In short, either Jesus was a sinner or my understanding of social sin is mistaken.

Not really. I have never said any one person must do everything to correct an evil system. Each person should do all God wants him or her to do. God's call on each individual's life varies. We sin as participants in evil social structures only if we understand something of their wickedness and then fail to do what God wants us to do to correct the evil. It is simply not true that Jesus did nothing to correct unjust structures. He spoke against economic oppressors. He condemned wicked rulers.[11] He formed a new community that began to live a new transformed lifestyle precisely in the area of economic sharing and neglect of the marginalized. And he rose from the dead and sent the Holy Spirit so his disciples would have the divine power to challenge evil in every form it takes.

It is also important to remember that Jesus lived under an imperialistic Roman dictatorship. He did not have the political opportunities of citizens living in a democracy. Furthermore, as the Jewish Messiah, he was called to live and minister among the Jews of Palestine, not to engage in direct action either to preach the Gospel in Rome or to correct Roman injustice.[12] Since Jesus was sinless, we can assume that he did all God wanted him to do to correct the injustice of his day.

Unfair systems and oppressive structures are an abomination to God, and "social sin" is the correct phrase to categorize them. Furthermore, as we understand their evil, we have a moral obligation to do all God wants us to do to change them. If we do not, we sin. That is the clear implication of Amos' harsh attack on the wealthy women of his day. It is also the clear implication of James 4:17: "Whoever knows what is right to do and fails to do it, for him it is sin."

The New Testament

In the New Testament,[13] the word cosmos (world) often conveys the idea of structural evil.[14] In Greek thought, the word cosmos referred to the structures of civilized life, especially the patterns of the Greek city state that were viewed as essentially good.[15] But the biblical writers knew that sin had invaded and distorted the structures and values of society.

Frequently, therefore, the New Testament uses the word cosmos to refer, in C. H. Dodd's words, "to human society in so far as it is organized on wrong principles."[16] "When Paul spoke of 'the world' in a moral sense, he was thinking of the totality of people, social systems, values, and traditions in terms of its opposition to God and his redemptive purposes."[17]

Before conversion, Christians follow the values and patterns of a fallen social order: "You were dead in your transgressions and sins, in which you used to live when you followed the ways of this world" (Eph. 2:1–2 NIV). Paul, in his letter to the Romans (12:1–2), and John, in his first epistle, urge Christians not to conform to this world's pattern of evil systems and ideas.

> Do not love the world or the things in the world. The love of the Father is not in those who love the world; for all that is in the world—the desire of the flesh, the desire of the eyes, the pride in riches—comes not from the Father but from the world. And the world and its desires are passing away, but those who do the will of God live forever. (1 John 2:15–17 NRSV)

Behind the distorted social structures of our world, Paul says, are fallen supernatural powers under the control of Satan himself. After Paul said that the Ephesians, before their conversion, had "followed the ways of this world," he added: "and of the ruler of the kingdom of the air, the spirit who is now at work in those who are disobedient" (Eph. 2:2 NIV). Paul warns that "our struggle is not against flesh and blood, but against the rulers, against the authorities, against the powers of this dark world and against the spiritual forces of evil in the heavenly realms" (Eph. 6:12 NIV).

Both Jews and Greeks in Paul's day believed that good and evil supernatural beings were behind the scenes influencing social and political structures.[18] To modern secular folk, that view of the supernatural belongs to George Lucas and Stephen King. But when I look at the demonic evil of social systems like Nazism, apartheid, and communism, or even the complex mixture of racism, unemployment, sexual promiscuity, substance abuse, and police brutality in American inner cities, I have no trouble believing that Satan and his gang are hard at work fostering oppressive structures and thus doing their best to destroy God's good creation.

These fallen supernatural powers twist and distort the social systems that we social beings require for wholeness. By seducing us into wrong choices that create evil systems, by working against attempts to overcome oppressive structures, and sometimes by enticing politicians and other leaders to use the occult, these demonic powers shape our world. Evil is far more complex than the wrong choices of individuals. It also lies outside us in oppressive social systems and in demonic powers that delight in defying God by corrupting the social systems that his human image-bearers need.

Pope John Paul II has rightly insisted that evil social structures are "rooted in personal sin." Social evil results from our rebellion against God and our consequent selfishness toward our neighbors. But the accumulation and concentration of many personal sins create "structures of sin" that are both oppressive and "difficult to remove."[19] When we choose to participate in and benefit from evil social systems, we sin against God and our neighbors.

God's Response

The prophets bluntly warned people about the way the God of justice responds to oppressive social structures. God cares so much about the poor that he works to destroy social systems that tolerate and foster poverty. Repeatedly God declared that he would destroy the nation of Israel because of two things: its idolatry and its mistreatment of the poor (see, for example, Jeremiah 7:1–15).

Attention to both of these is crucial. We dare not become so preoccupied with horizontal issues of social injustice that we neglect vertical evils such as idolatry. Modern Christians seem to have an irrepressible urge to fall into one extreme or the other. But the Bible corrects our one-sidedness[20] by making it clear that both lead to destruction. God destroyed Israel and Judah because of both their idolatry and their social injustice.

Here, however, our focus is on the fact that God destroys oppressive social structures. Amos's words, which could be duplicated from many other places in Scripture, make this divine response clear: "Behold, the eyes of the Lord God are upon the sinful kingdom, and I will destroy it from the surface of the ground" (9:8). Within a generation after Amos, the northern kingdom of Israel was completely wiped out.

Probably the most powerful statement of God's work to destroy evil social structures is in the New Testament—in Mary's Magnificat. Mary glorified the Lord who "has put down the mighty from their thrones, and exalted those of low degree; [who] has filled the hungry with good things, and the rich he has sent empty away" (Luke 1:52–53).

The Lord of history is working just as hard today to bring down sinful societies where wealthy classes live by the sweat, toil, and grief of the poor.

An Indian bishop once told me a story that underlines the importance of understanding social sin. A mental institution in his country had a fascinating way of deciding whether patients were well enough to go home. They would take a person over to a water tap, place a large water bucket under the tap, and fill the bucket with water. Then, leaving the tap on, they would give the person a spoon and say, "Please empty the bucket." If the person started dipping the water out one spoonful at a time and never turned the tap off, they knew he or she was still crazy!

Too often Christians, like the Indian mental patients, work at social problems one spoonful at a time. While working feverishly to correct symptoms, they fail to do anything to turn off the tap (e.g., change legal systems and economic policies that hurt people). And they remain confused and frustrated by how little progress they are making.

Understanding the biblical concept of social sin is essential to understanding the seriousness of unfair systems. At the same time, honest discussion should not leave people wallowing in guilt or feeling burdened to correct every global evil.

The proper response to sin is repentance. And genuine repentance leads to unconditional, divine forgiveness. Whenever we become aware of conscious participation in unjust systems, we should ask God's forgiveness. God does not want us to remain bogged down in feelings of guilt; he wants us to be forgiven. He wants us to rejoice in grace—and, in the power of the Spirit, to live differently.

However, living differently—doing all God wants us to do to change structural injustice—by no means involves trying to do everything. We each have our own unique gifts and calling. God wants many of us to fast and pray about social sin. Most should study, and many should write and speak out. Some should join and support organizations promoting social justice. Others should run for political office. All of us should ask how changes in our personal lifestyle could help model a better world. But God does not want anyone to feel guilty for not doing everything—or for taking time off for relaxation and recreation. Everyone should prayerfully ask God what limited, specific things God wants him or her to concentrate on. It was God, after all, who made us finite with only twenty-four hours each day. Being called to do all God wants us to do to correct social sin is not a heavy burden. It is an invitation to joy and meaning in life, an occasion for blessing our neighbors, and a wondrous opportunity to be a coworker with the Lord of history.

Study Questions

1. What was wrong about the situation at Edison High? Who was responsible?
2. How do Amos and Isaiah condemn both personal and social sin? If they were alive today, what might they say?
3. What happens when individuals or churches become preoccupied only with personal sin, or only with social sin? How balanced is your church?

PART THREE

What Causes Poverty?

Conservatives blame the poor for their misery. Liberals reject that view as hard-hearted and wrong-headed. Rather than blaming the victims, liberals argue, we should condemn the structures that create poverty. Conservatives scoff at such bleeding-heart liberals who cannot see or will not admit how sinful choices about sex, drugs, alcohol, and work contribute significantly to poverty.

Who is right? And wrong? Both. There is no single cause of poverty. Personal sinful choices and complex social structures cause poverty. So do misguided cultural ideas, natural and human disasters, and lack of appropriate technology. Whether one examines long-term poverty in U.S. cities or rural poverty in the Third World, the causes are complex.[1] Chapters 7 and 8 probe this complexity.

As we explore these many, interrelated, complex causes, a basic reminder is essential. No finite person knows enough to reach complete understanding. I do not pretend that these chapters contain the final word. They simply represent my best effort to listen as objectively as I can to careful, responsible scholars. Wherever I have failed to do that, I hope others will correct me.

It is essential that disagreement about the specific analysis in parts three and four not be confused with disagreement over parts one and two. I claim considerably more certainty about my conclusions in the first two parts of this book than in the following parts. Of course, even the biblical analysis in part two is less than perfect. But disagreement over complex economic issues is fundamentally different from disagreement about biblical principles.

7

POVERTY'S COMPLEX CAUSES

Lazy people should learn a lesson from the way ants live. . . .
Drunkards and gluttons will be reduced to poverty.

—PROVERBS 6:6; 23:21 TEV

Woe to those who make unjust laws . . . to
deprive the poor of their rights.

—ISAIAH 10:1–2 NIV

To reduce the suffering of the poor, it is essential to know what causes poverty. If we think most poverty results from laziness when, in fact, inadequate tools and unfair systems are major factors, our best efforts will fail. If we think unjust structures are the only cause of poverty when, in fact, personal choices play a role, we also will fail. To be successful, we have to start with truth.

Sinful Personal Choices

A few people are poor due to their own laziness, and some people are poor due to their own wrong choices. Choosing to misuse drugs, alcohol, and sex contributes significantly to poverty. To state that bluntly is not to join some callous conservative plot to ignore poor people or "blame the victim." It is simply to admit the truth. The Bible clearly teaches it (Prov. 6:6–11; 14:23; 23:21; 24:30–34), and reality regularly provides examples of

129

drug addicts, alcoholics, and sexually promiscuous persons whose tragically wrong choices have landed them in wrenching poverty.

Never, of course, do we make our choices in a vacuum. Lack of a good education, unemployment, racism, neglect in childhood—these and many other complex factors flow together to provide a setting in which sinful choices are easy and good choices are hard.

But to deny that persons make individual choices that help create poverty denies reality. It also obscures the fact that evangelism and divine transformation of rebellious sinners are central to the solution of some forms of poverty. When sinful personal choices contribute significantly to a person's poverty, no solution will work that does not include spiritual transformation.

Unbiblical Worldviews

Misguided cultural values and non-Christian worldviews also create poverty. For example, Hinduism's complex theology and practice of the caste system is a major cause of poverty in India, where more than 200 million "untouchables" live in agonizing poverty while the upper castes feel little obligation to change things. Why? Because the Hindu worldview teaches that people in the higher castes are there because of good choices in previous incarnations, and those in the lowest castes are there because of evil choices in earlier incarnations. If the untouchables submit to their lot, the reigning theology explains, they will do better in the next incarnation. This worldview nurtures fatalism among the poor and complacency among the powerful.

What India needs is a worldview that rightly names the gaping disparity as sinful and unjust and proclaims the equal worth and dignity of all people. In short, India's untouchables need the Gospel. They need to hear the biblical truth that all persons are created in the image of God. And that the God of history sides with the oppressed and invites them to be coworkers in shaping a just society for all.

Cultural values play a central role both in fostering poverty and in creating wealth. Those who think, as animists do, that the rivers and trees are living spirits, will not dam rivers to create hydroelectric power or cut forests to manufacture paper. Those who think, as some Eastern monists do, that the material world is an illusion to be escaped, will not waste much time creating material abundance. And those who think, as modern materialists do, that nothing exists except the material world, will search ever more frantically for meaning and joy in ever-increasing material possessions—even if the result is environmental destruction and neglect of the poor.

What we need is a biblical worldview—a genuinely biblical view of persons, history, and the material world. Then we will treasure material possessions without worshipping them. We will seek justice for all because every person bears the divine image. And we will respect God's creation as we exercise our God-given stewardship, using the rivers and trees to create sustainable civilizations of wholesome abundance.

Cultural values and underlying worldviews make a difference. Massachusetts Institute of Technology (MIT) economist Lester Thurow pointed out that China had the technology to create the industrial revolution and conquer the globe centuries before Europe did:

> At least eight hundred years before they were to occur in Europe, China had invented blast furnaces and piston bellows for making steel; gunpowder and the cannon for military conquest; the compass and rudder for world exploration; paper, movable type, and the printing press for disseminating knowledge; suspension bridges; porcelain; the wheeled metal plow, the horse collar, a rotary threshing machine and a mechanical seeder for improving agricultural yields; a drill that enabled them to get energy from natural gas; and the decimal system, negative numbers, and the concept of zero to analyze what they were doing. Even the lowly wheelbarrow and the match were used centuries earlier in China.[1]

But Confucian culture perceived innovation and technology as a threat rather than an opportunity. Western cultural values, rather than a Confucian worldview, shaped the industrial revolution and its amazing creation of wealth. Some of the results have been good, some evil. But they all are related to underlying Western cultural values, which are a strange mixture of historic Christianity and Enlightenment naturalism.

Disasters

Whether caused by nature or humanity, disasters cause poverty.

A raging hurricane brings widespread devastation, throwing hundreds of thousands of people into instant poverty. Floods, earthquakes, and drought also produce hunger and starvation. Sometimes environmental decay caused by human foolishness is partly to blame. But often it is merely the mysterious work of the wind and water. No one is to blame. No one needs to repent. We simply need to activate our relief networks as quickly as possible to prevent starvation.

Human disasters are different. Ethnic conflicts, religious wars, and tribal hostility today produce tens of millions of refugees abruptly snatched from their homes and livelihood. The result is hunger and starvation. Immediate relief assistance must go hand in hand with patient efforts to overcome ancient hostilities in our response to human disasters and the poverty they bring.

Lack of Knowledge and Technology

Some people are eager to work but lack the proper tools and knowledge. Because they do not have the seeds or implements, their agricultural production is too low to provide enough food to sustain a healthy life. Without the knowledge and skill to produce other things to exchange for food, they suffer, and sometimes die, of malnutrition.

Here the primary need is long-term community development[2]—helping to drill wells for irrigation, showing how to grow more productive strains of grain, or enabling people to fashion a better plow or storage bin.

Economists rightly insist that economics is not a zero-sum game, meaning that it is wrong to think of available wealth as a limited pie that must be recut into smaller portions if everyone is to have a piece. If that were the case, any gain on the part of the poor would mean a loss for the rich.

To the contrary, wealth can be created. Though ultimately the world is finite, there are vast possibilities, as the last couple of centuries have demonstrated, for producing many more of the things people need to

enjoy material abundance. Applying knowledge to nature produces astonishing new products. The black goo we know as crude oil was useless until
someone figured out how to use it to propel cars, airplanes, and electri-
cal generators. The result was vast new wealth (also, alas, environmental
destruction). Helping the poor acquire appropriate, sustainable technology is one central way to reduce poverty.

Great Inequalities of Power

Make no mistake. There is plenty of food in the world today. Powerlessness,
not famine, causes much of today's poverty. "Fundamentally," Bread for
the World says, "hunger is a political question: hungry people lack the
power to end their hunger."[3] In their influential book, *Why Nations Fail*,
economists Daron Acemoglu and James A. Robinson put it bluntly: "Poor
countries are poor because those who have power make choices that create poverty."[4] Many people today are poor and hungry largely because a
few people with enormous power neglect and/or mistreat the powerless.
Using their unequal power, they create structures that benefit themselves
and oppress others.

A large landowner in a poor village in Bangladesh, one of the poorest countries in the world, illustrates the problem. (In Bangladesh in the
mid-1990s, 65 percent of all children were malnourished, 87 percent of
the people lived in the countryside, and 86 percent of that rural population lived below the poverty level.) In an attempt to increase agricultural
output and reduce poverty, the World Bank financed an irrigation project in the rural village. The largest landowner in the area, however, was
also active in the ruling political party, and he managed to gain control of
the new irrigation project and get a monopoly on the new water supply.
Naturally, the benefits of the new technology flowed to this powerful
landowner, not to the poor. His agricultural output did expand, but this
did not help the most needy.[5]

The examples of abused power are everywhere. Europeans were the
first to apply gunpowder to warfare, using this enormous new power to
colonize everybody else. They largely annihilated the native peoples of
the Americas and forced millions of Africans into slavery.

Power itself is not evil. But as the famous British thinker Lord Acton said, "Power tends to corrupt and absolute power corrupts absolutely." Because of the Fall, sinful people regularly use great inequalities of power to oppress the weak. Again and again, the result is unfair social, economic, and political systems that produce poverty. If we are to understand one of the root causes of poverty, we must understand how unequal power nurtures social sin or structural injustice.

Local

The story of the Bangladeshi landowner is repeated—with local variation—almost everywhere. As Russia moved toward private ownership after the collapse of communism, formerly communist officials with inside knowledge and connections gained personal ownership of vast wealth. In many nations, a few people own vast amounts of land. Even when the poor do own land, they often do not have access to the resources needed to make it productive.

According to the United Nations Food and Agriculture Organization (FAO), 1.3 percent of all landowners in Latin America used to own 71.6 percent of the land.[6] Poor farmers who did not have much land often had to borrow money to purchase seed and fertilizer. Frequently, unscrupulous moneylenders were the only source of credit. But they often charged outrageous interest rates—sometimes even 20 percent per day.[7] Frequently, the poor farmer defaulted and lost his land—which was probably the moneylender's original goal.[8]

In addition, the poor regularly suffer from another abuse of power. The courts and the police are often weak and usually under the control of the powerful. As a result local elites regularly abuse and violently oppress their poor neighbors. That is why Gary A. Haugen and Victor Boutros insist in a powerful new book that "the end of poverty requires the end of violence."[9]

National

Wealthy elites—sometimes allied to corrupt, authoritarian rulers—dominate many poor nations.

The Philippines is a very poor nation where just under half (42 percent) of the people try to live on less than two dollars a day.[10] Many people try to earn a living from the land. But most people do not have any land. Most of the land is owned by large landowners and multinational companies.

For years President Marcos ruled the Philippines with a dictatorial fist, squelching efforts for land reform. Even when Mrs. Aquino won the hearts of the world with her brave, nonviolent victory over the brutal Marcos, little changed. Mrs. Aquino herself owned vast estates. And despite various attempts at land reform, poor peasants acquired almost no land. The most productive and fertile lands remain in the hands of wealthy elites.[11]

Angola is one of the richest developing nations in terms of natural resources. It is the second-largest sub-Saharan oil producer and the fourth-largest producer of diamonds in the world.[12] But 58 percent of the rural population live in poverty. One of ten children die before they are five.[13] Angola's main source of income is oil, accounting for 85 percent of GDP. Tragically, corruption and fraud have resulted in billions of dollars unaccounted for.[14] In 2013, the government spent 17 percent of its budget on "defense and security" (11 years after the country's civil war ended)—but only 8.9 percent on education and just 5.3 percent on health.[15]

Or consider the case of former president Mobutu, the fabulously wealthy ruler of Zaire (now the Democratic Republic of Congo) from 1965 to 1997. During the 1960s and 1970s, Belgium, France, and the U.S. sent cash and military forces to support Zaire's dictator, Mobutu Sese Seko, because he was a valuable opponent of communism in a strategic location. But the people of Zaire remained desperately poor, with 70 percent living in poverty. During the 1980s, per capita income in Zaire declined by an annual average of 1.3 percent. Meanwhile, there was good reason to believe that Mobutu stole $5 billion from the economy. Responsible government largely disappeared. Looting and riots became common. Mobutu fought every effort to move the country toward democracy. And twenty thousand soldiers protected this powerful dictator.[16]

Today in Egypt, vast numbers of people are poor. Why? "Precisely because it has been ruled by a narrow elite that have organized society for their own benefit at the expense of the vast mass of people." The former Egyptian president, Hosni Mubarak (who ruled as a dictator for about thirty years) reportedly accumulated a fortune of $70 billion.[17]

Peruvian economist Hernando de Soto has shown how small oligarchies in many countries like Peru control the economy for their benefit. They use their political power to create monopolies and complicated rules, fees, and procedures that make it almost impossible for new, smaller entrepreneurs to start businesses that would compete with and threaten their vested economic interests.[18] As a result, large numbers of gifted small entrepreneurs are forced into an informal economy where their rights and property are not protected by law. Poverty results from this abuse of power.

Or consider the U.S. In real dollars the minimum wage was worth less in 2014 than in 1984.[19] In inflation-adjusted dollars, the 1968 minimum wage would be worth over $10 an hour in 2014 instead of the current $7.25.[20] Powerful politicians propose drastic cuts in major programs that help poor Americans even while the United States has the highest poverty level of any industrialized nation.[21]

Meanwhile the richest 1 percent enjoy vastly expanding wealth. 95 percent of all the increase in national wealth from 2009–2012 went to the richest 1 percent.[22] The reasons for that are complex. But one significant factor is that many of the changes in tax policy in the last several decades have largely benefited the richest Americans.[23] Could the actions of the Washington politicians possibly be connected to the fact that most political donations come from the richest 1 percent?

Table 10 shows the distribution of income or consumption in a variety of nations. In South Africa, the poorest 20 percent receive only 3 percent of all income; the richest 20 percent get 68 percent. In the U.S., the richest 20 percent receive 46 percent, and the poorest 20 percent only 5 percent.

There is no obvious correlation between a country's total wealth and the gap between its rich and poor. In some rich countries, like the U.S. and Germany, the gap is quite large. In others, like Japan and Sweden, it is much less. Behind this simple table, however, lie enormous differences of power that profoundly shape the life of each nation.

Table 10—Percentage Share of Income or Consumption Distribution in Countries (listed in order of percentage of the richest 20 percent)

Country	Survey year	Gini Index[24]	Lowest 20%	Highest 20%
South Africa	2009	63	3	68
Honduras	2009	57	2	60
Colombia	2010	56	3	60
Brazil	2009	55	3	59
Chile	2009	52	4	58
Zimbabwe	1995	50	5	56
Panama	2010	52	3	56
Nigeria	2010	49	4	54
Mexico	2010	47	5	53
Kenya	2005	48	5	53
Uganda	2009	44	6	51
Philippines	2009	43	6	50
Russian Federation	2009	40	6	47
China	2009	42	5	47
United States	2000	41	5	46
Indonesia	2011	38	7	46
Israel	2001	39	6	45
United Kingdom	1999	36	6	44
India	2010	34	9	43
Switzerland	2000	34	8	41
Australia	1994	35	6	41
France	1995	33	7	40
Canada	2000	33	7	40
Sweden	2000	25	9	37
South Korea	1998	32	8	37
Norway	2000	26	10	37
Germany	2000	28	9	37
Japan	1993	25	11	36

Source: World Bank[25]

In *Why Nations Fail*, the authors show how a fundamental difference in how power (political and economic) was shared in the United States on the one hand and South America on the other helps explain why most people in South America remained in poverty for so long. When the Spanish and Portuguese conquered Latin America, politically powerful small elites received huge tracts of land. For centuries, these small elites used their vast economic and political power to organize society in a way that largely benefited them. In the U.S., on the other hand, the land (after it was stolen from Native Americans!) was divided up in a way that enabled the vast majority of Americans to own their own farms. That plus the early embrace of a democratic political order substantially decentralized power. That decentralization, these economists argue, is a primary reason why the American economy grew rapidly and why all Americans rather than just a few benefited from that growth.[26] Centralized power almost always leads to injustice and widespread poverty. Decentralized power is more likely to produce benefits for everyone.[27]

Global

The global financial crisis of 2008 and the resulting global recession provide a stark illustration of the imbalance of power and the results for the poor. A small group of very powerful, very wealthy Western bankers made reckless decisions that created the global financial crisis. The result was global economic decline and widespread recession in many countries. That, in turn, dramatically increased the number of people in poverty.[28]

Who suffered the most? Nobel laureate economist Joseph E. Stiglitz puts it bluntly: "The crisis emanated from the center and reached the periphery. Developing countries, and especially the poor in these countries, are among the hardest hit victims *of a crisis they had no role in making.*"[29]

The composition of important global institutions also illustrates centralized power. The five permanent members of the U.N. Security Council (U.S., Russia, Britain, France, and China) have veto power, and they regularly use that power for national advantage. With only 5 percent of the world's people, the U.S. controls 16 percent of the votes in the World Bank and 17 percent in the International Monetary Fund[30]—two powerful global institutions whose decisions regularly impact poorer nations. The *Stiglitz Report* points out that the majority of the world's countries (the developing countries) lack adequate voice and representation in the major global economic institutions.[31] Seven nations (U.S., Japan, Great Britain, France, Germany, Canada, and Italy) have only 11 percent of the world's people, but their annual summit (now called the G-7) is widely regarded as the most influential global economic institution.[32]

Western Colonialism

The history of European colonialism is a vivid historical example of how great inequalities of power foster injustice.

From the sixteenth century on, white Europeans have had more power—military power—than anyone else. They knew how to make guns. Asians, Africans, and Native Americans did not.[33] The rest is history. We wiped out most of the native peoples in North America; killed millions and decimated the rest in Latin America; enslaved millions of Africans; and divided up Asia, Africa, and the Americas as we pleased.

Economic historians still argue about the economic impact on colonized nations.[34] But it is now generally recognized by historians that many of the civilizations Europe "discovered" were highly developed in many ways; their most obvious "deficiency" was their lack of modern military technology. True, the civilizations of Asia, Africa, and the Americas were different in that they were not "Christian," but how Christian were the European colonizers?

The primary interest of colonial masters was the economic and political self-interest of the "Mother" country—even when that meant harm and destruction in the colonies. As the authors of *Why Nations Fail* point out, "the profitability of European colonial empires were often built on the destruction of independent polities and indigenous economies around the world."[35]

In the early eighteenth century, India produced and exported more textiles than any other country in the world. Britain's East India Company assisted this thriving Indian textile business by shipping large quantities for sale in Great Britain. But in the first two decades of the eighteenth century, British textile manufacturers persuaded the British parliament to outlaw the wearing of Indian textiles in Great Britain! The result was a dramatic contraction of the Indian textile industry and increased poverty in India. Soon, India was buying textiles made in Great Britain![36]

The Dutch had a similar impact on important parts of what is now Indonesia. In the sixteenth century, the Moluccan Archipelago (in modern Indonesia) was central to world trade because it was the only producer of spices like cloves, mace, and nutmeg. When the Dutch arrived, they decided to monopolize and control this lucrative trade in spices. Using their superior military power, they forced the people in some islands to become semi-slaves in order to produce spices cheaply. In order to control the production and sale of mace and nutmeg in the Banda Islands, the Dutch massacred almost all the population. They spared only a few "natives" to teach the new Dutch plantation owners (and the slaves they imported) how to produce the spices. In order to avoid a similar fate, a number of island rulers destroyed their production of spices. The result, as in India, was the reversal of indigenous economic development.[37]

Probably the worst effect of European colonialism came with the terrible destruction produced by the African slave trade. In the seventeenth and eighteenth centuries, more than ten million people were transported out of Africa as slaves. In addition to the devastation inflicted on the slaves themselves, the market for slaves produced destruction within Africa. Exchanging guns for slaves, the slave traders encouraged African political rulers to go to war to capture slaves to sell. "All laws and customs were distorted and broken to capture slaves and more slaves."[38]

Nor was it only the slave trade by Western colonial empires that harmed Africa. Development economists Acemoglu and Robinson point out that the political and economic institutions developed by colonial rulers to benefit narrow colonial elites were simply taken over and perpetuated by African leaders at independence. "Independence created an opening for unscrupulous leaders to take over and intensify the extraction that European colonialists presided over."[39]

A writer for *The Wall Street Journal* provides another example of the negative impact of colonialism. June Kronholz wrote an article examining the modern attempt of Gabon (a small country in Africa) to build a transnational railroad. Why, she asked, was one not built in colonial days?

The French built only what they needed to find and export Gabon's raw materials. In fact, colonials' habit of building only those roads and ports

140

and power plants that served their purposes, while ignoring the rest of the country, still stifles Third World economies. "[The leaders of the newly independent countries] inherited a legacy that condemned them to underdevelopment," complains the U.N.'s Mr. Doo Kingue, whose own country, Cameroon, was colonized by Germans, English and French.[40]

Whether in India, Indonesia, or Africa, the destructive effects of colonialism resulted from a huge imbalance of power.

It would be simplistic, of course, to suggest that the impact of colonialism and subsequent economic and political relations with industrialized nations was entirely negative. It was not. Among other things, literacy rates rose and health care improved.

I also thank God that opportunities to spread the gospel around the world increased during the colonial period. But think of how different colonial history would be if missionaries had challenged imperial injustice more often. Christian values sometimes undercut ancient social evils, such as the caste system in India, but what a tragedy that so much of the impact of the "Christian" North on the developing political and economic structures of the colonies was shaped by economic self-interest rather than the biblical principles of justice. If the whole biblical message had been shared and lived out in social and economic life, developing nations would know less misery today. If Christian attitudes toward property and wealth had ruled the colonizers' actions, if the principles of jubilee, the sabbatical year, and empowerment of the poor had been an integral part of the colonial venture and international economic activity, there would be less need for this book today.

Unfortunately, they were not. So the colonial legacy lingers. Not surprisingly, some of the injustices perpetuated in the early days of colonialism have become cemented in the institutions that govern contemporary economic activity.[41]

It would be silly, of course, to depict colonialism as the sole cause of present poverty. Wrong personal choices, misguided cultural values, disasters, and inadequate technology all play a part. So do gross inequalities of power and the unjust structures that they create and perpetuate. At every level—whether local, national, or global—people with great power use it for selfish purposes, enriching themselves and oppressing others. Widespread poverty is the result.

The abuse of power also helps explain a very recent development. Most very poor people used to live in the poorest countries. Today, the majority of people living below the international poverty level ($1.25 a day) live in middle income countries![42] Why? It is quite possible for a country to enjoy rapid economic growth without the poorer members of society enjoying the economic benefits.

India (where a huge share of today's poorest live) has experienced rapid economic growth of 7 percent or more per year since 1990. Yet almost half (48 percent) the children are stunted because of malnutrition. The powerful who controlled Indian governments did not choose to spend enough of its new wealth on nutritional and sanitation programs that could have substantially reduced widespread poverty and death among the poorest members of Indian society. Bangladesh on the other hand (in spite of much lower annual growth rates in GDP) chose to invest far more heavily in nutritional and health programs designed to reduce childhood malnutrition and death. The result? Bangladesh's rates of childhood stunting fell dramatically.[43]

Pope Francis is surely correct: "Growth in justice requires more than economic growth, while presupposing such growth; it requires decisions, programs, mechanisms and processes specifically geared to a better distribution of income, the creation of sources of employment and an integral promotion of the poor."[44]

One more crucial point about the causes of poverty is essential. Bryant Myers is right that ultimately, the most basic cause of poverty is spiritual.[45] Sin causes most poverty.[46]

Sin is the cause of the bad personal choices that create poverty. That is true not only—or even primarily!—about things like laziness and abuse of alcohol. It is also true of the complicated unjust structures that powerful elites create to benefit themselves at the expense of the weak. We should urge the powerful to repent.

Sin is also finally the cause of the destructive worldviews that oppress and immobilize vast numbers of poor people. Indian development specialist Jayakumar Christian shows how the powerful create religious systems, educational structures and judicial and political systems that not only oppress the weak but tell them that they are inferior, worthless and powerless. As the weak internalize these untrue (sinful) narratives about themselves, they are immobilized.[47] They need spiritual transformation—both biblical teaching about their worth as immeasurably invaluable persons made in the image of God, and the transforming presence of the Holy Spirit to empower them to reject all the ways that sin has impoverished them.

Study Questions

1. What causes of poverty do you and your friends emphasize? Why?
2. Do you agree or disagree with the explanation of poverty in this chapter? Why?
3. What parts of this chapter would be most widely challenged by your friends or the larger society? What arguments would you develop to respond to those challenges?

8

STRUCTURAL INJUSTICE TODAY

*Come now, you rich, weep and howl for the miseries that
are coming upon you. Your riches have rotted and your
garments are moth-eaten. Your gold and silver have rusted,
and their rust will be evidence against you and will eat
your flesh like fire. You have laid up treasure for the last
days. Behold, the wages of the laborers who mowed your
fields, which you kept back by fraud, cry out; and the cries
of the harvesters have reached the ears of the Lord of hosts.
You have lived on the earth in luxury and in pleasure:
you have fattened your hearts in a day of slaughter.*

—JAMES 5:1–5

*I read some time ago that Upton Sinclair, the author, read
this passage to a group of ministers. Then he attributed
the passage to Emma Goldman, who at the time was an
anarchist agitator. The ministers were indignant, and their
response was, "This woman ought to be deported at once!"*

—UNPUBLISHED SERMON [1 JUNE 1975] BY DR. PAUL E. TOMS,
FORMER PRESIDENT OF THE NATIONAL ASSOCIATION OF EVANGELICALS

Shortly after the first edition of this book was published, I was lecturing at an evangelical college about God's concern for the poor and the existence of unjust structures that help create poverty. In my chapel talk,

145

I suggested that some starvation results from economic structures that wealthy nations like the U.S. erect for their own advantage. The college chaplain did not see things that way. He invited me to his class. But before I spoke he made his position very clear when he said, as I recall his words, "I can hardly believe that my country could do anything wrong."

Years of global experience as president of World Vision led another evangelical leader to a starkly different conclusion. Stanley Mooneyham condemned "the stranglehold which the developed West has kept on the economic throats of the Third World." That, I believe, is to overstate the problem. But Mooneyham makes an important point in saying that "the heart of the problems of poverty and hunger are human systems which ignore, mistreat and exploit man. . . . If the hungry are to be fed, . . . some of the systems will require drastic adjustments while others will have to be scrapped altogether."[1] Such a conclusion should not surprise us in light of what we saw in the last chapter about the way abuse of power causes poverty. This chapter will explore that reality in more detail.

To do so, we must examine some complex economic ideas. I will try to use ordinary language rather than technical jargon. (After all, I am a theologian, not an economist.) However, the reader who has no interest in economics may want to skip to chapters 9 and 10, which deal with practical steps that individuals and churches can take to empower the poor.

Some critics of this chapter (and chapter 11) have suggested that I should have stayed with theology. Meddling theologians, they claim, never get their economics right. I have two responses. First, I have tried hard to listen to and learn from good economists. In fact, first-rate economists have provided extensive advice over the course of the several editions of this book, and their careful review of these sections and their advice have greatly improved chapters 8 and 11. Second, even brilliant economists disagree and make mistakes. Since economics is central to our world, non-economists like you and me will have to do our best to understand without being intimidated by the fact that our understanding is only partial.

In citing the disturbing data that follow, I do so with neither sadistic enjoyment of an opportunity to flagellate the affluent, nor with a desire to create feelings of irresolvable guilt. God has no interest in groundless "guilt trips." But I do believe the God of the poor wants us all to feel deep pain over the agony and anguish that torment our poor sisters and brothers. I also believe we must call sin by its biblical name.

As discussed in the previous chapter, the affluent North is not responsible for all the poverty in the world. There are many causes. But even if the rich did not cause any part of global poverty, we still would be responsible to help those in need. The story of the rich man and Lazarus (Luke 16:19–31) does not suggest that Lazarus's poverty resulted from oppression by his rich neighbor. The rich man merely neglected to help. His sin was one of omission. And it sent him to hell.

I do believe, however, that affluent nations have played a part in establishing economic structures that contribute to some of today's hunger and starvation. (Given what we know about two things—the sinful way that very powerful people regularly abuse their power, and second, the fact that Europeans and later also North Americans have been vastly more powerful militarily and then economically than the rest of the world—it would be utterly astonishing if this had not happened!) Surely our first responsibility is to understand and change what we are doing wrong.

How, then, are we a part of unjust structures that contribute to world hunger? A discussion of five issues will reveal our involvement: (1) market economies; (2) international trade; (3) natural resources and the environment; (4) multinational corporations in developing countries; and (5) discrimination and war.

Evaluating Market Economies

Do market economies help or hurt the poor? Our exploration of the structural causes of poverty must begin with this question. Democratic capitalism won the most dramatic economic/political debate of the twentieth century. Many, many countries in the world praise the ideal of democracy. Virtually every nation is taking steps toward "a market economy." Anybody concerned about the poor must struggle with how this momentous global embrace of market economies impacts the poorest.

But what is a market economy? Definition is crucial. There are a wide variety of actual market economies today. The "ideal type" of a pure laissez-faire economy (where the government never intervenes in economic life) does not exist in today's world.[2] Whether in North America, Western Europe, or the successful Asian Tigers (Taiwan, South Korea, Singapore, and Hong Kong), the government plays a substantial role in what everyone nevertheless calls market economies.[3]

A market economy, then, is an economic arrangement in which the bulk of the wealth and means of production are privately owned and most wages and prices are set by supply and demand. This does not mean that government never intervenes in the economy. It does today in all existing market economies—although in the U.S., for example, the government intervenes less than in Sweden.

Communist economies were fundamentally different. The state owned the means of production. State central planners determined wages, prices, and production. (There used to be a central office in Moscow that set twenty-five million prices every year!)[4]

By the beginning of the twenty-first century, it was clear that the modern world had rejected centrally planned economies in favor of market economies. Is that good news for the poor?

Yes, on balance, it is, although there are serious problems with the way present market economies are working.

Communism's state ownership and central planning did not work. They were inefficient and totalitarian. Market economies, on the other hand, have produced enormous wealth. And not only in Western nations. Many Asian countries have adopted market economies. The result has been a dramatic drop in poverty in the world's most populous continent. In 1970, chronic undernourishment plagued 35 percent of the people in all developing countries. In 2003—in spite of rapid population growth— only 17 percent of the people in developing countries were chronically undernourished.[5] And from 1990–1992 to 2011–2013, the hunger rate in developing countries dropped from 23.2 percent to 14.3 percent.[6]

Starting in the early 1980s, China began to introduce increasingly substantial aspects of a market economy. The result was stunning. In 1981, the poverty rate in China was 65 percent. By 2007, it was a mere 4 percent![7] Most poor developing countries in East Asia also embraced more market-oriented policies as did India in the 1990s. Today, almost all countries in the developing world embrace economic policies that apply market principles. And the result in many, many places has been rapid, even explosive, economic growth.[8]

It is important to underline the fact that the evidence on the success of market economies in no way supports the idea that the ideal is a purely laissez-faire economy—i.e., one where the government plays no role in empowering poor people. As we shall see at some length in chapter 11, the enormous success of early Asian market economies like South Korea, Taiwan, and Singapore was due to a significant degree precisely to the fact that government made land, and/or education and health care available to all.[9]

The evidence is overwhelming. Market economies are more successful than centrally owned and centrally planned economies at creating economic growth. China's phenomenal growth rate over the last three decades is clearly the result of its substantial adoption of free-market measures in both agriculture and substantial parts of industrial production.[10] Especially in Asia, but also in parts of Latin America (e.g., Chile) and Africa (e.g., Botswana), market economies are producing explosive economic growth.

Central to this growth is the expansion of exports and international trade. The rapid growth of the newer Asian market economies was directly related to their decision to reduce trade barriers and emphasize exports—along with substantial government activity. A World Bank report concluded: "A large empirical literature has documented that, on average, countries with market-friendly policies such as openness to international trade, disciplined monetary and fiscal policy and well-developed financial markets enjoy better long-run growth performance than countries where such policies are absent."[11]

International trade also tends to increase real wages in developing countries.[12] Wages in export-oriented firms in developing countries are, of course, very low in comparison to wages in developed nations. (That, after all, is a major part of why a poor nation can produce things more cheaply.) But those "low wages" are usually substantially higher—especially when trade unions have basic freedom—than the average wages in the country. Thus when international trading patterns use the advantage of low wages in poor nations, two beneficial things can result: poor people receive higher wages, and those of us who buy what they export pay lower prices for the products.[13]

International trade creates forces that tend to cause wages for labor with the same skills to equalize among trading partners.[14] Obviously, that hurts high-paid workers in industrialized nations who must compete with much lower-paid workers in Indonesia, Mexico, or China. But surely those most concerned with the poorest should support measures to improve wages in developing countries and then seek other ways (generous unemployment insurance and job training, for example) to help workers in rich nations who are hurt by global trade. In this way, developed nations focus more on areas where they have a comparative advantage.

The evidence of the last three decades clearly demonstrates that the widespread embrace of market economies has lifted vast numbers of poor people out of poverty. Tens of millions of very poor people in South Korea and Taiwan and more recently hundreds of millions of very poor people in China, Indonesia, India, and elsewhere are no longer poor. That fact merits celebration.

At the same time, we dare not overlook another reality. Merely increasing a country's GDP does not guarantee that the poorest benefit. In 1990, 90 percent of all the people living below the international poverty level ($1.25 per person per day) were living in low-income countries (i.e., with low per capita GDP). Today, about 70 percent of the people below this poverty level live in middle income countries![15] Why? Many countries (India for example) have experienced such a great increase in GDP that they have moved from low-income to middle-income status. But they have failed to implement the governmental policies that would ensure that everyone enjoyed the benefits of the growing economy.[16]

The first conclusion to draw, therefore, is that market economies are better at producing economic growth than present alternatives. Furthermore, since poor nations need economic growth in order to provide an adequate standard of living for the world's poorest people, those who care about the poorest should accept markets as an important, useful tool for empowering the poor.

Unfortunately, today's market economies also have fundamental weaknesses. When measured by biblical standards, glaring injustices exist. Precisely as we adopt a market framework as better than known alternatives, we must examine and correct problems that exist in today's market economies.

The first problem is that real life regularly lacks some of the basic features which economists assume in their model of an ideal market economy.[17] In that model, there are lots of producers and entry into any area is open and unrestricted so no one can acquire a monopoly and prevent competition. In real life, unfortunately, powerful people often organize a monopoly in an area of production or sales and benefit at the expense of the majority. Their monopoly prevents the emergence of competition which would benefit consumers but undermine their excessive profits. In the ideal economic model, everyone (both consumers and potential competitors) has full information so no one can be taken advantage of. In real life, vast numbers of people, especially the poor, lack the knowledge to make wise decisions (see below, the story of poor Brazilian women). In the ideal model, there are no "externalities" (e.g., real costs that affect others but are not accounted for in the company's costs). In real life, one company's pollution (e.g., of the air or water) harms everyone, but the company's balance sheet is not affected negatively by the "external" costs to all of us. If the ideal market economy of economic theorists always existed, market economies would be vastly more beneficial than they actually are. Tragically, in real life, existing market economies have major weaknesses. As a result, a few powerful people reap enormous benefit at the expense of the majority, especially the poor.

A second problem is that at least a quarter of the world's people lack the capital to participate in any major way in the global market economy. Land is still the basic capital in many agricultural societies. Money and education are far more crucial in modern capital-intensive, knowledge-intensive economies. Vast numbers of people in our world have almost no land, very little money, and virtually no education. All they have is their bodies to do physical labor. And for many, lack of adequate, nutritious food and access to health care, clean water, and sanitation means that even their bodies are inadequate.

The market's mechanism of supply and demand is blind to the distinction between basic necessities (even minimal food needed to avoid starvation) and luxuries desired by the wealthy. According to the United

Nations Development Programme, *Human Development Report 2005*, the richest one-fifth of the world enjoyed an income fifty times greater than the poorest fifth.[18] Left to itself, a market-driven economy will simply supply what the wealthy can pay for—even if millions of poor folk starve.

If we start with the present division of capital, the outcome of the market will be ghastly injustice. Only if private and public policies enable the poor to acquire capital (healthy bodies, land, education, and money to purchase more productive resources) will they be able to earn a decent living in our global market economy.

Third, in practice, market economies frequently create great extremes of income and wealth. As China embraced market mechanisms, a small group of enormously wealthy elites emerged. The same is true in most other market economies. The United States and Great Britain, the two oldest market economies, have also seen an enormous concentration of income and wealth in the past three decades.[19]

Why is this a problem? Not because making a great deal of money from a new invention that benefits many people is bad. (It is not.) Nor because the biblical norm is equality of income and wealth. (It is not.) But when inequality is so great that it hinders society from empowering its poorer members from acquiring the capital to improve their lot, that level of inequality is unacceptable. In addition, in a fallen world, sinful people will use highly centralized power for their selfish advantage.[20] Furthermore, there is increasing evidence that great inequality also hinders economic growth.[21]

Without corrective action, today's global markets appear to create unjust, dangerous extremes between rich and poor. Robert Frank, a Cornell University economist, argued in his book *Winner Take All* that complex developments (modern technology, the globalized economy, mass marketing, economies of scale, etc.) enable increasingly smaller numbers of people to acquire an ever-larger share of the wealth.[22]

Centralized wealth equals concentrated power. And that—as the conservative critics of communism rightly used to point out—is dangerous. It is not surprising that the relatively small numbers of wealthy people who control the largest corporations, which in turn own the media, also have vast political power. In the U.S., most of the private money for political campaigns comes from the richest 1 percent of the people. As a result, many politicians care more about the self-interest of their wealthy donors than about justice for the poor. Democracy is threatened and the poor suffer.

Fourth, pervasive cultural decline seems to follow the expansion of the market.[23] The most obvious perhaps is the sweeping materialism, consumerism, and individualism that flood the world as country after country joins the global market. Material possessions and the money that buys them become all-important to more and more people. The size of one's salary (and house) becomes more important than God, neighbor, and the creation. In fact, more and more people value making money above marriage, parenting, or even honesty.

It is easy to see how materialistic consumerism develops. The competitive drive to increase market share encourages ever-more seductive advertising. American historian William Leach's book *Land of Desire: Merchants, Power and the Rise of a New American Culture* tells how this happened.[24] The Puritan and other Christian traditions had shaped early nineteenth-century American culture to value thrift, frugality, and modest lifestyles. But that did not sell enough products. So large corporations developed advertising techniques to persuade us that joy and happiness come through fancy new clothes, the latest car models, and ever-more-sophisticated gadgets.

The director of research labs of General Motors, Charles Kettering, decided that business needed to create a "dissatisfied consumer." Annual model changes—planned obsolescence—was his solution. Success, according to advertising historian Roland Marchard, came to depend on "the virtue of qualities like wastefulness, self-indulgence, and artificial obsolescence."[25]

Diabolically clever advertising agencies use the most sophisticated combinations of beautiful women, gorgeous color, and splendid sound tracks to guarantee that self-indulgence and instant gratification replace frugality and simplicity.[26]

Television used to be the most important medium, but now it is digital media. The year 2013 was the first year Americans watched more digital media than television. Americans spent just 4.5 hours watching TV a day but 5 hours on their computers, smartphones, tablets, and videogames each day.[27] One study estimates that the typical American child age 2–11 watches more than 25,000 commercials each year.[28] Advertising on the Internet now accounts for 25 percent of advertising spending, up from just 5 percent in 2005.[29] Regardless of whether it is the TV or the Internet, the message is the same: "Buy something—do it now."

What started in the U.S. has spread around the world. Even the poorest kid in India knows that Coca-Cola refreshes. And Avon's slick advertising has persuaded desperately poor Brazilian women to buy expensive skin cream. Television ads showing sensuous, light-skinned women suggested that older women can shed their aging skin, tanned and wrinkled by years of hard labor in the sun. "Anew" costs thirty dollars a jar. And it works by burning off the top layer of skin. But Avon's communications director in Brazil has boasted that it works: "Women do everything to buy it. They stop buying other things like clothes, like shoes. If they feel good with their skin, they prefer to stop buying clothes and buy something that is on television."[30]

Global corporations own the global communications networks whose programs and advertising create a global lust for ever more consumption. Growing materialism creates growing markets and expanding profits. Tragically, this same materialism destroys social relationships and the creation. Increasingly, some people think the heart of parenting is supplying one's children with more and more material pleasures. And the consumptive overload pollutes the environment.[31]

The market also corrupts culture by rewarding immoral actions. If there is a demand for pornography and dishonest advertisements, the market generously rewards the producers—even if the process corrupts the character of both the producers and the recipients.

Cultural decay also flows from the imperialistic tendency of the market to dominate all of life. The efficiency that follows from making some relationships mere interactions of economic exchange based on supply and demand is frequently good. It is often fine to choose a television salesperson based on market prices. But should the same concern determine the choice of a spouse? Or the decision whether or not to have one parent stay at home with young children? It may be economically advantageous to pay a full-time nanny rather than have skilled professionals "waste" precious time on parenting. But something terribly precious has been lost. There should never be a market in sex or infants for adoption. "If sexuality is made a commodity of exchange, it becomes prostitution."[32] The market's imperialistic tendency to become the sole way to organize all of life corrupts and destroys character and culture.

The environmental crisis reveals a fifth problem with our global market economy. Our rivers and lakes are polluted, the ozone layer is depleted, and global warming has already begun. Unfortunately, markets pay little attention to the needs of future generations.[33] The market fails to account for environmental costs ("externalities" in the jargon of economists)— both because national accounting systems fail to notice the loss of natural capital and because companies seldom count pollution costs in their profit-and-loss statements. China has experienced explosive economic growth over the past three decades. But in the late 1990s, environmental degradation cost the country an estimated 13 percent of the GDP, per year.[34] A 2014 World Bank report showed that India lost $80 billion annually, or 5.7 percent of GDP because of environmental degradation.[35]

The market rewards polluters who pass their costs to neighbors— those who live downstream from where they dump polluted water into the river; those who live thousands of miles downwind from smokestacks that spew pollution into the air, which then quickly circles the globe; and all our grandchildren who will suffer the consequences of today's arrogant neglect. Unless governments compel all companies to pay the real costs of environmental destruction, the market will reward those who choose pollution and the quick profits it offers, not those who opt for the slower profits that result from environmental responsibility.

It is idolatrous nonsense to equate justice with the outcome of a pure laissez-faire economy. It is false to think that a market economy, if freed from all government interference, would create what the Bible means by justice. Masses of poor folk lacking capital are unable to afford even basic necessities. Concentrated wealth threatens democracy. Materialistic messages and practices corrode moral values, family life, and God's creation.

To do these things in the name of efficiency is idolatrous. Consumption is not the sole end of economic life. The economy is made for people, not people for an autonomous, efficient, ever-expanding economy. Wholesome family life and wise stewardship of God's garden matter more than economic efficiency. Yahweh is Lord even of economics.

International Trade

There is more international trade today than at any other time in human history. In 1800, international trade accounted for just 2 percent of global output, and in 1960 it was only 25 percent. But in 2011 international trade accounted for 60 percent of global output.[36] And developing countries are rapidly expanding their involvement in international trade. Developing countries' "share of world merchandise trade" increased from 25 percent to 47 percent between 1980 and 2010—and their share of world output increased from 33 percent to 45 percent in the same period.[37]

Economists nearly universally recognize that free international trade, under a certain set of conditions, is good for everyone, both rich nations and poor nations.[38] A 2007 Economic Report of the President estimated that free trade since WWII added about $10,000 in annual income to the typical American household of four.[39] China's market-oriented reforms included a massive expansion of its international trade, which accompanied the lifting of 500 million people out of poverty in just 20 years.[40] It is through international trade that Kenyan farmers can use Japanese cell phones to buy seeds with money wired from relatives working in the United States.

Trade encourages those places with a special advantage (for example, cheap labor or an ideal climate to grow bananas) to produce those things while other people produce what they can produce most cheaply. That lowers the prices for everyone and makes the best use of the world's limited resources. It also helps poor nations who often have plenty of people able to perform many tasks far more cheaply than workers in rich countries. Politicians may complain about "outsourcing" when jobs move from the U.S. to India. But outsourcing helps reduce poverty in India and also lowers prices for everyone.[41] For example, India earned $70 billion from exports in information technology in 2011–2012.[42] One study estimated that outsourcing reduced the cost of computers and communications equipment by 10 to 30 percent.[43]

The good news is that trade is more free now than at any time in history. The bad news is that industrialized nations continue to shape international trade agreements for their own economic benefit, often at the expense of the world's poorest nations.[44] A former chief economist of the World Bank wrote in 2005, "We now have an international trade regime which, in many ways, is disadvantageous to the developing countries."[45]

In colonial days, as we have seen, mother countries regularly made sure that economic affairs were organized to their own advantage.[46] Such advantage was largely achieved through manipulation of commodity trade. Western colonial nations adopted policies that increased the quantity of goods they wanted from their colonies and at the same time discouraged efforts in the colonies to develop or improve manufacturing capacities. As a result, many colonies became unnecessarily dependent on shipping primary products to and purchasing expensive manufactured products from their "mother" countries.[47] Unfortunately, these effects sometimes continued even after colonies gained independence.

Since WWII, global trade negotiations, first under the General Agreement on Tariffs and Trade (GATT) and now through the World Trade Organization (WTO), have dramatically increased free trade. In the early 1960s, the Kennedy round of tariff negotiations lowered the tariffs on goods traded among the rich industrial nations by 50 percent. But it did little to lower tariffs on goods from poorer countries. The relative situation of the poor countries actually grew worse.[48]

Global gains from the Uruguay Round of global trade negotiations, signed in 1994, were estimated to be between $200 and $500 billion, and a large portion was predicted to go to developing countries. Yet again, tariffs on goods from poorer nations remained up to four times higher than goods from industrialized nations. And the projected gains for the least developed countries turned into economic losses estimated at $600 million per year, or 5 percent of their annual GDP.[49]

Industrialized nations have continued to manipulate international trade through a range of barriers to keep out many of the goods produced in the less-developed countries and to give their producers an unfair advantage over producers in less-developed countries. For example, in 2008 the U.S. collected $1 billion in import taxes on products imported from Bangladesh and Cambodia, which is more than import taxes collected from the United Kingdom and France.[50] These protections are concentrated among products that low-income countries have an advantage producing: textiles, apparel, and agriculture.[51] These trade barriers and subsidies represent systemic injustice today.

The most glaring and irresponsible barriers to trade are the agricultural subsidies in the U.S., Europe, and Japan. OECD nations (i.e., the rich nations) spent $715 million a day on agricultural subsidies from 2011 to 2013.[52] The Environmental Working Group calculates that between 1995 and 2012, $292.5 billion were paid to U.S. farmers in the form of direct payments, crop insurance, and conservation subsidies.[53] These subsidies were originally designed to support small family farmers' dwindling wages. In fact, however, on average U.S. farmers earn $10,000 more than the typical U.S. household.[54] And most of the subsidies go, not to small family farmers, but to a few rich farmers. Sixty-two percent of farms in 2012 collected zero subsidies while 10 percent of farmers collected 75 percent of all the subsidies paid.[55] And 50 billionaires (worth $316 billion) were given a total of $11.3 million in subsidies in 2013![56]

How have these domestic subsidies affected international trade? These subsidies give farmers in rich countries an unfair advantage over farmers in developing countries. Cotton subsidies provide a striking example. Between 2001 and 2011, the EU, China and the U.S. paid $47 billion in subsidies to cotton growers; over half of that was paid to U.S. farmers.[57] A cotton grower in Mali earns $200 for the cotton he picks by hand on his hectare of ground; a cotton grower in the U.S. earns $250 per hectare in subsidies alone![58] These subsidies decrease the price of cotton by 10 to 14 percent, which costs cotton growers in West Africa $147 million each year—enough to feed 1 million people.[59] If those numbers are not absurd enough, consider that 18,600 cotton farms[60] in the U.S. shared $1.3 billion in subsidies in 2011.[61] That is $70,000 per farm! These farm subsidies both cost American taxpayers a lot of money and hurt poor farmers in developing countries.

In 2002, Brazil sued the U.S. through the WTO, claiming that U.S. cotton subsidies violated trade agreements. The Dispute Settlement Mechanism (DSM) of the WTO ruled in favor of Brazil. Rather than eliminate their illegal subsidies, the U.S. government decided to pay Brazilian cotton growers $147 million a year.[62] In addition to the huge sums of money going to U.S. cotton growers, the U.S. government was also subsidizing Brazilian cotton growers!

Significant trade barriers also exist in textiles and apparel. Perhaps no other commodity in history has seen such consistent trade barriers. In 18th century England, in order to protect the wool industry from cotton apparel imports, laws were passed mandating cotton to be worn only in summers and that persons must be buried in wool only.[63] Historically, textiles and apparel have played a key role in the economic development of many of the world's wealthiest nations including the U.K., the U.S., and Japan.[64] Today, low wages in countries that are poor give them an advantage in producing apparel. China, Bangladesh, India, Pakistan, and Indonesia make up half of the world's apparel exports.[65] The U.S. has an average applied tariff (a tax on imports) of 1.3 percent on all goods. But, the U.S. has an average applied tariff on apparel of 13.1 percent, with some items seeing tariffs as high as 32 percent.[66] For a country like Bangladesh with a per capita income of $770 in 2011, these tariffs are equivalent to a $4.61 tax on every Bangladeshi citizen.[67]

Quotas are also used to restrict trade in textiles and apparel. Quotas limit the number of goods imported. Apparel imports from China face quotas that allegedly protect American jobs. Because the amount of apparel that China can send to the U.S. is limited, the Chinese government sells quota licenses to Chinese exporters to allow them to send their goods to the U.S. Between 2004 and 2008, quota license fees for Chinese apparel imports amounted to $1.5 billion. Those fees raised the cost to American consumers by $1.5 billion and gave the Chinese government a gift of the same amount![68]

The current round of WTO trade negotiations, the Doha Development Round, is the first major attempt at addressing developing countries' trade needs. Talks have been slow and developing countries walked out of negotiations in the 2003 Cancun meeting. During 2013 meetings in Bali a trade facilitation agreement (e.g., upgrading ports in developing countries) was outlined. It is estimated to increase developing country exports by $570 billion and create 18 million new jobs in those countries.[69] It has not yet been ratified because India withdrew its support.[70] Even worse, the current agreements do not include any agreement by wealthy nations to end their harmful agricultural subsidies.

The legacy of fair trade agreements that have been in favor of industrialized nations continues to hinder WTO negotiations. It has been twenty years since a major trade deal was reached. Industrialized nations need to eliminate their subsidies and trade restrictions that unfairly target goods that developing countries have an advantage producing. Trade has the potential to lift many millions more out of poverty but only if industrialized nations take the first steps in making trade free and fair.

Destroying the Environment and the Poor

Our present behavior threatens the well-being of our grandchildren. Economic life today, especially in industrialized societies, is producing such severe environmental pollution and degradation that the future for everyone—rich and poor alike—is endangered. We are destroying our air, forests, lands, and water so rapidly that we face disastrous problems in the next one hundred years unless we make major changes.[71] Tragically, the poor are on the front lines when it comes to the harmful impacts of pollution and environmental degradation. In many instances they are the first to suffer, and they absorb the brunt of the destructive consequences due to their poverty and vulnerability.

What is causing these problems? We pollute our air, exhaust our supplies of fresh water, overfish our seas, and destroy precious topsoil, forests, and unique species lovingly shaped by the Creator. In many countries, chemicals, pesticides, oil spills, and industrial emissions degrade air, water, and soil. "Is it not enough for you to feed on the good pasture?" the Creator asks. "Must you also trample the rest of your pasture with your feet? Is it not enough for you to drink clear water? Must you also muddy the rest with your feet?" (Ezek. 34:18 NIV).

Always, of course, the poor suffer the most. This is true in two ways. They already suffer from reduced food production, unproductive land, polluted rivers, and toxic wastes that the rich do not want in their backyards. Furthermore, unless we can redirect economic life in a way that dramatically reduces environmental decay, it will be difficult to expand economic growth enough in poor nations to enable them to enjoy a decent standard of living without producing devastating, long-term environmental destruction.

The poor also damage the environment. Developing nations often use less-sophisticated technology and consequently consume fossil fuels less efficiently. Desperately poor people also try to farm marginal land and destroy tropical forests. Unless poverty is dramatically reduced around the world, we cannot win the war against environmental destruction.

Climate Change

The scientific evidence is now overwhelming. Human activity has already and will increasingly produce a rise in average global temperatures that will, unless we change, result in dramatic, probably devastating climate changes. (Greenhouse gases—especially carbon dioxide that results from burning fossil fuels, but also methane and nitrous oxide—hold heat in the lower atmosphere of the earth and thus slowly cause the temperature of the earth to rise. These gases trap the heat from the sun in a way similar to how a greenhouse prevents the heat from the sun from radiating back into the sky.) "The atmospheric concentrations of carbon dioxide, methane and nitrous oxide have increased to levels unprecedented in at least the last 800,000 years."[72] Rising sea levels, more devastating droughts and heat waves, and more severe storms and floods will cause much more fresh water scarcity, a drop in agricultural productivity, and more hunger, disease, malnutrition, poor health, and violent conflicts. And the poor will suffer the worst.

The Intergovernmental Panel on Climate Change (IPCC)—a large international body of the world's best environmental scientists—has been studying this issue since 1988. Their initial reports that global warming was already happening and that human activity was causing it were controversial. But each new report (1995, 2001, 2006, 2014) provided additional scientific evidence supported by more and more scientists.[73] (Interestingly, the chair of the IPCC's scientific panel for many years was Sir John Houghton, an evangelical Christian as well as a distinguished scientist.) Today, the scientific evidence is overwhelming. Global warming is happening. Unless we dramatically reduce the amount of greenhouse gases (especially CO_2 from the burning of fossil fuels) that we spew into the atmosphere, our children and their children will face new, devastating problems.

Tragically, some political conservatives and even some evangelical Christians refuse to accept this overwhelming scientific consensus.[74] Fortunately, a large group of evangelical leaders have issued a declaration

161

recognizing the scientific evidence and calling on Christians to urge government to act to reduce the emission of greenhouse gases.[75]

In *Global Warming and the Risen Lord*, Jim Ball outlines some of the major impacts of global warming for the poor, especially in developing nations.[76]

- Global warming will increase hunger and malnutrition by damaging rain-fed agriculture. The amount of agricultural land experiencing extreme drought will grow from 1–3 percent today to 30 percent by 2090. Tens, perhaps hundreds of millions will experience increased risk of hunger and malnutrition.[77]
- Growing scarcity of fresh water will result from more severe droughts and the loss of snowpack and glaciers (which are declining at a rapidly increasing pace). Globally, one billion people depend on water melting from glaciers, including one-quarter of the people in China.[78]
- Devastating floods caused by more severe storms and rising sea levels will produce more natural disasters.[79]
- Increasing temperatures and devastating floods will increase the likelihood that various diseases will expand and have major negative impacts on health, especially that of the poor.[80]
- Devastating climate changes will probably produce more violent conflicts between groups and many more refugees.[81]

Virtually everyone who talks about these and other devastating results of global warming point out that the poor will suffer the most. They often live in the most dangerous places. And they have the fewest resources to protect against or recover from these destructive situations. A 2012 report by the World Bank noted that "the poor will suffer most."[82] Again and again, the most recent report of the IPCC notes that the many devastating results that will come from climate change will especially harm the poor.[83] "Throughout the 21st century, climate change impacts are projected to slow down economic growth, make poverty reduction more difficult, further erode food security and prolong existing and create new poverty traps."[84]

The poor have done almost nothing to produce global warming. It is the rich, including the more recently rich, who have and continue to burn fossil fuels who are creating global warming. "If you live in a poor country and in an area that will be hit hard by global warming, then you are potentially the most vulnerable of all. You have done nothing to create this new vulnerability you must face. Others have put you at risk."[85]

Knowing that, those of us who live in rich nations whose wealth and abundance are based on activities that are producing destructive climate change have a special responsibility to take the lead in correcting these problems. In chapter 11, we will examine ways to do that.

Multinational Corporations in Developing Countries

Multinational corporations (MNCs) are large—often huge—businesses that operate in more than one country—and often in many. Most started in the affluent North (Europe, North America, and Japan) where they still have their headquarters—although more recently increasing numbers of MNCs have developed in countries like South Korea, China, India, and Brazil.

MNCs clearly help poorer nations in a number of ways:[86] (1) by providing new capital to develop new businesses; (2) by improving a country's balance of payments (both by bringing in new capital and also producing goods in the country which had previously been imported); (3) by paying local taxes and thus providing developing governments with additional tax revenues; (4) by creating new jobs; (5) by "technology transfer" as they introduce new technology and production methods and train local workers in new technical and managerial skills; (6) by providing local people with a wider choice of goods and services (often at lower prices than similar things imported from elsewhere).

These positive benefits are substantial. If the developing nations were equally powerful bargaining partners, and if the poor in developing countries shared equitably in the benefits, this might work well. Unfortunately, however, evidence shows that MNCs also have some negative effects on poor nations.

This should not surprise people with a biblical view of sin. MNCs, obviously, are interested primarily if not exclusively in profits for themselves. Powerful agents regularly dominate and take advantage of weaker ones.

And many MNCs are huge and therefore very powerful. Twenty-nine of the world's 100 largest economies are not countries but rather MNCs.[87] If Walmart were a country, its revenue would be larger than the GDP of 157 smaller countries! Amazon is bigger than Kenya. General Motors is bigger than Bangladesh. Walmart is bigger than Norway.[88]

This kind of power too often enables huge MNCs to benefit at the expense of poor people. They can coerce the governments of poor nations into providing special tax and other benefits including suppressing unions that might demand better wages. They can harm the environment, ignore health and safety concerns of workers and use complicated maneuvers (called "transfer pricing") to avoid taxes.

By manipulating prices and profits, dominating new technologies, and restricting potential competition, they avoid the qualification of their power that a freer market would impose. Anyone concerned with the dangers of centralized power should be concerned with the way huge MNCs have concentrated economic and political power.

MNCs can have negative effects in three areas: economics, politics, and culture.

MNCs can have negative as well as positive economic effects. Sometimes they borrow money from local banks and thus increase local interest rates and reduce funds available to local businesses. They can use "transfer pricing" to sell at a high price partly finished products made in a higher tax country to a subsidiary in a lower tax country and thereby increase their profit by making most of their profit in the low tax country. Increasingly, too, MNCs quickly pull out of one country and move to another with lower wages, taxes, and environmental regulations. The MNC increases its profits but the developing country losing a large business suffers an economic loss.[89] That is not to argue, of course, that moving manufacturing to a country with lower costs is wrong in itself. Precisely that action has lifted hundreds of millions of people in poor countries out of poverty.

MNCs can also use their power to avoid taxes in (and thus do economic harm to) their "home" country. Increasingly, MNCs based in Europe and North America have incorporated in "tax havens"—places like Bermuda or the Cayman Islands with very low or no corporate taxes. They do not have production facilities in the tax havens, just their legal place of incorporation. The prophet Amos would probably denounce this as an unjust legal technicality, but it saves MNCs billions and billions of tax dollars.

Second, MNCs can also have negative political results. Their vast power, and the threat of moving to another country, often gives them disproportionate influence on governments. That may result in especially favorable tax policies, lax environmental laws that enable MNCs to increase profits by not paying for environmental destruction, or even bribery of local governmental officials. With considerable frequency MNCs have worked with local governments to prevent or undermine strong unions who would have demanded higher wages and safer working conditions.[90] Many governments in developing nations have prevented union organizing so that wages will remain low and MNCs will remain happy.

The *New York Times* reported a glaring example in 1996: "Nike and thousands of other manufacturers have been lured to set up business in Indonesia by the low wages—and the assurance that the Government will tolerate no strikes or independent unions."[91] When Tongris Situmorang, a twenty-two-year-old worker in the Nike factory in Serang, tried to organize a union, he was fired. The military locked him in a room at the plant for seven days and questioned him about his labor activities.[92]

On the U.S.–Mexico border, there have been similar problems in the maquiladora assembly plants. (Maquiladoras are factories that produce goods for export to the U.S. market. They are located in Mexico very near the U.S. border to take advantage of cheap Mexican labor.) In 1987, "Ford Motor Company tore up its union contract, fired 3,400 workers, and cut wages by 45 percent. When the workers rallied around dissident labor leaders, gunmen hired by the official, government-dominated union shot workers at random in the factory."[93]

Third, there are also negative cultural effects. MNCs are on the cutting edge of industrialized nations' contact with the people of developing nations. MNCs thus communicate to poor people what life is like in affluent nations. But not only do they impress on the poor how affluent Northerners live; they also encourage them, through lavish advertising campaigns, to try to live the same way.

The result is that materialistic attitudes are spread everywhere, and many poor people are enticed into spending a disproportionate share of their incomes on goods of little value—whether Avon products or soft drinks.[94] Even more outrageous are the aggressive advertising campaigns of U.S. tobacco companies in poor nations. They seduce the poor into destroying their lungs with U.S. cigarettes.

One of the most well-known and pernicious cases involves a number of companies, including the Nestlé Corporation, that have marketed infant formula to Third World women who are better off nursing their children. Company representatives have sometimes dressed to look like nurses and then recommended to mothers that they feed their infants formula. Nestlé routinely handed out free samples of formula, frequently by donating supplies to hospital maternity wards. The use of formula soon causes a mother's milk to dry up, rendering her incapable of nursing even if she wants to. Parents then must buy formula. Tragically, they are often unable to read the instructions, lack access to sanitary water with which to mix it, or over dilute it in order to make it last longer.

Prepared improperly, formula milk lacks the nutrition babies require. Even under the best of circumstances, formula milk lacks immunological protection that breast milk provides. Frequently, the result has been "Bottle Baby Disease," severe malnutrition, and diarrhea. UNICEF reported that bottle-fed infants are much more likely to get sick and are as much as twenty-five times more likely to die in childhood than infants exclusively breast-fed for the first six months of life.[95] UNICEF reported that in 1990, one million infants died who would not have died if they had been exclusively breast-fed for their first six months. In some cases, there undoubtedly was good reason for the mothers to be absent, and therefore the baby needed infant formula. But many of those mothers were available to breast-feed their children, only to fall prey to powerful advertising.[96]

Promotion like that of Nestlé has drastically reduced the number of breast-fed babies in the developing nations. In its 1982–83 report, UNICEF noted that the percentage of breast-fed infants in Brazil declined from 96 percent in 1940 to 40 percent in 1974. In Chile it fell from 95 percent in 1955 to 20 percent in 1982–83.[97] In 1990, UNICEF reported that breast-feeding had continued to decline.

Fortunately, international opposition to such practices led to an international boycott of Nestlé products. The boycott was led by the International Baby Food Action Network (IBFAN). In 1981, the World Health Assembly adopted the "International Code of Marketing of Breast-milk Substitutes." In 1984, leaders of the boycott met with Nestlé and the company agreed to abide by the new code. The boycott was suspended. But evidence of continuing violations resulted in the relaunch of the boycott in 1989. In 2000, IBFAN presented evidence to the European Parliament that violations by Nestlé continued.

The global boycott certainly produced improvement in Nestlé's practices.[98] But problems continue. In 2011, nineteen prominent organizations (including Save the Children, Oxfam, and World Vision) in Laos charged Nestlé with violations of the code and launched a new boycott of Nestlé. IBFAN continues to provide updates.[99]

Too many big companies share the cynical attitude of H. W. Walter, chairman of the board of International Flavors and Fragrances:

> How often we see in developing countries that the poorer the economic outlook, the more important the small luxury of a flavored soft drink or smoke. . . . To the dismay of many would-be benefactors, the poorer the malnourished are, the more likely they are to spend a disproportionate amount of whatever they have on some luxury rather than on what they need. . . . Observe, study, learn. . . . We try to do it at IFF. It seems to pay off for us. Perhaps it will for you.[100]

The collapse of the Rana Plaza factory building in Bangladesh on April 24, 2013, illustrates the problem; 1,130 garment workers producing clothes for huge global MNCs like Walmart died. The story instantly became headline news around the world. Why had the owner of the building (who was a member of the local wing of the ruling political party in Bangladesh) been allowed to build the upper floors without the proper permits? Why had the Western MNCs who were able to buy clothes at low prices from Bangladeshi factory owners not been concerned to demand safe working conditions for thousands of poor working women? Why had Western consumers who profited from lower prices for their clothes not insisted that the companies that sold them the clothes demand safe working conditions for the workers who produced the clothes?

Are MNCs, on balance, good or bad for poor nations? They are certainly good for the wealthy elites who usually run poor nations. They have helped lift many, many millions of very poor people out of poverty. But MNCs also clearly have negative effects. For the purposes of this book, however, we do not have to know the answer to the question of their overall impact. It is enough to know that some specific MNCs do inflict significant damage on the poor in developing nations.

Once again we must ask, who is at fault? Is it the host governments and local governing elites who gladly cooperate with MNCs for their mutual benefit? Is it the MNCs, for being so one-sidedly focused on short-term profits? Is it the Christians who work in MNCs but fail to demand a change in MNCs' unfair policies? Is it the people in the developed world, for unknowingly supporting MNCs by purchasing their products or owning their stock? The answer is that all four share some responsibility for the negative impact of MNCs on developing countries.

Discrimination and War

Women

In most countries today, women suffer from discrimination. Womankind Worldwide (a U.K. charity dedicated to working internationally to raise the status of women) stated that "women work two-thirds of the world's working hours, produce half of the world's food, and yet earn only 10 percent of the world's income and own less than 1 percent of the world's property."[101] Obviously, that is only a rough estimate. What is perfectly clear, however, is that today, most women simply do not have equal opportunities—whether legal, educational, economic, or social. And the result is poverty. Seventy percent of the poor people in the world are women. The United Nations reports that 75 percent of the world's women cannot obtain bank loans or own property. In South Asia (India, etc.) 70 percent of employed women work in agriculture. According to the World Bank Vice President for Africa, 70 percent of African farmers are women but these hardworking women are "locked out of *land ownership due to customary laws.*"[102] They receive only 5 percent of all agricultural extension services. The United Nations Food and Agricultural Organization estimates that if these female farmers had the same access to agricultural extension services as men, they would produce 20–30 percent more crops. And the number of hungry people would drop by 12–17 percent![103]

The statistics on the number of women who die in pregnancy or childbirth illustrates the way that the equal value of women is widely violated. In *Half the Sky*, Nicholas D. Kristof and Sheryl WuDunn point out that the media seldom cover the fact that "five jumbo jets worth of women" die every day in childbirth. We have made huge progress in recent decades in reducing infant mortality and extending life expectancy. But the number of women who die in pregnancy or childbirth "has barely budged in thirty years."[104]

Tragically, discrimination sometimes starts with the family. Prejudice can limit women's educational opportunities. Table 11 shows that in 2011, adult men were more likely to be able to read than adult women in developing areas. In South Asia and sub-Saharan Africa, half of all adult women were still illiterate, whereas less than one-third of the men suffered the same tragedy.

Table 11—Adult Literacy Rate, 1990 and 2011 (Percentage age 15 and above of total population; developing countries only)

Regions	Male 1990	Male 2011	Female 1990	Female 2011
Eastern Asia and Pacific	88	97	72	92
Europe and Central Asia	97	99	92	97
Latin America and Caribbean	87	92	84	91
Middle East and N. Africa	68	85	44	70
South Asia	58	73	33	50
Sub-Saharan Africa	64	69	43	51

Source: World Bank's World Development Indicators 2014[105]

Especially tragic is the story of the "missing" women. In countries such as China and India, the ratio of males to females is 121–100 and 112–100, respectively. By contrast, the world average is 105 males for every 100 females. There is a similar problem in some West Asian countries.[106] In the early 1990s, former Harvard economist Amartya Sen estimated that in Asia there were 100 million women "missing."[107] Today, there are now 160 million "missing" women.[108] Since these societies value boys more than girls, female babies are aborted or abandoned. China's ghastly "one-child per family" policy has caused particularly discriminatory results against women in a culture that values men more than women. In one county in China, the ratio is 152 to 100.[109]

Finally, there is the horror of prostitution. Over four million women and girls around the world are trapped in prostitution.[110] Pimps and organized criminals traffic in hundreds of thousands of additional women and children that are tricked or forced into prostitution. In many countries, poor parents sell female daughters as prostitutes. Seventy percent of victims report that their trafficker was someone they knew.[111] Millions of poor women suffer this vile denial of their humanity.

Linda Tripp told about a young girl (I'll call her Rojana) who managed to get to World Vision's Distressed Women's Center in Bangkok, Thailand. When Rojana was eleven, her parents sold her into prostitution. From age eleven to age thirteen, Rojana worked in a brothel, serving as many as thirty different men a night. Then she ran away. The police found Rojana sleeping in a garbage dump. They brought her to the center, but Rojana was beyond help. Her body was too full of disease.[112] Rojana is a ghastly symbol of how discrimination against women contributes to poverty and death.

Racist, Religious, and Ethnic Hostility

Whether we think of Syria, South Africa, Central Africa, or the United States, the connections between racist, religious, and ethnic hostility on the one hand and poverty, hunger, and even starvation on the other are painfully clear. Thank God for the end of apartheid. But its deadly effects are still present in South Africa. If we treated white South Africa as a separate country, it would rank 12th in the Human Development Index— similar to Canada. Black South Africa would be 121st—near Honduras.[113]

What if we made the same comparison in the United States? U.S. Asians would be in a three-way tie for first in the world. U.S. Whites would rank sixth, right below Ireland. U.S. Hispanics would be twenty-fifth, next to Austria. And U.S. blacks would be down at the twenty-seventh spot, next to Singapore.[114]

Sudan's three-decade long civil war was rooted in ethnic and religious discrimination. Those in northern Sudan are predominantly Arab Muslims. Those in the South were black and Christian (or adherents of traditional African religions). The war between North and South has killed at least two million Sudanese and driven five million from their homes.[115] Fortunately, the war finally ended and South Sudan became an independent country. But tragically, post-independence tribal rivalries have led to further death and poverty.

In Brazil, 74 percent of all the households in the bottom 10 percent in income are of African descent.[116] In most countries members of racial, ethnic, and religious minorities are the farthest behind in reaching the Millennium Development Goals of reducing poverty, malnutrition, etc.[117]

Racial and ethnic bias, just like prejudice against women, becomes embedded in the legal, social, economic, and political systems in a way that produces poverty. And bloodshed.

War

War may not quite fit the category of structural injustice, but it results from a complex web of structural evils and certainly produces poverty and death.

Wars destroy agricultural productivity, hospitals, schools, transportation systems, and the environment. They produce instant death or refugee status for millions and long-term poverty and hunger for tens of millions. Natural disasters used to be a primary cause of famine and starvation. Today, human-made famines and poverty have become one of the primary causes of hunger, malnutrition, and starvation.[118] As I do the revision of this book, the terrible headlines about the civil war in Syria provide the most glaring current illustration. Today, about 1.5 billion people live in nations that are "fragile or conflict-affected." These fragile states have only 21 percent of the world's total population of 7 billion. But they have 77 percent of all primary age children not in school; 70 percent of all infant deaths; 65 percent of all people without safe water; and 60 percent of all the world's undernourished people.[119]

Many of these conflicts are civil wars within countries. According to the United Nations *Human Development Report 2013*, "While interstate conflicts appear to be on the decline since the early 1990s, the number of intrastate conflicts has increased since the mid-20th century . . . Conflicts in the post-Cold War era have claimed more than 5 million casualties, 95 percent of them civilians."[120] In fact, overall conflicts increased four-fold from 1952 to 1992, mostly driven by an increase in civil wars. And in 2010 and 2011 there were more intrastate conflicts than any year since the end of WWII.[121] These conflicts force many to flee for their lives. The United Nations Development Programme estimates there are 14 million refugees and 26 million internally displaced people because of conflicts.[122]

It is also important to know that to a significant degree war results from poverty. After careful studies on the correlation between an increase in poverty and a jump in armed conflict in Africa, scholars at Columbia University and University of California, Berkeley show that "poverty increases the risk of armed conflict for all Africans." In fact, the risk of war increases by 50 percent during years of economic recession.[123]

Often the conflicts result from a complex web of ethnic, tribal, racial, and religious factors plus economic and political motivations. Ancient ethnic, tribal, and religious hostilities explode in rape and massacre in Sudan, Syria, Pakistan, the Democratic Republic of the Congo, Central African Republic, and elsewhere. On and on the agonizing list goes.

Women and children suffer the most. The words of Amer Kuay, an African mother and refugee from the Southern Sudan, captures a little of their agony:

> We were attacked by cattle raiders working for the government. They took all of our cattle. They burned our houses. They took all our belongings . . . We were left with no tools and hardly any seed, so we harvested very little. By February we started to starve. There were still attacks . . . So we decided to cross the Nile to . . . where it was safer. We had to wait in the marshes for some time to get a fishing boat to take us across. We had no money to pay, so I had to give my daughter's clothes to the fisherman. Some of the people in our group were dying of hunger even as we started to walk from our village.

Young children and old people died. I lost my youngest girl. She was just two years old.[124]

In numerous complicated ways, you and I are involved in one way or another with unjust global structures. The mechanism of the market is a useful tool for organizing a great deal of economic life, but today's market economies also produce serious injustices that we must correct. International trade patterns contain injustice. Some current patterns of economic life threaten the global environment and the long-term economic opportunities of the developing world. Multinational corporations sometimes hinder rather than promote meaningful development in less-developed nations. And discrimination adds its own sometimes blatant, sometimes subtle oppression. The life of every person in developed countries is touched in some way by these structural injustices. Unless you have retreated to some isolated valley and grow or make everything you use, you participate in unjust structures that contribute directly to the desperate poverty of some of our billion suffering neighbors.

We should not, of course, conclude that international trade or investment by multinational corporations in poor countries is in itself harmful. Done right, both help the poor. Nor would the economies of the developed world be destroyed if present injustices in today's global economic system were corrected. The proper conclusion is that injustice has become deeply embedded in some of our fundamental economic institutions. Biblical Christians—precisely to the extent that they are faithful to Scripture—will dare to call such structures sinful.

Most of us wish that international economics were less complex and that faithful discipleship in our time had less to do with such a complicated subject. But former U.N. Secretary General Dag Hammarskjöld was right: "In our era, the road to holiness necessarily passes through the world of action."[125] To give the cup of cold water effectively in our age of affluence and poverty requires some understanding of international economic and political structures.

In March 1974, several Central American banana-producing countries agreed to demand a one-dollar tax on every case of bananas exported. Banana prices for producers had not increased in the previous twenty inflation-ridden years, but the costs for manufactured goods had constantly escalated. As a result, the purchasing power of the banana exporters had declined by 60 percent. This was a significant factor in the economy of Honduras and Panama because at least half of their export income came from bananas.

When the exporting countries demanded this one-dollar tax on bananas, the North American banana companies adamantly refused to pay. Since at that time three large companies (United Brands, Castle and Cooke, and Del Monte) controlled 90 percent of the marketing and distribution of bananas, they had powerful leverage. In Panama, the fruit company abruptly stopped cutting bananas, and in Honduras, the banana company allowed 145,000 crates of fruit to rot at the docks.

One after another the poor countries gave in. Costa Rica finally settled for twenty-five cents a crate, Panama for thirty-five cents, and Honduras agreed to a thirty-cent tax.[126]

In April 1975, North Americans learned that United Brands, one of three huge U.S. companies that grow and import bananas, had arranged to pay $2.5 million[127] in bribes to top government officials in Honduras to persuade them to tax bananas at a rate less than half what they had requested.[128] The Honduran government accepted the bribe and lowered the export tax, even though the money was desperately needed in Honduras.

A U.N. fact-finding commission concluded later that year: "The banana-producing countries with very much less income are subsidizing the consumption of the fruit, and consequently the development of the more industrialized countries."[129]

Why don't the poor demand change? They do. But too often they have little power. Until recently, dictators representing tiny, wealthy elites working closely with American business interests ruled many Latin American countries.

The history of Guatemala, also a producer of bananas for United Brands, shows why change is difficult. In 1954, the CIA helped overthrow a democratically elected government in Guatemala because it had initiated a modest program of agricultural reform that seemed to threaten unused land owned by the United Fruit Company (which later became United Brands and is now Chiquita Brands International). The U.S. secretary of state in 1954 was John Foster Dulles. His law firm had written the company's agreements with Guatemala in 1930 and 1936. The CIA director was Allen Dulles, brother of the secretary of state and previous president of United Fruit Company. The assistant secretary of state was a major shareholder in United Fruit Company.[130] In Guatemala and elsewhere change is difficult when U.S. companies work closely with wealthy local elites and the U.S. government to protect their mutual economic interests.

A case study in 2010 by a business school bluntly summarized the history of Chiquita. Chiquita, the authors said, was "for decades . . . synonymous with the notion of the rapacious multinational." Its farm workers worked long hours in dangerous conditions and "agrochemical runoff" contaminated water. "Since its founding more than a hundred years ago as United Fruit Company, Chiquita has been involved in paying bribes to Latin American government officials in exchange for preferential treatment, encouraging or supporting U.S. coups against smaller nations, putting in place dictatorships in Central America's 'banana republics,' exploiting local workers, creating an abusive monopoly, and now doing business with terrorists."[131]

Tragically, there will always be those eager to provide plausible rationalizations. Andrew M. Greeley, for years a prominent sociologist at the University of Chicago, has mocked those who condemn aspects of the United States' economic relationships with developing nations: "Well, let us suppose that our guilt finally becomes too much to bear and we decide to reform . . . We inform the fruit orchards in Central America that we can dispense with bananas in our diets . . . Their joy will hardly be noticed as massive unemployment and depression sweep those countries."[132]

One wonders if Greeley is naive or perverse. The point is not—and Greeley surely knows this—that we should stop importing bananas. Rather, it is that (1) multinational firms and huge agribusinesses, in complicity with all the buyers of bananas in the developed world, benefit from complex systems that make it more difficult for the poor to escape their poverty; and that (2) we should encourage the reorganization of economic structures and promote programs here and in Central America that will help poor people share more equitably in the benefits of agricultural production and trade.

The story of the bananas shows how all of us are involved in unjust international economic structures. The words of the apostle James speak directly to our situation.

> Come now, you rich, weep and howl for the miseries that are coming
> upon you . . . Your gold and silver have rusted, and their rust will be
> evidence against you . . . Behold, the wages of the laborers who mowed
> your fields, which you kept back by fraud, cry out; and the cries of the
> harvesters have reached the ears of the Lord of hosts. You have lived on
> the earth in luxury and in pleasure; you have fattened your hearts in a
> day of slaughter. (James 5:1–5)

Repentance

What should be our response? For biblical Christians, the only correct response to sin is repentance. We have become entangled, to some degree unconsciously, in a complex web of institutionalized sin. Thank God we can repent. God is merciful. God forgives. But only if we repent. And biblical repentance involves more than a hasty tear and a weekly prayer of confession. Biblical repentance involves conversion. It involves a whole new lifestyle. The One who stands ready to forgive us for our sinful involvement in economic injustice offers us his grace to begin living a generous new lifestyle that empowers the poor and oppressed.

Sin is not just an inconvenience or a tragedy for our neighbors. It is a damnable outrage against the almighty Lord of the universe. If God's Word is true, then all of us who dwell in affluent nations are trapped in sin. We have profited from systematic injustice—sometimes only half-knowing, sometimes only half-caring, and always half-hoping not to know. We are guilty of sin against God and neighbor.

But that is not God's last word to us. If it were, honest acknowledgment of our involvement would be almost impossible. If there was no hope of forgiveness, admission of our sinful complicity in evil of this magnitude would be an act of despair.[133] But there is hope. The One who writes our indictment is the One who died for us sinners.

John Newton was captain of a slave ship in the eighteenth century. A brutal, callous man, he played a central role in a system that fed tens of thousands to the sharks and delivered millions to a living death. But eventually, after he gave up his career as captain, he saw his sin and repented. His familiar hymn overflows with joy and gratitude for God's acceptance and forgiveness:

> *Amazing grace! How sweet the sound,*
> *that saved a wretch like me;*
> *I once was lost, but now am found,*
> *was blind but now I see.*
> *'Twas grace that taught my heart to fear,*
> *and grace my fears relieved;*
> *How precious did that grace appear*
> *the hour I first believed.*

John Newton became a founding member of a society for the abolition of slavery. The church he pastored, St. Mary Woolnoth in the city of London, was a meeting place for abolitionists. William Wilberforce frequently went to him for spiritual counsel. Newton delivered impassioned sermons against the slave trade, convincing many of its evil. He campaigned against the slave trade until he died in the year of its abolition, 1807. The stories of Newton and Wilberforce demonstrate powerfully that evil structures can be changed by dedicated Christians.

We are participants in structures that also contribute to the suffering and death of millions of people. If we have eyes to see, God's grace will also teach our hearts to fear and tremble, and then also to rest and trust.

But only if we repent. Repentance is not just coming forward at the close of a service. It is not just repeating a spiritual law. It is not just mumbling a liturgical confession. All of these things may help. But they are no substitute for the kind of deep inner anguish that leads to a new way of living.

Biblical repentance entails conversion, which means "turning around." The Greek word *metanoia* means "a total change of mind." The New Testament links repentance to a transformed style of living. Sensing the hypocrisy of the Pharisees who came seeking baptism, John the Baptist denounced them as a brood of vipers. "Bear fruit that befits repentance," he demanded (Matt. 3:8). Paul told King Agrippa that wherever he preached, he called on people to "repent and turn to God and perform deeds worthy of . . . repentance" (Acts 26:20).

Zacchaeus should be our model. As a greedy Roman tax collector, Zacchaeus was enmeshed in sinful economic structures. But he never supposed that he could come to Jesus and continue to enjoy the economic benefits of that evil system. Coming to Jesus meant repenting of his complicity in social injustice. It meant publicly giving reparations. And it meant a whole new lifestyle.

What might genuine, biblical repentance mean for affluent Christians entangled in sinful structures? And would not deep joy flow from obedient sharing that empowered others?

Study Questions

1. Are you convinced that present international economic structures involve us all in structural evil? How, specifically, does that happen?
2. What are the good and bad features of today's market economies?
3. How do tariffs, import quotas, and farm subsidies of industrialized countries hurt the poor?
4. What are the connections between environmental pollution and poverty?
5. What are the advantages and disadvantages of multinational corporations in reducing poverty?
6. How do discrimination and war contribute to poverty?
7. How does the original setting of "Amazing Grace" parallel the problems described here?
8. What were your strongest emotions as you read this chapter? Why?

PART FOUR

Implementation

A prominent Washington think tank once assembled a large cross-section of distinguished religious leaders to discuss the problems of world hunger. The conferees expressed deep concern. They called for significant structural change. But their words rang hollow. They were meeting at an exclusive resort in Colorado!

Simpler personal lifestyles are essential. But personal change is insufficient. I had a friend who forsook the city for a rural community. He grew almost all his own food, lived simply, and placed few demands on the poor of the earth. This person had considerable speaking and writing talents that could promote change in church and society, but he used them less than he might because of the time absorbed by his "simple" lifestyle.

We need to change at three levels. Appropriate personal lifestyles are crucial to symbolize, validate, and facilitate our concern for the hungry. The church must change so that its common life presents a new model for a divided world. Finally, both here and abroad, we must make the structures of society more fair.

Implementation demands specific proposals. But offering concrete suggestions is risky. We seldom know enough to be certain about the exact consequences of suggested changes. Broad generalizations, however, are not enough if we want to change our personal lifestyles, our churches, and our societies. So I have dared to be specific—even though I know I may be wrong.

If you question my suggestions, ask two questions: Are the suggestions grounded in biblical principles? Is the underlying social analysis valid? If the answers are yes, try the proposal. If no, develop a better way to solve the problem. Furthermore, let me know about your better proposal. Precisely because I want to empower God's poor, I am eager to abandon poor ideas—even my own!—as quickly as possible, and exchange them for effective ones.

TOWARD A SIMPLER LIFESTYLE: THE GRADUATED TITHE AND OTHER MODEST PROPOSALS

Before God and a billion hungry neighbors, we must rethink our values regarding our present standard of living and promote more just acquisition and distribution of the world's resources.[1]

—THE CHICAGO DECLARATION OF EVANGELICAL SOCIAL CONCERN, 1973

Those of us who live in affluent circumstances accept our duty to develop a simple life style in order to contribute more generously to both relief and evangelism.[2]

—LAUSANNE COVENANT, 1974

The rich must live more simply that the poor may simply live.[3]

—DR. CHARLES BIRCH, 1974

I once organized a lecture where a state senator from Pennsylvania argued that his constituents were so poor that they simply could not afford to pay another cent in taxes. He cited a letter from an irate voter as proof. This good person had written him announcing that her family could not possibly pay any more taxes. Why, she said, they already paid the government income taxes and sales taxes—and besides that they bought licenses for their two cars, summer camper, houseboat, and motorboat!

Many of us actually believe that we can barely get along on the fifty, sixty, or ninety thousand dollars that we make each year. We are in an incredible rat race. When our income goes up by another two thousand dollars, we convince ourselves we need that much more to live—comfortably.

How can we escape this delusion? Perhaps it will help to be reminded again that thousands of children starve every day. That over one billion people live in desperate poverty. And that another billion-plus are very poor. The problem, we know, is that the world's resources are not fairly distributed. North Americans, Western Europeans, and rich elites around the world are an affluent minority in a world where half the people are poor.

How will we respond to this inequity? Former President Richard Nixon enunciated one response in a June 13, 1973, speech to the nation: "I have made this basic decision: In allocating the products of America's farms between markets abroad and those in the United States, we must put the American consumer first."[4]

Such a statement may be good politics, but it certainly is not good theology.

But how much should we give? John Wesley gave a startling answer. One of his frequently repeated sermons was on Matthew 6:19–23 ("Lay not up for yourselves treasures upon earth" KJV).[5] Christians, Wesley said, should give away all but "the plain necessaries of life"—that is, plain, wholesome food, clean clothes, and enough to carry on one's business. One should earn what one can, justly and honestly. Capital need not be given away. But Wesley wanted all income given to the poor after bare necessities were met. Unfortunately, Wesley discovered, not one person in five hundred in any "Christian city" obeys Jesus' command. But that simply demonstrates that most professed believers are "living men but dead Christians." "Any 'Christian' who takes for himself anything more than the plain necessaries of life," Wesley insisted, "lives in an open, habitual denial of the Lord." He has "gained riches and hell-fire!"[6]

Wesley lived what he preached. Sales of his books often earned him fourteen hundred pounds annually, but he spent only thirty pounds on himself. The rest he gave away. He always wore inexpensive clothes and dined on simple food. "If I leave behind me ten pounds," he once wrote, "you and all mankind bear witness against me that I lived and died a thief and a robber."[7]

We need not agree with Wesley's every word and concrete standard to see that he was struggling to follow the biblical summons to share with the needy. How much should we give? Knowing that God wants every person to have the resources to earn a decent living, we should give until our lives truly reflect the principles of Leviticus 25 and 2 Corinthians 8. Surely Paul's advice to the Corinthians applies even more forcefully to rich Christians today: "I do not mean that others should be eased and you burdened, but that as a matter of equality your abundance at the present time should supply their want . . . that there may be equality" (2 Cor. 8:13–14).[8] Will we be that generous?

The God of North America

Why are we so unconcerned, so slow to care? We learn one reason from the story of the rich young ruler. When he asked Jesus how to obtain eternal life, Jesus told him to sell his goods and give to the poor. The man went away saddened because he had great possessions. The point of the story, as we are usually told, is that Christ alone must be at the center of the affections and plans of his followers. Whatever our idol—whether it be riches, fame, status, academic distinction, or membership in some "in" group—we must be willing to abandon it for Christ's sake. Riches just happened to be this young man's idol. Jesus, then, is not command-ing us to sell all our possessions; he is only demanding total submission to himself.

This interpretation is both unquestionably true and obviously inad-equate. To say no more is to miss the fact that possessions are the most common idol for rich Christians today. Jesus must have meant it when he added, "Truly I tell you, it will be hard for a rich person to enter the kingdom of heaven. Again I tell you, it is easier for a camel to go through the eye of a needle than for someone who is rich to enter the kingdom of God" (Matt. 19:23–24 NRSV).

We have become ensnared by unprecedented material luxury. Advertising constantly convinces us that we need one unnecessary luxury after another. Affluence is the god of twenty-first-century North Americans, and the adman is his prophet.

We all know how subtle the materialistic temptations are and how convincing the rationalizations. Only by God's grace and with great effort can we "Just say no!" to the shower of luxuries that has almost suffocated our Christian compassion.

All of us face this problem. Several decades ago, I spent about fifty dollars on an extra suit after persuading myself that it was a wise investment (thanks to the 75 percent discount). But that money would have fed a starving child in India for about a year. In all honesty we have to ask ourselves: Dare we care at all about current fashions if that means reducing our ability to help hungry neighbors? How many more luxuries should we buy for ourselves and our children when others are dying for lack of bread?

I do not pretend that giving an honest answer to some questions is easy. Our responsibility is not always clear. One Saturday morning as I was beginning to prepare a lecture (on poverty!), a poor man came into my office and asked for five dollars. He was drinking. He had no food, no job, no home. The Christ of the poor confronted me in this man. But I didn't have the time, I said. I had to prepare a lecture on the Christian view of poverty. I did give him a couple of dollars, but that was not what he needed. He needed somebody to talk to, somebody to love him. He needed my time. He needed me. But I was too busy. "Inasmuch as you did it not to the least of these, you did it not . . ."

We need to make some dramatic, concrete moves to escape the materialism that seeps into our minds via diabolically clever and incessant advertising. We have been brainwashed to believe that bigger houses, more prosperous businesses, and more sophisticated gadgets are the way to joy and fulfillment. As a result, we are caught in an absurd, materialistic spiral. The more we make, the more we think we need in order to live decently and respectably. Somehow we have to break this cycle because it makes us sin against our needy brothers and sisters and, therefore, against our Lord. And it also destroys us. Sharing with others is the way to real joy.

Some Examples

In the mid-1970s Graham Kerr was the Galloping Gourmet for two hundred million TV viewers each week. He was rich and successful, but his personal life was falling apart. In 1975 he came to Christ, and since then his family life has been miraculously restored. He abandoned his gourmet TV series and gave away most of his money.

For more than a decade Graham devoted his time and used his knowledge of nutrition to develop a new kind of agricultural missionary who both shares the gospel and helps very poor people in developing countries develop a better diet with locally available products.

In 1990 Graham returned to international television. He and his wife, Treena, continued to live with what they called "relative simplicity"—but not because they are ascetics. They lived simply because they wanted to share their lives and influence wherever possible. They cared deeply about those who did not enjoy the Gospel, good food, and good health. So they used their influence to encourage others to share out of abundance with those who are left out.[9]

Were Graham and Treena happy? They were immeasurably happier than before. Every time I saw them I saw joy and contentment flooding their lives. While living more simply, they were having the time of their lives.

Robert Bainum was a successful Christian businessman—in fact, a millionaire (decades ago when that was still a great deal of money). But when he read the first edition of this book, God called him to share more with the poor of the earth. He gave away half of his wealth and then devoted a major portion of his creative energy and organizational abilities to relief and development programs among the poor, both at home and abroad.[10]

In her delightful book *Living More with Less*, Doris Longacre gives us glimpses of several hundred Christians who are learning the joy of sharing more.[11] Some still live in what I consider substantial affluence. Others live far more simply than I do. But all are trying to spend less on themselves in order to share more with others.

Biblical Christians are experimenting with a variety of simpler lifestyles. More than two billion poor neighbors demand drastic change. But we must be careful to avoid legalism and self-righteousness. "We have to beware of the reverse snobbery of spiritual one-up-manship."[12]

The Graduated Tithe

The graduated tithe is one of many models that can help break the materialistic stranglehold. It is not the only useful model, but it has proved helpful in our family. Certainly it is not a biblical norm to be prescribed legalistically for others. It is just one family's story.

I tell it partly to show how the concept has evolved in our family. When our children hit the high school and college years we were astounded by how much more seemed right to spend on our family. We didn't always get it right, but we tried to be more concerned with persons (specifically our children's changing needs) than with some arbitrary "rule" or abstract theory.

When my wife, Arbutus, and I decided to adopt a graduated scale for our giving in 1969 right after I got my first full time job, we sat down and tried to calculate honestly what we would need to live for a year. We wanted a figure that would permit reasonable comfort but not all the luxuries. We decided that we would give a tithe (10 percent) on our base figure and then give a graduated tithe (15 percent or more) on income above that. For each thousand dollars above our base, we decided to increase our giving by another 5 percent on that thousand.

In 1969 our base figure was $7,000. By 1973 we had increased it to $8,000. And in 1982 we increased it again—to $10,000. (This time we decided to use an approximation of the 1982 federal poverty level: $9,862 for a family of four.)

Then came high school and college years. We decided that in our situation a Christian high school was important. That added major costs. So did college expenses. Soon we could no longer continue our original scheme, so we added costs for Christian education and college to our base.

What about taxes? At first we did not include taxes in our base figure. Obviously one would have to do that beyond a certain income, or the graduated tithe and taxes would eat up all income. So in 1979 we added taxes to our base.

Today we try to give 10 percent on a base figure that includes: (a) $30,000 (b) assistance to family; (c) genuine emergencies. On our income above this base, we apply the graduated tithe (see Table 12).

We don't always make it! But this is what we aim for.

Every family is unique. Housing costs vary enormously in different parts of the country and city. Probably the single most important decision on family expenses is where you decide to live. Our choice to live for thirty-seven years in a lower-income, interracial city neighborhood where housing and related expenses are vastly less than in the suburbs has helped us immensely. (It also lowered the children's sense of what they "needed.")

There is a near limitless set of variations. Some families need emergency counseling. Some children need special dental work. Some people with special entrepreneurial skills require large sums of capital for investment and should choose to count that as part of their base. What do you do about untaxed employer contributions to a pension fund? (We don't count it at all—but will when it appears as income during retirement.) What about employer-paid medical insurance?

Every family must work out its own answers to these questions. Our story is not a law for everyone—not even for one other person! Each person or family will need to develop an individualized plan, but the basic pattern is easy to follow. Through prayer, study, and conversation with sympathetic friends, decide what you should consider the base on which you will give 10 percent. Then for every $1,000 of income above the base, give an additional 5 percent. Table 12 shows how to do the calculations.

Table 12—Graduated Tithe

Total Income Base	Percent Given Away—10% of Base	Dollars Given Away—10% of Base
Base + $1,000	15% of last $1,000	10% of Base + 150
Base + 2,000	20% of last 1,000	10% of Base + 350
Base + 3,000	25% of last 1,000	10% of Base + 600
Base + 4,000	30% of last 1,000	10% of Base + 900
Base + 5,000	35% of last 1,000	10% of Base + 1,250
Base + 6,000	40% of last 1,000	10% of Base + 1,650
Base + 7,000	45% of last 1,000	10% of Base + 2,100
Base + 8,000	50% of last 1,000	10% of Base + 2,600
Base + 9,000	55% of last 1,000	10% of Base + 3,150
Base + 10,000	60% of last 1,000	10% of Base + 3,750
Base + 11,000	65% of last 1,000	10% of Base + 4,400
Base + 12,000	70% of last 1,000	10% of Base + 5,100
Base + 13,000	75% of last 1,000	10% of Base + 5,850
Base + 14,000	80% of last 1,000	10% of Base + 6,650
Base + 15,000	85% of last 1,000	10% of Base + 7,500
Base + 16,000	90% of last 1,000	10% of Base + 8,400
Base + 17,000	95% of last 1,000	10% of Base + 9,350
Base + 18,000	100% of last 1,000	10% of Base + 10,350

If you believe God is leading you to adopt the graduated tithe, here are a few suggestions.

First, discuss the idea with the whole family. Everyone needs to understand the reasons so that the family can come to a common decision. Second, put your plan in writing at the beginning of the year. It is relatively painless, sometimes even exciting, to work it out theoretically. After you have committed yourself to the abstract figures, it hurts less to dole out the cash each month. Third, discuss your proposal with a committed Christian friend or couple who share your concern for justice. Fourth, discuss major expenditures with the same people. It is easier for others to spot rationalizations than it is for you. They may also have helpful hints on simple living. Fifth, each year see if it is possible to reduce your basic figure and total expenditures. (This does not mean that you ignore the need for capital investment to increase productivity.)

This proposal for a graduated tithe is a modest one, so modest in fact that it verges on unfaithfulness to the apostle Paul. But at the same time it is sufficiently radical that its implementation would revolutionize the ministry and life of the church.

Some Christians are experimenting with far more radical attempts to win the war on affluence.

Communal Living

The model that permits the simplest standard of living is probably the commune. Housing, furniture, appliances, tools, and cars that would normally serve one nuclear family can accommodate ten or twenty people. Communal living releases vast amounts of money and time for alternative activities.

Some Christian communes have been initiated as conscious attempts to develop a more ecologically responsible, sharing standard of living. Others emerged as a spontaneous response to human need. Jerry Barker, a member of a Christian community in Texas, put it this way:

> It soon became obvious that the needs we were faced with would . . . take lots of resources and so we began to cut expenses for things we had been accustomed to. We stopped buying new cars and new televisions and things of that sort. We didn't even think of them. We started driving our cars until they literally fell apart, and then we'd buy a used car or something like that to replace it. We began to turn in some of our insurance policies so that they would not be such a financial drain on us. We found such a security in our relationship with the Lord that it was no longer important to have security for the future. . . . We never have had any rule about it, or felt this was a necessary part of the Christian life. It was just a matter of using the money we had available most effectively, particularly in supporting so many extra people. We learned to live very economically. We quit eating steaks and expensive roasts and things like that and we began to eat simple fare. . . . We'd often eat things that people would bring us—a box of groceries or a sack of rice.[13]

The standard of living in Christian communities varies. But almost all live far more simply than the average North American family. For many years at Chicago's Reba Place, for example, eating patterns were based on the welfare level of the city (see chapter 10). In the last few decades, Christian communes have had a symbolic importance out of all proportion to their numbers. They quietly question society's affluence. And they offer a striking alternative.

Communal living, of course, is not for everyone. In fact, I personally believe that it is the right setting for only a small percentage of Christians. We need many more diverse models.

No one model is God's will for everyone. God loves variety and diversity. Does that mean, however, that we ought to settle for typical Western individualism, with each person or family doing what is good in its own eyes? By no means.

Two things can help. First, we need the help of other brothers and sisters—in our local congregation, in our town or city, and around the world. We need a process for discussing our economic lifestyles with close Christian friends. We also need new ways to dialogue about the shape of a faithful lifestyle with poor Christians.[14]

Second, certain criteria can help us determine what is right for us.

Guidelines for Giving

I offer eight guidelines—as suggestions, not as norms or laws:

1. Move toward a personal lifestyle that could be sustained over a long period of time if it were shared by everyone in the world.
2. Distinguish between necessities and luxuries; withstand the desire to indulge regularly in luxuries and resist the inclination to blur the distinction.[15]
3. Distinguish between legitimate and non-legitimate reasons for spending/buying. (For example, expenditures to elevate or maintain our social status, feed our pride, stay in fashion, or "keep up with the Joneses" are wrong.)
4. Distinguish talents and hobbies from a curious interest in current fads. Allow expenditures that will develop talents

and hobbies, but don't indulge in all the latest recreational equipment simply because it is popular with those who seem "successful." Each person has unique interests and gifts. We should be able to express our creativity in those areas. (I love to fish!) But if we begin justifying lots of things in many areas, we should become suspicious.

5. Distinguish between occasional celebration and normal day-to-day indulgence. A turkey feast with all the trimmings at Thanksgiving to celebrate the good gift of creation is biblical (Deut. 14:22–27). Unfortunately, many of us overeat every day, and that is sin.

6. Resist buying things just because we can afford them. The amount we earn has nothing to do with what we need.

7. Seek a balance between supporting emergency relief, development, and broad structural change. Emergency food is important when people are starving. But more money needs to go for long-term community development so folk can feed themselves. It is especially crucial to give to organizations that increase understanding and promote just public policy and structural change (especially since so few Christians understand this last area). Part of a family's graduated tithe might very appropriately go to political campaigns to support candidates who will work for justice for the poor.

8. Do not neglect other areas of Christian work. Evangelism and Christian education are extremely important and deserve continuing support. Give approximately as much to support evangelism as you do for social justice activities. (Holistic programs that combine both are ideal.)[16]

Some Practical Suggestions

The following are hints, not rules, for living more simply. Freedom, joy, and laughter are essential elements of responsible living. (See the Appendix for addresses and information about books, groups, and organizations named.)

1. Question your own lifestyle, not your neighbor's
2. Reduce your food budget by:
   • Gardening: try hoeing instead of mowing.
   • Fasting regularly.
   • Setting a monthly budget and sticking to it.
3. Lower energy consumption by:
   • Keeping your thermostat (at the home and office) at 68 degrees Fahrenheit or lower during winter months.
   • Supporting public transportation with your feet and your vote.
   • Using bicycles, carpools, and, for short trips, your feet.
   • Making dish washing a family time instead of buying a dishwasher.
   • Buying a fan instead of an air conditioner.
   • Substituting plant-based protein for meat. It requires 11 times more fossil fuel energy to produce the same amount of animal-based protein as plant-based protein.[17]
4. Resist consumerism by:
   • Laughing regularly at TV commercials.
   • Developing family slogans like: "Who Are You Kidding?" and "You Can't Take It with You!"
   • Making a list of dishonest ads and boycotting those products.
   • Using the postage-paid envelopes of direct-mail advertisers to object to unscrupulous advertising.
5. Buy and renovate an old house in the inner city. (Persuade a few friends to do the same so you can enjoy Christian community.)
6. Reduce your consumption of nonrenewable natural resources by:
   • Resisting obsolescence (buy quality products when you buy).
   • Sharing appliances, tools, lawnmowers, sports equipment, books, even a car (this is easier if you live close to other Christians committed to living more simply).
   • Organizing a "things closet" in your church for items used only occasionally such as edger, clippers, cots for unexpected guests, lawnmowers, camping equipment, big ladder.

7. Determine how much of what you spend is for status and eliminate such spending.

8. Refuse to keep up with clothing fashions. (Very few readers of this book need to buy clothes—except maybe shoes—for two or three years.)

9. Enjoy what is free.

10. Live on a welfare budget for a month.

11. Examine *Shopping for a Better World* from the Council on Economic Priorities and *Alternatives Celebrations Catalog* published by Alternatives.[18] It provides exciting, inexpensive, ecologically sound alternative ideas for celebrating Christmas, Valentine's Day, Thanksgiving, and other holidays.

12. Give your children more love and time rather than more things.

That's enough for a beginning.

Evaluating Organizations

If 10 percent of all North American Christians adopted the graduated tithe, huge sums of money would become available to empower the poor. In fact, if just the committed Christians in the United States merely tithed, there would be an additional $46 billion available to do kingdom work.[19] Where would that money do the most good? Which relief and development agencies are doing the best job? This issue is important, but you must decide for yourself. Here are some general questions to ask:

1. Do the funds support holistic projects in poor countries, working simultaneously at an integrated program of evangelism, social change, education, agricultural development?

2. Do the funds support truly indigenous projects? In other words: (a) Are the leaders and most of the staff of the projects in the developing nations indigenous persons? (They should be.) (b) Do the projects use materials suited to the culture or have the leaders unthinkingly adopted Western ideas, materials,

and technology? (c) Did the project arise from the needs of the people rather than from an outside "expert"?

3. Are the projects primarily engaged in long-range development (including people development), or in emergency aid only?

4. Are the programs designed to help the poor understand that God wants sinful social structures changed and that they can help effect that change?

5. Do the programs work through and foster the growth of local churches?

6. Are the programs potentially self-supporting after an initial injection of seed capital? And do the programs from the beginning require commitment and a significant contribution of capital or time (or both) from the people themselves?

7. Do the programs aid the poorest people in the poorest developing countries?

8. Is agricultural development involved? (It need not always be, but in many cases it should be.)

9. Is justice rather than continual charity the result?[20]

10. Is the international agency through which you channel funds run efficiently and wisely? Ask these questions as you pick an organization: (a) Does the organization spend more than 10 or 15 percent of total funds on fund-raising and administration? (b) Are Third World persons, minority people, and women represented among the board and top staff? (c) Is the organization audited annually by an independent CPA firm? (d) Are the board members and staff persons of known integrity? Is the board paid? (It should not be.) (e) Are staff salaries consistent with the biblical call for jubilee among all God's people? (f) Does the organization object to answering these questions?[21]

The following example will help clarify the kind of holistic program that meets most of the above criteria:

Elizabeth Native Interior Mission [is] in southern Liberia. ENI is headed by Augustus Marwieh who became a Christian under Mother George, one of the first black American missionaries to Africa. Ten years ago Gus went to work at the struggling mission where he had been saved. The young people were leaving the villages to go to the capital city of Monrovia; there, most found only unemployment, alcohol, and prostitution. Local skills like log sawing, blacksmithing, and making pottery were dying out as the people became dependent on outside traders (usually foreigners) and became poorer and poorer. At least 90 percent of the people were illiterate, and many suffered from protein deficiency.

Today 160 churches have been started, and 10,000 people have become Christians. Eleven primary schools are operating, and they stress locally usable skills instead of the usual Liberian fare of Spot and Jane in English. A vocational school is forming that will help revive local trades and encourage new skills; and steps are being taken to form co-operatives which will avoid middlemen, replace foreign merchants, provide capital, etc.

One crucial element, especially in view of their protein shortage, is agriculture, and in the last ten years the people have made great strides. But they are so poor that often the only farming tool they have is a machete (a heavy knife). So Gus is burdened to start a revolving loan fund from which people can borrow to buy a hoe, a shovel, a water can, spraying equipment, a pick, or an ax. You and I buy tools like that on a whim for the garden in our backyards, but for these people such purchases are completely out of reach even though they need them to fight malnutrition. So next time you start feeling poor, remember Gus's people.[22]

When those words were written in 1976, there were not too many indigenous organizations of that kind. Today there are scores of similar holistic programs operated by biblical Christians in developing countries. They can use additional funds wisely and effectively. Organizations that channel assistance to such ministries in developing nations offer you and me a contemporary way to live the jubilee.

We also must ask: what kinds of programs (e.g., providing clean water to rural villages vs. providing laptops to poor children) do more to reduce poverty? *Christianity Today* asked development economist Bruce Wydick to answer this question. Fortunately in the last decade especially, development economists have applied much more rigorous methods (especially random-ized control trials) to see what kinds of programs actually reduce poverty.[23] So Bruce polled a bunch of prominent development economists and asked them to rate a number of different concrete strategies.

The most effective strategy? Providing clean water to rural villages. Every year, a million children die because they don't have clean drinking water. One famous study by the World Health Organization discovered that clean water in a rural village reduces the infant death rate by 35 to 50 percent—and it only costs $10 per person per year![24]

De-worming treatments for children ranked second. One of the early randomized control trials discovered that regular de-worming of school children in worm-infested areas reduced absence from school by 25 per-cent—at a tiny cost of 50 cents a year per student.[25]

Providing insecticide-treated bed nets to prevent malaria-carrying mosquitoes from biting people in their sleep ranked third. These bed nets reduce the instance of malaria by 50 percent and only cost 5–10 dollars. Also high on the list of effective interventions were child sponsorship and efficient wood burning stoves that reduce indoor air pollution that kills 1.6 million people prematurely each year.[26] Fair-trade coffee and laptops for kids were among the lowest rated interventions.

You can tell your favorite Christian development agency that you want to support these kinds of effective programs.

Opportunity International is one such organization. David Bussau was one of the founders. In my book *Cup of Water, Bread of Life*, I tell the amazing story of David's life. Forty years ago, David was a highly suc-cessful evangelical businessman in Australia.[27] Then he became one of the world's important bankers for the poor. For several years David and his family lived among the desperately poor in Indonesia. Slowly, they discov-ered that one of the very good ways to help is to make tiny loans at fair interest rates to poor people whom the banks ignore.

Today, Opportunity International has over 2.8 million active loans in 22 countries. In addition to small loans, Opportunity offers a wide range of services and products from savings accounts to insurance, from entre-preneurial support groups to business training. They have a successful track record with 98 percent of loans repaid. Ninety-three percent of loans go to women, helping some of the world's most vulnerable.[28] Over the past 15 years, Opportunity has created 10 million jobs through $6.8 billion in loans. Their goal is to create 20 million jobs by 2020.[29]

Opportunity's loans are a great investment. The average first loan is only $178.[30] With each loan, entrepreneurs are able to expand their businesses, spend more money on basic needs such as food, housing and school, and employ other workers who do the same. Once the money is paid back, it is reloaned to another person. Every dollar that is loaned turns into six dollars.[31]

In the Philippines, Opportunity's local partner, the Center for Community Transformation (CCT), combined evangelism and micro-loans. Teresita Duque's simple testimony shows how transforming this holistic ministry can be:

> My husband was a drunkard. I was a nagger. We were always hard
> up. My eight children had no one else. CCT sparked a hope within
> me. I obtained a loan for my fruit-vending business. What had gone
> to loan sharks now went into a savings account. Weekly Bible stud-
> ies gave me strength to quietly endure my husband's persecutions.
> I found rest for my soul knowing that God will never forsake me.
> My deepest joy was when my partner of 25 years and father of my
> children finally married me in a group wedding during CCT's anni-
> versary celebration.[32]

We have the money. Will we be generous? Almost every reader of this book could give $178 to provide a loan among the poor.

Donating money is not the only way to make loans and create jobs among the poor. Using one's investment fund is another.

Some people are investing some of their money in funds that make loans to empower very poor people. Initiated at the World Council of Churches' meeting in 1968 but now independent, Oikocredit pays 2 per-cent annual interest on money invested with it. Oikocredit then loans that money to poor entrepreneurs in 70 different countries. It's now the largest private financier of microfinance.[33] Mennonite Economic Development Associates (MEDA) has a similar program. Investors who loan money to their Sarona Risk Capital Fund receive an interest rate ranging from 0 to 4 percent. MEDA then uses that money to make loans to poor people, including gifted entrepreneurs who have the potential to start growing businesses that can employ others.[34]

Wise use of stocks can also help. Using our money (funds for retirement, for example) to purchase shares of companies that do not profit from things like tobacco, alcohol, abortion, and pornography and have solid track records concerning the poor, the environment, and workers' rights is a good way to promote the wholeness God desires. The Interfaith Center on Corporate Responsibility (see Appendix B) offers detailed information. The return on investment may not match the fastest-growing mutual funds, but by using the same funds to promote justice and prepare for retirement, we can accomplish two things with the same amount of dollars. God's Word and the world's needs call us to greater generosity both with how much money we give away and how we invest what we keep. Socially responsible investing is important.[35]

How Generous Are We?

Do you know how much the average person in the U.S. gives to all charitable causes? 2.3 percent of their income.[36] Church members do a little better. A recent study traced how much church members in the U.S. give to their local churches. In 2011, the figure was 2.3 percent of total income (see Table 13). Many church members also give to charities beyond their congregation. But even if the typical church member gave 2.3 percent to her local church and another 2 percent to other charities, the total figure would not be even close to the biblical standard of the 10 percent tithe.

Even more disturbing is that for most of the past forty-plus years, the percentage kept falling even though our income kept climbing. A careful study by John and Sylvia Ronsvalle provides the details. In the U.S., average per capita disposable income (i.e., after taxes) has more than doubled from 1968 to 2011.[37] (They take inflation into account and use constant 2005 dollars.) Tragically, the percent given to the church slowly declined. Table 13 shows how we gave less as we got richer.[38]

Table 13: Per Capita Member Giving[39]

Year	Giving as Percent of Income	Per capita disposable income (inflation adjusted 2005 dollars)
1968	3.11%	$14,136
1970	2.91%	$14,745
1975	2.73%	$16,375
1980	2.66%	$18,409
1985	2.60%	$20,955
1990	2.47%	$23,532
1995	2.43%	$25,082
2000	2.56%	$29,245
2005	2.52%	$31,343
2006	2.52%	$32,143
2007	2.53%	$32,524
2008	2.41%	$33,337
2009	2.48%	$31,863
2010	2.41%	$32,367
2011	2.32%	$32,653

One other statistic from the Ronsvalles' careful research is striking. They compare the giving of a cluster of evangelical denominations with a cluster of "mainline denominations active in the National Council of Churches." In 1968, the evangelical churches were giving almost twice as much (6.14 percent) as the NCC-related churches (3.3 percent). Tragically, the giving of the evangelical denominations has dropped precipitously. By 1985, the evangelical denominations were only giving 4.7 percent and by 2011 it was a mere 3.4 percent. (In 2011, the NCC related churches gave 2.65 percent.)[40]

What does God think of rich Christians whose church giving has fallen from 3.1 percent to 2.3 percent during exactly the same years that their average incomes have increased from $14,136 to $32,653?

Passing the Plate: Why American Christians Don't Give Away More Money is a stunning, powerful presentation of the puniness and possibility of American Christian giving. American Christians are the "most affluent single group of Christians in two thousand years of church history."[41] Over the course of the twentieth century, their per capita income (adjusted for inflation) increased four-fold. But the percent of that quadrupled income that we gave to charity actually declined.[42]

What makes *Passing the Plate* so stunning, however, is their amazing statistics on the tremendous good that American Christians could do if they just tithed. In fact, if just the "committed Christians" (those who attend church regularly or say they are "strong" Christians) tithed, there would be an additional 46 billion dollars available to do kingdom work. And they list dozens and dozens of astounding things that those additional dollars could accomplish each year:

- sponsor 150,000 new indigenous missionaries
- quadruple the total global resources currently spent on evangelism around the world
- fund 5,000,000 new microloans to poor entrepreneurs
- provide all the resources for a global campaign to prevent and treat malaria everywhere
- provide food, clothing, and shelter for all 6,500,000 current refugees in all of Africa, Asia, and the Middle East
- sponsor 20 million more needy children through Christian sponsorship organizations
- fund 1,000,000 new clean water well-drilling projects

That is just a *small fraction* of what new things "committed" American Christians could do if they simply tithed.[43]

I think God pleads with you and me to be far more generous. Start with a tithe if your current giving is less than that. Then ask God and a few Christian friends to help you develop your own version of the graduated tithe. But don't try to get there in one big jump. You may want to increase your giving (beyond the tithe) by 5 percent a year until you reach the level of generous sharing that you believe God wants you to enjoy.

That will not mean poverty. But it will mean giving up some luxuries. At the same time, if Jesus knew what he was talking about, it will lead to a new joy that will astonish you. And the additional resources your generosity offers to others will spread the Gospel and empower the poor.

This chapter has focused on monetary giving, but giving of ourselves is equally important. Some Christians choose low-paying jobs because the opportunity for service is great. Others decline opportunities to work overtime to be involved in more volunteer activity. Tens of thousands have volunteered a few days each year to help Habitat for Humanity build houses for the poor. Thousands of Christian doctors, teachers, farmers, and carpenters have given a few years to serve in developing countries or needy inner cities.

There is a great need for sensitive persons who will live with people in rural villages, showing the poor that God wants them to have both the tools to earn a decent living and the knowledge and power to change the unjust structures that oppress them. Agricultural workers who can share intermediate technological skills are in high demand. "One person with practical skills who's prepared to work and live in a remote village is generally worth a dozen visiting university professors and business tycoons."[44] Time is money. Sharing time is just as important as sharing financial resources.

We should be more generous with our money and our time. But that does not mean we should run ever more frantically at a dizzying pace so we can help the poor. Living a faithful lifestyle includes remembering the fourth commandment: "Observe the Sabbath day by keeping it holy, as the Lord your God has commanded you. . . . Remember that you were slaves in Egypt and that the Lord your God brought you out of there with a mighty hand and an outstretched arm. Therefore the Lord your God has commanded you to observe the Sabbath day" (Deut. 5:12, 15 NIV).

The Sabbath and Our Lifestyles

Genuine recovery of the Sabbath is just what both materialistic consumers and workaholic social activists need. One day out of seven, we should just stop. Stop feverish production of more gadgets. Stop even passionate pursuit of social justice. Just stop, pray, and enjoy.

God's provision of the Sabbath is not some harsh legalism but a divine reminder of our finitude and limitations. We are not God.[45] And we are not made to find our ultimate fulfillment in an ever-greater abundance of material things—or even an unlimited pursuit of justice for the poor.

Modern people have lost the biblical sense of human limitation. We want more and more faster and faster. And we destroy ourselves, our marriages, our families, and the environment to get it. God's Word is strikingly different: "Do not wear yourself out to get rich; have the wisdom to show restraint" (Prov. 23:4 NIV). The Sabbath is a divine mechanism to nurture restraint and moderation. It puts a halt to our frantic striving to produce more and more things—or even to work desperately to change the world for the sake of the poor!

Make no mistake. The material world is good and so is our work in creating wealth—not to mention empowering the needy. But God never intended us to forget our finitude and dependence on the Creator in our proper concern for shaping culture and doing mission. That's what the Sabbath is all about.

Once a week we are to stop, be quiet, and worship. It does not matter that for a whole day we fail to produce good things or even do good kingdom work. We are finite. Arrogantly thinking we must do it all is blasphemy. Just resting our bodies, enjoying our families, and praising our God is enough for one day out of seven.

If Christians could recover the practice of the Sabbath, it would help us turn away from the mad consumerism that is destroying people and the environment. Almost everything in our culture undermines what the fourth commandment wisely insists on preserving. If the spirit of the Sabbath would truly penetrate our minds and values, we would long to rest our tired psyches, enjoy our families and neighbors, and take quiet delight in the presence of our God—just "wasting" the whole day on worship and leisure! We would treasure this holy leisure more than the opportunity to use Sunday to accomplish still one more important task, or build one more balcony in our Tower of Babel. And in those quiet times in the divine presence, the God of the poor would transform our materialistic hearts and make us more generous.

A Call for Loyalty

I am convinced that simpler living is a biblical imperative for contemporary Christians in affluent lands. But we must remain clear about our reasons. We are not committed to a simple lifestyle. We have only one absolute loyalty, and that is to Jesus and his kingdom.[46] But the head of this kingdom is the God of the poor! And hundreds of millions of his children are desperately poor.

An age of hunger and poverty summons affluent people to a lower standard of living. But vague assent to this truth will not protect us from the daily seductions of Madison Avenue. Each of us needs a specific plan. The examples of Robert Bainum, David Bussau, and Graham and Treena Kerr provide suggestions. The graduated tithe and communal living are two other possibilities. There are many more.

By all means avoid legalism and self-righteousness. But have the courage to commit yourself to some specific method for moving toward a just personal lifestyle.

Will we dare to measure our living standards by the needs of the poor rather than by the lifestyles of our neighbors? Will we have the faith to believe Jesus' word that joy and happiness flow from sharing? Will rich Christians also be generous?

Study Questions

1. How does the graduated tithe work? How would you want to adapt it if you chose to use it in your life?
2. What other specific mechanisms could help Christians avoid materialism? Which ones do you think are: (a) most biblical; (b) most workable?
3. Which practical suggestions for consuming less did you find most helpful? Can you add others?
4. In the light of the criteria for giving, how do you evaluate your own giving? Your church's giving?
5. In what ways are you being challenged to change your spending patterns?
6. How did this chapter make you feel?

10

WATCHING OVER ONE ANOTHER IN LOVE

Extra ecclesiam, nulla salus.[1]

*Somehow the pressures of modern society were making it
increasingly difficult for us to live by the values we had
been taught. We thought our church should constitute
a community of believers capable of withstanding these
pressures, yet it seemed to go along with things as they were
instead of encouraging an alternative. The "pillars" of the
church seemed as severely trapped by material concerns
and alienation as most non-Christians we knew.*[2]

—DAVE AND NETA JACKSON

One day a man with a serious drinking problem dropped in to talk with
Virgil Vogt, one of the elders of Reba Place Fellowship in Evanston,
Illinois. When Virgil invited him to accept Christ and join the community
of believers, the man insisted that he simply wanted money for a bus ticket
to Cleveland.

"Okay," Virgil agreed, "we can give you that kind of help too, if that's all
you really want." He was quiet a moment, then he shook his head. "You
know something?" he said, looking straight at the man. "You've just

really let me off the hook. Because if you had chosen a new way of life in the kingdom of God, then as your brother I would have had to lay down my whole life for you. This house, my time, all my money, whatever you needed to meet your needs would have been totally at your disposal for the rest of your life. But all you want is some money for a bus ticket."[3]

The man was so startled he stood up and left, forgetting to take the money. But on Sunday he was back, this time sitting next to Virgil in the worship service.

The church should consist of communities of loving defiance. Instead it consists largely of comfortable clubs of conformity. A far-reaching reformation is necessary if the church is going to resist the materialism of our day and share God's concern for the poor.

If the analysis in the preceding chapters is even approximately correct, then the God of the Bible is calling Christians today to live in fundamental nonconformity to contemporary society, to confess and turn away from our obsession with materialism, sex, and economic success. Things have become more important to us than persons. Job security and salary increases matter more than starving children and poor peasants. Paul's warning to the Romans is especially pertinent: "Don't let the world around you squeeze you into its own mould" (Rom. 12:2 PHILLIPS). Biblical revelation summons us to defy many of the basic values of our materialistic, adulterous society.

But that is impossible! As individuals, that is. It is hardly possible for isolated believers to resist the anti-Christian values pouring from our radios, TVs, and billboards. The values of our affluent society seep slowly and subtly into our hearts and minds. The only way to defy them is to immerse ourselves in Christian fellowship so that God can remold our thinking as we find our primary identity with brothers and sisters who also are unconditionally committed to biblical values.

We should not be surprised that faithful obedience is possible only in the context of powerful Christian fellowship. The early church was able to defy the decadent values of Roman civilization precisely because it experienced Christian fellowship in a mighty way. For the early Christians, *koinonia* was not the "frilly fellowship" of church-sponsored, biweekly bowling parties. It was not tea, cookies, and sophisticated small talk in the

Fellowship Hall after the sermon. It was an almost unconditional sharing of their lives with other members of Christ's body.

When one member suffered, they all suffered. When one rejoiced, they all rejoiced (1 Cor. 12:26). When a person or church experienced economic trouble, the others shared generously. And when a brother or sister fell into sin, the others gently restored the straying person (Matt. 18:15–17; 1 Cor. 5; 2 Cor. 2:5–11; Gal. 6:1–3).[4] The sisters and brothers were available to each other, liable for each other, and accountable to each other—emotionally, financially, and spiritually.

The early church, of course, did not always live out the New Testament vision of the body of Christ. There were tragic lapses. But the network of tiny house churches scattered throughout the Roman Empire did experience oneness in Christ so vividly that they were able to defy and eventually conquer a powerful, pagan civilization.

John Wesley's early Methodist class meetings captured something of the spirit alive in the early church. Every week they gathered together in houses, "united in order to pray together, to receive the word of exhortation, and to watch over one another in love, that they may help each other to work out their salvation."[5] The overwhelming majority of churches today, however, do not provide a context in which brothers and sisters can encourage, admonish, and disciple each other. We desperately need new structures for watching over one another in love, new settings that will help us live like Jesus rather than like our broken culture.

A Sociological Perspective

Sociologists of knowledge have studied the relationship between ideas and the social conditions in which they arise and have discovered that the plausibility of ideas depends on the social support they have: "We obtain our notions about the world originally from other human beings, and these notions continue to be plausible to us in a very large measure because others continue to affirm them."[6]

This underlines the importance of Christian community for those who long to conform to Jesus rather than to the world. An Amish youth who migrates to New York City will soon begin to question earlier values.

The sociological reason for this change is that the "significant others" who previously supported his ideas and values are no longer present.

The complicated network of social interactions in which people develop and maintain their view of reality is called a plausibility structure. It consists of ongoing conversation with "significant others" as well as specific practices, rituals, and legitimations designed to support the validity of certain ideas. As long as these continue, people tend to accept the corresponding beliefs as true or plausible. But if the supportive structures disappear, doubt and uncertainty arise.

Hence the difficulty of small groups of people who hold a set of beliefs that differ sharply from the majority view in their society. (Sociologists call such people a cognitive minority.) Because they constantly meet people who challenge their fundamental ideas, members have difficulty maintaining their distinctive beliefs. According to well-known sociologist Peter Berger, these groups maintain their unpopular ideas only if they have a strong community structure:

> Unless our theologian has the inner fortitude of a desert saint, he has only one effective remedy against the threat of cognitive collapse in the face of these pressures. He must huddle together with like-minded fellow deviants—and huddle very closely indeed. Only in a counter-community of considerable strength does cognitive deviance have a chance to maintain itself. The countercommunity provides continuing therapy against the creeping doubt as to whether, after all, one may not be wrong and the majority right. To fulfill its function of providing social support for the deviant body of "knowledge," the countercommunity must provide a strong sense of solidarity among its members.[7]

Berger's analysis relates directly to contemporary Christians determined to follow biblical teaching on the poor and possessions. Berger analyzed the problem of orthodox Christians who defy the dominant "scientific" ideas of contemporary secularism and maintain a biblical belief in the supernatural. But his analysis pertains just as clearly to the problem of living the ethics of Jesus' kingdom in a world that follows different standards. Most of our contemporaries—both inside and outside the churches—accept the dominant values of our consumption-oriented, materialistic culture. Genuine Christians, on the other hand, are committed to the very different norms revealed in Scripture. It should not surprise us that only a faithful remnant clings to these values. And the fact that genuine Christians are a minority upholding un-popular beliefs alerts us to the need for strong Christian community.

This does not mean that most Christians should imitate the Amish and retreat to isolated rural solitude. We must remain at the center of contemporary society in order to challenge, witness against, and, hopefully, even change it. But precisely as we are in the world but not of it, the pressure to abandon biblical norms in favor of contemporary values will be intense. Hence the need for new forms of Christian community.

The ancient Catholic dictum *extra ecclesiam, nulla salus* ("outside the church there is no salvation") contains a significant sociological truth. Certainly it is not impossible for individual Christians to maintain biblical beliefs even if a hostile majority disagrees. But if the church is to consist of communities of loving defiance in a sinful world, it must pay more attention to the quality of its fellowship and find new models of Christian community.

New Patterns of Christian Community

At the mere mention of Christian community, some people instantly think of Christian communes. This is unfortunate. Communes are only one of many forms for genuine Christian fellowship today. Discipleship and mission groups within larger congregations, individual house churches, and small traditional churches all offer excellent contexts for living out the biblical vision of the church.

I am convinced, however, that the overwhelming majority of Western churches no longer understand or experience biblical *koinonia* to any significant degree. As mentioned earlier, the essence of Christian community is far-reaching accountability to and liability for sisters and brothers in the body of Christ. That means that our time, our money, and our very selves are available to one another.

Such fellowship rarely happens in groups of one hundred or more persons. It requires small communities of believers like the early Christian house churches. The movement that conquered the Roman Empire was a network of small house churches. The apostle Paul frequently mentioned "the church that meets in the house of . . ." (Rom. 16:5, 23; 1 Cor. 16:19; Col. 4:15; Phil. 2; see also Acts 2:46; 12:12; 20:7–12). The structure of the early church fostered close interaction and fellowship.[8] Only in the latter part of the third century did Christians start to construct church buildings.

When God grants the gift of genuine Christian fellowship, deep, joyful sharing replaces the polite prattle typically exchanged by Christians on Sunday morning. Sisters and brothers begin to discuss the things that really matter to them. They disclose their inner fears, their areas of peculiar temptation, their deepest joys. And they begin to challenge and disciple each other according to Matthew 18:15–17 and Galatians 6:1–3.

In that kind of setting—and perhaps only in that kind of setting—the church today will be able to forge a faithful, generous lifestyle for rich Christians in a time of hunger and wealth. In small house-church settings, brothers and sisters can challenge each other's affluent lifestyles. They can discuss each other's finances and annual budgets. Larger expenditures (like those for houses, cars, and long vacations) can be evaluated honestly in terms of the needs of both the individuals involved and God's poor around the world. They can exchange tips for simple living, discuss voting patterns that liberate the poor, support jobs that are ecologically responsible, and encourage charitable donations that build self-reliance among the needy. These and many other issues can be wrestled with openly and honestly by persons who have pledged themselves to each other as brothers and sisters in Christ.

A Congregation of House Churches

Congregations composed of clusters of house churches make up, in my opinion, a viable alternative to the typical congregation. Here are two examples.

Koinonia Fellowship[9]

Forty-five years ago Koinonia Fellowship was a typical, successful Pentecostal church with a large, growing congregation of several hundred people. The church had a young dynamic pastor, a packed schedule of meetings, a full repertoire of church committees, and, according to the pastor, little real Christian fellowship.

In 1970 the church decided to change drastically. It dropped all existing activities except the Sunday morning worship service and urged everyone to attend "home meetings," where twelve to twenty people met weekly for study, prayer, worship, and discipling.

For a couple of years they wondered if they had made a gigantic mistake. "To move from a pew to a living room chair and look at people face-to-face was terrifying," one of the pastors told me. But a breakthrough occurred when the leaders of the home meetings realized that most people did not know how to meet each other's needs. The leaders started making suggestions: "Would you two please go to Jane Brown's house and make dinner for her because she is sick?" "Would you three people paint Jerry's apartment on Saturday?"

Oneness and caring began to develop. The weekly gatherings became the center of spiritual activity. Counseling, discipling, even evangelistic outreach, began to happen primarily in the home meetings. One result was rapid growth. As soon as a home meeting reached twenty-five persons, it was divided into two home meetings. By the mid-seventies, thirteen to fourteen hundred people were attending weekend services. There were fifty home meetings and four Sunday services.

Several new congregations evolved. One met on Sunday morning in the original downtown sanctuary. Another rented space from another church and held a service on Sunday afternoon. As a result they avoided costly building programs and kept financial resources available for more important matters.

Genuine Christian community emerged from this drastic restructuring, and leaders could confidently assert that all their members received personal, pastoral care because every home meeting knew and dealt with each person's individual troubles.

Financial sharing was not part of the original vision, but it began to happen in a significant way. Members of home meetings dug into savings and stocks to provide interest-free loans for two families who purchased house trailers for homes. When members went to sign the papers for an interest-free mortgage for another family's house, the unusual agreement

211

left secular folk present for the transfer totally perplexed! If a member of a home meeting needed a small amount of financial assistance, the other members helped out. A congregational fund met larger needs. A food co-op and a store for used clothing and furniture supplied some basic needs inexpensively. Eventually, a sizable portion of total congregational giving went to economic sharing in the church.

Koinonia Fellowship also began to develop a deeper concern for the poor. The leaders preached about social justice. The church began to work in a major way with refugees from Southeast Asia and to contribute thousands of dollars each year to relieve world poverty.

An interracial subcongregation of 150 persons also developed. It started with an evangelistic outreach in the poorest Hispanic section of the city. Drug rehabilitation, job counseling, emergency food distribution, and ministry to battered women were all part of this holistic outreach. Some church members then relocated to this needy area to continue with evangelism and discipling. Eventually they developed a large holistic health center, ministering to one of the poorest inner-city neighborhoods.

Koinonia Fellowship has demonstrated that a traditional congregation can be transformed into a cluster of house churches. And the result can be growth—in discipleship, community, and numbers.

Church of the Savior

At the end of World War II, the Church of the Savior in Washington, D.C., pioneered the small-group model.[10] All members had to be in one of its many mission groups. Prospective members took five classes over a period of about two years. The membership covenant, renewed annually, committed every member to four disciplines: daily prayer, daily Bible study, weekly worship, and proportionate giving, beginning with a tithe of total gross income.

Consisting of five to twelve persons, the mission groups were the heart of the Church of the Savior. They were not merely prayer cells, Bible studies, encounter groups, or social action committees (although they were all of these). Gordon Cosby, founder and long-time pastor of Church of the Savior, insisted that it was in the mission groups that the members experienced the reality of the body of Christ: "The mission group embodies the varied dimensions of church. It is total in scope. It is both inward and outward. It requires that we be accountable to Christ and to one another for the totality of our lives. It assumes that we share unlimited liability for one another."[11]

Via verbal or written reports, each member of a mission group reported weekly on failure or success in following the covenanted disciplines, on new scriptural insight, and on the problems and joys of the week.

Economics figured prominently in the membership commitment. Part of the membership covenant read, "I believe that God is the total owner of my life and resources. I give God the throne in relation to the material aspect of my life. God is the owner. I am the ower. Because God is a lavish giver, I too shall be lavish and cheerful in my regular gifts."[12]

The church has held out the goal of accountability to each other in the use of personal finances. Some mission groups shared personal income tax returns as a basis for discussing family budgets and finances. Concern for simpler lifestyles has been a part of their life together.

The goal of many of the mission groups has been empowerment of the poor. One group, Jubilee Housing, has renovated deteriorating housing in inner-city Washington. Along with other mission groups (Jubilee Jobs, Columbia Road Health Service, Family Place), they have brought hope of genuine change to hundreds of people in the inner city. For Love of Children has fought for the rights of neglected children through court action, legislation, and monitoring of local and federal governmental activity. Several of the church's mission groups have dedicated themselves to peace and justice in the international arena. The Church of the Savior International Good Neighbors has made it possible for several hundred Americans to serve in Thailand refugee camps. They also provided direct relief to Central American refugees driven by violence from their homes into neighboring countries and the United States. At the same time, several mission groups worked to change U.S. foreign policy, which was contributing to the Central American refugee problem.

Increasing size, however, threatened genuine community at Church of the Savior. In 1994, the church divided into eight (later nine) faith communities. Each is legally and formally separate and has a distinct name, but all are informally linked together. Each community has approximately

130 members and 40 to 50 intern members. The original Church of the Savior no longer exists as a church body or as a directing board for the faith communities. Instead, the principles started by Gordon Cosby and implemented so successfully in the Church of the Savior over the past sixty-plus years live on in the life of the separate faith communities. Like Koinonia Fellowship, Church of the Savior preferred to subdivide into small congregations rather than risk diluting Christian community.

Thousands of churches today have small groups—encounter groups, biweekly fellowship groups, serendipity groups, prayer cells, and an almost infinite variety of action groups. They all claim to promote fellowship. Do these small groups fulfill the same function as Koinonia Fellowship's home meetings and Church of the Savior's mission groups? Hardly ever.

Though the numerous small groups flourishing in churches today are useful and valuable, they seldom go far enough. Participants may agree to share deeply in one or two areas of life, but they do not assume responsibility for the other brothers' and sisters' growth toward Christian maturity in every area of life. Hardly ever do they dream that truly being sisters and brothers in Christ means costly, sweeping economic liability for each other or responsibility for the economic lifestyles of the other members. The crucial question is, have the participants committed themselves to be brothers and sisters to each other so unreservedly that they enjoy far-reaching liability for and accountability to each other?

Almost everyone expects small groups to dissolve in six months or two years and that life will then continue as before. These short-term, "limited liability" groups serve a purpose, but people today desperately need a church that functions as the church—a body of believers who accept liability for one another, are available to one another, and make themselves accountable to one another.

The Individual House Church

Another structure where true Christian community can happen, and which involves virtually no expense, is the individual house church. When it is impossible to find genuine Christian community in any other way, small groups of Christians should begin meeting in their own homes. (But they should promptly seek a relationship with other bodies of Christians. Lone rangers are not God's will for his church!)

An ideal house church arrangement is to have several families or single persons purchase houses within a block or two of each other. In many inner-city locations, especially in changing neighborhoods, inexpensive houses change hands rapidly. Living across the street or down the block from each other makes it convenient to share such things as cars, washers and dryers, freezers, and lawnmowers (or gardening equipment). Living close also encourages Christian community by creating open relationships that foster honest, mutual searching for a responsible standard of living.

In his book on church structures, Howard A. Snyder proposed that denominations adopt the house church model for church planting, especially in the city. This structure is flexible, mobile, inclusive, and personal. It can grow by division, is an effective means of evangelism, and needs little professional leadership.[13]

"All Things in Common"

Reba Place Fellowship in Evanston, Illinois, began in 1957 with three people.[14] In 2014, there were 46 adult covenant members living with a common treasury. Some live in large households, but many have their own apartments. They live close to one another in three neighborhoods.

In addition to those who share a common treasury, another several hundred persons are part of two separate, but related congregations. These have their own private budgets but share a calling to faithfully embrace the astonishing teachings of Jesus about how we should handle our money and how much we are to love one another. An emphasis on community pervades the entire fellowship.

Those who share a common treasury place their earnings in a central fund. The central fund pays directly for large expenditures like housing, utilities, transportation, medical, and educational expenses. Each month, every family and single person receives an allowance for food ($126 a month for each adult), clothing, and incidentals. This allowance is based on family size and is adjusted for special needs. It has nothing to do with how much the individual contributed to the common treasury. The sharing of equipment such as cars, lawnmowers, and washing machines makes it possible for people to function effectively and efficiently at substantial savings.

The community forgoes most insurance policies, except those required by law. And generally they choose to disperse extra funds rather than to accumulate them. Trusting God for future needs while living simply results in having remarkable amounts of money available to respond to the needs of others in the immediate neighborhood and around the world.

Although not for everyone, Reba Place and other Christian communes offer one setting in which widespread liability for and accountability to other brothers and sisters can become a reality.[15] They are one means of living biblically in our increasingly materialistic society.

Many communal experiments occurred in the 1960s and 1970s. The fact that many did not survive indicates that this model is not easy to follow. More recently a number of new Christian communal groups have emerged.[16] Although communal living is certainly not a requirement for faithful discipleship, it does represent an alternative way of life for Christians dissatisfied with today's individualistic, materialistic society.

Glass Cathedrals in an Age of Hunger?

In early 1976, Eastminster Presbyterian Church in suburban Wichita, Kansas, had an ambitious church construction program in the works. Their architect had prepared a $525,000 church building program. Then a devastating earthquake struck in Guatemala on February 4, destroying thousands of homes and buildings. Many evangelical congregations lost their churches.

When Eastminster's board of elders met shortly after the Guatemalan tragedy, a layman posed a simple question: "How can we set out to buy an ecclesiastical Cadillac when our brothers and sisters in Guatemala have just lost their little Volkswagen?"

The elders courageously opted for a dramatic change of plans. They slashed their building program by nearly two-thirds and settled instead for church construction costing $180,000. Then they sent their pastor and two elders to Guatemala to see how they could help. When the three returned and reported tremendous need, the church borrowed $120,000 from a local bank and rebuilt twenty-six Guatemalan churches and twenty-eight Guatemalan pastors' houses.

I talked with Eastminster's pastor, Dr. Frank Kirk. He told me that Eastminster stayed in close touch with the church in Central America and later pledged $40,000 to an evangelical seminary there. In the years after their unusual decision, Eastminster Presbyterian experienced tremendous growth—in spiritual vitality, concern for missions, and even in attendance and budget. Dr. Kirk believes that cutting their building program to share with needy sisters and brothers in Guatemala "meant far more to Eastminster Presbyterian than to Guatemala."

The Eastminster Presbyterian congregation asked the right questions. They asked whether their building program was justified at this moment in history given the particular needs of the body of Christ worldwide and the mission of the church in the world. The question is not, Are gothic (or glass) cathedrals ever legitimate? Of course they are. The right question is: Is God calling our congregation to spend millions on church construction when more than a billion people have not yet heard of Jesus Christ and over one billion people are starving or malnourished?

The Triple Five Plan

If a congregation wants to increase their giving, how can they begin? Denominational offices, Christian relief and development organizations, Bread for the World, Evangelicals for Social Action, and many other groups (see the Appendix) all have helpful materials.

One simple approach is the Triple Five Plan.[17] After careful study of biblical teaching and world poverty, a congregation could decide to expand their giving and volunteer time to empower the poor by 5 percent each year for three successive years. They could also urge each member to do the same. After they have completed the first three-year cycle, the congregation could then write to political leaders asking government to expand effective programs for the poor by 5 percent each year for three years. To add authority to their appeal to government, the congregation could report their three years of growing church commitment to the poor and promise that as a congregation they will expand their church giving in the same way in the next three years. Politicians might listen to that kind of appeal.

The Bible and the daily newspaper issue the same summons. Faithful, generous people in an age of hunger, poverty, and wealth must adopt simpler lifestyles and change unjust economic structures. But that is not a popular path to tread in an affluent society. Unless Christians anchor themselves in genuine Christian community, they will be unable to live the radical nonconformity commanded by Scripture and essential in our time. Our only hope is a return to the New Testament vision of the body of Christ. If that happens, the Lord of the church may again create communities of loving defiance able to withstand and conquer today's powerful, pagan civilizations worshipping at the shrine of Mammon.

Study Questions

1. What is Christian community? Why is it so important for helping the poor?
2. What specific structures encourage closer Christian community? Which ones are most biblical? Which are most workable?
3. How close is your local church to the ideal of Christian community? What do you think God is leading you to do about that?

11

MAKING THE WORLD
MORE FAIR

Let justice roll down like waters, and
righteousness like an everflowing stream.

—AMOS 5:24

A group of devout Christians once lived in a small village at the foot of a mountain. A winding, slippery road with hairpin curves and steep precipices wound its way up one side of the mountain and down the other. There were no guardrails, and fatal accidents were frequent. The Christians in the village's three churches decided to act. They pooled their resources and purchased an ambulance so they could rush the injured to the hospital in the next town. Week after week, church volunteers gave faithfully, even sacrificially, of their time to operate the ambulance twenty-four hours a day. They saved many lives, although some victims died and others remained crippled for life.

One day a visitor came to town. Puzzled, he asked why they did not close the road over the mountain and build a tunnel instead. Startled, the ambulance volunteers quickly pointed out that this approach, though technically possible, was not realistic or advisable. After all, the narrow mountain road had been there for a long time. Besides, the mayor would bitterly oppose the idea. (He owned a large restaurant and service station halfway up the mountain.)

219

The visitor was shocked that the mayor's economic interests mattered more to these Christians than the many human casualties. Somewhat hesitantly, he suggested that perhaps the churches ought to speak to the mayor. After all, he was an elder in the oldest church in town. Perhaps they should even elect a different mayor if he proved stubborn and unconcerned.

Now the Christians were shocked. With rising indignation and righteous conviction they informed the young radical that the church dare not become involved in politics. The church is called to preach the Gospel and give a cup of cold water, they said. Its mission is not to dabble in worldly things like changing social and political structures.

Perplexed and bitter, the visitor left. As he wandered out of the village, one question churned in his muddled mind. Is it really more spiritual, he wondered, to operate ambulances that pick up the bloody victims of destructive social structures than to try to change the structures themselves?

Ambulance Drivers or Tunnel Builders?

An age of affluence and poverty demands compassionate action and simplicity in personal lifestyles. But compassion and simple living apart from structural change may be little more than a gloriously irrelevant ego trip or proud pursuit of personal purity.

By itself, living on less will not feed a single starving child. If millions of North Americans and Europeans reduce their consumption but do not act politically to change public policy, the result will not necessarily be less starvation in the developing world. To be sure, if people give the money saved to private agencies promoting economic development in poor nations, the result may be less hunger. But if local elites and the patterns of international trade trample and destroy the newfound hope of the poor, our simple personal lifestyles and model churches will help very little. Changes in public policy are also essential. If justice is to roll down like an ever-flowing stream, structural change is necessary.

Many questions promptly arise. What specific structural changes are consistent with biblical principles and economic facts? Indeed, are biblical principles pertinent to secular society? Israel, after all, was a theocracy. Can we really expect unbelievers to live according to biblical ethics?

220

The Bible does not directly answer all these questions. Although biblical revelation tells us that God and his faithful people are always at work liberating the oppressed, Scripture gives us no comprehensive blueprint for a new economic order. We do find, however, important principles about justice in society.

Certainly the first application of biblical truth concerning just relationships should be to the church. As the new people of God, the church should be a new society incarnating in its common life the biblical principles on justice (Gal. 3:6–9; 6:16; 1 Peter 2:9–10). Indeed, only as the church itself is a visible model of transformed socioeconomic relationships will any appeal to government possess integrity. Too much Christian social action is ineffective because Christian leaders call on the government to legislate what they cannot persuade their church members to live.

Biblical principles, however, are also relevant to secular societies as well as to the church. We must be careful, of course, to remember that church and state are two distinct institutions with different tasks and roles. The state should not make every item of Christian ethics a law. But biblical principles of justice are not arbitrary rules relevant only for believers. Therefore, a carefully developed political philosophy is essential.[1] The Creator revealed basic principles about social justice because he knew what would lead to lasting peace, social harmony, and happiness for his creatures.

The Bible is full of material that suggests the kind of social order God wills. And the church is supposed to be a model (imperfect, to be sure) of what the final kingdom of perfect justice and peace will be like. Thus, as the church models the coming kingdom, it exercises a powerful leavening influence in society (Luke 13:20–21).

Furthermore, the more faithfully and appropriately any secular society applies the biblical norms on justice in society, the more peace, happiness, and harmony that society will enjoy. Obviously, sinful persons and societies will never get beyond a dreadfully imperfect approximation. But social structures do exert a powerful influence on saint and sinner alike. Christians, therefore, should exercise political influence to make societal systems more fair.

That the biblical authors did not hesitate to apply revealed standards to persons and societies outside the people of God supports this point.

Amos announced divine punishment on the surrounding nations for their evil and injustice (Amos 1–2). Isaiah denounced Assyria for its pride and injustice (Isa. 10:12–19). The book of Daniel shows that God removed pagan kings like Nebuchadnezzar in the same way he destroyed Israel's rulers when they failed to show mercy to the oppressed (4:27). God obliterated Sodom and Gomorrah no less than Israel and Judah because they neglected to aid the poor and feed the hungry (Ezek. 16:49). The Lord of the universe applies the same standards of social justice to all nations.

This last principle bears directly on the issues of this chapter. Some countries, like the United States, Russia, Canada, and Australia, have a bountiful supply of natural resources within their national boundaries. Do they therefore have an absolute right to use these resources solely for the advantage of their own citizens? Not according to the Bible.[2] If we believe Scripture, we must conclude that the human right of all persons to have the opportunity to earn a just living clearly supersedes the right of the rich nations to use resources exclusively for themselves. We are only stewards, not absolute owners. God is the only absolute owner, and he insists that the earth's resources be shared.

Before sketching specific steps for applying these principles to today's economic structures, I must register one disclaimer and one clarification.

We must constantly remember the large gulf between revealed principles and contemporary application. There are many valid ways to apply biblical principles. The application of biblical norms to socioeconomic questions today leaves room for creativity and honest disagreement among biblical Christians. Objecting to my application of biblical ethics to contemporary society is not at all the same as rejecting biblical principles. Of course, not all applications are equally valid. But humility and tolerance of one another's views are imperative.[3] We can and must help one another see where we are unfaithful to biblical revelation and inadequately grounded in social analysis. We must combine biblical norms and solid study of society.

One clarification is also necessary. To argue that Christians should work politically to change aspects of our economic structures that are unjust is not to call for a violent revolution that would forcibly impose a centralized, statist society. I believe that the way of Jesus is the way of nonviolent love, even for enemies. I therefore reject the use of lethal violence.[4] The exercise of political influence in a democratic society, of course, involves the use of nonlethal pressure (or force). When we legislate penalties for drunken driving or speeding, we use an appropriate kind of nonlethal "force." The same is true when we pass legislation that changes a nation's foreign policy toward poor nations, makes trade patterns more just, restricts the unfair practices of multinational corporations, or increases foreign economic aid. In a democratic society, of course, such changes can occur only if a majority agrees.

As we work to correct unjust economic structures, it is important constantly to promote decentralized, democratic decision-making and control. Marxist totalitarianism clearly, and multinational corporations to a lesser but dangerous degree, centralize power in the hands of a tiny group of individuals. Often, the choices of these powerful elites reflect their own self-interest, not what is good for the majority. Biblical people will work both for a decentralization of economic power and a more just economy built on the basic biblical affirmation that God is on the side of justice for all and therefore has a special concern for the poor and oppressed.

That can be done! Change is possible. Just think of what has happened since this book first appeared almost forty years ago. Communism has fallen. Apartheid collapsed. Democratically elected governments have replaced dictators in many nations. A much smaller percentage of the world's people suffer from chronic malnutrition.

Societies can change. We can correct unjust structures. Our challenge today is to take the next practical, concrete steps to empower the poor.

This chapter explores measures that could make economic structures more fair: corrections in today's market economies; changes in international trade; restoring our global environment; and improving economic foreign aid.

Who Will Be Helped?

Before we examine those issues, however, we must face a complex question. Given the great imbalance of power in many poor nations today, who would benefit from increased foreign aid, expanded exports to rich nations, or a growing economy?

Would a growing economy automatically help the poor? The most obvious structural solution to hunger is rapid economic development in poorer nations. Macro-economic growth in nations (China, for example) has lifted hundreds of millions of people out of poverty. As a result these countries can produce more of their own food and basic necessities or trade for them on the world market. Macroeconomic growth is essential.

Throughout the fifties and sixties and into the seventies however, this was almost the exclusive focus of people concerned about poor nations. Economists advocated, and many governments in developing countries implemented, economic programs designed to produce economic growth, which at that time was thought to be synonymous with economic development. As the GNP of a country grew, people expected the forthcoming benefits eventually to "trickle down" to the poor so that the entire society would benefit. The poor would obtain jobs in a growing economy, and poverty would vanish.

Over the years, however, it became evident that even when the GNP increased, the conditions of the poor did not automatically improve.[5] In light of the experience of the last several decades, it is now widely recognized that this trickle-down approach to development benefits the middle and upper classes but does much less to help the poor. This is why in 1990, 90 percent of those living below the international poverty level of $1.25 per day lived in poor countries but today 70 percent of those poorest folk live in middle income countries.[6] Countries like India have experienced enormous economic growth and moved up to be middle income countries. But the poorest have not benefited very much. What is needed is political decisions that devote more resources for health care, education, and economic opportunity for the poorest. That does not happen as much as it should because of the unfair distribution of power.

Compelling, recent research by economists has demonstrated that the distribution of power—both political and economic—decisively determines whether nations fail or succeed in creating sustained economic growth that benefits most people.[7] Economic development specialists Daron Acemoglu (MIT) and James A. Robinson (Harvard) distinguish between 'extractive' and 'inclusive' political and economic institutions. Extractive economic institutions are ones where small elites are able to control the economy so it largely benefits a tiny group of powerful people. Inclusive economic institutions provide genuine opportunity for everyone. "To be inclusive, economic institutions must feature secure private property, an unbiased system of law, and a provision of public services that provides a level playing field in which people can exchange and contract; it must also permit the entry of new businesses"—i.e., no monopolies or complicated rules designed to prevent new entrepreneurs from challenging current businesses.[8]

But it is precisely politics which determines whether the economic institutions benefit everyone or only a few. For most people to benefit, political power must be decentralized. "It is politics and political institutions that determine what economic institutions a country has."[9] And it is only when political power is decentralized so small elites cannot manipulate the economy for the benefit of the few that sustained economic growth happens.[10]

The industrial revolution happened first in Great Britain where rapid economic growth continued over many generations. Central to this development was a political revolution that limited the power of the king and the aristocracy. As political power was increasingly decentralized, democratic institutions and independent courts emerged and grew. And that in turn led to economic institutions that worked for and benefited more and more people, encouraging innovation and investment and thus sustained economic growth. Similar things happened in the United States.[11] "Almost all of the countries that have enjoyed good economic performance across generations are countries that have stable democratic governments."[12]

Decentralization of power is crucial. That helps explain why Nobel Laureate economist Amartya Sen says the expansion of freedom for everyone (which decentralizes power) is the primary end and the principle means of development.[13]

The summary by the authors of *Why Nations Fail* of what creates sustained economic growth similarly underlines the crucial significance of decentralizing power:

> Inclusive economic institutions that enforce property rights, create a
> level playing field, and encourage investments in new technologies and
> skills are more conducive to economic growth than extractive economic

institutions that are structured to extract resources from the many by [and for] the few and that fail to protect property rights or provide incentives for economic activity. Inclusive economic institutions are in turn supported by, and support, inclusive political institutions, that is those that distribute political power widely. . . . Similarly extractive economic institutions are synergistically linked to extractive political institutions, which concentrate power in the hands of a few, who will then have incentives to maintain and develop extractive economic institutions for their benefit and use the resources they obtain to cement their hold on political power.[14]

Those who want to end widespread poverty must oppose highly centralized political and economic power.

Wealthy nations should provide more foreign aid and reduce trade barriers against poorer countries. But that will not necessarily benefit the poorest half of the developing countries one iota. As we saw in chapter 7, North Americans and Europeans are not to blame for all the poverty in the world today. Sin is not just a white European phenomenon. Wealthy elites, largely unconcerned about the suffering of the poor masses in their lands, rule many developing countries.[15] They often own a large percentage of the best land, on which they grow cash crops for export to earn the foreign exchange they need to buy luxury goods from the developed world. Meanwhile, the poorest 30 to 70 percent of the people face grinding poverty. More recently these wealthy elites own the new corporations engaged in global trade. More foreign aid and expanding exports might simply enable these wealthy elites to strengthen their repressive regimes.[16]

Does that mean that North Americans and Europeans can wash their hands of the whole problem? Not at all. In many cases over the past decades, the wealthy elites continued in power partly because they received massive military aid and diplomatic support from the United States and other industrial nations.[17] The United States actually trained large numbers of military officers and police who then tortured thousands of people working for social justice in many countries in Latin America.[18] In 1996, the Pentagon finally released a manual that had been used for many years at the U.S. Army's School of the Americas, which trained about sixty thousand Latin American police and military officers. The manual recommended "interrogation techniques like torture, execution, blackmail and arresting relatives."[19] Western-based multinational corporations have worked closely with repressive governments. The histories of Brazil, Chile, El Salvador, and the Philippines demonstrate that the United States supported dictatorships that used torture and did little for the poorest one-half as long as these regimes were friendly to U.S. investments and foreign policy objectives.[20]

A Change in Foreign Policy

What can be done? Citizens of industrialized countries could demand a major reorientation of foreign policy. We could insist that our nations unequivocally focus on justice for the poor and decentralization of power.

If we truly believe that all people are created equal, then our foreign policy must be redesigned to promote the interests of all people and not just the wealthy elites in developing countries or our own multinational corporations. We should use our economic and diplomatic power to promote justice for all, especially the poorest. That would mean placing greater weight in U.S. foreign policy on democracy and human rights; free, effective trade unions; correcting abuses of MNCs; and foreign aid that reaches the poorest.

Poor majorities in many countries eagerly seek to end repressive regimes that benefit primarily wealthy elites in their nation. The U.S. and other developed nations could use their vast diplomatic and economic power far more than they do to decentralize power by promoting human rights, encouraging democracy, and nurturing a civil society in which thousands of private voluntary organizations can flourish. Vast numbers of popular people's organizations have sprung up in Africa, Asia, Latin America, and the former Soviet Union as more democratic, pluralistic governments have replaced repressive regimes.[21] This should be encouraged so the poor can demand new opportunity and power.

Trade unions in poor countries are one crucial piece of the puzzle. Honest, democratic trade unions decentralize power. Developed nations should work hard to strengthen workers' rights and trade unions in negotiations over international trade. Unfortunately, precisely the opposite has happened. A working paper for the U.S. Congress Joint Economic Committee pointed out that labor is the only significant factor "which did not receive special protection in the [earlier] Uruguay Round of trade negotiations."[22] They are not a part of the current Doha Round negotiations either.[23] We must insist that a concern for workers' rights including independent unions play a significant part in all U.S. trade negotiations.

Insisting on ethical norms for multinational corporations would also help. This is difficult, of course, precisely because MNCs are large and international. But most MNCs have their headquarters in North America, Western Europe, or Japan—although a growing number are in countries like South Korean, China, India, and Brazil. Citizens in rich nations have a particular responsibility to see that the impact of MNCs on poor nations is positive rather than negative.

Unfortunately, U.S. foreign policy has usually supported the economic interests of U.S. MNCs rather than the poor in the developing nations. In May 1981, for instance, the United States was the only nation in the world to vote in the World Health Organization against a code to control the advertising and marketing of infant formula by MNCs in the developing world (the vote was 119–1). In spite of worldwide documentation of the evil effects of the marketing activities of Nestlé and other MNCs,[24] the Reagan administration voted no because it said the code might damage "free enterprise."[25]

A foreign policy that seeks biblical justice for the poor will have to be willing to try to place ethical controls on the operations of MNCs, even if that is not in the short-term economic interest of the MNC and its U.S. shareholders. Both by political activity and by well-designed citizen protests like the Nestlé boycott, Christian citizens can help reduce the negative impact of MNCs on the poor of the earth.[26]

We should also insist that our foreign aid benefit primarily the poorest in the most needy nations, and that those nations become more democratic and work for "growth with equity." Aid to countries whose governments care little about improving the condition of the poor will likely end up in the pockets of the rich.

Our nation's foreign policy ought to have a special focus on the poorest.

Only then will proposed structural changes in areas like international trade and foreign aid programs actually improve the lot of the poorest billion people.

Social Change and Conversion

A fundamental change in our policy toward developing nations is imperative. But it is not enough. In addition, the poor in those nations must somehow find the courage to demand sweeping structural changes in their own lands.

Such changes, however, can happen only if a fundamental transformation of values occurs. In a scholarly book on land tenure in India, Robert Frykenberg of the University of Wisconsin lamented the growing gulf between rich and poor. "No amount of aid, science, and/or technology," he concluded, "can alter the direction of current processes without the occurrence of a more fundamental 'awakening' or 'conversion' among significantly larger numbers of people . . . Changes of a revolutionary character are required, changes which can only begin in the hearts and minds of individuals."[27]

At precisely this point the Christian Church—and evangelistic activities in particular—can play a crucial role. Two things are important: first, evangelism; and second, the whole message of Scripture. Evangelism is central to social change. Nothing so transforms the self-identity, self-worth, and initiative of a poor, oppressed person as a personal, living relationship with God in Christ. Discovering that the Creator of the world lives in each of them gives new worth and energy to people psychologically crippled by centuries of oppression.[28]

The second important component is sharing the whole biblical vision. Some religious worldviews tend, as we saw in chapter 7, to create a fatalistic attitude toward poverty. Hinduism, for instance, teaches that those in the lower castes (usually also the poorest) are there because of sinful choices in prior incarnations. Only by patiently enduring their present lot can they hope for a better life in future incarnations. In addition, some Eastern religions deemphasize the importance of history and material reality, considering them illusions to be escaped.

Biblical faith, on the other hand, affirms the goodness of the created, material world and teaches that the Creator and Lord of history demands justice now for the poor of the earth. As missionaries and others share this total biblical message, they can make a profound contribution to the battle against hunger, poverty, and injustice.[29] To be sure, missionaries cannot engage directly in political activity in foreign countries. But they can and must teach the whole Word for the whole person. Why have missionaries so often taught the New Testament Epistles but not the Old Testament Prophets to new converts in poor lands? If it is true, as we argued in Part 2, that Scripture constantly asserts that God is on the side of the poor, then missionaries should make this biblical theme a central part of their teaching. If we accept our Lord's Great Commission to teach "all that I have commanded you," then we dare not omit or deemphasize the biblical message of justice for the oppressed, even if it offends ruling elites.

Cross-cultural missionaries need not engage directly in politics. But they must carefully and fully expound for new converts the explosive biblical message that God has a special concern for the poor and oppressed. The poor will quickly learn how to apply these biblical principles to their own oppressive societies. The result will be changed social structures in developing countries.

A recent, widely praised article by Professor Robert Woodberry in the *American Political Science Review* (the most prestigious scholarly journal in political science) demonstrates how "conversionary" Protestant missions contributed significantly to the decentralization of power and the emergence of democratic institutions in Africa and Asia.[30] Wanting everyone to be able to read the Bible, nineteenth and early twentieth century Protestant missionaries promoted mass education, widespread printing of newspapers, religious freedom, and voluntary organizations. All of these things decentralized power and prevented local elites from monopolizing wealth and political power. Using sophisticated statistical analyses, Woodberry demonstrates that conversionary Protestant missions "explain about half the variation in democracy outside Europe." Christians today need to discover anew how the power of the Gospel decentralizes power in a way that promotes better political and economic institutions.

Thus far we have looked at two things: a fundamental change in the foreign policy of rich nations, and a mass movement of social change rooted in new religious values in the poorer countries. Christians should promote both.

What else needs to happen?

First, we need to correct problems in market economies. Second, we should make international trade more fair. Third, we need to care for God's creation so God's poor and our grandchildren can enjoy a sustainable environment. And finally, we must be willing to help with wisely targeted and administered economic foreign aid, which will help prevent starvation during emergencies and empower the poor to earn their own way.

Correcting Weaknesses of Market Economies

Market economies have been far more successful than existing alternatives in creating wealth. Those who care about the poor should endorse market-oriented economies—rather than state-owned, centrally planned ones—as the best basic framework currently known for economic life. This does not mean we uncritically embrace everything done in the name of market reform. Nor does it mean we endorse a libertarian view that condemns virtually all government intervention in the economy. But it does mean we support a decentralized economic system in which the bulk of productive resources are privately owned, and in which supply and demand rather than a centralized government bureaucracy determines most prices and wages.

There are, however, glaring weaknesses in present market economies, as we saw in chapter 8.[31] Here I outline four specific corrective measures: providing the poor with basic capital so they can participate in economic life; insisting on the right kind and amount of government intervention; finding new measures for economic life; and redefining the good life.

Capital for the Poor

We must end the outrage of Christians celebrating the market economy and then failing to provide the poorest with access to the capital they need to earn a decent living in the global market. The mechanism of supply and demand pays no attention whatsoever to whether the purchaser wants to buy basic food to keep her children from starving or luxury items to parade social status. The market only rewards purchasing power.

We do know, of course, what to do to strengthen the purchasing power of the poorest. They need capital. The poorest billion have hardly any capital except their bodies, so they and their children waste away in malnutrition and starvation. To endorse market economies without redistributing resources so the poorest have access to the capital to earn a decent living is damnable defiance of the biblical God of justice.

Today's wealth is divided in a way that flatly contradicts the Bible. God wants every family to have the basic capital—land, money, knowledge—to earn their own way and be dignified, participating members of society.[32] (See the discussion in chapter 4.) If we want to implement this biblical teaching on economic justice—and enable market economies to operate justly—we must fundamentally change the terrible injustice of allowing many of the world's people to exist with little or no capital. The poorest billion-plus have virtually no capital. Another two billion have very little. That is why the richest 20 percent of the world's people receive 83 percent of world income while the poorest 20 percent get only 1 percent.[33]

According to a 2014 Oxfam report, the richest 1 percent have 65 times more wealth than the bottom half of the world. In fact, the richest 85 individuals in the world have more wealth than 3.5 billion people![34]

Christians today must insist on economic empowerment—through both private voluntary efforts and effective government programs.[35] That means programs that truly enable the poorer members of society to acquire more capital.

What kind of capital do people need? It varies with the situation. In a largely agricultural society, land reform is essential. In an information society, equality of educational opportunity is the most basic way to empower the poor. Wise schemes to enable the poor to acquire the money needed to buy a house, start a small business, or prepare for retirement are also important.[36]

Providing capital so the poor have economic opportunity to earn their own way can happen through both private voluntary programs and the activities of democratic governments.

In the last several decades, microfinance (providing tiny loans to very poor people) has grown from initial experiments to a huge global effort. Mohammed Yunus, a Bangladeshi economist, was one of the early pioneers. He discovered that providing a tiny loan of $50, $75, or $120 to buy a cow, plow, or small irrigation pump could help lift a poor family out of poverty. Yunus' Grameen Bank eventually made millions of tiny loans—and won him the Nobel Peace Prize in 2006. Large numbers of Christian organizations—led by Opportunity International—embraced microfinance and invested hundreds of millions of dollars in this popular approach. Kiva is a fairly new, rapidly growing microfinance organization that uses loans that investors are repaid to make loans to poor people.[37] By 2014, roughly 200 million borrowers were receiving microloans.

Microfinance, however, is not the silver bullet to end all global poverty. In fact, a number of recent sophisticated studies have suggested that microfinance does not produce as significant a decrease in poverty as had been thought.[38] Microfinance does help the poor acquire capital that helps them expand small businesses and smooth out the ups-and-downs of uncertain incomes. In some cases, it does help produce somewhat higher incomes for borrowers. But increasing numbers of careful studies do not find a significant increase in income for borrowers. An article in the prestigious magazine, *Foreign Affairs*, goes so far as to say that "there is only a limited increase in entrepreneurial activity [from microloans]—and no measurable decrease in poverty rates."[39] That is undoubtedly too pessimistic.[40] Distinguished development specialists continue to recommend microloans.[41]

But there are many other ways to help poor people acquire capital.

One quite new approach that is stunningly successful according to initial evaluations is to use recent innovations in cell phone banking to make direct unconditional cash grants to very poor people. Current cell phone technology makes it possible to transfer money directly to a person's cell phone account. That person can then access the money by cell phone. (The World Bank reports that mobile signals now reach 90 percent of the world's poor—and inexpensive cell phones are spreading rapidly among the poor.)[42]

GiveDirectly (started by Christian economist Paul Niehaus) illustrates the approach. They select households with thatched roofs (a good measure of poverty) in poor communities in East Africa and give each household a one-time gift of $1000—no strings attached. The person can spend the money on anything he/she chooses!

I must confess that my initial reaction was one of considerable suspicion! Would the money just be wasted? But GiveDirectly has been evaluated using a sophisticated randomized procedure to select the recipients and a control group. They were able to compare households that received the cash with very similar households that did not. The results were quite astounding. There is no increased spending on things like alcohol and tobacco. They discovered a 33 percent drop in days children in the recipient households went without food and a 116 percent increase in household investment in land, farm inputs, livestock, and housing.[43] Because of this different strategy, GiveDirectly has very little overhead. Ninety-two percent of all donations actually get to poor recipients.

GiveWell is a prominent organization that rates charity organizations. GiveWell has recommended only 1 percent of all the organizations they have reviewed. And GiveDirectly is GiveWell's number one most highly recommended charity!

It is certainly too early to know how significant this new strategy will eventually prove to be. That will be more clear in ten and twenty years. But GiveDirectly has been evaluated using the most sophisticated techniques currently available for evaluating results. All the current evidence (and that evidence continues to grow rapidly) points to a promising new approach.[44] It will be important to examine the results carefully as more organizations apply this new strategy.

The young innovators who started GiveDirectly illustrate what people are increasing calling "social entrepreneurship." Social entrepreneurs use the disciplines of the corporate world (rigorous assessment of results, adaptation, innovation, and risk-taking) to solve social problems.[45] Public good rather than private profit is their goal. Students of social entrepreneurship often cite Mohammad Yunus of the Grameen Bank as a good earlier example. Social entrepreneurs are developing a whole new range of innovative organizations to empower poor people.

Two of the most important ways to provide the poor with capital is to provide them with better education and better health care. A careful study from Kenya shows how good health is a significant form of capital. Many Kenyan children have intestinal worms that consume a good deal of the nutrients in the food they eat. Worms deprive the children of healthy bodies and minds. The program to treat children for worms costs only $1.36 per child per year. One study compared the long-term effects of school children being treated for worms for two years rather than one year—and therefore being better nourished for two years rather than one. The effect? The children treated for two years earned 20 percent more ($3,269 US dollars) every year as adults![46] Both private agencies and government programs can provide that kind of capital to poor kids.[47]

Effective government programs are also absolutely essential if we want to end the injustice of billions of people who lack the capital to participate effectively in our global market economy. Even when microloans and cash grants work very well, tiny entrepreneurs cannot flourish if they lack fair legal systems, reliable infrastructure (such as roads and communication systems), wise macroeconomic policies, and public systems of education and health care.[48] That means we must tax those with resources to guarantee basic goods like education and health care to everyone, especially the poorest members of society. Some government programs, of course, are disastrously ineffective. We should promptly abolish them! We must avoid both libertarian views that reject almost all government intervention in the economy and statist approaches that seek to abandon a basic market framework.

Measures such as the Pell Grants and the Earned Income Tax Credit (EITC) in the U.S. illustrate the kind of government redistribution program that works well. Pell Grants to college students from poor families do not encourage long-term welfare dependency. They end in a semester or two if the student fails to study and flunks out. And they create capital for a lifetime. The EITC subsidizes the income of low-income workers who faithfully carry out their responsibility to work but can find only low-paying jobs that do not provide a living wage.[49] Republican President Ronald Reagan called the EITC "the best anti-poverty, the best pro-family, the best job creation measure to come out of Congress"—precisely because it rewarded work and responsibility and worked within the market framework.

Both private and public programs to provide capital so that the poor have genuine opportunity to earn their own way are absolutely indispensable if today's market economies are to work with even minimal justice.

Failure to do that would be like freeing illiterate slaves and then providing no land, money, or education.[50]

Government Activity

What works and what doesn't? The history of communist societies clearly demonstrates that consolidating economic and political power in the same hands brings totalitarianism. We must avoid that kind of centralized power. But it is also clear today that the largest corporations and the elites who control them also wield vast political power. Highly centralized power inevitably threatens democratic life. We need intensive study of how much and what kind of government activity promotes both political freedom and economic justice. Through painstaking analysis and careful experimentation, we must discover how government can work within a basic market framework to empower the poor and restrain those aspects of today's markets that are destructive.

Libertarian views that condemn all government intervention make nonsense of twentieth-century economic history. In the U.S., most elderly folk are no longer in poverty precisely because of government-sponsored social security and Medicare. A number of antipoverty measures have failed and need drastic reform. But others—such as Pell Grants and the Earned Income Tax Credit—have been very successful.

The lesson of the Asian Tigers is not that the market will produce magic if governments will just get out of the way. Governments played a major role in the "economic miracles" of South Korea, Taiwan, and many other Asian countries. Economist Michael Todaro insists that "public-private cooperation, and not the triumph of free market and laissez-faire economics, is the real lesson of the success stories of South Korea, Taiwan, and Singapore."[51]

The South Korean miracle started with government-organized land reform. From 1952 to 1954, the percentage of farmers who owned land (rather than working as tenants) jumped from 50 to 94 percent.[52] Something similar happened in Taiwan. The governments of both countries invested heavily in health, education, and job training. The result? Their people were ready to use the most recent technologies. The productivity of labor has been growing by 10 percent a year—and half of that growth results from the state's investment in education and technical skills.[53] An activist government was central to the economic growth of South Korea and Taiwan.

Equally important was the way these governments intervened in the economy. They worked with the market rather than against it. They encouraged private enterprise and the growth of exports and refused—over the long haul—to protect the nations' companies from international competition. The right kind of market-friendly government activity is essential.[54]

The contrast between South Korea and Brazil (until 2003) is striking. Both countries have experienced rapid economic growth since 1960. The South Korean government invested heavily in health care and education for the poor, but the Brazilian government did not (until 2003). The result? In Brazil, tens of millions of poor individuals remained stuck in poverty, benefiting very little from the country's growing economy. In South Korea, by contrast, the poorest gained ground significantly (and the economy also grew faster!). By 1998, the richest one-fifth of the Korean population had about four and one-half times as much income as the poorest one-fifth. In Brazil, the ratio was worse than 30 to 1.[55] Harvard economist Amartya Sen called Brazil's pattern "unaimed opulence" and South Korea's "participatory growth." The Korean government's far greater investment in public health and education was a key to this strikingly different outcome.

But things changed in Brazil in 2003 when the people elected Luis Lula da Silva as President. Actually, the decisive movement toward a decentralization of power happened in the preceding several decades as unions and other institutions in civil society slowly grew stronger.[56] As a long-time union organizer, President da Silva was determined to reallocate substantial government resources to empower poor Brazilians. He launched a program called Zero Hunger designed to enable each Brazilian to be able to afford three meals a day. His national school feeding program provided nutritious meals to over 36 million school children—and also boosted the income of the 80,000 small family farmers who provided the food. Rural poverty rates declined and school attendance improved. Da Silva's Bolsa Familia program targeted the poorest families, providing conditional cash grants. Beneficiaries received the cash only if they agreed to do concrete things. Pregnant women had to get regular checkups. Parents had to have their children attend school and get immunizations.

In addition to allocating large new resources to empower poor Brazilians, da Sliva also maintained a strong market economy. And the economy grew at a rapid rate.

The result? Since 2004, the income of poor families has grown seven times as fast as that of the richest. From 2004–2009, extreme poverty in Brazil dropped from 10 percent to 2 percent of the total population. By 2009, income inequality in Brazil had fallen to a 50-year low.[57] The right kind of government programs combined with a vibrant market economy produces economic growth and economic empowerment of the poor.

Even the World Bank insists that "markets in developing countries cannot generally be relied upon to provide people—especially the poorest—with adequate education (especially primary education), health care, nutrition, and family-planning services."[58] The World Bank has stated bluntly: "No country has achieved significant improvement in child mortality and primary education without government involvement."[59] Governments, the World Bank says, should do less where markets work and more where they don't:

> Above all this means [government] investing in education, health, nutrition, family planning, and poverty alleviation: building social, physical, administrative, regulatory, and legal infrastructure of better quality; mobilizing the resources to finance public expenditures; and providing a stable macroeconomic foundation, without which little can be achieved. Government intervention to protect the environment is necessary for sustainable development.[60]

Nobel laureate economist Amartya Sen underlines the importance of governmental policies for overcoming poverty by reminding us that that is exactly what happened in those countries that are rich today. "In the past of the rich countries of today we can see quite a remarkable history of public action, dealing respectively with education, health care, land reforms and so on. The wide sharing of these social opportunities made it possible for the bulk of the people to participate directly in the process of economic expansion."[61]

Growing market economies do not automatically help the poor. The right kind and amount of government activity is also essential if the poor are to benefit from an expanding GNP. Recent history demonstrates that government is an essential partner along with private business if we want just, participatory growth that empowers the poorest.

Pope Francis is surely right in his insistence on a proper role for government to correct the injustice in market economies that neglect the poor while making a few exceedingly rich. "While the earnings of a minority are growing exponentially, so too is the gap separating the majority from the prosperity enjoyed by those happy few. This imbalance is the result of ideologies which defend the absolute autonomy of the market place and financial speculation. Consequently, they reject the right of states, charged with vigilance for the common good, to exercise any form of control. A new tyranny is born."[62]

New Measures of Social and Economic Well-Being

Is society better off when a huge oil spill costs a billion—or 30 billion—dollars to clean up? Or when a wealthy person hires expensive lawyers to arrange a complicated divorce? Obviously not. And yet the common (mis) understanding of the GDP would tell us that it is! In the minds of many, the GDP is our basic measure of economic progress. They assume that if the economy is growing, society is improving. This widespread notion is absurd.

Even though politicians often use it as such, the Gross Domestic Product (GDP), as we saw in chapter 8, is a poor measure of economic or social well-being.[63] To begin with, the GDP measures only economic transactions (i.e., activity where money changes hands). It does not count unpaid work in the family or the community at all! If one parent leaves paid employment to stay home to parent children, the GDP actually goes down. If Mom and Dad get a divorce—and in doing so pay lawyers, pay realtors to sell one house and buy two others, pay for "professional" childcare, etc.—GDP goes up! Volunteering to improve one's local community does not count at all.

The GDP also counts many negatives as positive growth. Indirectly, crime actually raises the GDP. How? More lawyers, police, judges, prisons, plus all kinds of crime-prevention devices, all raise the GDP. When TV and home videos replace storytelling by parents and grandparents, the

GDP goes up. When cigarette advertising creates addictive smoking, the GDP goes up. Gambling, alcoholism, and pornography all have the same wonderful result.

Environmental pollution raises the GDP twice! Once when a factory creates products with byproducts that pollute, and again when the nation spends billions to clean up the toxic site.

Equally bad is the fact that the GDP does not tell us anything about whether the current level of economic activity is sustainable. The GDP goes up today if we greatly increase economic activity by burning vast amounts of coal—even though that fills the atmosphere with much higher levels of carbon dioxide that will in turn produce devastating climate change that will decrease economic output in the future.[64]

Obviously we need a better measure of social and economic well-being. The Genuine Progress Indicator (GPI), produced by people in an organization called Redefining Progress, offers a good start.[65] Their GPI measures more than twenty things the GDP ignores.

Parents at home to care for children or grandparents get counted. So do volunteer workers in the community. These things raise the GPI.

Destructive things lower the GPI, including expenses that result from crime and any environmental pollution that damages health, agriculture, beaches, or buildings. If people work longer hours for the same pay, that also lowers the GPI. The GPI counts a nation's use of nonrenewable resources in the same way a private business does, not the way government does. When a private company uses up its nonrenewable resources, it counts that as a cost. But when a nation does the same thing to its oil and other minerals, the GDP counts it as a gain.

GPI studies have now been done for 17 different countries that together include 53 percent of the world's total production—including the U.S., Germany, India, and China. Several countries, the European Union, and a couple states in the U.S. now take the GPI into account as they examine their economic well-being.

Striking things have become clear when one compares a longitudinal study over time of the growth (or decline) of both GDP and GPI. Since 1950, with very short breaks and exceptions, the GDP of almost all countries has continued to climb. But after an initial rise of GPI as GDP increased, the GPI has leveled off or even declined. In the U.S., both GDP and GPI increased steadily until about 1978. After that, GDP continued to grow but the overall quality of life measured by the GPI did not continue to improve.[66] In China, the GDP and GPI rose together from about 1978 to 1997. Since 1997, the GDP has continued to climb dramatically but the GPI has not as pollution, the depletion of non-renewable resources, crime, and family breakdown have all increased.[67]

This pattern also holds at the global level. GDP of course, climbs ever higher. But globally, overall economic welfare has not improved since 1978. "If we hope to achieve a sustainable and desirable future, we need to rapidly shift our policy focus away from maximizing production and consumption (GDP) towards improving genuine human well-being (GPI or something similar)." That means more attention to "environmental protection, full employment, social equity, better product quality and durability."[68]

The people at Redefining Progress may or may not have all the details right.[69] We need not accept their detailed findings to recognize that they have raised a very basic issue. Indeed, in the last two decades, many people, including the World Bank and most European nations, have been working on better ways to measure social and economic growth.[70]

One potential result of this kind of new analysis is that it has the possibility of bringing environmentalists and social conservatives closer together. Environmentalists deplore the way an unrestricted market economy destroys the environment. Social conservatives denounce the way a preoccupation with economic growth (which demands ever-more consumption) destroys the family and communal life.

Redefining Progress has raised some fundamental issues about the nature of "economic growth." But the problem really lies deeper than they indicate. During the eighteenth-century Enlightenment, a human-centered, pseudoscientific view of reality replaced the historic God-centered view. The autonomous individual replaced God as the source of ethics. The scientific method became the only avenue to truth. Nature, according to naturalistic scientist Carl Sagan, is all that exists.

Tragically, this new view abandons the limits of economic growth imposed by historic Christian faith. In a God-centered, biblical worldview, persons, family, and God's good creation matter more than money and unlimited material consumption. The scientific method, however, cannot measure love or joy in the family. But it can measure a growing bank account, larger cars, and increasingly sophisticated gadgets. Modern folk cast aside the limits imposed on economic life by the biblical truth that Yahweh is Lord even of economics. The result has been preoccupation with economic growth that is now devastating the family, community life, and the environment.

Jesus' question is still relevant: Do we want to worship God and therefore accept God's perspective on everything, including the fact that quality family life is more important than economic growth and more gadgets? Or do we prefer to absolutize the material world and the things that scientific technology can produce?

Getting a more accurate measure of social and economic well-being via some new Genuine Progress Indicator will not answer that fundamental question. But it will make it easier for us to think about it more carefully if we really want to choose God rather than mammon.

Redefining the Good Life

It is idolatrous nonsense to suggest that human fulfillment comes from an ever-increasing supply of material things. Genuine, lasting joy comes from a right relationship with God, neighbor, self, and the earth. As body-soul beings created for community, we do need significant material resources. But looking for happiness in ever-expanding material wealth is both theologically heretical and environmentally destructive. It also hardens our hearts to the cries of the poor.

We must redefine "the good life." We must develop a theology of enough. We must meditate on Proverbs 23:4 until it seeps deep into our psyches: "Do not wear yourself out to get rich; have the wisdom to show restraint" (NIV). We must develop models of simpler lifestyles; corporate policies that permit people to choose parenting, leisure, and community service over maximizing income and profits; and macroeconomic policies and advertising practices that discourage overconsumption. Unlimited economic growth is an economic Tower of Babel, not a biblical goal.

The developed world should consume less and pollute less. But there are complications. As MIT economist Lester Thurow has pointed out, given today's economic structures, environmental crusades that reduce growth and advocate greater pollution control may well benefit the middle and upper classes at the expense of the poor. Under current structures, reducing growth may lead to a rise in unemployment, which hits the poor (both here and abroad) harder than the rich. Increased pollution-control equipment may raise the prices of goods needed by the poor. Furthermore, a cleaner environment may well raise the standard of living of the wealthier classes who retain their jobs and have enough money to get out and enjoy the enhanced environment."

Few economists doubt the validity of this analysis. But that does not mean we should ignore environmental pollution as we seek to help the poor. Rather, Thurow's warning illuminates the size and complexity of the obstacles we must overcome.

The pervasive notion that increased consumption leads to greater happiness is at the heart of our dilemma. In fact, even some economists understand that economic growth and rising affluence do not guarantee greater happiness. Economist Richard Easterlin has argued that people tend to measure their happiness by how much they consume relative to their neighbors. As all try to get ahead, he argued, most tend to rise together so everyone is frustrated by their unsuccessful efforts to achieve happiness by getting ahead of the others! Easterlin concluded: "To the outside observer, economic growth appears to be producing an ever-more affluent society, but to those involved in the process, affluence will always remain a distant, urgently sought, but never attained goal."[72]

Growth occurs, the earth is used and abused—but happiness is still beyond one's grasp. To Christians this should be no surprise. We should be the first to reject this rat race in which everyone is trying to surpass the other guy. Knowing that material goods are not what brings ultimate happiness, we should be the first to experiment with simpler lifestyles. As we reduce our demand for dwindling resources that pollute the environment, we witness to others that happiness is not found primarily in material possessions.

As we move in this direction, however, we need to be alert to Thurow's warning. If, in our advanced state of technology, significant numbers of people consume less, there will be less need for production. Declining demand will signal a decline in the need for workers. Therefore, we need long-term structural changes if displaced workers are to find other jobs. Due to the monumental proportions of the changes needed, they must be made slowly and gradually. The suggestions I offer, therefore, are for both the immediate and the more distant future.

In the short run, a simpler lifestyle lived by Christians will mean more money not being spent on consumption goods. If large numbers of people save rather than spend this income, severe unemployment might ensue. If, however, we donate the income we have saved to Christian agencies promoting development in poor nations, a major reduction in employment is unlikely. Aid recipients will spend the money on goods they need to create wealth and attain an adequate level of material well-being. As they do, many of the dollars spent on these goods will eventually return to buy things from businesses in industrialized nations. As the developed nations consume less and share more, we will also spur indigenous development in the developing nations, thus fostering a more just distribution of goods and assets.

As we adopt this short-run approach, Christians all over the world ought to reexamine priorities at a still deeper level. Suppose that by a miracle of God's grace we succeeded in ending the scandal of a world where a billion people live in grinding poverty while the affluent live like kings. Even if we reached the biblical norm of distributional justice, we would have to ask ourselves the next question: Should we again pursue the same sort of economic growth we formerly did? The obvious answer is no. The earth's resources are limited, and we dare not destroy the environment.

Christians must strive to redirect the demand for goods and services away from heavy resource usage and environment-damaging goods toward goods and services that make less demand on the earth's carrying capacity. Christians could spend more of their time and money creating vibrant, active Christian churches. Everyone could spend more money on the arts (drama, music, and other creative expressions), thus creating an incentive for more people to engage in these activities instead of in the production of more material goods. People could work fewer hours at their jobs, and in their new leisure they could do volunteer work in their community or spend more time with their families or in constructive hobbies.[73]

In the long run, sweeping changes will eventually come. Hopefully, Christians will lead the way in redefining the good life by returning to a biblical understanding of what produces joy and happiness.[74]

I am not a pessimist. Continued wise use of modern technology and market economies can offer new hope to those who are still poor. It is possible, within the framework of market economies, to empower most of the world's people to enjoy a generously adequate level of material well-being without creating environmental catastrophe. But to accomplish that we must make sure that the poor have access to capital, that government plays its proper role, and that society rediscovers the ancient faith that persons do not live by bread alone.

Making International Trade More Fair

We saw in chapter 8 how unfairness in international trade hurts poor countries. According to a recent estimate, restriction on free trade cost poor countries $291 billion a year—over twice what rich nations provide in foreign aid.[75] Developed nations should drastically reduce or eliminate trade barriers on imports from the developing countries.

Trade barriers hurt not only poor nations but also the average person in rich nations. Without trade barriers, we could buy many imported goods more cheaply. Trade barriers cost Americans tens of billions of dollars every year. That means a loss of hundreds of dollars for every family.[76] Without those barriers, of course, the developing nations could be better off because they could increase both their production and income via increased exports.

Rich nations must end their agricultural subsidies. Unfortunately, this is easier said than done. First, because powerful political interests in rich nations lobby hard to defend their subsidies. Second, because these subsidies actually make the global price of some food cheaper. Abrupt, across the board cuts would shock the global food system in a potentially harmful way. And third, eliminating agricultural subsidies in rich nations does not automatically mean increased incomes for developing nations. Many developing nations lack the infrastructure and technical capacity to rapidly expand their agricultural output.[77] Changes to these subsidies need to be done in a way that allows global markets to adjust in a gradual way.

Professor Joseph Stiglitz, a prominent economist, gives three "key components" for eliminating agricultural subsidies.[78] First, the trade barriers imposed by rich nations on products that are primarily produced in developing countries should be rapidly eliminated. This would increase the income developing countries receive with the least increase on consumer prices in developing countries. Cotton would fall into this category; removing cotton subsidies in the United States and the European Union would increase West African cotton exports by $250 million annually.[79] Second, subsidies that have lowered the price of grains (such as wheat, soybeans, and corn) should be reduced gradually. Many developing countries currently rely on imports of these grains and time is needed to allow developing countries to expand production of these vital food sources. Third, the subsidies in rich nations that protect the environment and protect farmers from natural disasters must be redesigned. For example, the current U.S. crop insurance program costs taxpayers $9 billion annually, but no limits are put on how much a single farmer can earn and farmers are not required to adopt environmental protections.[80]

Studies that predict the global gains from making all trade free suggest that over half of the gains will come from eliminating barriers to agricultural trade.[81] This will benefit the most poor people because 75 percent of people who are poor in developing countries live in rural areas and most depend on agriculture for their livelihood. Addressing barriers to agricultural trade is also the most effective because growth in the agricultural sector of the economy is at least twice as effective in reducing poverty as growth in other sectors.[82]

Rich nations must also end their tariffs and import quotas, especially on those goods that developing countries have a special advantage producing. One study demonstrated that if the complex tariff and quota rules governing apparel imports to the U.S. had been removed, the exports of clothing from Africa would have been five times greater.[83]

Ending agricultural subsidies and eliminating tariffs and quotas on imports from developing countries, however, is not enough. We should work to make all trade freer and fairer. According to a recent analysis, if seven broad proposals that were a part of the Bali meeting (2013) of the Doha Round negotiations are enacted, global exports may increase by $2 trillion and over 34 million jobs may be supported.[84]

Unfortunately, there is no guarantee whatsoever that the Doha Round of trade negotiations will succeed. Year after year, for the past twenty years, the Doha Round has failed to achieve significant progress. Parliaments and congresses in rich nations will have to make wise but painful decisions if the poor are to benefit.[85]

Powerful interests in rich nations will fight back, desperately trying to protect their narrow self-interest. They have, after all, been very successful—every dollar spent by the agricultural lobby yields $2,000 in government transfers.[86] Only if concerned citizens in rich nations develop the political will to demand that their politicians remove these trade barriers will there be any substantial change. It depends on you and me. We must tell our congressional leaders and presidential candidates that we demand the end of trade barriers against poor nations.

It is politically difficult to remove such trade restrictions because the people employed in the businesses protected by them will suffer. Although the numbers would be relatively small, considering the size of our total economy, some people (especially lower income workers) will lose their jobs. But there is a remedy for this problem. It is called adjustment assistance.[87] Adjustment assistance is a government program designed to facilitate the movement of unemployed workers into new areas of employment. It compensates workers for the period during which they are unemployed, and it helps them to relocate and find jobs with comparable pay.

A relatively modest sacrifice by rich Northerners would produce major benefits in the South. And in the long run, economists expect, the North would not even lose jobs. As developing nations turn to industrialized countries to spend their new income, the businesses they patronized would need to hire the displaced workers to meet the new demand. In the short run, however, there will be a cost to removing trade barriers. Will Christian voters be more concerned about hungry people abroad or economic convenience at home?

Merely removing restrictions on imports, however, does not guarantee that the poor in developing nations will enjoy the benefits. If local governing elites seize the land of peasants so that they and multinational corporations can grow crops for export, only the rich benefit. If local governing elites suppress labor unions so that the workers who manufacture the goods for export receive very low wages, only the rich benefit.

How, then, can we remove our trade barriers in such a way that the poorest people will benefit? We can use diplomacy and economic aid to encourage democratic institutions, strengthen civil society, and nurture free, strong trade unions. Improving working conditions is especially important.

The good news is that study after study has shown that increased trade results in higher wages, both in developed and developing countries. Studies have also shown that trade ultimately leads to better working conditions.[88] We can work to facilitate decent standards for workers at four levels: international, national, corporate, and as individual consumers.

International standards are especially important. Otherwise, individual nations with despicable working conditions have a comparative advantage.[89]

The International Labor Organization's conventions provide a good starting point internationally. These standards include: (1) the right and freedom of association; (2) the right to organize and bargain collectively; (3) prohibitions against forced labor; (4) standards for wages and worker safety; and (5) a minimum age for child labor.[90] Most nations have endorsed these standards. But they are often ignored because there is no global enforcement mechanism. That is needed.[91]

Developed nations can also do far more. I have already shown that the U.S. has largely ignored the rights of workers in its global trade negotiations. That needs to change. A concern for unions and working conditions should become a central focus of concern and aggressive action in the trade policy of all developed nations. That will help workers in both poor and rich nations.

Corporations can also play a significant role—and you and I can encourage them! Some large corporations have already adopted codes of conduct to improve workers' rights and environmental protection in their global operations. Christian executives can encourage that from the inside. Consumers can do the same from the outside—with letters and conscientious decisions about where to buy things.[92]

Fair labor practices around the globe are essential if the poor are to receive their fair share of the benefits of growing international trade.

Making Multinational Corporations More Just

At one level just to write such a headline sounds like utopian dreaming. MNCs' huge size give them enormous power (29 of the world's 100 largest economies are corporations.[93]) Their global reach means that no one country can regulate them because they have the power to move their operations to other countries that offer more favorable conditions.

MNCs have, increasingly in the last several decades, "outsourced" their production of all kinds of things to countries where wages were low, unions weak, and environmental and safety regulations poor to nonexistent. Repeatedly, stories have emerged of factories in developing nations producing products for famous brands like Nike and Apple where the workers worked very long hours at low wages in dangerous situations.

One of the most obvious ways to regulate MNCs would be via the many global trade agreements. Tragically, people representing workers' concerns and environmental issues have had only a very small role in the negotiation of international trade agreements. In the early 1990s, there were three major advisory committees in the U.S. for global trade negotiations. They had a total of 111 members. But 92 represented individual corporations and 16 represented trade associations. Only two represented unions and only one represented environmental groups.[94] That must change. People representing the interests of workers and the environment must play a far more important role in all international trade negotiations. Citizens of industrialized nations can demand that their politicians appoint such people to the relevant bodies and make workers' rights and environmental concerns far more important in international trade negotiations.

A second way to pressure MNCs to change is via the people who purchase companies' stocks. Increasingly, people have embraced "ethical investing" and are buying stocks that have been screened to avoid companies involved with tobacco, alcohol, or bad labor and environmental practices.[95] In addition, many people with stock have joined shareholder actions in which groups of shareholders attend a corporation's annual meeting to protest unjust corporate action and demand change. The Interfaith Center on Corporate Responsibility has a long, distinguished history of leading shareholder actions and providing excellent information on how to pressure MNCs to be more fair.[96]

One of the more effective ways of pressuring MNCs to correct bad practices has been the boycotts, protests, and media campaigns by a wide variety of organizations in civil society. The response of two huge MNCs, Nike and Nestlé, demonstrates that such activity can compel significant change.

For decades, Nike has manufactured all its famous running shoes in factories owned and operated by others in poor countries with low wages, bad working conditions, and weak unions. During one year in the mid-1990s, the famous American basketball player Michael Jordan made as much money advertising Nike sneakers as 18,000 factory workers in Indonesia made in producing many of those shoes.[97] When one of the Indonesian factory workers tried to organize a union to demand better wages and treatment for the workers, he was fired. And the Indonesian military locked him up for seven days.[98] A 1997 audit showed that workers manufacturing Nike's sneakers in Vietnam were paid less than the minimum wage, were exposed to dangerous chemicals, and were subject to sexual harassment.[99]

Then activists launched a massive campaign. University students led protests and boycotts. In 1999, forty-five human rights organizations wrote to Nike demanding an end to low wages and human rights abuses in factories producing Nike's shoes. At first, Nike said it had no responsibility for the conditions in factories owned and operated by others who contracted to produce its shoes. But the protests began to damage Nike's image—and bottom line.

Nike decided to accept responsibility for the labor practices of its suppliers. In a May 1998 speech at the national Press Club, Nike's CEO (Phil Knight) admitted that "the Nike product has become synonymous with slave wages, forced overtime, and arbitrary abuse."[100] In 2000, Nike's CEO was the only American CEO to attend UN Secretary General Kofi Annan's launch of the Global Compact to promote more responsible business practices. Nike called for mandatory global standards—thus pressuring its competitors to "share the financial burden of securing a regulated level of worker conditions in global supply chains."[101] An article in the *Harvard*

Business Review has shown how Nike moved from denying responsibility for working conditions in the factories of its suppliers to accepting responsibility to correct bad conditions there.[102] That is not to say that all problems have been solved. But Nike has improved the working conditions in its supply chains—thanks to the vigorous protest by a variety of civil society organizations. Sustained public protest can change even huge MNCs.

In chapter 8, we saw how Nestlé, the huge Swiss MNC, has used manipulative practices around the world to persuade poor mothers to buy infant formula instead of breast-feeding, which is far cheaper and more healthy. Here, too, a massive global boycott has pressured Nestlé to make significant changes. There are still problems with Nestlé. But in 2013, the person whose book played a key role in launching the Nestlé boycott in 1974 thanked Nestlé's CEO for the progress they had made.[103]

In a somewhat parallel fashion, there has been a global response of outrage to the collapse of the Rana Plaza building in 2013 in Bangladesh where 1,129 poorly paid garment workers died. Global public opinion has forced both European and American MNCs to agree to take at least some responsibility for safety and other working conditions in the factories where the clothes are produced.[104]

Protests, boycotts, and advocacy by groups in civil society can pressure MNCs to correct some unjust practices. Christians should add their voices by using the resources of major advocacy groups working to promote more just labor, safety, and environmental practices by MNCs.[105]

Preserving the Earth and Empowering the Poor

We have polluted the environment so severely that everyone, especially the poor, faces grave dangers (see chapter 8). What can be done?

There are a lot of promising steps for improving our environment. But they all cost money! In the short run, therefore, the temptation is to continue old patterns even though they pollute cities, destroy our forests and lakes, and lead to likely disaster in the next one hundred years.

Restoring environmental integrity is a task for individuals and governments, children and adults, churches and businesses. It can be worked on at every level. Each family can make a difference by practicing the three Rs: reduce, reuse, and recycle (in that order). Churches can teach biblical principles—like temperance, patience, justice, and self-restraint— which are essential if we are to develop a sustainable society. Businesses must prepare to shoulder more costs, and politicians must dare to adopt more courageous public policies.[106]

The basic direction we need to travel is fairly clear. We want to make decisions now that will allow our grandchildren and their grandchildren to have a decent, sustainable life. We want their future to be one where they can continue to rejoice in the earth's goodness and splendor. Therefore, we must end the degradation of the environment by making changes in the way we think, believe, and act. Some changes, such as using public transportation and buying a fuel-efficient vehicle, are a matter of individual choice. Others (e.g., the availability of good public transportation) involve forces and institutions that no individual or family can change by themselves. Yet all these changes are necessary, and they all will be difficult.

Government action is essential. Without rules that apply to all, businesses that invest in pollution controls and environmental sanity are at a competitive disadvantage with callous competitors who continue dumping on everyone. In the short run, the market ignores environmental costs. Therefore, legislation that justly compels all businesses to end pollution places all competitors on an even playing field.

If this is true for businesses, it is also true for nations. Pollution does not respect international boundaries. For many countries, a great deal of the pollution degrading their nation comes from abroad. And they in turn export much of the pollution they produce. So if one country decides to spend the money to reduce pollution, and surrounding nations refuse, the investment improves the lives of ornery, selfish neighbors as well as its own citizens.

International standards are essential. Some things can be done only by strengthened global institutions like the United Nations. Obviously, it would be unwise to centralize vast power in any one global agency. (Centralized power in a fallen world is always dangerous.) But that does not mean we can ignore the need for strengthened global institutions to deal with our inextricably interrelated countries on planet Earth. While we do that, however, we must be careful both to do all we can on a local level and also to make sure there are careful checks and balances for the centralized global institutions that the environmental crisis requires.

The good news is that not just scientists but business leaders have come to the conclusion that we must act vigorously to combat climate change. A cover story in *Business Week* (August 16, 2004) pointed out that business is "far ahead of Congress and the White House." In 2007, 150 global firms (including Shell Oil, General Electric, and DuPont) joined in "a call for a comprehensive, legally binding United Nations framework to tackle climate change."[107] In 2013, the President and CEO of Walmart praised President Obama for his commitment to renewable energy and conservation and noted that the Environmental Protection Agency had named Walmart the number one user of onsite renewable energy.[108] And in June 2014, President Obama announced significant plans to cut carbon pollution from U.S. power plants by 30 percent from 2005 levels by the year 2030.

That is the good news. The bad news is that enormous opposition to substantial proposals to dramatically cut carbon emissions exists in many countries around the world. No binding global agreement to reduce greenhouse gas emissions enough to avoid dramatic climate change has emerged in spite of the increasingly dire warnings by our best scientists. In fact, "in the first decade of this century, emissions actually grew at twice the pace of the preceding three decades."[109]

We must act now if we want to pass on a livable world to our grandchildren. Our scientists tell us that to avoid catastrophic climate change, we must reduce greenhouse gas emissions enough so that global temperatures will not rise more than 2° Celsius (3.6° Fahrenheit) above what they were before the Industrial Revolution began.

There are many ways to work at reducing the carbon emissions that occur when we burn fossil fuels (coal, oil, gas). We need to greatly expand the use of renewable energy—i.e., more generation of electricity using energy from the sun, wind, and water. And we need to learn how to use less energy by making our transportation systems, cars, appliances, and buildings more efficient.

These changes will require action at every level: our personal lives, our churches, and our governments.

We can organize our lives so that it is easier and more desirable to walk,

253

bike, carpool, and use public transportation more and personal vehicles less. When we move, we can choose a location that accomplishes the same. When a new passenger vehicle is required, we should purchase the most fuel-efficient and least polluting vehicle available that truly fits our needs and does not significantly threaten our safety or the safety of others.

Christian business leaders should encourage their employees to use public transportation and participate in ride-share programs, avoid subsidized parking, and purchase fuel-efficient business vehicles.

Local churches should educate their congregations about public transportation options available both for their daily activities and for church services, and create ride-share programs to transport members to worship services and church activities. Churches, denominations, and Christian organizations should educate their members that transportation choices are moral choices.

Christians and Christian organizations and denominations should advocate for government policies that make it easy for individuals to do the right thing when it comes to transportation. This includes:

- making communities pedestrian- and bike-friendly;
- making public transportation easily accessible, readily available, and affordable;
- requiring new passenger vehicles to be more fuel efficient by raising fuel economy (CAFÉ) standards significantly (President Obama made great strides in this area, but CAFÉ standards need to continue to demand more fuel efficiency);
- supporting research and development for hydrogen fuel cells and other promising alternative technologies;
- promptly implementing government policies that dramatically reduce greenhouse gas emissions.

There are a variety of ways that governments can act to reduce carbon emissions (e.g., "cap and trade" policies and a carbon tax). But a carbon tax is almost certainly the best. A carbon tax would be the most efficient and market-friendly. Even the CEO of Exxon Mobil, the huge oil company, has said he supports a carbon tax on greenhouse gas emissions.[110]

The calculations would not be exact, but scientists and economists could estimate the real costs of fossil fuels—including all the negative environmental results of the present pollution and the future costs of global warming. Since coal produces the most carbon, the tax on coal would be the highest—then oil, then gas. Renewable energies, such as that from sun and wind, produce no carbon emissions and therefore would suffer no tax. A carbon tax would mean the market would then work to apply the real costs of pollution. Having it be revenue-neutral (i.e., the government could offset any tax increase by decreasing other taxes by the same amount) would mean that those who do the right thing and reduce their use of fossil fuels would actually get a tax cut (if the laws were written properly).

A serious carbon tax that would truly make a difference must be steep. Many economists suggest that gasoline prices in the U.S. should double. That kind of change would be politically difficult, but less so once the revenue-neutral aspect is successfully communicated. It is time for the U.S. to enact a steep carbon tax—although it should be phased in over a number of years to give people and businesses time to adjust.

The U.S. should take the lead since for decades the U.S. was the largest producer of carbon emissions. North America and Western Europe have created the problem. Any successful effort to avoid catastrophic global warming, of course, must include all countries. (China recently passed the United States as the largest producer of carbon emissions.) But acknowledging that we have been largely responsible for creating the problem and then taking the lead to correct the problem will help us persuade all nations, especially the newly industrializing nations like China, India, and Brazil, to join in a global agreement to avoid devastating global warming.

Doomsayers predict that cutting greenhouse gas emissions enough to prevent the earth from warming more than 2° Celsius above pre-industrial levels would have devastating economic consequences. But they are wrong. The Intergovernmental Panel on Climate Change (IPCC) is the global body that almost everyone recognizes as providing the best current information. And their most recent report indicates that taking the steps now to avoid more than a 2° Celsius rise in temperatures would only slow down economic growth by .14 percent—a mere fraction of the typical annual growth of 3–4 percent.[111] Surely we can make that kind of modest sacrifice for our grandchildren and the poor.

At the same time, we must invest more seriously in effective programs to end widespread global poverty. We cannot preserve the earth without empowering the poor because poverty contributes to environmental degradation (see chapter 8). Poor, desperate people chop down rain forests and damage marginal lands unsuited for farming. Rich nations must understand that to preserve a decent global environment, they must do more than recycle garbage or collect expensive carbon taxes. They must also use some of their abundance to reduce the poverty of desperate people driven to environmentally destructive behavior because they have no other way to feed their children. We cannot have environmental integrity without justice.

Does Foreign Aid Help?

Two things complicate any discussion of foreign aid in the United States. First, Americans think that the U.S. is already spending a huge percent of the federal budget on foreign aid, and they want major cuts. And second, there are a number of harsh critics who charge that most foreign aid is wasted and/or useless.

For decades, polls have consistently shown that most Americans think that the U.S. devotes 20–25 percent of the federal budget to foreign aid. In a November 1995 poll, the *Washington Post* discovered that the average respondent thought the United States spends 26 percent of the federal budget on foreign aid. They suggested that 13 percent would be more reasonable. The actual figure for official development assistance was 0.5 percent—only 1/52 of what the people thought.[112] A 2001 poll by the University of Maryland found similar results: "Most Americans think the United States spends about 24 percent of its annual budget on foreign aid."[113] More recent polls show the same thing. The 2013 poll by the highly respected Kaiser Family Foundation found that on average, Americans think 28 percent of the federal budget goes to foreign aid![114]

In fact, the U.S. typically spends less than 1 percent of the federal budget on foreign economic aid. That is vastly less than the 20–28 percent that most Americans think—and even vastly less than the 10–13 percent they sometimes say would be fine.

In reality, the U.S. is one of the least generous among industrialized nations when foreign aid is measured as a percent of the total economy of a country. The U.S. gives a mere one-fifth of one percent (.19) of its total Gross National Income (GNI) in overseas development assistance, whereas Norway gives 1.07 percent, Sweden 1.02 percent, and Great Britain .72 percent.[115]

Net ODA in 2013 — as a Percentage of GNI

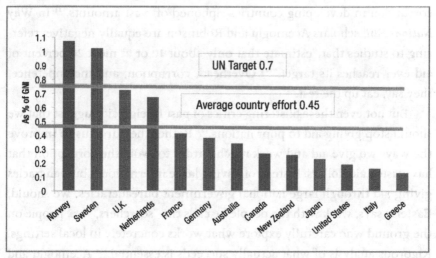

Source: OECD, 2014[116]

Measured in terms of a nation's total economy, the U.S. is one of the most stingy countries in the developed world in terms of its official economic development assistance.

It is also true that because the U.S. has the largest economy in the world, even .2 percent of our GNI is a lot of money. In actual dollars, the U.S. is by far the largest donor of official economic development assistance. Another important part of the total picture is that American religious agencies annually give many billions (perhaps at least $7.5 billion) to combat global poverty.[117] Globally, the amount and percent of total development assistance coming from private NGOs has increased dramatically—from 5 percent of total development assistance in 1992 to 27 percent by 2008.[118] And the U.S. contributes almost two-thirds of that total private contribution.[119]

The U.S. is more generous in helping poor nations than is sometimes said. But in comparison to what would be possible, we are still far from generous.

What about the second issue—the charge that U.S. foreign aid is largely wasted or even counter-productive? In *The White Man's Burden*, William Easterly argues that much of the $2.3 trillion in Western foreign aid given in the last five decades to poor countries has been wasted. Foreign experts worked with national elites in poor countries in a top-down approach that failed to understand what was needed on the ground.[120] Widespread corruption in developing countries siphoned off vast amounts.[121] In *Why Nations Fail*, scholars Acemoglu and Robinson are equally negative, referring to studies that "estimate that only about 10 or at most 20 percent of aid ever reaches its target."[122] Overhead, corruption, and incompetence, they say, eat up the rest.

But not even these blistering critics of past foreign aid suggest that we should stop giving aid to poor nations.[123] Rather they urge us to improve the ways we give aid and work much harder to avoid the corruption that has wasted aid dollars. Instead of having large international bureaucracies giving aid through large national government bureaucracies, we should, Easterly says, work with the people he calls the "searchers," i.e., people on the ground who carefully explore what works concretely in local settings. Rigorous analysis of what actually succeeds is essential.[124] Acemoglu and Robinson stress the importance of channeling aid in such a way that it helps to decentralize power and promotes democracy and the reduction of corruption.[125]

While it is true that too much development assistance has been wasted and ineffective, the harsh critics overlook truly fantastic progress in reducing poverty and improving health in poor nations. There has been enormous success. In 1967, smallpox killed two million people in the world. By 1981, smallpox had totally disappeared. Why? A massive coordinated program to eradicate this killer by governments, donors, and health researchers. Millions of dollars in U.S. foreign aid helped defeat smallpox.[126] Millions of Africans are living with instead of dying of AIDS because of President George W. Bush's PEPFAR program, which has devoted billions of dollars to treating Africans who have AIDS. Global immunization programs supported by the United States save the lives of more than two million children every year.[127] Industrialized nations greatly expanded their foreign aid (by 275 percent!) from 2001–2010. Aid to sub-Saharan Africa jumped from $12 billion in 2000 to $42 billion by 2010. Over that decade nine of the ten countries experiencing the largest progress in human development (less poverty, better health) were in sub-Saharan Africa—precisely the countries that received especially large amounts of foreign development assistance.[128] The United States is the largest donor of food aid. Since the program began in 1961, three billion people have received food aid.[129]

Foreign aid has helped billions of people and saved many tens of millions of lives. We should continue, even increase it, not cut it. But it certainly can and should be improved. How can we do that?

Here are nine suggestions for improving governmental foreign aid.

1. *Focus on the poorest of the poor.* The purpose of economic foreign aid should be to enable the most vulnerable people in the poorest nations to meet their own basic needs. Since most poor people live in rural areas (although increasing numbers now live in urban slums), the focus must be on integrated rural development with sustainable activities. This usually means land reform; agricultural extension services including credit, improved seeds, and fertilizer; rural public works programs such as irrigation projects; agricultural research; introduction of appropriate technology; and the development of light industry and improved infrastructure to complement the agricultural development.

It is particularly important that basic, minimal health care, education, and a secure and nutritious food supply be available to rural communities.[130] This is essential, first for the sake of justice and second because it is especially effective. For one thing, it is a crucial part of slowing the population explosion. Furthermore, the American Feed the Future initiative reports that "growth in the agriculture sector is at least twice as effective in reducing poverty as growth in other sectors."[131] A study by the World Bank concluded, "In all developing countries, policies [that] succeed in improving the conditions of life for the poor, and in providing education and employment opportunities for women, are likely to reduce fertility. An improvement in the welfare of the poor appears to be essential before fertility can fall to developed country levels."[132]

Such a conclusion should not surprise the Christian. If, as the Bible teaches, God is at work in history liberating the poor and oppressed, then we should expect that an effective development strategy would be one that brings justice to poor people. At the same time this approach to development focused on the poorest of the poor provides a decisive answer to "lifeboat" theorists. Foreign aid to promote rural development is not a foolish gesture that sustains millions now only to doom even more later. Rather, foreign aid that encourages sustainable agricultural production, thus improving livelihoods, as well as (at the least) minimal education and health care among the rural masses, especially women, is probably the best way to slow down population growth. Justice and effectiveness coincide.

Tragically, a great deal of U.S. economic assistance has not gone to the truly poor. A great deal of U.S. foreign aid has been heavily concentrated in countries where the United States has strong political or security interests. The same is true for other nations.[133] From 2006 to 2012, the three countries that received the most economic aid from the U.S. were Afghanistan ($21.7 billion); Israel ($18.7 billion); Egypt $11.6 billion).[134] Afghanistan (where the U.S. has huge political interests) is certainly poor but it has a smaller population than Bangladesh, which only received $1 billion. Israel is a *tiny rich* country but received the second largest amount of U.S. economic assistance! Egypt and Ethiopia have about the same number of people, but Egypt's per capita income is seven times greater than that of Ethiopia.[135] In spite of being much richer, Egypt received more than twice as much economic development assistance as Ethiopia—because of Egypt's cooperation with Israel. Political connections trump need.

2. Channel more aid through local organizations while at the same time promoting more effective, transparent governmental institutions free from corruption. Strengthening civil society by empowering local, indigenous NGOs decentralizes power. So does strengthening local governmental agencies so that they and indigenous NGOs are decisively involved in planning and implementing all programs.[136] At the same time, fostering transparent, effective national governmental institutions is also essential because sustainable development requires effective governmental structures able to deliver essential services and public goods to its citizens.

3. Focus on empowerment. Development assistance should empower the powerless. Empowerment of the poor will often mean land reform. It will certainly mean, as Gary Haugen says so powerfully in *The Locust Effect*, working to end the political corruption by which the powerful maintain oppressive systems.[137] It will mean an end to the violation of human rights. And it will also involve the promotion of unions and other civil society organizations that enable the poor to exercise influence in shaping their societies. Obviously, empowering the poor will threaten some oppressive corrupt elites currently in power—in the local village, the state, the nation, and the globe. But only if development assistance empowers the poor so that they can shape their own destiny will it foster justice rather than dependence. Our government-to-government assistance ought to go primarily to countries that agree to an overall development strategy to empower the absolutely poor by means of land reform, secure human rights, secure property rights, and an open democratic process.

4. Deemphasize the donor's political and economic interests. Short-term economic and political considerations have hindered the effectiveness of foreign aid.[138] Too much aid continues to go to nations because they are currently of geopolitical interest to the donor. The long-range goal of a global society free of widespread hunger and poverty, rather than immediate political or economic concerns, should govern the granting of aid.

One big problem is the fact that the United States has "tied" a good portion of its aid, especially food aid, demanding that the money be used to purchase U.S. goods and services.[139] In 2012, the U.S. provided about $2 billion in food aid helping to save millions of lives. But most food aid in the American Food for Peace program must be grown in the U.S.—thanks to lobbying by American farmers. Usually, however, it is quite possible to purchase locally or regionally grown food. That helps farmers in developing countries and it is on average, 30 percent cheaper. So the same money will buy more food and save more lives!

Also problematic is the fact that current law requires that half of all U.S. food aid be shipped on American vessels—thanks to lobbying by U.S. shipping interests. That typically adds 60 cents to every dollar spent on food aid and delays delivery—sometimes the food takes six months to arrive via U.S. ships!

Ending these two areas of "tying aid" would not significantly harm U.S. economic interests. U.S. food aid is less than 1 percent of total American agricultural exports. And food aid shipped in U.S. vessels is a tiny fraction of all U.S. shipping. In order to make American food aid more efficient and save more lives, U.S. citizens should demand that our legislators end this kind of "tying" aid.[140]

5. *Nurture economic sustainability.* We dare not continue destroying the world's soil, water, and forests. Northern capital-intensive farming, for instance, is frequently not a model to promote in developing nations. Our aid should promote appropriate technology and a labor-intensive approach that is sensitive to preserving a sound global ecosystem.[141]

6. *Emphasize developing country ownership.*[142] The U.S. foreign aid program was not designed to foster local ownership. Too often, a few foreign "experts" decided what developing communities needed. Congressional earmarks and Presidential initiatives continue to determine the shape of much U.S. development assistance.[143] Developing countries can take it or leave it.

All U.S. development agencies should involve local actors in shaping every stage of development assistance, starting with the initial planning. There should be far fewer Congressional earmarks and Presidential directives. "The U.S. government should actively promote and invest in developing country-led efforts to ensure that all citizens, including the poorest, marginalized populations, and women and girls, can participate in the process of setting development priorities that inform both donor and country budget allocation decisions."[144] Local developing country institutions (governments, civil society organizations) should be the normal option for delivering assistance. "Local capacity building and local agenda-setting" should become standard.[145] The Obama administration's Feed the Future initiative stresses "country-led" development.

7. *Separate development aid from military aid.* U.S. citizens are sometimes confused because military aid and economic assistance both appear in the annual U.S. foreign aid bill appropriating money for developing countries.[146] Military aid should be appropriated separately from development aid.

8. *Emphasize better education, nutrition, and health care for women and their*

young children. Poverty affects more women than men. A major cause of female and child poverty is that women are neglected in agricultural extension services. Female farmers provide more than 50 percent of all the food grown in the world—up to 80 percent in Africa; 60 percent in Asia. But women receive only 5 percent of all the agricultural extension services. And women have legal title to only 2 percent of the land in the world. If we paid more attention to these female farmers, both they and their children would benefit. Because, as the Gates Foundation says, "women are much more likely than men to spend additional income on food and healthcare."[147]

That is why a focus on women will also help countries with the widespread problem of childhood malnutrition and death. More recent studies demonstrate that the first 1,000 days of life (starting from conception) are the most crucial for a child's life-long well-being. And we know what to do about it. Pregnant women must have essential nutrients. New mothers should breast-feed exclusively for six months. Young children need treatment for worms and diarrheal diseases. They also need supplemental vitamins and minerals. A recent study reported that the crucial package of actions could reduce malnutrition by 36 percent. And it would only cost $100 per child. Focusing on women and their babies could significantly reduce global poverty.

It would also slow population growth. The data clearly show that improving the lot of women is the best way to slow population growth. "Educating girls is three times more likely to lower family size than educating boys."[148] Educated women often delay marriage and/or childbearing to finish school, reducing the number of births. For every additional year of schooling for women in poor countries, infant mortality rates decline by 5 to 10 percent.[149] Table 14 makes the point vividly. High infant mortality rates and high fertility go along with low levels of education for women. High educational levels go hand in hand with low rates of infant mortality and population growth. Women are generally the ones who take care of the children, so when they learn about hygiene and family planning, the results are greater. The gender development index in the following table shows the correlation between female education, infant mortality, and the fertility rate.

Table 14—Under-five mortality rate and total fertility rate by mother's education level

In selected countries, most recent year available since 2005

Country	Survey Year	Under-five mortality rate (per 1,000 live births)				Total Fertility rate (births per woman)			
		No education	Primary	Secondary or higher	Overall	No education	Primary	Secondary or higher	Overall
Bangladesh	2007	93	73	52	74	3.0	2.9	2.5	2.7
Egypt	2008	44	38	26	33	3.4	3.2	3.0	3.0
Ethiopia	2005	139	111	54	132	6.1	5.1	2.0	5.4
Ghana	2008	103	88	67	85	6.0	4.9	3.0	4.0
India	2005/2006	106	78	49	85	3.6	2.6	2.1	2.7
Indonesia	2007	94	60	38	51	2.4	2.8	2.6	2.6
Liberia	2009	164	162	131	158	7.1	6.2	3.9	5.9
Mali	2006	223	176	102	215	7.0	6.3	3.8	6.6
Niger	2006	222	209	92	218	7.2	7.0	4.8	7.0
Nigeria	2008	210	159	107	171	7.3	6.5	4.2	5.7
Rwanda	2007/2008	174	127	43	135	6.1	5.7	3.8	5.5
Uganda	2006	164	145	91	144	7.7	7.2	4.4	6.7
Zambia	2007	144	146	105	137	8.2	7.1	3.9	6.2

Note: Data Refer to the period 10 years before the survey year.[150]

9. *Reduce military aid.* In 2012, the U.S. designated $31.2 billion in economic assistance and $17.2 billion in military assistance.[151] Much more of the $17.2 billion in military assistance should be spent on long-term development. Poor nations don't need more tanks and bullets. They need more help to win an effective war on poverty.

Improving the way we give foreign aid can help reduce hunger, poverty, and injustice. But how much aid is needed?

Bombs, Bread, and Illusions

The world faces a crucial choice. We have made substantial progress to reduce global poverty. But to continue that progress requires major sums of money.

As we saw earlier, the U.S. government spends less than 1 percent of its total budget on foreign development assistance. After World War II, we were far more generous. Between 1947 and 1952, the United States poured $23 billion (approximately $102 billion in terms of 2014 dollars) into Western Europe under the Marshall Plan.[152] One has only to look at the material prosperity of Western Europe today to realize that it was one of the most successful aid programs the world has ever seen.

The plight of over a billion poor people today is more desperate than that of the people of war-ravaged Europe in the late 1940s. Yet we give a vastly smaller percentage of our wealth to today's needy even though our wealth has grown enormously. And we regularly hear politicians demanding that we cut foreign aid even more.

For a time after the end of the Cold War and the collapse of the Soviet Union, it appeared that global military expenditures would drop dramatically. In fact, there was a significant reduction between 1987 and 1998. Since September 11, 2001, however, the war on terrorism has provoked and vastly increased U.S. military expenditures. In fiscal year 2013, the U.S. spent $640 billion on military expenditures—37 percent of all global military expenditures.[153] That $640 billion is 29 times more than the U.S. government spent on foreign aid to specifically address poverty. Is that the balance U.S. citizens want?

Global military expenditures today are $1,747 billion annually, four times more than the total annual income of the poorest one billion people in the world.[154] President Eisenhower's words, spoken many years ago, are still relevant: "Every gun that is made, every warship launched, every rocket fired signifies, in the final sense, a theft from those who hunger and are not fed, those who are cold and are not clothed."[155]

Government budgets reflect fundamental values and priorities in the same way that church and family budgets do. What kind of national values do we want reflected in our foreign aid and military budgets? Will Christians act to persuade fellow citizens that budgets should reflect wise generosity toward the poor?

Organizations That Make a Difference

The tasks outlined in this chapter seem vast and overwhelming. Only as individuals join with other concerned citizens can they effectively promote the necessary structural changes. Here are a few organizations working to change public policy:

Bread for the World (BFW) is a nationwide Christian citizens' movement that seeks justice for the world's hungry people by lobbying our nation's decision makers. BFW has members in every congressional district across the country and has organized local groups at the grassroots level in many of those. BFW's newsletter, published eight times a year—and various Action Alerts and Quicklines—keep members up-to-date on current issues and legislation affecting hungry people. Members influence legislation by calling, writing, or visiting government officials, especially their own congressional representatives.

Bread for the World is an explicitly Christian organization. Local groups are encouraged to open their meetings with prayer and Bible study, and the national staff gathers for worship every Friday morning. Both BFW's founder, Arthur Simon, and its current president, David Beckmann, are Lutheran pastors. BFW makes a conscious effort to involve Catholics, Orthodox, evangelicals, and mainline Protestants at every level, including its staff and board. BFW's local activities are carried out by volunteer activists, of whom there are some 2,500 across the nation. Founded in 1974, BFW has grown to 50,000 members, including 2,500 churches whose membership fees and additional contributions supply the bulk of the support required to keep the organization going.

Because BFW has 50,000 "lobbyists" working at the local level, it has been very successful in affecting public policy on behalf of hungry people. Over the years, BFW staff and members have developed, helped introduce, and greatly facilitated passage of numerous pieces of legislation that have benefited poor and hungry people both in the U.S. and in the developing world.

BFW's Christian activists make a difference. In 1999–2000, BFW joined with dozens of other organizations and famous people like Bono to win a huge debt relief program for heavily indebted countries, especially in Africa. Because of huge debt repayments to Western nations, many African countries were dramatically reducing their expenditures on education, health care, and poverty reduction. One African president asked: "Must we starve our children to pay our debts?"

BFW and thousands of other activists lobbied the U.S. government. The same thing happened in many other countries. The result? Twenty nations (plus the World Bank and the International Monetary Fund) forgave $69 billion of essentially unrepayable debts. That gave poor nations about $4 billion a year more for education and poverty reduction. As a result, "20 million more poor children in Africa are going to school, and families in thirty-three different countries have more food, better housing and better health care."[156]

Dr. Kim, the President of the World Bank, has said that tremendous economic growth in African countries in the last decade is because of this debt relief program plus numerous efforts to combat AIDS. In addition, because the debt forgiveness agreements required the receiving nations to involve civil society organizations in how the new funds would be used, the process also promoted democratic institutions.[157]

In 2003, vigorous lobbying by BFW helped persuade Congress to establish the Millennium Challenge Account as a new international assistance initiative focused on poverty reduction. The $2 billion increase in poverty-focused development assistance—up 33 percent over the previous year—was the largest U.S. government funding increase in decades to combat hunger, poverty, and disease in the developing world.

In 2011, there were powerful efforts in the U.S. congress to slash both domestic and international anti-poverty programs. Again BFW played a central role in organizing many organizations (e.g., U.S. Conference of Catholic Bishops, Sojourners, The Salvation Army, Evangelicals for Social Action) to oppose the cuts. That effort preserved tens of billions of dollars in effective anti-poverty programs.[158]

We can persuade politicians to authorize, expand, and protect programs that reduce poverty. Well-organized citizen action works!

Evangelicals for Social Action (ESA) is a biblical movement helping Christians combine social transformation with evangelism and spiritual formation. ESA believes that prayer and radical dependence on the Holy Spirit must be central to any successful movement to bring structural change in society.

ESA's materials, including its weekly online ePistle, regularly deal with issues of global and domestic poverty. ESA's membership is a network of biblical Christians who seek to change the world and empower the poor because they know and love the God of the poor.[159]

Jubilee USA Network is an alliance of more than 75 U.S. organizations, 400 faith communities, and 50 global partners. Jubilee promotes an economy that "serves, protects and promotes participation of the most vulnerable around the world."[160]

Numerous other organizations attempt to change public policy. Here, I can mention only a few.

The Interfaith Center on Corporate Responsibility (ICCR) provides information to help people understand the impact of multinational corporations on the poor, the environment, and society. For many decades, the ICCR has used shareholder resolutions, careful research, and public pressure to make corporations more responsible.[161]

Other citizen lobbies include Network, an organization staffed by Catholic sisters who publish a monthly newsletter, a quarterly, and a hunger packet; and Friends Committee on National Legislation, which also issues a monthly newsletter. The United States Catholic Conference's Department of Social Development and World Peace works extensively and produces helpful materials on questions of poverty and justice. (To contact see the appendix.)

Let Justice Ring

In this chapter I have called for the reform of present economic structures. At a time when Marxism has collapsed and democratic capitalism is in danger of an overconfident neglect of its own failures, we must continue to re-examine economics from a thoroughly biblical perspective. We need economists immersed in biblical faith who will rethink economics as if poor people mattered. As a theologian and ethicist, I have only a very incomplete idea of what a modern version of the year of jubilee might look like. But at the heart of God's call for jubilee is a divine demand for socioeconomic structures that provide all people with the opportunity to acquire the capital necessary to earn their own way. We must discover new, concrete models for applying this biblical principle in our interdependent world. I hope and pray for a new generation of economists and political scientists who will devote their lives to formulating, developing, and implementing a contemporary model of jubilee.

The Liberty Bell hanging in historic Philadelphia could become a powerful symbol for citizens working to share resources with the poor of the world. The inscription on the Liberty Bell, "Proclaim liberty throughout the land," comes from the biblical passage about the jubilee (Lev. 25:10). To Hebrews enslaved in debt, these words promised the freedom and the land necessary to earn a living. Billions today long for the same opportunity. The God of the Bible still demands institutionalized mechanisms that will offer everyone the opportunity to earn a just living. The jubilee inscription on the Liberty Bell issues a ringing call for international economic justice.

Do Christians today have the generosity and courage to demand and implement the structural changes needed to make that ancient inscription a contemporary reality?

Study Questions

1. Chapter 11 starts with a parable. Which character in the parable do most Christians you know most identify with and imitate?
2. Chapters 9 and 10 discuss how we can respond as individuals and churches. Are these two responses enough? If not, why not?
3. Do biblical norms apply to modern secular societies? If so, how?
4. What are the strengths and weaknesses of the structural changes suggested in this chapter?
5. How much difference would it make if we ended trade barriers to goods from poor nations? Why don't we?
6. How can we reduce environmental pollution?
7. How does this chapter underline chapter 9's call for living more simply?
8. Should foreign aid be given to poor nations? If so, how could it be more effective?
9. Should we redirect money from military expenditures to reducing poverty? What typical objections do people raise to this suggestion? How would you respond?
10. How do you sense God calling you to work for structural change in our world?

EPILOGUE

We live at one of the great turning points in history. The present division of the world's resources must not continue. And it cannot. Either generous Christians will persuade their affluent neighbors to transform today's market economies so that everyone can share the good earth's bounty, or growing divisions between rich and poor will lead not only to more starvation and death but also to increasing civil strife, terrorism, and war.

Christians should be in the vanguard. The world will change if Christians obey the One we worship. But to obey will mean to follow. And he lives among the poor and oppressed, seeking justice for those in agony. In our time, following in his steps will mean more simple personal lifestyles. It will mean transformed churches with a corporate lifestyle consistent with worship of the God of the poor. It will mean costly commitment to building societal systems that work fairly for all.

Do Christians today have that kind of generosity and courage? Will we pioneer new models of sharing in our interdependent world? Will we dare to become the pioneers in the struggle for more just societies?

I am not pessimistic, in spite of widespread materialism. God regularly accomplishes his will through faithful remnants.[1] Even in affluent nations, there are millions of Christians who love their Lord Jesus more than houses and lands.

271

If at this moment in history a few million generous Christians blessed with material abundance dare to join hands with poor neighbors around the world, we will decisively influence the course of world history. Together we must strive to be a biblical people ready to follow wherever Scripture leads. We must pray for the courage to bear any cross, suffer any loss, and joyfully embrace any sacrifice that biblical faith requires in an age of affluence and poverty.

If you want to be a member of God's generous minority, I invite you to do one simple thing each day. It will only take a minute, but it might change your life. Daily, stop for a moment, look into the face of Jesus Christ, and whisper softly, "Lord Jesus, teach my heart to share your love for the poor."

We know that our Lord Jesus is alive! We know that the decisive victory over sin and death has occurred. We know that the Sovereign of the universe wills an end to hunger, injustice, and oppression. The resurrection of Jesus is our guarantee that, in spite of the massive evil that sometimes almost overwhelms us, the final victory will surely come.[2] Secure on that solid rock, we will plunge into this unjust world, changing now all we can and knowing that the Risen King will complete the victory at his glorious return.

APPENDIX A

General Works

Acemoglu, Daron and James Robinson. *Why Nations Fail: The Origins of Power, Prosperity, and Poverty*. New York: Crown Business, 2012.

Ball, Jim. *Global Warming and the Risen Lord: Christian Discipleship and Climate Change*. Washington, D.C.: Evangelical Environmental Network, 2010.

Banerjee, Abhijit Vinayak. *Making Aid Work*. Cambridge: MIT Press, 2007.

Banerjee, Abhijit Vinayak and Esther Duflo. *Poor Economics: A Radical Rethinking of the Way to Fight Global Poverty*. New York: PublicAffairs, 2011.

Bauer, P. T. *Equality, the Third World, and Economic Delusion*. Cambridge, MA: Harvard Univ. Press, 1981.

Beisner, Calvin E. *Prospects for Growth: A Biblical View of Population, Resources, and the Future*. Westchester: Crossway Books, 1990.

Bello, Walden. *Dark Victory: The United States, Structural Adjustment, and Global Poverty*. Oakland, CA: Pluto Press, 1994.

Benne, Robert. *The Ethic of Democratic Capitalism: A Moral Reassessment*. Philadelphia: Fortress Press, 1981.

Berger, Peter. *Pyramids of Sacrifice*. New York: Basic Books, 1975.

Birch, Bruce C., and Larry L. Rasmussen. *The Predicament of the Prosperous*. Philadelphia: Westminster Press, 1978.

Bornstein, David and Susan Davis. *Social Entrepreneurship: What Everyone Needs to Know*. Oxford University Press, 2010.

Brandt, Willy, et al. *North-South: A Program for Survival*. Cambridge, MA: MIT Press, 1980.

Bread for the World Institute. *2013 and 2014 Hunger Reports.* Bread for the World Institute, 2013, 2014. (A superb annual publication.)

Byron, William, ed. *The Causes of World Hunger.* New York: Paulist Press, 1982.

Carlson-Thies, Stanley W., et al. *Welfare in America: Christian Perspectives on a Policy in Crisis.* Grand Rapids, MI: Eerdmans, 1996.

Câmara, Dom Hélder. *Revolution Through Peace.* New York: Harper & Row, 1971.

Chinweizu. *The West and the Rest of Us.* New York: Random House, 1975.

Christian Aid, Banking on the Poor: The Ethics of Third World Debt. London: Christian Aid, 1988.

Cobb, John. *For the Common Good: Redirecting the Economy Toward Community, the Environment and a Sustainable Future.* Boston: Beacon Press, 1989.

Conway, Gordon. *One Billion Hungry: Can We Feed the World?* Ithaca: Cornell University Press, 2012.

Corbett, Steve and Brian Fikkert. *When Helping Hurts: How to Alleviate Poverty Without Hurting the Poor . . . and Yourself.* 2nd ed. Chicago, IL: Moody Publishers, 2012.

Cromartie, Michael, ed. *The Nine Lives of Population Control.* Washington, DC: Ethics and Public Policy Center, 1995.

Davis, Shelton H. *Victims of the Miracle: Development and the Indians of Brazil.* Cambridge: At the University Press, 1977.

De Jesús, Carolina María. *Child of the Dark.* Trans. David St. Clair. New York: Signet Books, 1962. An explosive personal account of urban Brazilian poverty.

Dreze, Jean, and Amartya Sen. *Hunger and Public Action.* New York: Oxford Univ. Press, 1989.

Duchrow, Ulrich. *Alternatives to Global Capitalism.* Utrecht: International Books, 1995.

Duchrow, Ulrich. *Global Economy: A Confessional Issue for the Churches?* Geneva: WCC Publications, 1987.

Easterly, William. *The White Man's Burden: Why the West's Efforts to Aid the Rest Have Done So Much Ill and So Little Good.* New York: Penguin Books, 2006.

Eberly, Don. *The Rise of Global Civil Society: Building Communities and Nations from the Ground Up.* New York: Encounter Books, 2008.

Fisman, Raymond and Edward Miguel. *Economic Gangsters: Corruption, Violence, and the Poverty of Nations.* Princeton University Press, 2008.

Food and Agriculture Organization. *The State of Food Insecurity in the World 2013.* Rome: United Nations, 2013. An excellent annual publication.

Freudenberger, C. Dean, and Paul M. Minus Jr. *Christian Responsibility in a Hungry World.* Nashville: Abingdon Press, 1976.

Gay, Craig M. *With Liberty and Justice for Whom? The Recent Evangelical Debate over Capitalism.* Grand Rapids, MI: Eerdmans, 1991.

George, Susan. *Debt and Hunger*. Minneapolis: American Lutheran Church Hunger Program, 1987.

Gheddo, Piero. *Why Is the Third World Poor?* Maryknoll, NY: Orbis Books, 1973.

Gilder, George. *Wealth and Poverty*. NY: Basic Books, 1981.

Goudzwaard, Bob. *Aid for the Overdeveloped West*. Toronto: Wedge, 1975.

———. *Capitalism and Progress: A Diagnosis of Western Society*. Trans. Josina Van Nuis Zylstra. Grand Rapids, MI: Eerdmans, 1979.

Goudzwaard, Bob, and Harry de Lange. *Beyond Poverty and Affluence: Toward an Economy of Care*. Grand Rapids, MI: Eerdmans, 1995.

Griffiths, Brian. *Morality and the Market Place: Christian Alternatives to Capitalism and Socialism*. London: Hodder and Stoughton, 1982.

———. *The Creation of Wealth: A Christian's Case for Capitalism*. Downers Grove, IL: InterVarsity, 1984.

Grudem, Wayne and Barry Asmus. *The Poverty of Nations: A Sustainable Solution*. Wheaton, IL: Crossway, 2013.

Hall, Tony. *Changing the Face of Hunger: One Man's Story of How Liberals, Conservatives, Republicans, Democrats, and People of Faith are Joining Forces in a New Movement to Help the Hungry, the Poor, and the Oppressed*. Nashville, TN: Thomas Nelson, 2006.

Halteman, James. *The Clashing Worlds of Economics and Faith*. Scottdale: Herald Press, 1995.

———. *Market Capitalism & Christianity*. Grand Rapids, MI: Baker Book House, 1988.

Hawken, Paul. *The Ecology of Commerce: A Declaration of Sustainability*. New York: Harper Business, 1993.

Hay, Donald. *Economics Today: A Christian Critique*. Grand Rapids, MI: Eerdmans, 1989.

Jegen, Mary Evelyn, and Charles K. Wilbur, eds. *Growth with Equity*. New York: Paulist Press, 1979.

Korten, David C. *When Corporations Rule the World*. West Hartford: Kumarian Press Inc., 1996.

Lutz, Charles P., ed. *Farming the Lord's Land: Christian Perspectives on American Agriculture*. Minneapolis: Augsburg, 1980.

Kutzner, Patricia. *Who's Involved with Hunger: An Organization Guide for Education and Advocacy*. Washington, DC: World Hunger Education Service/BFWI, 1995.

McGinnis, James B. *Bread and Justice: Toward a New International Economic Order*. New York: Paulist Press, 1979.

Millett, Richard. *Guardians of the Dynasty: A History of the U.S. Created Guardia Nacional de Nicaragua and the Somoza Family*. Maryknoll, NY: Orbis Books, 1977.

Morgan, Elizabeth, Van Weigel and Eric DeBaufre. *Global Poverty and Personal Responsibility*. New York: Paulist, 1989.

Myrdal, Gunnar. *The Challenge of World Poverty*. New York: Random House, 1971.

Nelson, Jack A. *Hunger for Justice: The Politics of Food and Faith*. Maryknoll, NY: Orbis Books, 1981.

Olsen, Gregg M. *Power and Prosperity: A Comparative Introduction*. Oxford University Press, 2011.

Rau, Bill. *Feast to Famine: The Course of Africa's Underdevelopment*. Washington, DC: Africa Faith and Justice Network, 1985.

Rich, William. *Smaller Families Through Social and Economic Progress*. Washington, DC: Overseas Development Council, 1973.

Rodney, Walter. *How Europe Underdeveloped Africa*. London: Bogle-L'Ouverture, 1972.

Sachs, Jeffrey D., ed. *Developing Country Debt and the World Economy*. Chicago: University of Chicago Press, 1989.

Sachs. Jeffrey D. *The End of Poverty: Economic Possibilities for Our Time*. New York: Penguin, 2005.

Schlossberg, Herbert, Vinay Samuel, and Ronald J. Sider, eds., *Christianity and Economics in the Post-Cold War Era: The Oxford Declaration and Beyond*. Grand Rapids, MI: Eerdmans, 1994.

Schor, Juliet B. *The Overworked American: The Unexpected Decline of Leisure*. New York: BasicBooks, 1992.

Schumacher, E.F. *Small Is Beautiful: Economics as If People Mattered*. New York: Harper & Row, 1973.

Sen, Amartya. *Development as Freedom*. New York: Alfred A Knopf, Inc., 1999.

Simon, Arthur. *Bread for the World*. Grand Rapids, MI: Eerdmans; New York: Paulist Press, 1975.

————. *The Rising of Bread for the World: An Outcry of Citizens Against Hunger*. Mahwah, NJ: Paulist Press, 2009.

Simon, Julian L. *Population and Development in Poor Countries*. Princeton: Princeton University Press, 1992.

Sivard, Ruth Leger. *World Military and Social Expenditures*. Leesburg, VA: World Priorities. An annual publication from 1974–1996.

Skillen, James W. *International Politics and the Demand for Global Justice*. Sioux Center, IA: Dordt College Press, 1981.

Smith, Christian and Michael O. Emerson with Patricia Snell. *Passing the Plate: Why American Christians Don't Give Away More Money*. Oxford University Press, 2008.

Spykman, Gordon, et al. *Let My People Live: Faith and Struggle in Central America*. Grand Rapids, MI: Eerdmans, 1988.

Stackhouse, Max L., et al. *On Moral Business: Classical and Contemporary Resources for Ethics in Economic Life.* Grand Rapids, MI: Eerdmans, 1995.

State of the World 2013. Washington: Worldwatch Institute. An annual publication.

Stiglitz, Joseph E. *The Price of Inequality: How Today's Divided Society Endangers Our Future.* New York: W. W. Norton & Company, Inc., 2012.

Stiglitz, Joseph E. *The Stiglitz Report: Reforming the International Monetary and Financial Systems in the Wake of the Global Crisis.* New York: The New Press, 2010.

Stiglitz, Joseph E., Amartya Sen, and Jean-Paul Fitoussi. *Mismeasuring Our Lives: Why GDP Doesn't Add Up.* New York: The New Press: 2010.

Tamari, Meir. *With All Your Possessions: Jewish Ethics and Economic Life.* New York: The Free Press, 1987.

Taylor, John V. *Enough Is Enough.* London: SCM Press, 1975.

Thurow, Lester C. *The Future of Capitalism: How Today's Economic Forces Shape Tomorrow's World.* New York: William Morrow and Company, 1996.

Todaro, Michael P. and Stephen C. Smith. *Economic Development. Twelfth Edition.* Boston: Addison Wesley, 2014.

UNICEF. *The State of the World's Children 2014.* New York: UNICEF, 2014. An important annual publication.

United Nations Development Program. *Human Development Report 2013.* New York: UNDP, 2013. An important annual report.

Wilkinson, Loren, ed. *Earthkeeping: Christian Stewardship of Natural Resources.* Grand Rapids, MI: Eerdmans, 1980.

Williams, Robert G. *Export Agriculture and the Crisis in Central America.* Chapel Hill: University of North Carolina Press, 1986.

World Bank. *Globalization, Growth and Poverty.* Washington: World Bank, 2003.

World Bank. *World Development Indicators 2014.* Washington: World Bank, 2014. An annual report.

World Bank. *World Development Report 2014.* New York: Oxford Univ. Press, 2014. Annual.

World Bank. *Mainstreaming the Environment.* Washington, DC: World Bank, 1995.

World Hunger Program, Brown University. *Hunger in History: Food Shortage, Poverty, and Deprivation.* New York: Basil Blackwell, 1990.

Lifestyle

Alexander, John. *Your Money or Your Life: A New Look at Jesus' View of Wealth and Power.* San Francisco: Harper and Row, 1986.

Bascom, Tim. *The Comfort Trap: Spiritual Dangers of the Convenience Culture.* Downers Grove, IL: InterVarsity Press, 1993.

Conn, Harvie M. *Bible Studies on World Evangelization and the Simple Lifestyle.* Phillipsburg, NJ: Presbyterian and Reformed Publishing, 1981.

Eller, Vernard. *The Simple Life: The Christian Stance Toward Possessions.* Grand Rapids, MI: Eerdmans, 1973. It is important to read Eller's warning against legalism, but the overall effect is to give aid and comfort to our carnal inclination to rationalize our sinful affluence.

Ewald, Ellen Buchman. *Recipes for a Small Planet.* New York: Ballantine Books, 1973. Recipes for delicious, meatless dishes.

Foster, Richard J. *Freedom of Simplicity.* New York: Harper & Row, 1981.

Fuller, Millard. *The Theology of the Hammer.* Macon, GA: Smyth & Helwys, 1994.

Greenway, Roger S., ed. *Discipling the City: A Comprehensive Approach to Urban Mission.* 2nd ed. Grand Rapids, MI: Baker Book House, 1992.

Jones, Ellis. *The Better World Shopping Guide.* Gabriola, B.C.: New Society Publishers, 2012.

Irwin, Kevin W., et al. *Preserving the Creation: Environmental Theology and Ethics.* Washington, DC: Georgetown University Press, 1994.

Kerr, Graham. *The Graham Kerr Step-by-Step Cookbook.* Elgin, IL: David C. Cook, 1982.

Lappé, Frances Moore. *Diet for a Small Planet.* Rev. ed. New York: Ballantine, 1975.

Longacre, Doris Janzen. *More-with-Less Cookbook.* Scottdale, PA: Herald Press, 1976. 25th Anniversary ed., 2000.

———. *Living More with Less.* Scottdale, PA: Herald Press, 1980.

McGinnis, James, and Kathleen McGinnis. *Parenting for Peace and Justice.* Maryknoll, NY: Orbis Books, 1981.

Ronsvalle, John L., and Sylvia Ronsvalle. *The State of Church Giving Through 2011.* Champaign: Empty Tomb Inc., 2013. The 23rd edition of an important annual.

Schlabach, Joetta Handrich. *Extending the Table: Recipes and Stories from Afghanistan to Zambia.* Rev. Ed. Scottdale: Herald Press, 2014.

Schneider, John. *Godly Materialism: Rethinking Money & Possessions.* Downers Grove, IL: InterVarsity Press, 1994.

Shannon-Thornberry, Milo. *Alternate Celebrations Catalogue.* Washington, DC: Alternatives, 1982.

Hollister, Benjamin, Rosalyn Will and Alice Tepper Marlin. *Shopping for a Better World.* Sierra Club Books, 1994.

Sider, Ronald J., ed. *Lifestyle in the Eighties: An Evangelical Commitment to Simple Lifestyle.* Philadelphia: Westminster, 1982.

———. *Living More Simply: Biblical Principles and Practical Models.* Downers Grove, IL: InterVarsity Press, 1980.

Sine, Tom. *Why Settle for More and Miss the Best?* Waco, TX: Word, 1987.

Wuthnow, Robert. *God and Mammon in America*. New York: The Free Press, 1994.

Theology, Biblical Studies, and the Church

Armerding, Carl E., ed. *Evangelicals and Liberation*. Nutley, NJ: Presbyterian and Reformed, 1977.

Banks, Robert J. *Paul's Idea of Community*. Grand Rapids, MI: Eerdmans, 1980.

Batey, Richard. *Jesus and the Poor: The Poverty Program of the First Christians*. New York: Harper & Row, 1972.

Baum, Gregory. *The Priority of Labor: A Commentary on Laborem Exercens; Encyclical Letter of Pope John Paul II*. New York: Paulist, 1982.

Beckman, David and Arthur Simon. *Grace at the Table: Ending Hunger in God's World*. Mahwah, NJ: Paulist Press, 1999.

Beisner, E. Calvin. *Prosperity and Poverty: The Compassionate Use of Resources in a World of Scarcity*. Westchester, IL: Crossway, 1988.

Bloomberg, Craig. *Neither Poverty Nor Riches: A Biblical Theology of Material Possessions*. Grand Rapids: Eerdmans, 1999.

Boerma, Conrad. *The Rich, the Poor—and the Bible*. Philadelphia: Westminster, 1979.

Brueggemann, Walter. *The Land*. Philadelphia: Fortress Press, 1977.

Byron, William J. *Toward Stewardship: An Interim Ethic of Poverty, Pollution and Power*. New York: Paulist Press, 1975.

Carroll, M. Daniel, *Christians at the Border: Immigration, The Church and the Bible*. Grand Rapids, Baker, 2008.

Cannon, Mae Elise. *Social Justice Handbook: Small Steps for a Better World*. Downers Grove: InterVarsity Press, 2009.

Cesaretti, C.A., and Stephen Cummins, eds. *Let the Earth Bless the Lord: A Christian Perspective on Land Use*. New York: Seabury Press, 1981.

Cosby, Gordon. *Handbook for Mission Groups*. Waco, TX: Word Books, 1975.

Cone, James H. *God of the Oppressed*. New York: Seabury Press, 1975.

Dayton, Donald W. *Discovering an Evangelical Heritage*. NY: Harper & Row, 1976.

De Santa Ana, Julio. *Good News to the Poor: The Challenge of the Poor in the History of the Church*. Geneva: WCC Publications, 1977.

Economic Justice for All: Pastoral Letter on Catholic Social Teaching and the U.S. Economy. Washington, DC: National Conference of Catholic Bishops, 1986.

Escobar, Samuel. *The New Global Mission: The Gospel From Everywhere to Everyone*. Downers Grove: InterVarsity Press, 2003.

———. *Changing Tides: Latin America And World Mission Today*. Maryknoll, NY: Orbis, 2002.

Escobar, Samuel, and John Driver. *Christian Mission and Social Justice*. Scottdale, PA: Herald Press, 1978.

Finn, Daniel R., and Pemberton L. Prentiss. *Toward a Christian Economic Ethic: Stewardship and Social Power.* Minneapolis: Winston, 1985.

Gill, Athol. *Life on the Road: The Gospel Basis for a Messianic Lifestyle.* Homebush West (Australia): Anzea Publishers, 1989.

Gollwitzer, Helmut. *The Rich Christians and Poor Lazarus.* Trans. David Cairns. New York: Macmillan, 1970.

Gremillion, John, ed. *The Gospel of Peace and Justice: Catholic Social Teaching Since Pope John.* Maryknoll, NY: Orbis Books, 1976.

Grigg, Viv. *Cry of the Urban Poor.* Monrovia, CA: Mission Advanced Research and Communication Center, 1992.

Haugen, Gary. *Good News About Injustice.* Downers Grove: InterVarsity Press, 1999.

Hendricks, Jr., Obery M. *The Politics of Jesus.* New York: Doubleday, 2006.

Hengel, Martin. *Poverty and Riches in the Early Church: Aspects of a Social History of Early Christianity.* Philadelphia: Fortress Press, 1974.

Johnson, Luke T. *Sharing Possessions.* Philadelphia: Fortress Press, 1981.

Keith-Lucas, Alan. *The Poor You Have Always with You: Concepts of Aid to the Poor in the Western World from Biblical Times to the Present.* St. Davids, PA: North American Association of Christians in Social Work, 1989. (Box S-90, St. Davids, PA 19087).

Keller, Timothy J. *Ministries of Mercy: the Call of the Jericho Road.* Second ed. Phillipsburg, N.J.: RoR Publishing, 1997.

Kerans, Patrick. *Sinful Social Structures.* New York: Paulist Press, 1974.

Kirk, Andrew. *Liberation Theology: An Evangelical View from the Third World.* Atlanta: John Knox Press, 1979.

Kraybill, Donald B. *The Upside Down Kingdom.* Scottdale, PA: Herald Press, 1978.

Kreider, Carl. *The Rich and the Poor: A Christian Perspective on Global Economics.* Scottdale, PA: Herald Press, 1987.

Lernoux, Penny. *Cry of the People.* Garden City, NY: Doubleday, 1980.

Ludwig, Thomas E. et al. *Inflation, Poortalk and the Gospel.* Valley Forge, PA: Judson Press, 1981.

Lyon, Jo Anne. *The Ultimate Blessing: Rediscovering The Power of God's Presence.* Indianapolis: Wesleyan Publishing House, 2003.

Meeks, M. Douglas. *God the Economist: The Doctrine of God and Political Economy.* Minneapolis: Fortress, 1989.

Mott, Stephen C. *Biblical Ethics and Social Change.* New York: Oxford, 1982.

Novak, Michael. *Will It Liberate? Questions About Liberation Theology.* New York: Paulist, 1986.

Owensby, Walter L. *Economics for Prophets: A Primer on Concepts, Realities, and Values in Our Economic System.* Grand Rapids, MI: Eerdmans, 1988.

Padilla, C. Rene. *Mission Between the Times.* Grand Rapids, MI: Eerdmans, 1985.

Perkins, John. *With Justice for All.* Glendale, CA: Regal, 1982.

Pilgrim, Walter E. *Good News to the Poor: Wealth and Poverty in Luke–Acts.* Minneapolis: Augsburg, 1981.

Preston, Ronald H. *Religion and the Ambiguities of Capitalism.* London: SCM Press, 1991.

Ronsvalle, John and Sylvia. *Behind the Stained Glass Window: Money Dynamics in the Church.* Grand Rapids, MI: Baker, 1996.

Samuel, Vinay. *The Meaning and Cost of Discipleship.* Bombay: Bombay Urban Industrial League for Development, 1981.

Samuel, Vinay and Albrecht Hauser, eds. *Proclaiming Christ in Christ's Way: Studies in Integral Evangelism.* Oxford: Regnum Books, 1989.

Samuel, Vinay and Chris Sugden, eds. *Evangelism and the Poor: A Third World Study Guide.* Oxford: Regnum, 1982.

Scott, Waldron. *Bring Forth Justice.* Grand Rapids, MI: Eerdmans, 1980.

Seccombe, David Peter. *Possessions and the Poor in Luke–Acts.* Studien zum Neuen Testament und seiner Umwelt, 1982.

Sider, Ronald J., ed. *Cry Justice: The Bible Speaks on Hunger and Poverty.* Downers Grove, IL: InterVarsity Press; New York: Paulist Press, 1980. (1997 edition: *For They Shall Be Fed.* Dallas: Word.)

———. *Good News and Good Works: A Theology for the Whole Gospel.* Grand Rapids: Baker, 1999.

———. *Cup of Water, Bread of Life.* Grand Rapids, MI: Zondervan, 1994.

———. *Just Politics: a Guide for Christian Engagement.* Grand Rapids: Baker, 2012.

———. *Living Like Jesus.* Grand Rapids, Baker, 1999.

Sine, Tom. *The Mustard Seed Conspiracy.* Waco, TX: Word, 1981.

Slade, Peter, Charles Marsh and Peter Goodwin Heltzel, eds. *Mobilizing for the Common Good: The Lived Theology of John M. Perkins.* Jackson, MS: University Press of Mississippi, 2013.

Stearns, Richard. *The Hole in Our Gospel.* Nashville: Nelson, 2009.

Sugden, Chris. *Seeking the Asian Face of Jesus.* Oxford: Regnum, 1997.

Taylor, Richard K. *Economics and the Gospel.* Philadelphia: United Church Press, 1973.

Tizon, Al. *Transformation After Lausanne: Radical Evangelical Mission in Global-Local Perspective.* Oxford: Regnum, 2008.

———. *Missional Preaching: Engage, Embrace, Transform.* Valley Forge, PA: Judson Press, 2012.

Villafane, Eldin. *The Liberating Spirit: Toward an Hispanic American Pentecostal Social Ethic.* Grand Rapids, MI: Eerdmans, 1993.

Wallis, Jim. *Agenda for Biblical People.* New York: Harper & Row, 1976.

———. *The Call to Conversion: Recovering the Gospel for These Times.* New York: Harper & Row, 1981.

—————. *The (Un)Common Good: How the Gospel Brings Hope to a World Divided.* Grand Rapids: Baker, 2014.

Westphal, Carol. "Covenant Parenting for Peace and Justice." Office of Family Life, Reformed Church of America. (Write RCA Distribution Center, 18525 Torrence Avenue, Lansing, IL 60438.)

White, John. *The Golden Cow: Materialism in the Twentieth-Century Church.* Downers Grove, IL: InterVarsity Press, 1979.

Woodley, Randy. *Living in Color: Embracing God's Passion for Diversity.* Grand Rapids, MI: Chosen Books, 2001.

Wright, Christopher J. H. *An Eye for An Eye: The Place of Old Testament Ethics Today.* Downers Grove, IL: InterVarsity, 1983.

—————. *God's People in God's Land: Family, Land and Property in the Old Testament.* Grand Rapids, MI: Eerdmans, 1990.

Ziesler, J. A. *Christian Asceticism.* Grand Rapids, MI: Eerdmans, 1973.

Development

Batchelor, Peter. *People in Rural Development.* Exeter: Paternoster, 1981.

Freire, Paulo. *Pedagogy of the Oppressed.* Trans. Myra B. Ramos. New York: Herder and Herder, 1970.

Goulet, Denis. *A New Moral Order.* Maryknoll, NY: Orbis Books, 1974.

Myers, Bryant L. *The Changing Shape of World Mission.* Monrovia, CA: Mission Advanced Research and Communication Center, 1993.

—————. *Exploring World Missions.* Monrovia, Ca. World Vision, 2003.

—————. *Walking with the Poor. Principles and Practice of Transformational Development.* Maryknoll: Orbis, 1999. Revised edition, 2011.

Perkins, John M. *Beyond Charity: The Call to Christian Community Development.* Grand Rapids, MI: Baker Book House, 1993.

Perkins, John M., ed. *Restoring At-Risk Communities.* Grand Rapids, MI: Baker, 1995.

Samuel, Vinay and Chris Sugden. *The Church in Response to Human Need.* Monrovia, CA: Missions Advanced Research Communication Center, 1983.

Sider, Ronald J., ed. *Evangelicals and Development: Toward a Theology of Social Change.* Philadelphia: Westminster, 1982.

Sinclair, Maurice. *The Green Finger of God.* Exeter: Paternoster, 1980.

Yamamori, Tetsunao, et al. *Serving with the Poor in Asia.* Monrovia: MARC, 1995.

Periodicals

Creation Care Magazine. www.creationcare.org/magazine. A biblical environmental magazine.

Multinational Monitor. www.multinationalmonitor.org/. It reports on large corporations, especially in the Third World.

The New Internationalist. www.newint.org/. An influential development periodical.

Sojourners Magazine. 3333 14th St., N.W, Suite 200 Washington, D.C., 20010. www.sojo.net/magazine. A biblical magazine with regular articles on economic justice, discipleship, and community.

Transformation Magazine published by the Oxford Center on Mission Studies (www.ocms.oc.uk). One of the best places to listen to all parts of the worldwide evangelical community.

Numerous other religious journals regularly carry related items: *Christian Century, Commonweal, Christianity Today, Engage, Relevant, World.*

Audiovisuals

A vast array of excellent audiovisuals are available. For lists, write to almost any of the organizations listed in Appendix B.

APPENDIX B

Organizations

American Enterprise Institute. www.aei.org. An influential conservative think tank on a wide range of public policy issues, including hunger.

American Friends Service Committee. www.afsc.org. An established Quaker relief, development and justice agency.

Amnesty International. www.amnesty.org. Amnesty's focus is human rights.

Bread for the World. www.bread.org. An effective Christian citizens' lobby (see description in chapter 11).

Canadian Hunger Foundation. www.chf.ca.

Catholic Relief Services. www.crs.org. The major Catholic relief and development agency.

Christian Community Development Association. www.ccda.org.

Church World Service. www.cwsglobal.org. CWS is the relief, development, refugee assistance and global education arm of the NCCC.

Compassion International. www.compassion.com.

Cooperative League of the U.S.A. www.ncba.coop/ncba-clusa/home.

Corporate Accountability International (formerly Infact). www.stopcorporateabuse.org.

Council on Economic Priorities (CEP), 30 Irving Place, New York, NY 10003. 212-420-1133. Social and environmental research on corporations for consumers, investors, managers, employees and activists.

Crop Hunger Walk. www.cropwalk.org.

Ecumenical Bank: see World Council of Churches.

Educational Concerns for Hunger Organizations (ECHO). www.echonet.
org. Provides agricultural information, seeds, and training to agricultural
missionaries and development workers.

Environmental Defense Fund. www.edf.org.

Evangelical Environmental Network. www.creationcare.org.

Evangelicals for Social Action. www.evangelicalsforsocialaction.org.

Fair Labor Association. www.fairlabor.org/about-us.

Food and Agricultural Organization (FAO). www.fao.org. A United Nations
agency.

Friends Committee on National Legislation. www.fcnl.org. Newsletter and
legislative updates.

Global Reporting Initiative. www.globalreporting.org.

Habitat for Humanity. www.habitat.org.

Interfaith Center on Corporate Responsibility. www.iccr.org. See chapter 11 for
description.

Mennonite Central Committee. www.mcc.org. A large Mennonite relief and
development agency heavily involved in long-range development. The
Washington office (www.mcc.org/get-involved/advocacy/washington)
publishes an excellent newsletter, *Washington Memo*.

Mennonite Economic Development Associates (MEDA). www.meda.org.

Micah Network. www.micahnetwork.org.

Multinational Monitor. http://multinationalmonitor.org/

Network. www.networklobby.org. A citizen lobby staffed by Catholic sisters
who publish regularly on hunger issues.

OPPORTUNITY International. www.opportunity.org. An excellent
microenterprise development organization.

World Concern. www.worldconcern.org.

World Council of Churches. www.oikoumene.org. Books, pamphlets, and
newsletters on a wide range of hunger and development issues.

World Relief. www.worldrelief.org. The international relief and development
arm of the National Association of Evangelicals.

World Vision. www.worldvision.org.

Worldwatch Institute. www.worldwatch.org.

NOTES

Chapter 1

1. "Iracema's Story," *Christian Century*, November 12, 1975.
2. "Committing to Child Survival: A Promise Renewed 2013 Progress Report," United Nations Children's Fund (UNICEF), (September 2013), 4.
3. Robert L. Heilbroner, *The Great Ascent: The Struggle for Economic Development in Our Time* (New York: Harper & Row, 1963), 33–36.
4. "Poverty and Equity Data," The World Bank, last updated on April 12, 2013, accessed April 18, 2014, http://povertydata.worldbank.org/poverty/home/. Figures are estimates for the year 2010.
5. "PovcalNet: the on-line tool for poverty measurement developed by the Development Research Group of the World Bank," http://iresearch.worldbank.org/PovcalNet/index.htm. Data updated on April 12, 2013. Figures are 2010 estimates. 2.4 billion global poor divided by global population (in 2010) of 6.9 billion equals 34.7 percent. Population figure from: http://www.prb.org/Publications/Datasheets/2010/2010wpds, accessed February 18, 2014.
6. "Committing to Child Survival: A Promise Renewed 2013 Progress Report," United Nations Children's Fund (UNICEF), (September 2013), 4.
7. K. von Grebmer, et al, *2013 Global Hunger Index: The Challenge of Hunger: Building Resilience to Achieve Food and Nutrition Security*, (Bonn, Washington, DC, and Dublin: Welthungerhilfe, International Food Policy Research Institute, and Concern Worldwide, 2013), 11.

8. *Poor Economics* (New York: Random House, 2013), xii. This does not include housing and the statistics are from 2005, but they illustrate the depth of the deprivation.
9. Bread for the World Institute (BFWI), *2014 Hunger Report* (Washington, DC: Bread for the World Institute, 2013), 152.
10. BFWI, *2013 Hunger Report*, 34.
11. United Nations Development Program (UNDP), *Human Development Report 2013: The Rise of the South: Human Progress in a Diverse World* (New York: United Nations, 2013), 12.
12. Ibid., 23.
13. Ibid., 26.
14. Ibid., 23.
15. Ibid., 26.
16. Ibid., 13.
17. Ibid., 46.
18. GDP growth (annual percent). World Bank national accounts data, and OECD National Accounts data files. Data retrieved from World Development Indicators online database, accessed February 27, 2014, http://povertydata.worldbank.org/poverty/home/.
19. UNDP, *Human Development Report 2013*, 56.
20. Klaus von Grebmer, et al. *2012 Global Hunger Index* (Bonn/Washington, DC/ Dublin: IFPRI/Concern Worldwide/Welthungerhilfe and Green Scenery, 2012), 3.
21. BFWI, *2013 Hunger Report*, 194. Earlier figure comes from Food and Agriculture Organization, *The State of Food Insecurity in the World 2003* (Rome: United Nations, 2003), 6.
22. Food and Agriculture Organization, *The State of Food Insecurity in the World 2003* (Rome: United Nations, 2003), 31–32. Earlier figures come from BFWI, *Hunger 1995*, 10–15; BFWI, *Hunger 1997*, 15.
23. BFWI, *2013 Hunger Report*, 190, 193.
24. Ibid., 13.
25. Abhijit V. Banarjee and Esther Duflo, *Poor Economics* (New York: Random House, 2013), 1.
26. World Bank, "How We Classify Countries," accessed February 27, 2014, http://data.worldbank.org/about/country-classifications. "Note that these are preliminary estimates and may be revised. Country classifications are determined once a year and remain fixed, regardless of subsequent revisions to their estimates of their GNI per capita." http://data.worldbank.org/news/new-country-classifications. GNI refers to the "sum of value added by all resident producers plus any product taxes (less subsidies) not included in the valuation of output plus net receipts of primary income

(compensation of employees and property income) from abroad." See http://data.worldbank.org/indicator/NY.GNP.PCAP.CD/countries for more information.

27. World Development Indicators, "Population Dynamics," accessed April 18, 2014, http://wdi.worldbank.org/table/2.1.

28. World Development Indicators, "GNI per capita, Atlas method (current US$)," accessed February 27, 2014, http://data.worldbank.org/indicator/NY.GNP.PCAP.CD/countries.

29. World Bank Health Nutrition and Population Statistics. Data retrieved from World Development Indicators online database, accessed February 27, 2014, http://data.worldbank.org/.

30. 2010 estimate. World Development Indicators, "Education Statistics – All Indicators," accessed February 27, 2014, http://data.worldbank.org/.

31. World Development Indicators, "Population Dynamics," accessed April 18, 2014, http://wdi.worldbank.org/table/2.1.

32. World Development Indicators, "GNI per capita, Atlas method (current US$)," accessed February 27, 2014, http://data.worldbank.org/indicator/NY.GNP.PCAP.CD/countries.

33. World Development Indicators, "Population Dynamics," accessed April 18, 2014, http://wdi.worldbank.org/table/2.1.

34. World Development Indicators, "GNI per capita, Atlas method (current US$)," accessed February 27, 2014, http://data.worldbank.org/indicator/NY.GNP.PCAP.CD/countries.

35. World Development Indicators, "Population Dynamics," accessed April 18, 2014, http://wdi.worldbank.org/table/2.1.

36. World Development Indicators, "GNI per capita, Atlas method (current US$)," accessed February 27, 2014, http://data.worldbank.org/indicator/NY.GNP.PCAP.CD/countries.

37. World Bank, "World Development Report 1990" (Washington, DC: World Bank, 1990), 8, table I.I.

38. World Bank stopped calculating for this aggregate region in 2009.

39. World Bank national accounts data, and OECD National Accounts data files. Figures based on author's calculations from data retrieved from World Development Indicators online database, accessed March 24, 2014, http://databank.worldbank.org/data/home.aspx.

40. World Bank national accounts data, and OECD National Accounts data files. Figures based on author's calculations from data retrieved from World Development Indicators online database, accessed April 9, 2014, http://databank.worldbank.org/data/home.aspx.

41. James Brooke, "Brazilians Vote Today for President in a Free and Unpredictable Election," *New York Times*, November 15, 1989.

42. BFWI, *2013 Hunger Report*, 44. In 2009, the richest 20 percent of the population received 58.6 percent of the country's income, while the poorest 60 percent received 22.4 percent. World Bank, World Development Indicators: Brazil," accessed April 9, 2014, http://povertydata.worldbank.org/poverty/country/BRA.

43. World Bank national accounts data, and OECD National Accounts data files. Figures based on author's calculations from data retrieved from World Development Indicators online database, accessed April 9, 2014, http://databank.worldbank.org/data/home.aspx.

44. World Bank, Development Research Group. Data are based on primary household survey data obtained from government statistical agencies and World Bank country departments. Data retrieved from World Development Indicators online database, accessed February 27, 2014, http://povertydata.worldbank.org/poverty/home/.

45. World Bank, Poverty and Inequality Database, accessed March 24, 2014, http://databank.worldbank.org/data/home.aspx.

46. BFWI, *2013 Hunger Report*, 20.

47. BFWI, *2014 Hunger Report*, 153.

48. W. Stanley Mooneyham, *What Do You Say to a Hungry World?* (Waco, TX: Word, 1975), 38–39. The specific figures on income are now outdated, but the agony is still there for hundreds of millions in 2015.

49. Lester R. Brown, *In the Human Interest* (New York: Norton, 1974), 55–56.

50. AIDS is also contributing to famine. See Alex de Wool and Alan Whiteside, "New Variant Famine: AIDS and Food Crisis in Southern Africa," *Lancet* 362 (October 11, 2003): 1234–37.

51. World Bank, World Development Indicators, accessed April 9, 2014, http://data.worldbank.org/indicator/SH.DYN.MORT/countries/XM-XD?display=graph.

52. UNICEF, "Committing to Child Survival," 19.

53. BWFI, *2013 Hunger Report*, 5.

54. K. von Grebmer, et al, *2013 Global Hunger Index*, 13.

55. WHO, UNICEF, & World Bank, *State of the World Vaccines and Immunizations*, (Geneva, World Health Organization, 2009),10. Available from http://whqlibdoc.who.int/publications/2009/9789241563864_eng.pdf?ua=.

56. *Child of the Dark: The Diary of Carolina Maria de Jesus* (New York: Dutton, 1962), 42.

57. Mooneyham, *What Do You Say to a Hungry World?*, 191.

58. Donald Hay, *Economics Today* (Leicester: InterVarsity, 1989), 257.

59. World Bank, World Development Indicators, accessed April 9, 2014, http://data.worldbank.org/indicator/SE.ADT.LITR.ZS/countries/ IN-PK?display=graph. Latest available figure.

60. UNESCO Institute for Statistics. Data retrieved from World Development Indicators online database, accessed April 9, 2014, http://databank. worldbank.org/data/home.aspx.

61. "The Millennium Development Goals Report, 2013" United Nations, 17. Available from http://mdgs.un.org/unsd/mdg/Resources/Static/ Products/Progress2013/English2013.pdf.

62. UNESCO Institute for Statistics. Figure based on author's calculations of data retrieved from World Development Indicators online database, accessed April 9, 2014, http://databank.worldbank.org/data/home.aspx.

63. "The Millennium Development Goals Report, 2013," 34.

64. World Bank, "2.21 World Development Indicators: Mortality," accessed April 10, 2014, http://data.worldbank.org/indicator/SP.DYN.IMRT.IN.

65. Ibid.

66. Ibid.

67. World Bank, "Highlights: World Development Indicators, 2014," 10.

68. World Health Organization, Global Health Observatory Data Repository, data retrieved June 7, 2014, http://apps.who.int/gho/data/node.main.

69. "Committing to Child Survival: A Promise Renewed 2013 Progress Report," United Nations Children's Fund (UNICEF), (September 2013), 4. Diarrhea can be inexpensively and effectively treated. Pneumonia is more expensive to treat and prevent, but a plan has been developed by the World Health Organization. See "Immunization Highlights 2008–2009," World Health Organization, November 2010, 13. Available from http:// whqlibdoc.who.int/hq/2010/WHO_IVB_10.11_eng.pdf?ua=1.

70. World Health Organization, Global Health Observatory Data Repository, data retrieved June 7, 2014, http://apps.who.int/gho/data/node.main.

71. Poverty-Environment Partnership, "Linking Poverty Reduction and Water Management," updated November 2008, 40, available from http://esa. un.org/iys/docs/san_lib_docs/povety%20reduction%20and%20water. pdf. See the cited study for specific figures on a range of interventions and their associated economic benefits: G. Hutton and L. Haller, *Evaluation of the Costs and Benefits of Water and Sanitation Improvements at the Global Level* (Geneva: World Health Organization, 2004), 26, 34, available from http:// www.who.int/water_sanitation_health/wsh0404.pdf.

72. "Weight Loss Market in U.S. Up 1.7% to $61 Billion," PRWeb, April 16, 2013, accessed April 10, 2014, http://www.prweb.com/releases/2013/4/ prweb10629316.htm.

73. BFWI, *2013 Hunger Report*, 5.

74. Mooneyham, *What Do You Say to a Hungry World?*, 191.

75. *2013 Hunger Report*, 5.

76. World Health Organization, *Health Conditions in the Americas* (Pan-American Health Organization, Scientific Publication Series, no. 427, 1982), 102.

77. World Health Organization, "Adults and Children Estimated to be Living with HIV, 2012," accessed April 10, 2014, http://www.who.int/gho/hiv/epidemic/hiv_001.jpg.

78. Mead Over and Yuna Sakuma, "A Question of Quality: Why Retention Matters for AIDS Treatment," accessed April 11, 2014, http://www.cgdev.org/blog/question-quality-why-retention-matters-aids-treatment. US data is from CDC's June 2013 "Today's HIV/AIDS epidemic." Africa estimates are derived by Over and Sakuma from Elvin Geng's PEPFAR SAB presentation (October, 2012) which credits Sydney Rosen and Matthew P. Fox, "Retention in HIV Care between Testing and Treatment in Sub-Saharan Africa: A Systematic Review," *PLoS Med* 8, no. 7 (2011): e1001056; Sydney Rosen and Matthew P. Fox, "Patient Retention in Antiretroviral Therapy Programs up to Three Years on Treatment in sub-Saharan Africa, 2007–2009: Systematic Review," *Tropical Medicine & International Health* 2010-Jun:15 Suppl 1:1–15.

79. World Health Organization, Global Health Observatory Data Repository, accessed April 10, 2014, http://apps.who.int/gho/data/node.main.619?lang=en.

80. World Bank, World Development Indicators, accessed April 10, 2014. Data is from 1990–2012.

81. United Nations, "Millennium Development Goals Report 2013," 36.

82. Opportunity International's Impact, October, 2003.

83. "Global Report: UNAIDS report on the global AIDS epidemic 2013," (UNAIDS, 2013), 68.

84. Ibid., 15.

85. Ibid., 46.

86. "The 2013 DATA Report: Executive Summary," One.org, 2013, 10. Available from http://one-org.s3.amazonaws.com/us/wp-content/uploads/2013/05/ONE_DataReport_2013_Summary.pdf.

87. Ibid.

88. UNICEF, The State of the World's Children 1995, 21.

89. "Measles Data by WHO Region," World Health Organization, accessed April 11, 2014, http://apps.who.int/gho/data/view.main.1520_62?lang=en.

90. WHO, UNICEF, World Bank. State of the world's vaccines and immunization, 3rd ed. Geneva, World Health Organization, 2009, XIX, XXIV.

91. Lara J Wolfson, et al, "Estimating the costs of achieving the WHO–UNICEF Global Immunization Vision and Strategy, 2006–2015," *Bulletin of the World Health Organization* 86, no. 1 (January 2008), 35. Available from http://www.who.int/bulletin/volumes/86/1/07-045096.pdf?ua=1.

92. Lara J Wolfson, et al, "Estimating the cost . . ." 35.

93. World Bank, World Development Report 1993, 19.

94. Melinda Henry, Global Alliance for Vaccines and Immunization (Gavi) (World Health Organization, March 2001–2002), http://www.who.int/mediacentre/factsheets/fs169/en/.

95. "25 Years: The MECTIZAN® Donation Program," Merck, last modified 2012, accessed April 11, 2014, http://www.merck.com/about/featured-stories/mectizan1.html#nojs.

96. Bruno de Benoist, "Iodine deficiency in 2007: Global progress since 2003," *Food and Nutrition Bulletin* 29, no. 3 (2008): 195. Available from http://www.who.int/nutrition/publications/micronutrients/FNBvol29N3sep08.pdf?ua=1.

97. "Micronutrient Deficiencies," World Health Organization, accessed April 11, 2014, http://www.who.int/nutrition/topics/idd/en/.

98. "The 10 Most Expensive Weapons in the World," 24/7 Wall St., January 9, 2012, accessed April 16, 2014, http://247wallst.com/special-report/2012/01/09/the-10-most-expensive-weapons-in-the-world/3/

99. "Micronutrients - Iodine, Iron and Vitamin A," UNICEF, last updated May 6, 2003, accessed April 11, 2014, http://www.unicef.org/nutrition/index_iodine.html.

100. Jennifer Bryce, Oliver Fontaine, Roeland Monasch, and Cesar G. Victoria, "Reducing Deaths from Diarrhea through Oral Rehydration Therapy," Bulletin of the World Health Organization (New York: World Health Organization, 2000), 1250.

101. "Committing to Child Survival: A Promise Renewed Progress Report 2013," UNICEF, 25.

102. "Oral Rehydration Salts ORS," Rehydration Project, updated August 2013, accessed April 16, 2014, http://rehydrate.org/ors/.

103. UNICEF, The State of the World's Children 1995, 10, 13.

104. "Polio Eradication & Endgame Strategic Plan 2013–2018," GPEI (World Health Organization, 2013), 1.

105. "Polio Eradication & Endgame Strategic Plan 2013–2018," GPEI (World Health Organization, 2013), 2, 6.

106. "Global Report: UNAIDS report on the global AIDS epidemic 2013," (UNAIDS, 2013), 4.

107. UNAIDS, "Update: How Africa Turned AIDS Around," May 2013, 15.

108. World Health Organization, "Number of Deaths Due to HIV/AIDS," accessed April 10, 2014, http://www.who.int/gho/hiv/epidemic_status/ deaths_text/en/.

109. "Global Report: UNAIDS report on the global AIDS epidemic 2013," (UNAIDS, 2013), 48.

110. "Humanitarian Action for Children 2014: Overview," UNICEF, 5. Available from http://www.unicef.org/appeals/files/HAC_Overview_2014_WEB. pdf.

111. "The 10 Most Expensive Weapons in the World," 24/7 Wall St., January 9, 2012, accessed April 16, 2014, http://247wallst.com/ special-report/2012/01/09/the-10-most-expensive-weapons-in-the-world/3/.

112. "2011 World Population Data Sheet," Population Reference Bureau, July 2011, accessed April 17, 2014, http://www.prb.org/pdf11/2011-world- population-data-sheet-presentation.pdf.

113. United Nations, Department of Economic and Social Affairs, Population Division (2013). *World Population Prospects: The 2012 Revision, Key Findings and Advance Tables*. Working Paper No. ESA/P/WP.227, 2.

114. United Nations, Department of Economic and Social Affairs, Population Division (2013). *World Fertility Report 2012* (United Nations publication), 1.

115. Ibid., ix, 3.

116. Ibid., ix.

117. "2011 World Population Data Sheet," Population Reference Bureau, July 2011, accessed April 17, 2014, http://www.prb.org/pdf11/2011-world- population-data-sheet-presentation.pdf.

118. United Nations Population Division. World Population Prospects; United Nations Statistical Division. Population and Vital Statistics Report (various years); and Census reports and other statistical publications from national statistical offices. Figure retrieved from World Development Indicators online database, Accessed April 17, 2014, http://databank.worldbank.org/ data/home.aspx.

119. United Nations, Department of Economic and Social Affairs, Population Division (2013). *World Population Prospects: The 2012 Revision, Key Findings and Advance Tables*. Working Paper No. ESA/P/WP.227, 1.

120. Ibid., 1.

121. United Nations, Department of Economic and Social Affairs, Population Division (2013). World Population Prospects: The 2012 Revision, DVD Edition.

122. Quoted in *BFW Newsletter*, July 1976. This issue has an excellent refutation of Hardin and Paddock's call for triage and lifeboat ethics.

123. See the critique in Amartya Sen, "Population, Delusion and Reality," *New York Review of Books*, September 22, 1994; reprinted in Mike Cromartie, ed., *The Nine Lives of Population Control* (Grand Rapids: Eerdmans, 1995), 101ff.

124. World Development Indicators, Accessed April 17, 2014, http://povertydata.worldbank.org/poverty/home/.

125. United Nations, Department of Economic and Social Affairs, Population Division (2013). World Population Prospects: The 2012 Revision, DVD Edition. Estimate based on "No Change" in fertility or mortality rates.

126. "Desertification: The Invisible Front Line," United Nations Convention to Combat Desertification, January 2014, 4.

127. "Desertification, Land Degradation, and Drought, (DLDD) – Some Global Facts and Figures," United Nations Convention to Combat Desertification, June 17, 2012, accessed April 18, 2014, http://www.unccd.int/Lists/SiteDocumentLibrary/WDCD/DLDD%20Facts.pdf.

128. Supplement to *Radar News*, January 1975, 3–4.

Chapter 2

1. Hélder Câmara, *Revolution Through Peace* (New York: Harper & Row, 1971), 142.

2. *New York Times*, July 12, 1949. Quoted in Jules Henry, *Culture Against Man* (New York: Random House, 1963), 19.

3. For the adverting figure see, U.S. Census Bureau, *Statistical Abstract of the United States 2003*, 1274. For the education statistic see, U.S. Census Bureau, *Statistical Abstract of the United States 2012*, 220.

4. "Marketing Fact Pack: 2014 Edition," *Advertising Age*, December 30, 2013, 14. In 2010, we spent $289 billion on public higher education, *Statistical Abstract of United States 2012*, 220.

5. "Marketing Fact Pack: 2014 Edition," *Advertising Age*, December 30, 2013, 15.

6. Richard K. Taylor, "The Imperative of Economic De-Development," *The Other Side* 10, no. 4 (July–August 1974): 17.

7. Common Sense Media, "Advertising to Children and Teens: Current Practices," Spring 2014, 5.

8. Nielsen, "State of the Media: U.S. Consumer Usage Report," 2012.

9. Common Sense Media, "Advertising to Children and Teens: Current Practices," Spring 2014, 5. Advergaming refers to games created for the explicit purpose of advertising a company's product.

10. Robert Bellah, *The Broken Covenant: American Civil Religion in Time of Trial* (University of Chicago Press, 1992), 134.

11. *Newsweek*, October 28, 1974, 69.

12. John V. Taylor, *Enough Is Enough* (London: SCM Press, 1975), 71.

13. Patrick Kerans, *Sinful Social Structures* (New York: Paulist Press, 1974), 80–81. See further, chapter 6.

14. See the helpful comments on this in Art Gish, *Beyond the Rat Race* (Scottdale, PA: Herald Press, 1973), 122–26.

15. UNDP, *Human Development Report 1999*, 3; UNDP, *Human Development Report 2005*, 36.

16. Rob Clark, "World Income Inequality in the Global Era: New Estimates, 1990–2008," *Social Problems* 58, No. 4 (November 2011): 587–588.

17. Oxfam, "Working For the Few: Political Capture and Economic Inequality," January 20, 2014, 5; cf. Isabel Ortiz and Matthew Cummins, "Global Inequality," 20.

18. Economists use three terms: Gross Domestic Product (GDP), Gross National Product (GNP), and Gross National Income (GNI). GDP refers to the total value of goods and services produced in a particular geographical area (e.g., country). GNP refers to the actual income earned by the nationals of a particular country (including income from foreign investments and minus local profits sent to the home country by foreign owners of local enterprises). See Michael P. Todaro and Stephen C. Smith, *Economic Development*, 8th ed. (New York: Addison Wesley, 2003), 542. GNP and GNI are very similar. The World Bank has replaced GNP with GNI (see http://data.worldbank.org/indicator/NY.GNP.PCAP.CD).

19. World Bank, World Development Indicators, "Size of the Economy," accessed April 21, 2014, http://wdi.worldbank.org/table/1.1.

20. Ibid.

21. The price of a haircut in Bangladesh is based on personal communication with Rosalind Hawlader, June 23, 1996.

22. See above, n. 18.

23. Figures come from using xe.com currency converter on April 23, 2014.

24. World Bank, World Development Indicators, "Size of the Economy," accessed April 21, 2014, http://wdi.worldbank.org/table/1.1; "Table 1: Human Development Index and its Components," *Human Development Report 2013*, 144–147.

25. Sue J. Goldie, et al. "Working Paper 1: Priority Research Areas for Basic Science And Product Development for Neglected Diseases," *Global Health 2035*, November 26, 2013, 7. Available from http://globalhealth2035.org/working-papers.

26. "Percent of consumer expenditures spent on food, alcoholic beverages, and tobacco that were consumed at home, by selected countries, 2012," USDA, Economic Research Service, accessed April 23, 2014, http://www.ers.usda.gov/data-products/food-expenditures.aspx#26636.

27. Ibid.

28. "Obesity and Overweight," U.S. Centers for Disease Control and Prevention, last updated November 21, 2013, accessed April 23, 2014, http://www.cdc.gov/nchs/fastats/overwt.htm.

29. "Global and regional food consumption patterns and trends," World Health Organization, accessed April 24, 2014, http://www.who.int/nutrition/topics/3_foodconsumption/en/. Sub-Saharan Africa excludes South Africa.

30. Figures have been updated using the U.S. Bureau of Labor Statistics' Consumer Price Index Inflation Calculator, accessed May 23, 2014, http://www.bls.gov/data/inflation_calculator.htm, to reflect the difference in inflation from 1974 to 2014.

31. "Middle Class? Not on $15,000 a Year," *Philadelphia Inquirer*, October 28, 1974, 9a. I have updated Arnett's figures to account for inflation. He actually spoke of $15,000 and $18,000. But $15,000 in 1974 equals $72,100 in 2014, and $18,000 in 1974 equals $86,600 in 2014.

32. *Newsweek*, September 21, 1977, 30–31. Figures have been updated to reflect inflation.

33. Quoted in Juliet B. Schor, *The Overworked American* (New York: HarperCollins, 1992), 116. Figure has been updated to reflect inflation.

34. George Stephanopoulos, "EXCLUSIVE – Romney on Debates: Obama Will 'Say Things That Aren't True,'" September 14, 2012, accessed April 25, 2014, http://abcnews.go.com/blogs/politics/2012/09/exclusive-romney-on-debates-obama-will-say-things-that-arent-true/.

35. For 1993 Figures: UNICEF, *The State of the World's Children 1995* (New York: Oxford University Press, 1995), 68–69. For 2003 figures: Organization for Economic Co-operation and Development, Official Development Assistance (ODA) from 2000 to 2003. For 2013 figures: Organization for Economic Co-operation and Development, "Preliminary Data – Official Development Assistance (ODA) data for 2013," updated April 8, 2014, accessed April 25, 2014, http://www.oecd.org/dac/stats/data.htm.

36. See Chapter 11, nn. 112–15 and findings released on February 2, 2001, at http://www.pipa.org/onlinereports/bfw/finding1.html.

37. John Norris, "Five Myths About Foreign Aid," *Washington Post*, April 28, 2011, accessed April 25, 2014, http://www.washingtonpost.com/opinions/five-myths-about-foreign-aid/2011/04/25/AF00z05E_story.html.

38. Paul A. Laudicina, *World Poverty and Development: A Survey of American Opinion* (Washington, DC: Overseas Development Council, 1973), 21.

39. "The 0.7% ODA/GNI Target - A History," OECD, accessed April 28, 2014, http://www.oecd.org/dac/stats/the07odagnitarget-ahistory.htm.

40. "Aid to Developing Countries Rebounds in 2013 to Reach an All-Time High," OECD, April 8, 2014, accessed April 25, 2014, http://www.oecd.org/development/aid-to-developing-countries-rebounds-in-2013-to-reach-an-all-time-high.htm.

41. World Bank, World Development Indicators 2014, accessed February 16, 2015. Growth in terms of average GDP growth for High Income – OECD countries for given years.

42. UNDP, Human Development Report 1994, 48, and World Bank, "World Development Report 2004," 184.

43. In 2003, world military spending was $956 billion (current dollars) according to The Stockholm International Peace Research Institute. See also David Fickling, "World Bank Condemns Defense Spending" (*Guardian*, February 14, 2004), http://www.guardian.co.uk/print/0,3858,4858685-103681,00.html.

44. UNDP, *Human Development Report 2013*, 165. Military spending figure in 2005 PPP dollars and was calculated by multiplying percent of GDP spent on military by total GDP. Combined income of 1.2 billion earning $1.25 for 365 days equals $547 billion and for the 1.2 billion earning $2 equals $876 billion.

45. UNDP, *Human Development Report 1995*, 8.

46. Figures based on author's calculations of Stockholm International Peace Research Institute (SIPRI) and Yearbook: Armaments, Disarmament and International Security data retrieved from World Development Indicators 2014 online database, accessed April 28, 2014, http://data.worldbank.org/.

47. Michael Renner, "Peacekeeping Budgets Equal Less Than Two Days of Military Spending," World Watch Institute, March 31, 2014, accessed April 28, 2014, http://vitalsigns.worldwatch.org/vs-trend/peacekeeping-budgets-equal-less-two-days-military-spending.

48. Garrett Hardin, "Lifeboat Ethics: The Case Against Helping the Poor," *Psychology Today* 8, no. 4 (September 1974): 38ff. See also William and Paul Paddock, *Famine 1975!* (Boston: Little, Brown and Co., 1967), reprinted in 1976 under the title *Time of Famines: America and the World Food Crisis*.

49. Brown, *In the Human Interest*, 113–14.

50. See Michael Cromartie, ed., *The Nine Lives of Population Control* (Grand Rapids: Eerdmans, 1995), 101–27.

51. BFWI, *Hunger 95*, 63.

52. The right kind of aid often encourages labor-intensive development and intermediate technology. See E. F. Schumacher, *Small Is Beautiful* (New York: Harper Touchbooks, 1973), 161–79.
53. UNDP, Do You Know That (Quotable Facts from HDR), United Nations Development Programme, 2003, accessed 1 January 2005; available from http://www.undp.org/hdr2003/know_that.html.
54. Robert H. Schuller, *Your Church Has Real Possibilities!* (Glendale, CA: Regal Books, 1974), 117.

Introduction to Part Two

1. Quoted in *Post-American*, 1, no.4 (Summer 1972), 1.
2. Paul A. Laudicina, *World Poverty and Development: A Survey of American Opinion* (Washington, D.C.: Overseas Development Council, 1973), 21.
3. Ronald J. Sider, *For They Shall Be Fed* (Dallas: Word, 1997). An earlier edition was called *Cry Justice: The Bible Speaks on Hunger and Poverty* (New York: Paulist Press; Downers Grove, IL: InterVarsity, 1983).

Chapter 3

1. See, for instance, Enzo Gatti, *Rich Church—Poor Church?* (Maryknoll, NY: Orbis Books, 1974), 43. Liberation theology in general leans in this direction. For excellent evaluations of liberation theology, see J. Andrew Kirk, *Liberation Theology: An Evangelical View from the Third World* (Atlanta, GA: John Knox Press, 1980); and Harvie Conn's two excellent chapters (8 and 9) on liberation theology in Stanley N. Gundry and Alan F. Johnson, eds., *Tensions in Contemporary Theology* (Chicago: Moody Press, 1976).
2. Ernst Bammel, "ptochos," in Gerhard Kittel and Gerhard Friedrich, eds., *Theological Dictionary of the New Testament*, trans. Geoffrey W. Bromiley, 10 vols. (Grand Rapids, MI: Eerdmans, 1968), 6:888. Hereafter called *TDNT*.
3. A. Gelin, *The Poor of Yahweh* (Collegeville, MN: Liturgical Press, 1964), 19–20.
4. *TDNT*, VI, 885ff. Penes is used only once and means a humble workman with no property (*TDNT*, VI, 37ff). For an excellent discussion on the biblical teaching on the poor and material possessions, see Craig L. Blomberg, *Neither Poverty Nor Riches: A Biblical Theology of Material Possessions* (Grand Rapids: Eerdmans, 1999).
5. See the helpful distinctions among those who are poor because of (1) sloth, (2) calamity, (3) exploitation, and (4) voluntary choice in R. C. Sproul, "Who Are the Poor?" *Tabletalk* 3, no. 6 (July 1979). See also the discussion of the "spiritual poor" below, note 12.

6. Unlike some liberation theologians who take the Exodus merely as an inspirational device, I assert that in the Exodus God was both liberating oppressed persons and also calling out a special people to be the recipients of his special revelation. Yahweh called forth a special people so that through them he could reveal his will and salvation for all people. But his will included, as he revealed even more clearly to his covenant people, that his people should follow him and be very concerned for justice for the poor and oppressed. The fact that Yahweh did not liberate all poor Egyptians at the exodus does not mean that God was not concerned for the poor everywhere any more than the fact that he did not give the Ten Commandments to everyone in the Near East means that God did not intend them to have universal application. Because God chose to reveal himself in history, he disclosed to particular people at particular points in time what he willed for all people everywhere.

7. John Bright, *A History of Israel* (Philadelphia: Westminster Press, 1959), 240–41.

8. Ibid.

9. Roland de Vaux, *Ancient Israel* (New York: McGraw Hill, 1965), 2:72–73.

10. So also in the case of Judah; compare Ezekiel 20, Jeremiah 11:9–10.

11. Preaching the gospel and seeking justice for the poor are distinct, equally important dimensions of the total mission of the church; see my "Evangelism, Salvation and Social Justice: Definitions and Interrelationships," *International Review of Mission*, July 1975, 251ff. (esp. 258); my "Evangelism or Social Justice: Eliminating the Options," *Christianity Today*, 8 October 1976, 26–29; and, more recently, *Good News and Good Works* (Grand Rapids: Baker, 1999) and *Cup of Water, Bread of Life* (Grand Rapids Zondervan, 1994).

12. This is not to deny that a "spiritual" usage of the term "the poor" emerged in the intertestamental period. But even then, the material, economic foundation was never absent. See my "An Evangelical Theology of Liberation," in Kenneth S. Kantzer and Stanley N. Gundry, eds., *Perspectives on Evangelical Theology* (Grand Rapids: Baker, 1979), 122–24.

13. See also Revelation 7:16.

14. Richard Batey, *Jesus and the Poor* (New York: Harper & Row, 1972), 7.

15. This paragraph represents a change from the first three editions. I think John Schneider's critique at this point is partly correct. See his *Godly Materialism* (Downers Grove, IL: InterVarsity, 1994), 103–121 (esp. 107–110).

16. Martin Hengel, Property and Riches in the *Early Church: Aspects of a Social History of Early Christianity* (Philadelphia: Fortress Press, 1974), 38.

17. Batey, *Jesus and the Poor*, 6. Again, however, I think Schneider is right (*Godly Materialism*, 110) that my earlier editions overstated the marginality of Nazareth.

18. See also Psalm 107:35–41. See the "Pious Poor" section, chapter 5, for a discussion of the different versions of the beatitudes in Matthew 5 and Luke 6.

19. I do not overlook, of course, the biblical teaching that obedience brings prosperity. See "Biblical Balance" in chapter 5, for a discussion of this theme.

20. Bright, *History of Israel*, 306. For a similar event, see Daniel 4 (esp. v. 27).

21. See also Micah 2:1–3.

22. Joachim Jeremias, *The Parables of Jesus* (London: SCM Press, 1954), 128–30, and others have argued that Jesus' point was an entirely different one. But I am still inclined to follow the usual interpretation; see, for instance, *The Interpreter's Bible*, 8:288–92.

23. Ibid., 290.

24. Clark H. Pinnock, "An Evangelical Theology of Human Liberation," *Sojourners*, February 1976, 31.

25. "The Bible and the Other Side," *The Other Side* 11, no. 5 (September– October 1975): 57.

26. See J. A. Motyer, *The Day of the Lion: The Message of Amos* (Downers Grove, IL: InterVarsity, 1974), 129–37, for a good exegesis of these verses. See also Micah 6:6–8; James 2:14–17.

27. This is not to say that God is unconcerned with true worship. Nor does Amos 5:21–24 mean that God is saying, "I do not want you to defend my rights, real or imaginary; I want you to struggle and expend your energies in advancing the rights of the poor and oppressed" (Gatti, *Rich Church—Poor Church?*, 17). Such a dichotomy ignores the central prophetic attack on idolatry. God wants both worship and justice. Tragically, some people today concentrate on one, some on the other. Few seek both simultaneously.

28. See for example Craig S. Keener, *A Commentary on the Gospel of Matthew* (Grand Rapids: Eerdmans, 1999), 605–606.

29. G. E. Ladd, *A Theology of the New Testament* (Grand Rapids: Eerdmans, 1974), 133. For this whole topic of whether Matthew 25, 1 John 3, and so on must be limited in their application to Christians, see the superb discussion of Stephen C. Mott, *Biblical Ethics and Social Change* (New York: Oxford Univ. Press, 1982), 34–36.

30. Todd M. Johnson, ed., *World Christian Database* (Leiden/Boston: Brill, accessed May, 8 2014). For GDP of low and lower-middle income countries, World Bank, World Development Indicators, accessed May 8, 2014.

31. God does not desire the salvation of the poor more than the salvation of the rich. I disagree strongly with Gatti's assertion: "They [the poor and oppressed] are the ones that have the best right to that word [of salvation]; they are the privileged recipients of the Gospel" (*Rich Church—Poor Church?*, 43). God desires all people—oppressors and oppressed alike—to be saved. No one has any "right" to hear God's Word. We all deserve death. It is only by contrast with the sinful perversity of Christians who prefer to minister in the suburbs rather than the slums that Jesus and Paul seem to be biased in favor of preaching to the poor.
32. See chapter 6.
33. See my articles on the resurrection listed in note 2 of the epilogue.

Chapter 4

1. I adapt here some material from my article, "Toward a Biblical Perspective on Equality," *Interpretation*, April 1989, 156–69.
2. See Roland de Vaux, *Ancient Israel: Its Life and Institutions*, trans. John McHugh (London: Darton, Longman and Todd, 1961), I, 164.
3. H. Eberhard von Waldow, "Social Responsibility and Social Structure in Early Israel," *CBQ* 32 (1970), 195.
4. Albrecht Alt, "Micah 2. 1–5: Ges Anadasmos in Juda." *Kleine Schriften zur Geschichte des Volkes Israel* (Munich: C.H. Beck, 1959), III, 374.
5. In his study of early Israel, Norman Gottwald concluded that Israel was "an egalitarian, extended-family, segmentary tribal society with an agricultural-pastoral economic base . . . characterized by profound resistance and opposition to the forms of political domination and social stratification that had become normative in the chief cultural and political centers of the ancient Near East." *The Tribes of Yahweh: A Sociology of the Religion of Liberated Israel 1250-1050 BCE* (London: SCM Press, 1979), 10.
6. For a survey of the literature on Leviticus 25, see R. Gnuse, "Jubilee Legislation in Leviticus: Israel's Vision of Social Reform," *Biblical Theology Bulletin* 15 (1983), 43–48.
7. Also Ezekiel 47:14. See the discussion and the literature cited in Mott, *Biblical Ethics and Social Change*, 65–66; and Stephen Charles Mott, "Egalitarian Aspects of the Biblical Theory of Justice," in the *American Society of Christian Ethics*, Selected Papers 1978, ed. Max Stackhouse (Newton, MA: American Society of Christian Ethics, 1978), 8–26.
8. See the excellent book edited by Loren Wilkinson, *Earthkeeping: Christian Stewardship of Natural Resources*, 2nd ed. (Grand Rapids: Eerdmans, 1980), esp. 232–37.

9. See in this connection the fine article by Paul G. Schrotenboer, "The Return of Jubilee," *International Reformed Bulletin*, Fall 1973, 19ff. (esp. 23–24).

10. See also Ephesians 2:13–18. Marc H. Tanenbaum points out the significance of the day of atonement in "Holy Year 1975 and Its Origins in the Jewish Jubilee Year," *Jubilaeum* (1974), 64.

11. For the meaning of the word liberty in Leviticus 25:10, see Martin Noth, *Leviticus* (Philadelphia: Westminster, 1965), 187: "Deror, a 'liberation' . . . is a feudal word from the Accadian (an)duraru—'freeing from burdens.'"

12. Roland de Vaux reflects the scholarly consensus that Leviticus 25 "was a Utopian law and it remained a dead letter" (*Ancient Israel*, 1:177). Tanenbaum ("Holy Year 1975," 75–76) on the other hand, thinks it was practiced. The only other certain references to it are in Leviticus 27:16–25, Numbers 36:4, and Ezekiel 46:17. It would be exceedingly significant if one could show that Isaiah 61:1–2 (which Jesus cited to outline his mission in Luke 4:18–19) also refers to the year of jubilee. De Vaux doubts that Isaiah 61:1 refers to the jubilee (*Ancient Israel*, 1:176). The same word, however, is used in Isaiah 61:1 and Leviticus 25:10. See John H. Yoder's argument in *Politics of Jesus* (Grand Rapids: Eerdmans, 1972), 64–77; see also Robert Sloan, *The Acceptable Year of the Lord* (Austin, TX: Scholar Press, 1977); and Donald W. Blosser, "Jesus and the Jubilee" (Ph. D. diss., Univ. of St. Andrews, 1979).

13. My understanding of the centrality of the land in Israel's self-understanding owes a good deal to Christopher J. H. Wright, *An Eye for an Eye: The Place of Old Testament Ethics Today* (Downers Grove, IL: InterVarsity, 1983), esp. chapters 3 and 4. Walter Brueggemann's *The Land* (Philadelphia: Fortress Press, 1977) is also a particularly important work on this topic.

14. De Vaux, *Ancient Israel*, 1:173–75.

15. Leviticus 25 seems to provide for emancipation of slaves only every fiftieth year.

16. See Jeremiah 34 for a fascinating account of God's anger at Israel for their failure to obey this command.

17. Some modern commentators think that Deuteronomy 15:1–11 provides for a one-year suspension of repayment of loans rather than an outright remission of them. See, for example, C. J. H. Wright, *God's People in God's Land* (Grand Rapids: Eerdmans, 1990), 148 and S. R. Driver, *Deuteronomy, International Critical Commentary*, 3d ed. (Edinburgh: T. and T. Clark, 1895), 179–80. But Driver's argument is basically that remission would have been impractical. He admits that v. 9 seems to point toward remission of loans. So too Gerhard von Rad, *Deuteronomy* (Philadelphia: Westminster, 1966), 106.

18. See de Vaux, *Ancient Israel*, 1:174–75, for discussion of the law's implementation. In the Hellenistic period, there is clear evidence that it was put into effect.

19. Ibid., 1:171.

20. John Mason has done some masterful work on the type of "welfare system" suggested by the Old Testament; see "Biblical Teaching and Assisting the Poor," *Transformation*, 4 (April–June, 1987), 1–14, and his essay, "Biblical Teaching and the Objectives of Welfare Policy in the United States," in Stanley W. Carlson-Thies and James W. Skillen, eds., *Welfare in America: Christian Perspectives on a Policy in Crisis* (Grand Rapids: Eerdmans, 1996), 145–85.

21. This is an extremely complicated problem, which has been debated throughout church history. The long dispute among Lutherans over the "third use of the law" is one example of the perennial debate.

22. De Vaux, *Ancient Israel*, 1:171.

23. Ibid., 170; Taylor, *Enough Is Enough*, 56–60.

24. Driver, Deuteronomy, 178.

25. For a highly fascinating, scholarly account of the entire history, see Benjamin Nelson, *The Idea of Usury: From Tribal Brotherhood to Universal Otherhood*, 2d ed. (Chicago: Univ. of Chicago Press, 1969).

26. See the excellent discussion by Bob Goudzwaard, *Capitalism and Progress: A Diagnosis of Western Society* (Grand Rapids: Eerdmans, 1979).

27. See Matthew 4:23; 24:14; Mark 1:14–15; Luke 4:43; 16:16; and see the long discussion of the prophetic hope and the Gospel of the kingdom in my *Good News and Good Works*, chapters 3–4.

28. For this common interpretation, see Batey, *Jesus and the Poor*, 3, 9, 100, note 8; J. A. Ziesler, *Christian Asceticism* (Grand Rapids: Eerdmans, 1973), 45; TDNT 3:796; *Interpreter's Bible*, 8:655, 690; Carl Henry, "Christian Perspective on Private Property," in *God and the Good*, ed. C. Oriebeke and L. Smedes (Grand Rapids: Eerdmans, 1975), 98.

29. See also Batey, *Jesus and the Poor*, 8.

30. Taylor, *Economics and the Gospel*, 21.

31. See D. Guthrie et al., ed., *The New Bible Commentary Revised* (Grand Rapids: Eerdmans, 1970), 980; Batey, *Jesus and the Poor*, 38.

32. TDNT, 3:796.

33. The key verbs are *epipraskon* and *diemerizon* (Acts 2:45) and *epheron* (Acts 4:34). See *Interpreter's Bible*, 9:52; Batey, *Jesus and the Poor*, 33, 105, note 9.

34. Ziesler, *Christian Asceticism*, 110.

35. Batey, *Jesus and the Poor*, 36, 96–97.

36. See Keith F. Nickle, *The Collection: A Study of Paul's Strategy, Studies in Biblical Theology*, no. 48 (Naperville, IL: Allenson, 1966), 29; and *Interpreter's Bible*, 9:153.

37. See Diane MacDonald, "The Shared Life of the Acts Community," *Post-American*, July 1975, 28.
38. See *Interpreter's Bible*, 9:150–52, for a summary of the reasons for accepting the reliability of this account.
39. See Nickle, *The Collection*, 68–69.
40. See *TDNT*, 3:804ff.
41. In fact, Paul was probably at Jerusalem to deliver the gift mentioned in Acts 11:27–30. See *Interpreter's Bible*, 9:151.
42. See *TDNT*, 3:807–8.
43. See also the striking use of *koinonos* in Philemon 17–20. As fellow Christians, the slave Onesimus; his master, Philemon; and Paul are all partners (*koinonoi*). This common fellowship means that Paul can ask Philemon to charge Onesimus's debt to his own account. But Paul and Philemon are also partners in Christ. Furthermore, Philemon owes Paul his very soul. Therefore, Paul suggests there is no need for anyone to reimburse Philemon. Their fellowship in Christ cancels any debt that Onesimus might otherwise owe. See *TDNT*, 3:807.
44. For example, Proverbs 6:6–11; 10:4–5. See my "Towards a Biblical Perspective on Equality," esp. 164, and my *Fixing the Moral Deficit* (Downers Grove, IL: IVP Books, 2012), 57–59.
45. Quoted in Hengel, *Property and Riches in the Early Church*, 42–43.
46. Ibid., 42–44.
47. Quoted in ibid., 45.
48. On August 21, 2012, Huffington Post reported a study that showed Americans waste $165 billion in food each year. See, "Food Waste: Americans Throw Away Nearly Half Their Food, $165 Billion Annually, Study Says," accessed May 12, 2014, http://www.huffingtonpost.com/2012/08/21/food-waste-americans-throw-away-food-study_n_1819340.html. Using the figure for the income of Christians in Africa from Todd M. Johnson, ed. *World Christian Database* (Leiden/Boston: Brill, accessed May 12, 2014), I estimated that $165 billion in food waste is 29.7 percent of $555 billion in African Christian income.
49. Total construction spending by religious institutions in the US was $840 billion according to U.S. Department of Commerce: Census Bureau, "Total Construction Spending: Religious," accessed May 21, 2014, http://research.stlouisfed.org/fred2/graph/?g=BiN. According to the Pew Research Center's Religion and Public Life Project, accessed May 21, 2014, http://religions.pewforum.org/reports, 78.4 percent of Americans are Christians. 78.4 percent of $840 billion is $659 billion.

50. See Helmut Gollwitzer, *The Rich Christians and Poor Lazarus*, trans. David Cairns (New York: Macmillan, 1970), 5, and Arthur C. Cochrane, *Eating and Drinking with Jesus* (Philadelphia: Westminster Press, 1974).

Chapter 5

1. Quoted in *Discernment*, Spring, 1995, 3. For good discussion of the themes of this chapter, see Blomberg, *Neither Poverty Nor Riches*.
2. Carl F. H. Henry, "Christian Perspective on Private Property," 97; Hengel, *Property and Riches in the Early Church*, 15.
3. See further Emil Brunner, *Justice and the Social Order*, trans. Mary Hottinger (London: Lutterworth Press, 1945), 42ff., 133ff.; and E. Clinton Gardner, *Biblical Faith and Social Ethics* (New York: Harper & Row, 1960), 285–91.
4. Adam Smith, *The Wealth of Nations* (1776; reprint ed., New York: Modern Library, 1937).
5. See, for example, Gary North, "Free Market Capitalism," *Wealth and Poverty: Four Christian Views of Economics*, ed. Robert G. Clouse (Downers Grove, IL: InterVarsity, 1984).
6. See Goudzwaard, *Capitalism and Progress*.
7. Henry, "Christian Perspective on Private Property," 97.
8. Hengel, *Property and Riches in the Early Church*, 12.
9. Walther Eichrodt, "The Question of Property in the Light of the Old Testament," *Biblical Authority for Today*, ed. Alan Richardson and W. Schweitzer (London: SCM Press, 1951), 261.
10. Ibid., 271.
11. Dom Helder Câmara, *Revolution Through Peace* (New York: Harper & Row, 1971), 142–43.
12. *TDNT*, 6:271. Taylor (*Enough Is Enough*, 45) suggests that the word connotes "excess" or "wanting more and more."
13. For a discussion of church discipline, see my "Watching Over One Another in Love," *The Other Side* XI, no. 3 (May–June, 1975): 13–20, 58–60 (esp. 59).
14. For a good discussion of this issue, see Ziesler, *Christian Asceticism*.
15. See the biblical texts in my *Cry Justice*, 175–87 for the former and 148–53 for the latter.
16. See Gordon D. Fee, "The New Testament View of Wealth and Possessions," *New Oxford Review* (May 1981): 9: "It is only as one is righteous—i.e., walks in accordance with God's law—that one is promised the blessing of abundance and family. But to be righteous meant especially that one cared for or pleaded the cause of the poor and the oppressed."
17. Taylor, *Enough Is Enough*, chapter 3.
18. See further the twenty references in Batey, *Jesus and the Poor*, 92.

19. Ziesler, *Christian Asceticism*, 52. See further my "An Evangelical Theology of Liberation," 122–25.

20. See further Gardner, *Biblical Faith and Social Ethics*, 276–77. Also, see the "Oxford Declaration on Christian Faith and Economics" in Herbert Schlossberg, Vinay Samuel, and Ronald J. Sider, eds., *Christianity and Economics in the Post-Cold War Era* (Grand Rapids: Eerdmans, 1994), 11–32.

21. *Interpreter's Bible*, 7:320; see also 1 Timothy 6:17–19.

22. A. W. Argyle, Matthew, *The Cambridge Bible Commentary* (Cambridge: Cambridge Univ. Press, 1963), 53. *Interpreter's Bible*, 7:318.

Chapter 6

1. Quoted in Richard K. Taylor, *Economics and the Gospel* (Philadelphia: United Church Press, 1973), 45.

2. "Edison High School—A History of Benign and Malevolent Neglect," *Oakes Newsletter* 5, no. 4 (14 December 1973):1–4; and "Northeast High Took the Glory Away," *Sunday Bulletin*, 27 January 1974, sect. 1, 3.

3. Rodney Stark et al., "Sounds of Silence," *Psychology Today*, April 1970, 38–41, 60–67.

4. See my "Evangelicals and Structural Injustice: Why Don't They Understand It and What Can Be Done?" in Daniel K. Darko and Beth Snodderly, eds., *First the Kingdom of God: Global Voices on Global Mission* (Pasadena, CA: William Carey International University Press, 2014), 257–263.

5. Bright, *History of Israel*, 241, note 84.

6. Compare Isaiah 3:13–17.

7. Schneider, *Godly Materialism*, 113.

8. Ronald J. Sider, "Racism," *United Evangelical Action*, Spring, 1977, 11.

9. Schneider, *Godly Materialism*, 114.

10. Ibid., 115.

11. See my *Good News and Good Works* for a discussion of "Jesus and Politics" (152–54).

12. Ibid.

13. This section is taken from my *Good News and Good Works*, 150–51; see further, 146–54.

14. See Mott, *Biblical Ethics and Social Change*, 4–6. For an excellent, extended treatment of systemic evil (including a discussion of the Pauline concept of the "principalities and powers"), see Mott, *Biblical Ethics and Social Change*, chapter 1.

15. Ibid., 4; *TDNT*, III, 868.

16. Quoted in Mott, *Biblical Ethics*, 6. Sometimes, of course, cosmos simply means God's good creation (e.g., John 1:9–10a). See Richard Mouw's delightful distinction in *Called to Holy Worldliness* (Philadelphia: Fortress, 1980), 75.

17. Clinton E. Arnold, *Powers of Darkness: Principalities and Powers in Paul's Letters* (Downers Grove, IL: InterVarsity, 1992), 203.
18. See Mott, *Biblical Ethics*, 6–10; Arnold, *Powers of Darkness*, esp. 87–210; and the massive, three-volume work by Walter Wink published by Fortress Press: *Naming the Powers* (1984); *Unmasking the Powers* (1986); *Engaging the Powers* (1992).
19. John Paul II, *Sollicitudo Rei Socialis* (Dec. 30, 1987), sect. 36. John Paul insists that we cannot gain a "profound understanding of the reality that confronts us" in our complex world without the ethical category of *"structures of sin"* (my italics).
20. See my *Good News and Good Works*. See also the call for biblical balance in every area that runs through my *Living Like Jesus* (Grand Rapids: Baker Books, 1999).

Introduction to Part Three

1. See, for an analysis of the long-term causes of poverty in the U.S., my *Just Generosity: A New Vision for Overcoming Poverty in America*, 2nd edition (Grand Rapids: Baker, 2007), 40–50.

Chapter 7

1. Lester C. Thurow, *The Future of Capitalism* (New York: Morrow, 1996), 15.
2. This is not to deny the universality of sin and therefore everyone's need to hear the Gospel. Nor is it to overlook the significance of cultural values in the adoption of technology.
3. BFWI, *Hunger 1995*, 22.
4. *Why Nations Fail: The Origins of Power, Prosperity and Poverty* (New York: Crown Business, 2012), 68. See also John Friedmann, *Empowerment: The Politics of Alternative Development* (Cambridge: Blackwell, 1992) where Friedmann argues that the lack of "social power" is what creates poverty. Also related to the issue of power is Amartya Sen's understanding of poverty as the absence of freedom to make meaningful choices. *Development as Freedom* (New York: Alfred A. Knopf, 1999). Very frequently this lack of freedom results from the abuse of power by others.
5. BFWI, *Hunger 1995*, 25.
6. Todaro, *Economic Development*, 1994, 292–95.
7. Ibid., 608.
8. Ibid., 296–97.
9. Gary A. Haugen and Victor Boutros, *The Locust Effect: Why the End of Poverty Requires the End of Violence* (Oxford University Press, 2014).

10. "Poverty & Equity Data: Philippines," Poverty and Inequality Database, accessed February 25, 2014, http://povertydata.worldbank.org/poverty/country/PHL.

11. "Property Rights and Resource Governance: Philippines," USAID, January 2011, accessed April 28, 2014, http://usaidlandtenure.net/philippines.

12. "Oil and Natural Gas in Sub-Saharan Africa," U.S. Energy Information Administration, August 1, 2013, accessed May 23, 2014, http://www.eia.gov/pressroom/presentations/howard_08012013.pdf; Nienke Oomes and Matthias Vocke, "Diamond Smuggling and Taxation in Sub-Saharan Africa," IMF Working Paper, Research Department and African Department, August 2003, 5.

13. World Bank, World Development Indicators 2014, accessed April 28, 2014, http://databank.worldbank.org.

14. "Angola," *The World Factbook 2013–14*, (Washington, DC: Central Intelligence Agency, 2013), accessed April 28, 2014, https://www.cia.gov/library/publications/the-world-factbook/geos/ao.html; "Angola: Oil Wealth Eludes Nation's Poor," Human Rights Watch, April 13, 2010, accessed April 28, 2014, http://www.hrw.org/news/2010/04/12/angola-oil-wealth-eludes-nation-s-poor.

15. "Angola Parliament Approves 2013 Budget in Final Vote," Reuters, February 14, 2013, accessed April 28, 2014, www.reuters.com/article/2013/02/14/angola-budget-idUSL5N0BECIM20130214; Colin McClelland, "Angola Approves $69 Billion Budget With $4.1 Billion Deficit," Bloomberg, February 14, 2013, accessed April 28, 2014, http://www.bloomberg.com/news/2013-02-14/angola-approves-69-billion-budget-with-4-1-billion-deficit.html.

16. UNDP, *Human Development Report 1994*, 43.

17. Acemoglu and Robinson, *Why Nations Fail*, 3.

18. Hernando de Soto, *The Other Path: The Invisible Revolution in the Third World* (New York; Harper and Row, 1989).

19. "The Facts," Raise the Minimum Wage, (A project of the National Employment Law Project), accessed April 29, 2014, http://www.raisetheminimumwage.com/facts/entry/amount-with-inflation/.

20. "Federal Minimum Wage," National Employment Law Project, accessed April 29, 2014, http://www.nelp.org/index.php/site/issues/category/federal_minimum_wage/.

21. See my *Fixing the Moral Deficit: A Balanced Way to Balance the Budget* (Downers Grove: IVP Books, 2012).

22. Rana Foroohar, "Time to Talk about the I Word," *Time*, February 10, 2014, 23.

23. *Fixing the Moral Deficit*, 32–38.
24. The Gini index measures the extent to which the distribution of income deviates from a perfectly equal distribution; 0 = perfect equality and 100 = perfect inequality.
25. World Bank, World Development Indicators, 2014: "2.9 Distribution of Income or Consumption," accessed April 29, 2014, http://wdi.worldbank.org/table/2.9#.
26. *Why Nations Fail*, 33–40, 120.
27. See also Mancur Olson, *Power and Prosperity: Outgrowing Communist and Capitalist Dictatorships* (New York: Basic Books, 2000).
28. Simon Johnson and James Kwak, *13 Bankers: The Wall Street Takeover and the Next Financial Meltdown* (New York: Vintage Books, 2011).
29. Joseph E. Stiglitz, et al., *The Stiglitz Report: Reforming the International Monetary and Financial Systems in the Wake of the Global Crisis* (New York: The New Press, 2010), 1; my italics.
30. For the World Bank, the figure is an average of U.S. voting power in each of the four World Bank organizations. See "Voting Powers," World Bank, accessed April 29, 2014, http://go.worldbank.org/AXK8ZEAD10; For the IMF, see "IMF Members' Quotas and Voting Power, and IMF Board of Governors," International Monetary Fund, updated April 29, 2014, accessed April 29, 2014, http://www.imf.org/external/np/sec/memdir/members.aspx#U.
31. Stiglitz, et al,. *Stiglitz Report*, 121ff.
32. For a time, the G-7 became the G-8 when Russia was included, but Russia was excluded in 2014 because of its actions in Ukraine.
33. The Chinese apparently knew how, but chose not to.
34. For a Marxist view of the impact of colonialism, see Walter Rodney, *How Europe Undeveloped Africa* (London: Bogle-L'Ouverture, 1972). Rodney argues that European nations found culturally sophisticated African nations and under colonial practices gradually stripped them of their cultural, social, and economic vitality. It would be foolish, of course, to accept uncritically Marxist scholars who explain all history in terms of class struggle, but there is equal danger in denying the importance of history as a crucial explanatory factor. P. T. Bauer, for example, in *Equality, the Third World, and Economic Delusion* (Cambridge, MA: Harvard University Press, 1981), disregards history and argues instead that current economic inequalities are almost totally due to differences in ingenuity, effort, and resource distribution rather than to historical misuses of political and economic power. For a balanced criticism of Bauer from a rather traditional economist, see Amartya Sen, "Just Desserts," a review of Bauer's book in the *New York Review of Books*, March 4, 1982. David

Beckmann, a Christian economist who formerly worked at the World
Bank, attributes a good deal of Third World poverty to colonial and
other exploitative practices, *Where Faith and Economics Meet* (Minneapolis:
Augsburg Press, 1981).

35. *Why Nations Fail,* 271.

36. *Why Nations Fail,* 199–201, 272–273.

37. Ibid., 245–250.

38. Ibid., 254.

39. Ibid., 116.

40. June Kronholz, "Gabon's Been Working on Its New Railroad, but Pay Day
Is Far Off," *Wall Street Journal,* July 30, 1981, 1ff.

41. Joan Robinson has argued that trade structures and land and labor
institutions in the Third World, as well as international financial
structures, all developed substantially from the foundation that was laid
in the colonial era. Robinson, *Aspects of Development and Underdevelopment*
(Cambridge: University Press, 1979).

42. Bread for the World Institute, *Within Reach: Global Development Goals, 2013
Hunger Report* (Washington: Bread for the World Institute, 2012), 3.

43. Ibid., 12.

44. Pope Francis, *The Joy of the Gospel: Evangelii Gaudium 204* (Washington: U.S.
Conference of Catholic Bishops, 2013), 103.

45. *Walking with the Poor* (2nd ed.; Maryknoll: Orbis, 2011), chapter 4.

46. Not all. Natural disasters and much lack of knowledge about better
technology to create wealth are not the result of sin.

47. See Jayakumar Christian, "Powerlessness of the Poor," (Ph.D. dissertation,
Fuller Theological Seminary, 1994) and *God of the Empty-Handed: Poverty,
Power and the Kingdom of God* (Monrovia: MARC, 1999); and Myers, *Walking
with the Poor,* 123–131.

Chapter 8

1. Mooneyham, *What Do You Say to a Hungry World?,* 117, 128.

2. Chile and Estonia are countries that lean more strongly than most in this
direction.

3. See the helpful distinction of different types of economies today in
Transformation, July–September 1995, 18.

4. Another possibility, democratic socialism, refers to a society in which
politically there is a democratic rather than a totalitarian political
arrangement, but the economy is largely centrally planned and
state-owned.

5. The Food and Agriculture Organization of the United Nations, The State of Food Insecurity in the World 2003 (Rome: Food and Agriculture Organization, 2003), 31.

6. BFWI, 2014 Hunger Report, 154.

7. Ibid., 34.

8. UNDP, Human Development Report 2013, 2, 13.

9. See chapter 11, nn. 50–61.

10. For a careful analysis of the complexity of the Chinese model, see Yasheng Huang, *Capitalism With Chinese Characteristics: Entrepreneurship and the State* (Cambridge University Press, 2008).

11. World Bank, World Development Report 2000/01: Attacking Poverty (New York: World Bank and Oxford University Press, 2001), 63, also available at http://siteresources.worldbank.org/INTPOVERTY/Resources/WDR/English-Full-Text-Report/ch4.pdf. This is not to forget that when a country opens its markets, there may be local and regional economic dislocations that harm some people. See Bread for the World Institute, Hunger Report 2003: Agriculture in the Global Economy (Washington, DC: BFWI, 2003), 22.

12. World Bank, World Development Report 1995, 5. One study covering 1970–1990 compared 37 countries where the relative importance of the country's exports was falling with 32 countries where exports were rising. Real wages grew an average of 3 percent per year in countries where exports were rising and fell where exports were declining in importance. In the first set of countries, the ratio of exports to GNP was falling; in the latter, this ratio was rising (Ibid.).

13. Other possible negative factors may also occur. Local elites that work with global corporations to prevent poor workers from developing unions reduce or prevent the benefit of increasing wages. And unnecessary shipping of materials around the world is environmentally foolish.

14. Paul Samuelson's "factor price equalization theorem," articulated decades ago, has been confirmed repeatedly.

15. BFWI, 2013 Hunger Report, 3, 12, 20.

16. See chapter 7, nn. 42–43, and chapter 11, nn. 5–16, 51–61.

17. I owe this section to development economist Bruce Wydick, who has provided advice on chapters 8 and 11.

18. UNDP, *Human Development Report 2005*, 36.

19. For the U.S. see Joseph E. Stiglitz, *The Price of Inequality* (New York: W.W. Norton, 2012), especially chapter 1.

20. See my *Fixing the Moral Deficit* (Downers Grove, IL: IVP Books, 2012), 57–59.

21. Stiglitz, *The Price of Inequality*, especially chapter 4.

22. Robert Frank and Philip J. Cook, *Winner Take All* (New York: Free Press, 1995). See also Lester C. Thurow, *The Failure of Capitalism* (New York: Morrow, 1996).

23. Not all cultural change is bad. A small, poor nation with twenty small tribes, twenty different languages, and no modern sense of time will be unable to participate in the global economy. Certainly they are welcome to retain their traditional culture, but they should not then blame the rest of the world for their poverty.

24. New York: Vintage, 1994.

25. Quoted in Juliet B. Schor, *The Overworked American* (New York: Harper Collins, 1992), 120.

26. See the powerful discussion of manipulative advertising in Peter Ubel, *Free Market Madness: Why Human Nature is at Odds with Economics—and Why it Matters* (Harvard Business Review Press, 2008).

27. "Marketing Fact Pack: 2014 Edition," *Advertising Age* (December 20, 2013), 20.

28. Common Sense Media, "Advertising to Children and Teens: Current Practices," Spring 2014, 7, 9–12.

29. "Marketing Fact Pack: 2014 Edition," *Advertising Age* (December 20, 2013), 16.

30. Ibid., 158.

31. For a good critique of consumerism, see William Cavenaugh, *Being Consumed: Economics and Christian Desire* (Grand Rapids, MI: Eerdmans, 2008).

32. M. Douglas Meeks, *God the Economist* (Minneapolis: Fortress, 1989), 39.

33. This is not to say communist societies did better. In fact, the environmental destruction in the former Soviet bloc was much worse than in the West.

34. Vaclav Smil and Mao Yushi, "The Economic Costs of China's Degradation," American Academy of Arts & Sciences, 1998, accessed April 30, 2014, https://www.amacad.org/content/Research/researchproject.aspx?d=961&t=4&s=0. A more scientific study showed that China lost 4.1 percent of the GDP to land degradation alone in 1999. See Hao, Fang-hua, et al. "Assessment of China's Economic Loss Resulting from the Degradation of Agricultural Land in the End of the 20th Century," *Journal of Environmental Sciences* 16, no. 2 (2004): 199–203.

35. "India: Green Growth - Overcoming Environment Challenges to Promote Development," The World Bank, March 6, 2014, accessed April 30, 2014, http://www.worldbank.org/en/news/feature/2014/03/06/green-growth-overcoming-india-environment-challenges-promote-development?cid=SAR_TTWBSAREN_EXT.

36. *Human Development Report 2013*, 43.

37. Ibid., 2. "Between 1980 and 2011, South-South trade as a share of world merchandise trade rose from 8.1% to 26.7%, with growth particularly remarkable in the 2000s. Over the same period, the share of North-North trade declined from about 46% to less than 30% (Ibid., 45). And the increase in trade has not just been in raw materials. "Removing fuel, metals and ores from aggregate trade statistics means that the share of South-South trade in world trade rose from 6.3% in 1980 to 26.1% in 2011 and that the share of North-North trade declined from 50.6% in 1980 to 31.4% in 2011" Ibid., 126, fn 13).

38. The logic underlying the benefits of international trade is, as economist Herman E. Daly and theologian John B. Cobb Jr. note, "unassailable." *For the Common Good: Redirecting the Economy Toward Community, the Environment, and a Sustainable Future*, 2nd ed. (Boston, Beacon Press, 1994), 209. David Coates makes a similar statement in "Free Trade and Fair Trade," in David Coates, ed., *The Oxford Companion to American Politics* (Oxford University Press, 2012), 405.

39. As quoted in David Coates, "Free Trade and Fair Trade," 407. Similarly, Robert J. Carbaugh, *International Economics* 13th ed. (Mason, OH: South-Western, Cengage Learning, 2011), 22, puts the gains for U.S. households between $7,000 and $13,000.

40. *Human Development Report 2013*, 12.

41. See the *Economist*, May 5, 2001, 59–62. See also, Carbaugh, *International Economics*, 59.

42. *Human Development Report 2013*, 70.

43. Carbaugh, *International Economics*, 59.

44. Developing countries have also shown that the capacity to increase exports is not a given. For example, the EU's Everything but Arms initiative (EBA) and the U.S.'s African Growth and Opportunity Act (AGOA) established special trade agreements with the least developed countries in Africa. But Africa's share of world exports has actually decreased. See Joseph E. Stiglitz and Andrew Charlton, *Fair Trade For All: How Trade Can Promote Development* (Oxford University Press, 2005), 9.

45. Stiglitz and Charlton, *Fair Trade For All*, 13.

46. For one summary, see Gheddo, *Why Is the Third World Poor?*, 69–100.

47. William Easterly, in *White Man's Burden*, gives an interesting additional layer to this period in history. His point is that alongside the more sinister motives of exploiting from the colonies whatever the colonists wanted, European colonists were simply inept. They came to African and Asian shores certain that they knew best how to govern and how to farm. They

changed traditional farming techniques in favor of what worked in Europe. Or they imported new inappropriate technologies. See pages 278–282 for this discussion.

48. James P. Grant, "Can the Churches Promote Development?" *Ecumenical Review* 26 (January 1974), 26.

49. Joseph E. Stiglitz and Andrew Charlton, *The Right to Trade: Rethinking the Aid for Trade Agenda* (London, UK: Commonwealth Secretariat, 2013), 3–4. See also, World Bank, *World Development Report 1995*, 57.

50. Stiglitz and Charlton, *The Right to Trade*, 21. According to the United States International Trade Commission's interactive trade database (accessed September 22, 2014), this has happened every year from 2010–2013. See the Interactive Tariff and Trade DataWeb at http://dataweb.usitc.gov/.

51. Dwight H. Perkins, Steven Radelet, and David L. Lindauer, *Economics of Development*, 6th ed. (New York: W.W. Norton & Co., 2006), 750.

52. OECD, "Producer and Consumer Support Estimates", OECD Agriculture statistics (database), accessed September 22, 2014. doi: 10.1787/agr-pcse-data-en. Figure includes only "Producer Support Estimate," which includes things like direct payments and price support.

53. See "EWG Farm Subsidies," Environmental Working Group, accessed September 1, 2014, http://farm.ewg.org/region.php?fips=00000.

54. E. Wesley F. Peterson, *A Billion Dollars A Day: The Economics and Politics of Agricultural Subsidies* (Malden, MA: Wiley-Blackwell, 2009), 127; "Farm Income Data Debunks Subsidy Myth," Environmental Working Group, May 2012, 2010, accessed September 1, 2014, http://www.ewg.org/agmag/2010/05/farm-income-data-debunks-subsidy-myths.

55. According to the USDA 2012 Census of Agriculture, of the 2,109,303 farms only 811,387 received subsidies—only 38 percent. The Census of Agriculture can be accessed at http://www.agcensus.usda.gov/Publications/2012/.

56. Alex Rindler, "Forbes Fat Cats Collect Taxpayer-Funded Farm Subsidies," Environmental Working Group, November 7, 2013, accessed September 1, 2014, http://www.ewg.org/research/forbes-fat-cats-collect-taxpayer-funded-farm-subsidies.

57. "The Great Cotton Stitch-Up," A Fairtrade Foundation Report (November 2010), 5.

58. Ibid. 3.

59. Ibid., 14.

60. http://www.cotton.org/edu/faq/.

61. http://farm.ewg.org/progdetail.php?fips=00000&progcode=cotton.

62. Mike Lavender, "Will Cotton Subsidies Ignite New Trade Disputes?" Environmental Working Group, January 24, 2014, accessed September 5, 2014, http://www.ewg.org/agmag/2014/01/will-cotton-subsidies-ignite-new-trade-dispute. The U.S. paid Brazil from 2010 to September 2013. The recently passed 2014 Farm Bill does not appear to resolve the dispute.
63. Pietra Rivoli, *The Travels of a T-Shirt in the Global Economy: An Economist Examines the Markets, Power, and Politics of World Trade*, 2nd ed. (Hoboken, NJ: John Wiley & Sons, 2009), 208–209.
64. Ibid., 92–104.
65. World Trade Organization, "International Trade Statistics 2012: Merchandise Trade," 4.6 Clothing, Table II.69, accessed September 23, 2014, http://www.wto.org/english/res_e/statis_e/its2012_e/its12_merch_trade_product_e.htm.
66. 2012 data. Dan Ikenson, "Washington's Coddling of U.S. Textile Industry Is Hurting Shoppers," *Forbes*, July 23, 2013, accessed September 12, 2014, http://www.forbes.com/sites/danikenson/2013/07/23/textile-protectionism-in-the-trans-pacific-partnership/.

    The effects of these trade barriers are vastly complex. Rivoli outlines various effects, including: Confusion. The rules are so complex and ever changing that producers have trouble keeping up. Limited investment. With confusing and changing rules, it is difficult for entrepreneurs to take the risk of opening up new factories or expanding into new markets. Limited choices. The rules dictate (or do not dictate) what kind of fabric or thread can come from what country and be processed in what country. Depending how a particular piece of clothing is produced it may or may not be subject to a quota or a tariff. This makes it difficult to source fabric inputs for U.S. apparel manufacturers. In some cases the rules are at cross-purposes and self-defeating. See Rivoli, *Travels of a T-Shirt*, 150–154.
67. Sanchita B. Saxena, "American Tariffs, Bangladeshi Deaths," *New York Times*, December 11, 2012, accessed September 23, 2014, http://www.nytimes.com/2012/12/12/opinion/american-tariffs-bangladeshi-deaths.html?_r=0.
68. Pietra Rivoli, *The Travels of a T-Shirt*, 181.
69. Gary Hufbauer and Jeffrey Schott, "Payoff From the World Trade Agenda 2013," Report to the ICC Research Foundation, April 2013, 12.
70. "Bailing Out From Bali," *The Economist*, August 9, 2014, accessed September 27, 14, http://www.economist.com/news/finance-and-economics/21611088-indias-scuppering-latest-trade-talks-leaves-no-one-better-bailing-out?zid=301&ah=e8eb01e57f7c9b43a3c864613973b57f.

71. See the annual *State of the World* publication (including those for 2011 and 2012) by World Watch Institute; Ben Lowe, *Green Revolution: Coming Together to Care for Creation* (Downers Grove, IL: InterVarsity Press, 2009); and Jonathan A. Moo and Robert S. White, *Let Creation Rejoice: Biblical Hope and Ecological Crisis* (Downers Grove, IL: IVP Academic, 2014) for recent overviews of the current environmental degradation. Pp. 149–160 of the 2005 edition of *Rich Christians in an Age of Hunger* contained a then current summary of this data.

72. IPCC, Climate Change 2013, Headline Statements from the Summary for Policy Makers, January 30, 2014; www.climatechange2013.org.

73. See the detailed evidence cited in my *Just Politics*, 223–224 (n.1). For the most recent (March 2014 report from the IPCC, see http://ipcc-wg2.gov/AR5/images/uploads/WG2AR5_SPM_FINAL.pdf.

74. E.g., Wayne Grudem in his *Politics According to the Bible* (Grand Rapids: Zondervan, 2010), 371. See my critique in *Just Politics*, 171-2).

75. http://christiansandclimate.org. See also Katharine Hayhoe and Andrew Farley, *A Climate for Change: Global Warming Facts for Faith-Based Decisions* (New York: Faith Works, 2009).

76. Jim Ball, *Global Warming and the Risen Lord: Christian Discipleship and Climate Change* (Washington: The Evangelical Environmental Network, 2010), 99–128.

77. IPCC, AR4, WG2, Ch 5, p. 300; see discussion p. 298, where the worst case is 1.3 billion would suffer hunger. All of the modeling simulations of impacts on agriculture may be too rosy, i.e., too conservative, in their projections due to what is not included in the modeling: the impacts of increased pests, reduced crop pollinators, extreme weather events (e.g., floods, strong storms, intense heat) of modest duration, and sea level rise. See also National Academy of Sciences (NAS), National Research Council, Advancing the Science of Climate Change (National Academies Press: May 2010): pp. 229–30; http://books.nap.edu/openbook.php?record_id=12782&page=R1#; and National Academy of Sciences (NAS), *Climate Stabilization Targets: Emissions, Concentrations, and Impacts over Decades to Millennia*, Prepublication Copy (National Academies Press, Washington, DC: July 2010): http://www.nap.edu/catalog/12877.html, where it states that "other processes have not been adequately quantified. These include responses of weeds, insects, and pathogens; changes in water resources available for irrigation; effects of changes in surface ozone levels; effects of increased flood frequencies; and responses to extremely high temperatures. Moreover, most crop modeling studies have not considered changes in sustained droughts, which are likely

to increase in many regions (Wang, 2005; Sheffield and Wood, 2008), or potential changes in year-to-year variability of yields. The net effect of these and other factors remains an elusive goal, but these are likely to push yields in a negative direction" (p. 130); United Nations Development Programme (UNDP), Kishan Khoday, "Climate Change and the Right to Development: Himalayan Glacial Melting and the Future of Development on the Tibetan Plateau," Occasional Paper, (UNDP, May 2007): pp. 4, 6; http://hdr.undp. org/en/reports/global/hdr2007- 2008/papers/Khoday_Kishan.pdf. See also the IPCC, *Climate Change 2014*, "Summary for Policy Makers," http://ipcc-wg2.gov/AR5/images/uploads/WG2AR5_SPM_FINAL.pdf.

78. Stern, *Economics of Climate Change*, 63–64; IPCC, Climate change 2014, 15.
79. Ball, *Global Warming*, 104–108.
80. Ibid., 109; IPCC, *Climate Change 2014*, 20.
81. Ball, *Global Warming*, 115–126; IPCC, *Climate Change 2014*, 20–21.
82. The World Bank, *Turn Down the Heat: Why a 4°C Warmer World Must Be Avoided* (November 2012), http://documents.worldbank.org/curated/en/2012/11/17097815/turn-down-heat-4%C2%B0c-warmer-world-must-avoided. See also p. 2.
83. IPCC, *Climate Change 2014*, 8, 12, 13, 19.
84. Ibid., 21.
85. Ball, *Global Warming and the Risen Lord*, 92.
86. See Todaro and Smith, *Economic Development* (2009), 719–720; Jagdish Bhagwati, "Do Multinational Corporations Hurt Poor Countries?" the *American Enterprise*, June 2004, 28–30; "Impact of Multinational Companies on the Host Country," Triple a LEARNING, accessed May 30, 2014, http://www.gregglee.biz/ftp/student/businessOrg/page-144.htm.
87. See Brian Roach, "Corporate Power in a Global Economy," a teaching module from Tufts University's Global Development and Environment Institute, accessed May 30, 2014, http://ase.tufts.edu/gdae/education_materials/modules/Corporate_Power_in_a_Global_Economy.pdf.
88. Vincent Trivett, "25 US Mega-Corporations: Where They Rank if They Were Countries," accessed May 30, 2014, http://www.businessinsider.com/25-corporations-bigger-tan-countries-2011-6?op=1.
89. "Impact of Multinational Companies," triple a LEARNING.
90. Ibid. See also the earlier discussion by Donald Hay, *Economics Today: A Christian Critique* (Grand Rapids: Eerdmans, 1989), 264–66.
91. *New York Times*, "An Indonesian Asset Is Also a Liability," March 16, 1996, B1, B36.
92. Ibid.
93. Korten, *When Corporations Rule the World*, 129.

94. Ivan Illich, author of "Outwitting the 'Developed' Countries," *The Political Economy of Development and Underdevelopment*, ed. Charles K. Wilber (New York: Random House, 1979), 436–44, is a development ethicist who is particularly galled by the proliferation of soft drinks in the LDCs.

95. UNICEF, *The State of the World's Children 1990*, 26.

96. UNICEF, *The State of the World's Children 1995*, 20.

97. UNICEF, *The State of the World's Children 1982–83*, 3–4.

98. See Mike Muller (whose 1974 report *The Baby Killer* was a major factor in the beginning of the boycott) "Nestle Baby Milk Scandal has Grown Up But Not Gone Away," *The Guardian*, February 13, 2013, accessed May 29, 2014, http://www.theguardian.com/sustainable-business/ nestle-baby-milk-scandal-food-industry-standards.

99. See www.babymilkaction.org/nestlefree; accessed May 29, 2014.

100. H. W. Walter, "Marketing in Developing Countries," *Columbia Journal of World Business* (Winter 1974), quoted in Lappe and Collins, *Food First*, 309.

101. Claudia Kennedy, "Light in the Midst of Darkness: Two Views of Global Poverty" March 5, 2004, http://mediamavens.com/Speech_GlobalPoverty. htm. Linda Tripp, a vice president of World Vision Canada, made a similar estimate: "A Voice for Women," *Transformation*, January–March 1992, 21.

102. "How Africa Can Transform Land Tenure, Revolutionize Agriculture, and End Poverty," International Land Coalition: Africa, December 4, 2013, accessed June 24, 2014, http://africa.landcoalition.org/how-africa-can- transform-land-tenure-revolutionize-agriculture-and-end-poverty/.

103. BFWI, *2013 Hunger Report*, 46.

104. Nicholas D. Kristof and Sheryl WuDunn, *Half the Sky: Turning Oppression into Opportunity for Women Worldwide* (New York: Alfred A Knopf, 2009), 98.

105. United Nations Educational, Scientific, and Cultural Organization (UNESCO) Institute for Statistics. Data retrieved from World Bank, World Development Indicators, accessed June 10, 2014, http://databank. worldbank.org/.

106. Mara Hvistendahl, *Unnatural Selection: Choosing Boys Over Girls, and the Consequences of a World Full of Men* (New York: Public Affairs, 2011), 5–6.

107. UNDP, *Human Development Report 1995*, 35.

108. Mara Hvistendahl, *Unnatural Selection*, 5–6.

109. Ibid., 19. Hvistendahl, in *Unnatural Selection*, makes the intriguing case that ties many of the top down approaches to population control by the governments (in India and China, for example) to a 1952 Colonial Williamsburg meeting on population control that was largely funded by the Rockefeller Foundation. The evidence shows many examples of blatant

racism and eugenics that was essentially imposed upon these countries in exchange for development assistance. The line might be very thin between well-intentioned activists (who genuinely thought the world could not support many more billions of people) and racist bigots who simply wanted to strengthen their economic privilege through oppressive means.

Related, the author makes the case that poverty may have contributed to the underlying thinking that favors boys. And, sadly, that increased development actually increases abortions because it gives people increased access to more resources to ensure that they got a son (i.e., ultrasounds, abortion, etc.).

110. "21 million people are now victims of forced labour, ILO says," International Labour Organization, June 1, 2012, accessed June 25, 2014, http://www.ilo.org/global/about-the-ilo/newsroom/news/WCMS_181961/lang--en/index.htm.

111. Mara Hvistendahl, *Unnatural Selection*, 184.

112. Tripp, "A Voice for Women," *Transformation*, January–March, 1992, 23.

113. Vusi Gemede, "Social and Economic Inclusion in Post-Apartheid South Africa," in *2011 Transformation Audit: From Inequality to Inclusive Growth*, Jan Hofmeyr, ed. (Cape Town: Institute for Justice and Reconciliation, 2011), 91. This report gives estimated HDI figures, which I then compared to the *Human Development Report 2013* list.

114. Raúl Segura and Kurt Birson, "The Human Development Index: How Do Puerto Ricans Measure Up?," Center for Puerto Rican Studies (May 2013), 2–3.

115. Richard Wolffe, "On the Road to Nowhere," *Newsweek*, May 3, 2004, 42–43.

116. BFWI, *2013 Hunger Report*, 45.

117. Ibid.

118. BFWI, *Hunger 1996*, 95.

119. BFWI, *2013 Hunger Report*, 40.

120. UNDP, *Human Development Report 2013*, 39–40.

121. *Human Security Report* (Vancouver: Human Security Press, 2013), 24 90. This figure refers to internationalized intrastate conflicts (i.e., civil wars where foreign countries get involved).

122. UNDP, *Human Development Report 2009*, 26.

123. Raymond Fisman and Edward Miguel, *Economic Gangsters: Corruption, Violence and the Poverty of Nations* (Princeton: Princeton University Press, 2008), 122–125.

124. BFWI, *Hunger 1996*, 11.

125. Dag Hammarskjöld, *Markings* (New York: Knopf, 1964), xxi.

126. See "Bananas," *New Internationalist*, August 1975, 32.

127. Only $1.25 million was actually paid.
128. *Philadelphia Inquirer*, April 10, 1975, 1–2.
129. "Action," *New Internationalist*, August 1975, 32.
130. Carl Oglesby and Richard Schaull, *Containment and Change* (NY: Macmillan, 1967), 104; and Stephen Schlesinger and Stephen Kinzer, *Bitter Fruit: The Untold Story of the American Coup in Guatemala* (Garden City, NY: Doubleday, 1982).
131. Andreas Schotter and Mary Teagarden, "Blood Bananas: Chiquita in Columbia," 1,5; *Thunderbird School of Global Management Case Study* (2010).
132. "America's World Role: Should We Feel Guilty?" *Philadelphia Inquirer*, July 18, 1974, 7a.
133. See the helpful comments on this in Patrick Kerans, *Sinful Social Structures* (New York: Paulist Press, 1974), 47–51.

Chapter 9

1. Ronald J. Sider, ed., *The Chicago Declaration* (Carol Stream, IL: Creation House, 1974), 2.
2. J. D. Douglas, ed., *Let the Earth Hear His Voice: International Congress on World Evangelization, Lausanne, Switzerland* (Minneapolis: World Wide Publications, 1975), 6, sect. 9.
3. "Creation, Technology, and Human Survival," Plenary Address, WCC's Fifth Assembly, December 1, 1975. This is a recent rendition of Elizabeth Seton's statement, "Live simply that others may simply live."
4. *New York Times*, June 14, 1973.
5. This sermon was one of the series of sermons that constituted the standard doctrines of the early Methodists. See *The Works of John Wesley*, 14 vols. (1872; reprinted, Grand Rapids: Zondervan, n.d.), 5:361–77.
6. Ibid., 365–68.
7. J. Wesley Bready, *England: Before and After Wesley* (London: Hodder and Stoughton, n.d.), 238.
8. I do not conclude from this and the rest of the Bible that absolute equality of income is the biblical norm. See my *Fixing the Moral Deficit*, 57–59. But St. Paul's text surely calls us to dramatic sharing.
9. See his moving testimony, "From Galloping Gourmet to Serving the Poor," in my *Lifestyle in the Eighties*, 174–82; and more recently, "The Graham Kerr Story: From Galloping Gourmet to Kingdom Cook," *PRISM*, September–October, 1996, 16–19.
10. See Gene M. Daffern, "One Man Can Make a Difference," *These Times*, September 1982, 6–11.

11. Doris Longacre, *Living More with Less* (Scottdale, PA: Herald Press, 1980). See also the personal testimonies in Ronald J. Sider, ed., *Living More Simply: Biblical Principles and Practical Models* (Downers Grove, IL: InterVarsity, 1980), 59–159.

12. Ginny Hearn and Walter Hearn, "The Price Is Right," *Right On*, May 1973, 1, 11.

13. Michael Harper, *A New Way of Living* (Plainfield, NJ: Logos International, 1973), 93.

14. See my suggestions on this in "Living More Simply for Evangelism and Justice," in Sider, *Lifestyle in the Eighties*, 32–35.

15. See my response to the critique of this distinction in John Schneider, *Godly Materialism* (Downers Grove, IL: InterVarsity, 1994), in "Rich Christians in an Age of Hunger—Revisited," *Christian Scholars' Review*, xxvi:3 (Spring 1997), 328.

16. For great examples, see my *Cup of Water, Bread of Life* (Grand Rapids: Zondervan, 1994), and my *Good News and Good Works: A Theology for the Whole Gospel* (Grand Rapids: Baker, 1999). In addition, *Transformation* and *PRISM* regularly publish holistic models of evangelism and social concern.

17. David Pimentel and Marcia Pimentel, "Sustainability of meat-based and plant-based diets and the Environment," *American Society for Clinical Nutrition* 78(suppl), (2003): 661S–662S.

18. Both are now old, but they still contain useful ideas.

19. See nn. 41–43.

20. I owe much to John F. Alexander in the development of these criteria.

21. Criteria a, c, d, and f are adapted from Edward R. Dayton, "Where to Go from Here," *Fuller Seminary's Theology News and Notes*, October 1975, 19.

22. Quoted from a fund-raising piece written by John F. Alexander. Much has changed in Liberia since John wrote these words in 1976, but they still illustrate the criteria I have listed.

23. See for example Abhijit V. Banerjee and Esther Duflo, *Poor Economics* (New York: Random House, 2013), 9–21 and elsewhere.

24. Wydick published his results in a World Bank blog: "Evaluating the Best Ways to Give to the Poor: Guest Post by Bruce Wydick," February 27, 2012, http://blogs.worldbank.org/impactevaluations/evaluating-the-best-ways-to-give-to-the-poor-guest-post-by-bruce-wydick, accessed December 23, 2013.

25. Ibid., 2.

26. Ibid., 2. See also Bruce Wydick, "Want to Change the World? Sponsor a Child," *Christianity Today*, June 2013: 20–25.

27. See my *Cup of Water, Bread of Life* (Grand Rapids: Zondervan, 1994), chapter 7, and Philippa Tyndale, *Don't Look Back: The David Bussau Story* (St. Leonards, New South Wales, Australia: Allen and Unwin, 2004).

28. "Approach to Microfinance," Opportunity International, accessed May 20, 2014, http://opportunity.org/what-we-do/microfinance.

29. Opportunity International 2012 Annual Report (Oak Brook, IL: Opportunity International), 1.

30. Opportunity International 2012 Annual Report, 6.

31. "Approach to Microfinance," Opportunity International.

32. *Impact* (a newsletter of Opportunity International), October 2003.

33. http://oikocreditusa.org/home. Oikocredit USA, 1701 K Street N.W., Suite 1201, Washington, DC, 2006.

34. Correspondence with Amie McPhee on April 7, 2014; see also *http://www. meda.org/annual-report*.

35. See Mary Naber, "Christ's Returns," *Christianity Today*, September 3, 2001, 79ff. See also the Forum for Sustainable and Responsible Investment (*www. ussif.org*) and its biannual publication.

36. I calculated this from two figures. The first is from Giving USA, "2013 Highlights," 1, which estimates total charitable contributions in the U.S. to be $316 billion. The second is from the Bureau of Economic Analysis, "National Data: Table 2.1 Personal Income and Its Disposition," accessed May 20, 2014, www.bea.gov, which estimates U.S. personal income for 2012 to be, as an average of each quarter reported, $13,743 billion. Giving divided by personal income is 2.3 percent.

37. Unfortunately, while the *average* per capita income has grown substantially, many people have not experienced this growth because more and more of the growth in U.S. income has gone to the richest 20 percent (especially the richest 1 percent) in the last thirty years. See my *Fixing the Moral Deficit*, 21–42.

38. John L. and Sylvia Ronsvalle, *The State of Church Giving Through 2011* (Champaign, IL: Empty Tomb, Inc.: 2013), 15-22.

39. Adapted from *The State of Church Giving Through 2011*, 17, 21.

40. Ronsvalle, *The State of Church Giving Through 2011*, 31–32.

41. Christian Smith, Michael O. Emerson, and Patricia Snell, *Passing the Plate* (New York: Oxford University Press, 2008), 3. I read the book in manuscript and suggested the title: *Stingy Christians in an Age of Affluence!*

42. Ibid., 48–49.

43. Smith, Emerson, and Snell, *Passing the Plate*, 13–18; the list goes on for five pages!

44. Larry Minear, *New Hope for the Hungry* (New York: Friendship Press, 1975), 79.

45. See the superb development of this truth by Tyler Wigg-Stevenson, *The World is Not Ours to Save: Finding the Freedom to Do Good* (Downers Grove, IL: IVP Books, 2013).

46. See my *I Am Not a Social Activist: Making Jesus the Agenda* (Scottdale: Herald Press, 2008).

Chapter 10

1. The Latin phrase means, "Beyond the church, there is no salvation."

2. Dave Jackson and Neta Jackson, *Living Together in a World Falling Apart* (Carol Stream, IL: Creation House, 1974), 15.

3. For a discussion of Reba Place, see Jackson and Jackson, *Living Together in a World Falling Apart*, esp. 36–39, 230–33. I received more recent information through personal corrrespondence with Virgil Vogt, one of Reba Place's oldest leaders.

4. See my "Spare the Rod and Spoil the Church," *Eternity*, October, 1976.

5. From John Wesley's account (1748) of the origin of the class meetings (*The Works of John Wesley*, 8:269).

6. Peter Berger, *A Rumor of Angels* (Garden City, NY: Anchor Books, 1970), 34 (also 6–37). See also Peter Berger and Thomas Luckman, *The Social Construction of Reality* (Garden City, NY: Doubleday, 1956).

7. Berger, *A Rumor of Angels*, 17. See further 41ff for Berger's rejection of the common idea that the sociology of knowledge leads inexorably to thoroughgoing relativism.

8. See Floyd Filson, "The Significance of the Early House Churches," *Journal of Biblical Literature* 58 (1939):105–12.

9. This is not its real name. The congregation (which I have known for almost forty years) has experienced some difficult struggles in the last twenty years, but those problems are not the result of its exciting exploration of genuine Christian community.

10. I have relied largely on Gordon Cosby's *Handbook for Mission Groups* (Waco, TX: Word, 1975) for this discussion. See also Elizabeth O'Connor's several books, all of which are rooted in the experience of Church of the Savior, including: *Call to Commitment* (New York: Harper & Row, 1963), *Journey Inward, Journey Outward* (New York: Harper & Row, 1968). See also "Who Is the Church of the Savior," http://www.io-sermons.org/church-history, accessed February 15, 2014.

11. Cosby, *Handbook for Mission Groups*, 63.

12. Ibid., 140.

13. Howard A. Snyder, *The Problem of Wineskins: Church Structure in a Technological Age* (Downers Grove, IL: InterVarsity, 1975), 140–42. See

also his *Liberating the Church: The Ecology of Church and Kingdom* (Downers Grove, IL: InterVarsity, 1983).

14. See Jackson and Jackson, *Living Together in a World Falling Apart*, esp. 36–39, 230–33.

15. For a good historical perspective on Christian communes and an excellent bibliography, see Donald G. Bloesch, *Wellsprings of Renewal: Promise in Christian Communal Life* (Grand Rapids: Eerdmans, 1974). For a handbook by a Catholic charismatic, see Stephen B. Clark, *Building Christian Communities* (Notre Dame, IN: Ave Maria Press, 1972). And more recently, David Janzen, et al., *Fire, Salt and Peace: Intentional Christian Communities Alive in North America* (1996); also David Janzen *The Intentional Christian Community Handbook: For Idealists, Hypocrites, and Wannabe Disciples of Jesus* (Brewster, MA: Paraclete Press, 2012).

16. See for example Jonathan Wilson-Hartgrove, *New Monasticism: What It Has to Say to Today's Church* (Grand Rapids, MI: Brazos Press, 2008) and the many books and articles by Shane Claiborne, who is a key founder of The Simple Way Community in Philadelphia, PA.

17. I owe this idea to a lively conversation with a good friend, Malcolm Street, who asked, after I was arrested in Washington, D.C. for protesting cuts in government programs for the poor, why I did not challenge the churches just as strongly!

Chapter 11

1. See my "Toward an Evangelical Political Philosophy," in David P. Gushee, ed., *Christians and Politics: Beyond the Culture Wars* (Grand Rapids, Baker, 2000), 79–96; and *Just Politics: A Guide for Christian Engagement* (Grand Rapids: Brazos Press, 2012).

2. See *Just Politics*, 184–187.

3. See my plea for tolerance and understanding of the specific reasons for disagreement in "A Plea for More Radical Conservatives and More Conserving Radicals," *Transformation*, January–March 1987, 11–16.

4. See my *Nonviolent Action: What Christian Ethics Demands but Most Christians Have Never Really Tried* (Grand Rapids: Baker, 2015); *Nuclear Holocaust and Christian Hope* (Downers Grove, IL: InterVarsity, 1982), co-authored with Richard K. Taylor; and earlier my *Christ and Violence* (Scottdale, PA: Herald Press, 1978).

5. See, for example, the section titled "Uneven Distribution" and its corresponding notes in chapter 1.

6. BFWI, *2013 Hunger Report*, 20.

7. See especially, Acemoglu and Robinson, *Why Nations Fail* (2012) and Olson, *Power and Prosperity* (2000).

8. *Why Nations Fail*, 74–75.

9. Ibid., 43.

10. Olson, *Power and Prosperity*, especially 1–44.

11. Acemoglu and Robinson, *Why Nations Fail*, especially 102–113, 191–212; also Olson, *Power and Prosperity*, 30-43.

12. Olson, *Power and Prosperity*, 43.

13. *Development as Freedom*, xii and chapter 6, 146ff.

14. Acemoglu and Robinson, *Why Nations Fail*, 429–430. Recent studies show that good governance has been a crucial factor in producing success at meeting the Millennium Development Goals (BFWI, *Hunger Report 2014*, 163).

15. See for example Raymond Fisman and Edward Miguel, *Economic Gangsters: Corruption, Violence and the Poverty of Nations* (Princeton: Princeton University Press, 2008).

16. The right kind of foreign aid does help the poor. See nn. 123–129.

17. See, for instance, Ogelsby and Shaull, *Containment and Change*, 72–111.

18. Amnesty International, *Report on Torture* (New York: Farrar, Straus, and Giroux, 1975), especially the special report on Chile on 243ff. See also Fred B. Morris, "Sustained by Faith Under Brazilian Torture," *Christian Century*, January 22, 1975, 56–60; Latin America and Empire Report 10, no. 1, January 1976; and BFWI, "Military Aid, the World's Poor and U.S. Security." The School of the Americas (SOA), in Georgia, trains military personnel from other countries. Among its graduates: Manuel Noriega, currently serving forty years for drug trafficking. Also, a 1992 international human rights tribunal in Colombia cited 246 officers for human rights violations; 100 of them were SOA graduates. *At the Crossroads: The Future of Foreign Aid* (Silver Spring, MD: BFWI, 1995), 15. More recently, Grace Livingstone, *America's Backyard: The United States and Latin America from the Monroe Doctrine to the War on Terror* (London: Zed Books, 2009); Lesley Gill, *The School of the Americas: Military Training and Political Violence in the Americas* (Durham, NC: Duke University Press, 2004). There is a website dedicated to closing the School of the Americas (now called Western Hemisphere Institute for Security Cooperation (WHINSEC)). See http://soaw.org/index.php. The website for WHINSEC is http://www.benning.army.mil/tenant/whinsec/index.html.

19. "School of the Dictators," *New York Times*, September 28, 1996, 22.

20. Penny Lernoux, *Cry of the People* (New York: Penguin, 1982).

21. See for example, Don Eberly, *The Rise of Global Civil Society: Building Communities and Nations From the Bottom Up* (New York: Encounter Books, 2008). David C. Korten has been promoting "global people's organizations" for years: *Getting to the 21st Century: Voluntary Action and the Global Agenda* (West Hartford: Kumarian Press, 1990) and *Globalizing Civil Society: Reclaiming Our Right to Power* (New York: Seven Stories Press, 1998).

22. William E. Spriggs and Robert E. Scott, "Economists' Views of Workers' Rights and U.S. Trade Policy," working paper, U.S. Congress Joint Economic Committee, reprinted by the Center for International Business Education and Research (1996), 14, http://www.bmgt.umd.edu/Ciber/wp60.html. I owe this reference to a former student, Fred Clark.

23. "Subjects treated under the Doha Development Agenda," World Trade Organization, accessed June 28, 2014, http://www.wto.org/english/tratop_e/dda_e/dohasubjects_e.htm.

24. See UNICEF, *The State of the World's Children 1982–83*, 3–4.

25. "The Breast vs. the Bottle," *Newsweek*, June 1, 1981, 54.

26. This is not to argue that the total impact of MNCs is negative. For Nestlé, see chapter 8, nn. 95–99, and below, n. 103.

27. Robert E. Frykenberg, ed., *Land Tenure and the Peasant in South Asia: An Anthology of Recent Research* (Madison, WI: Land Tenure Center, 1976), 14.

28. See the discussion in my *Good News and Good Works*, 113–18, and all the stories in my *Cup of Water, Bread of Life*. See also Myers, *Walking With the Poor*, 2nd ed., especially 177–180.

29. See the interesting Indian case study, Saral K. Chatterji, *Religious Values and Economic Development: A Case Study*, Social Research Series, no. 5 (Bangalore: Christian Institute for the Study of Religion and Society, 1967).

30. "The Missionary Roots of Liberal Democracy," *American Political Science Review*, 106, no. 2 (May 2012): 244–274. See also Nathan Nunn's chapter, "Gender and Missionary Influence in Colonial Africa," in E. Akyeampong, R. Bates, N. Nunn and J. A. Robinson, *Africa's Development in Historical Perspective* (Cambridge University Press, forthcoming).

31. See also the excellent article by John P. Tiemstra, "The Road to Serfdom Runs Both Directions," *Perspectives: A Journal of Reformed Thought*, November–December, 2013, accessed June 27, 2014, http://www.perspectivesjournal.org/novemberdecember2013/essay/the-road-to-serfdom-runs-both-directions.

32. I am using the word capital in a broader sense than do most economists. I use it as a shorthand for "productive resources."

33. Isabel Ortiz and Matthew Cummins, "Global Inequality: Beyond The Bottom Billion," UNICEF Social and Economic Policy Working Paper (April 2011), 12; http://www.unicef.org/socialpolicy/files/Global_Inequality.pdf.

34. Oxfam, "Working For the Few: Political Capture and Economic Inequality," January 20, 2014, 5; cf. Isabel Ortiz and Matthew Cummins, "Global Inequality," 20.

35. In some fundamental sense, that means redistribution. People with resources need to find effective ways to enable those who have very little capital to acquire more. Taxing richer people to provide the funds for effective government programs that truly empower poor people is one important part of the agenda. But the goal is neither state ownership of the bulk of the means of production nor the equalization of wealth. The goal is the empowerment of poor people which has the effect of decentralizing power.

36. One interesting example is the Central Provident Fund in Singapore (see the *Economist*, January 13, 1996, 38).

37. "About Us," Kiva, accessed June 13, 2014, http://www.kiva.org/about.

38. See the several recent studies cited by Nathan Fiola, "Can Microenterprises Grow Through Finance?," Development Impact, November 13, 2013, accessed June 28, 2014, http://blogs.worldbank.org/impactevaluations/node/1061; and Michael Strong, "Beyond Microfinance," *Carnegie Council for Ethics in International Affairs*, accessed January 4, 2014, https://www.carnegiecouncil.org/publications/ethics_online/0026.html/:pf_printable; Niels Hermes and Robert Lensink, "Microfinance: Its Impact, Outreach and Sustainability," *World Development* (2011), doi: 1016/j.worlddev.2009.10.021.

39. Jake Kendall and Rodger Voorhies, "The Mobile Finance Revolution," *Foreign Affairs*, March/April 2014, 9. See also Banerjee and Duflo, *Poor Economics*, chap. 9.

40. See the results of the study by Nathan Fiola in n. 38 above.

41. E.g., Gordon Conway, *One Billion Hungry: Can We Feed the World?* (Cornell: Cornell University Press, 2012), especially the last chapter.

42. Kendall and Voorhies, "The Mobile Finance Revolution," 10.

43. "2012 Annual Report," Give Directly, accessed July 2, 2014, https://www.givedirectly.org/pdf/2012AnnualReport.pdf, 7.

44. See also Johannes Haushofer and Jeremy Shapiro, "Policy Brief: Impacts of Unconditional Cash Transfers," October, 24, 2013, accessed July 2, 2014, http://www.princeton.edu/~joha/publications/Haushofer_Shapiro_Policy_Brief_2013.pdf; and Bruce Wydick, "Why Shouldn't we GiveDirectly?," *Prism* (Spring, 2014).

45. See David Bornstein and Susan Davis, *Social Entrepreneurship: What Everyone Needs to Know* (Oxford: Oxford University Press, 2010).

46. Banerjee and Duflo, *Poor Economics*, 57, 401.

47. For a private agency, see The Worm Project started by Claude Good (www. wormproject.org).

48. Bureaucratic regulations designed to favor special groups must also be abolished. See Hernando de Soto, *The Other Path: The Invisible Revolution in the Third World* (New York: Harper, 1989).

49. For the EITC, see my *Just Generosity: A New Vision for Overcoming Poverty in America*, 2nd ed., (Grand Rapids: Baker, 2007), 126–130.

50. This is precisely what American society did in the 1860s.

51. Todaro, *Economic Development* (1994), 590.

52. United Nations, *Human Development Report 1993*, 30.

53. Ibid., 38.

54. World Bank, *World Development Report 1991*, 5–11. See its helpful summary of criteria for market-friendly government activity.

55. See Jean Dreze and Amartya Sen, *Hunger and Public Action* (New York: Oxford University Press, 1989), 13; and table 10 in chapter 7.

56. Acemoglu and Robinson, *Why Nations Fail*, 455–460.

57. BFWI, *2013 Hunger Report*, 44.

58. World Bank, *World Development 1991*, 6.

59. World Bank, *World Development Report 2004*, 11.

60. World Bank, *World Development 1991*, 9. One of the committees from the Third Oxford Conference on Christian Faith and Economics offered an excellent summary of what the market does well and poorly; see sections 3 and 4 of "The Market Economy," *Transformation*, July 1995, 12.

61. *Development as Freedom*, 143. See also Banerjee and Duflo, *Poor Economics*, 46–58, 81–104, 394–401.

62. Pope Francis, *The Joy of The Gospel (Evangelii Gaudium)*, 56; Washington: United States Conference of Catholic Bishops, 2013, 29.

63. See for example, Joseph E. Stiglitz, Amartya Sen, and Jean-Paul Fitoussi, *Mis-Measuring Our Lives: Why GDP Doesn't Add Up* (New York: The New Press, 2010).

64. See Stiglitz, et al., *Mis-Measuring Our Lives*, 8, 19, and 97ff.

65. See "If the GDP Is Up Why Is America Down?" *Atlantic Monthly*, October 1995, 59–78. See their 2004 update: Jason Venetoulis and Cliff Cubb, *The Genuine Progress Indicator 1950–2002* (2004 update) (Oakland: Redefining Progress, 2004); Ida Kabiszewski, et al., "Beyond GDP: Measuring and Achieving Global Genuine Progress," *Ecological Economics* 93 (2013), 57–68; and the vast bibliography there; and the regular reports from Redefining Progress (http://rprogress.org/sustainability_indicators/genuine_progress_indicator.htm).

66. Kabiszewski, et al., "Global Genuine Progress," 66.

67. Ibid., 61–62.
68. Ibid., 67.
69. See a response to some of the criticism in Kabiszewski, et al., "Beyond GDP," 58.
70. For example, the UNDP Human Development Index uses statistics on health and education as well as income to measure human development. See *Human Development Report 2013*, 23–34.
71. Lester C. Thurow, *The Zero-Sum Society* (New York: Viking, 1981), 103–7.
72. Richard A. Easterlin, "Does Money Buy Happiness?" *The Public Interest*, no. 3 (Winter 1973): 10. See also Martin Bolt and David G. Myers, "Why Do the Rich Feel So Poor?" in *The Human Connection* (Downers Grove, IL: InterVarsity, 1984); and Paul L. Wachtel, *The Poverty of Affluence: A Psychological Portrait of the American Way of Life* (New York: Macmillan, 1983); and David Meyers, "Money and Misery," in *The Consuming Passion: Christianity and the Consumer Culture* (Downers Grove, IL: InterVarsity, 1998).
73. See the concrete suggestions in Mark and Lisa Scandrette, *Free: Spending Your Time and Money on What Matters Most* (Downers Grove, IVP Books, 2013).
74. Christians ought to provide powerful counterevidence to Francis Fukuyama's prediction that democratic consumer capitalism will prevail everywhere by offering happiness through material abundance and overwhelm all claims that persons do not live by bread alone. See Francis Fukuyama, "The End of History," *The National Interest* (Summer 1989), 3–18.
75. Kym Anderson, et al, "Distortions to World Trade: Impacts on Agricultural Markets and Farm Income," *Review of Agricultural Economics* 28, no. 2 (2006): 180. According to the OECD, "Aid Statistics" accessed September 29, 2014, http://www.oecd.org/dac/stats/totaldacflowsataglance.htm, total Official Development Assistance in 2011 was $127 billion.
76. "How to Make the World $600 Billion Poorer," *The Economist* February 22, 2014, accessed September 29, 2014, http://www.economist.com/news/leaders/21596934-barack-obamas-unwillingness-fight-free-trade-expensive-mistake-how-make-world; World Bank, *World Development Report 1987*, 150.
77. In 2003, the UNCTAID Secretary General said, "Trade liberalization is no panacea for developing countries. For many of them, it involves considerable adjustment and social costs. There is a need for synergy and proper sequencing—between the capacities of the developing countries, the level of obligations they are to take on, the cost of implementation, and the adequacy of financial and technical resources available to them." Quoted in Stiglitz, "Right to Trade," 8. It is appropriate, then, that the WTO has focused on the Millennium Development Goal 8, which is related to capacity building in developing countries.

78. *Fair Trade For All*, 123-124.
79. "The Great Cotton Stitch-Up," 3.
80. See "The Case for Farm Subsidy Reform," Environmental Working Group, accessed October 3, 2014, http://www.ewg.org/farming-and-the-environment/the-case-for-farm-subsidy-reform. Some environmental protections would inherently reduce a farmer's risk to natural disaster. For example, organic no-till farming has proven to produce higher yields than conventional no-till during drought years. Read about the 30-year farming system trial conducted by the Rodale Institute at http://rodaleinstitute.org/our-work/farming-systems-trial/farming-systems-trial-fst-fast-facts/.
81. See, for example, the summary in Peterson, *A Billion Dollars a Day*, 121. This includes developing countries eliminating their barriers to trade as well. See also Antoine Bouët "The Expected Benefits of Trade Liberalization for World Income and Development: Opening the 'Black Box' of Global Trade Modeling," *Food Policy Review 8*, (Washington, DC: IFPRI, 2008), 91.
82. "Agriculture and Food Security," USAID, last modified August 11, 2014, accessed October 3, 2014, http://www.usaid.gov/what-we-do/agriculture-and-food-security.
83. David A. Gantz, *Liberalizing International Trade After Doha: Multilateral Plurilateral, Regional and Unilateral Initiatives* (Cambridge University Press, 2013), 55 fn 21.
84. Gary Hufbauer and Jefferey Schott, "Payoff from the World Trade Agenda 2013," 7.
85. For example, the U.S. Congress should give the president "fast-track" trade promotion authority (which previous presidents have had) in order to streamline the negotiating process. See "How to Make the World $600 Billion Poorer."
86. E. Wesley Peterson, *A Billion Dollars a Day*, 149.
87. For some alternatives to trade adjustment assistance, see chapter 11 by George R. Neumann in *International Trade and Finance: Readings*, ed. Robert E. Baldwin and David J. Richardson, 2d ed. (Boston: Little, Brown, 1981). For the need to improve this important safety net see Ryan Avent, "Better Safety Nets Needed," *The Economist*, February 22, 2011, accessed October 7, 2014, http://www.economist.com/blogs/freeexchange/2011/02/trade_1.
88. "Trade, Growth, and Jobs," OECD Trade and Agriculture Directorate, May 2012, accessed October 3, 2014, http://www.oecd.org/tad/tradedev/50447052.pdf.

89. I am not ignoring or rejecting the comparative advantage that poor nations have because all labor costs there are much lower than in rich nations. As I pointed out earlier, using this comparative advantage is one way greater global justice emerges. But it is important that just labor laws and active unions exist in poor nations so that workers receive a fair share of the benefits from global trade.

90. Spriggs and Scott, "Economists' Views of Workers' Rights and U.S. Trade Policy," 2.

91. Perhaps via trade sanctions through the World Trade Organization.

92. See the Interfaith Center on Corporate Responsibility, http://www.iccr.org (see appendix) as well as these Web sites: http://www.equalexchange.com; http://www.nosweatapparel.com; http://www.fairtradefederation.org.

93. Brian Roach, "Corporate Power in a Global Economy," A GDAE Teaching Module, Social and Environmental Issues in Economics (Global Development and Environmental Institute, Tufts University, 2007), accessed June 3, 2014; http://ase.tufts.edu/gdae/education_materials/modules/Corporate_Power_in_a_Global_Economy.pdf.

94. Ibid., 28.

95. See Thomas M. Anderson, "The 7 Top Funds for Ethical Investing," *Kiplinger*, July 2010, accessed June 3, 2014, http://www.kiplinger.com/article/investing/T041-C000-S002-the-7-top-funds-for-ethical- investing.html. See also the series of ethical investment stock market indices produced by the FTSE Group (http://ethicalinvestment.co.uk/FTSE_4_Good.htm).

96. See www.iccr.org.

97. Korten, *When Corporations Rule the World*, 111, and personal communication with Jeff Ballinger of Press for Change, a corporate watchdog group, on May 22, 1996. It is also true that the wages these 18,000 workers earned (around $2.50 per day) were higher than prevailing Indonesian wages.

98. "An Indonesian Arrest is Also a Liability," *New York Times*, March 16, 1996, B1, B36.

99. Roach, "Corporate Power," 13.

100. Quoted in Doug Guthrie, "Building Sustainable and Ethical Supply Chains," *Business*, March 9, 2012, accessed June 3, 2014, http://www.forbes.com/sites/dougguthrie/2012/03/09/building-sustainable-and-ethical-supply-chains/.

101. Simon Zadek, "The Path to Corporate Responsibility," *Harvard Business Review*, December 2004, 8.

102. Ibid.

103. Mike Muller, "Nestlé Baby Milk Scandal," *The Guardian*, February 13, 2013, accessed May 29, 2014, http://www.theguardian.com/ sustainable-business/nestle-baby-milk-scandal-food-industry-standards.

104. Imara Jones, "Lessons from the Bangladeshi Factory Collapse," *Colorlines*, May 22, 2014, accessed June 3, 2014, http://colorlines.com/ archives/2014/05/lessons_from_the_bangladeshi_factory_collapse.html.

105. See the Fair Labor Association (http://www.fairlabor.org/about-us); Global Reporting Initiative (https://www.globalreporting.org); Multinational Monitor (http://multinationalmonitor.org/); Corporate Accountability International (formerly Infact) (http://www. stopcorporateabuse.org/).

106. In the U.S., the national Religious Partnership for the Environment has helpful materials (www.nrpe.org). The Evangelical Environmental Network integrates biblical principles in its material to help Christians work effectively to protect the environment (www.creationcare.org).

107. Sam Kim, "Multinationals Push for New Greenhouse Gas Emissions Regulations," Center for Effective Government, December 4, 2007, accessed June 26, 2014, http://www.foreffectivegov.org/node/3548.

108. The White House Blog, June 27, 2013, accessed June 27, 2014, http://www.whitehouse.gov/blog/2013/06/27/ business-leaders-support-president-obamas-plan-reduce-carbon-pollution.

109. Eduardo Porter, "A Paltry Start in Curbing Global Warming," *New York Times*, June 4, 2014, B1, B5.

110. "Opinion Leaders," Carbon Tax Center, accessed June 26, 2014, http:// www.carbontax.org/services/supporters/opinion-leaders/; and Ben Klayman, "UPDATE 2-Market-based energy policy would aid U.S.-Exxon CEO" Reuters, December 11, 2008, accessed June 26, 2014, http://www. reuters.com/article/2008/12/11/exxon-tillerson-idUSN1127815320081211.

111. Porter, "Paltry Start in Curbing Global Warming," B5.

112. BFWI, *Reality of Aid*, 201. Other polls also include the same gross misunderstanding (e.g., *At the Crossroads: The Future of Foreign Aid*, 14).

113. Catholic Relief organization, "The Power of Perception" (Catholic Relief Organization, 2003), http://www.catholicrelief.org/get_involved/ advocacy/grass_roots/handout%205.pdf.

114. "2013 Survey of Americans on the U.S. Role in Global Health," Kaiser Family Foundation, November 7, 2013, accessed July 24, 2014, http://kff.org/global-health-policy/ poll-finding/2013-survey-of-americans-on-the-u-s-role-in-global-health/.

115. BFWI, *2013 Hunger Report*, 60.

116. Organization for Economic Co-operation and Development, "Preliminary Data – Official Development Assistance (ODA) data for 2013," updated April 8, 2014, accessed April 25, 2014, http://www.oecd.org/dac/stats/data. htm.

117. Don Eberly, *The Rise of Global Civil Society*, 53.

118. BFWI, *2013 Hunger Report*, 67.

119. Sixty-two percent according to Eberly, *The Rise of Global Civil Society*, 53. See also Eberly's larger discussion of other American contributions in *ibid.*, 51–58.

120. New York: Penguin Books, 2006.

121. Eberly, *The Rise of Global Civil Society*, 65–73.

122. P. 245.

123. Easterly, *White Man's Burden*, 5, 11, 22, 269, 370, 382ff; Acemoglu and Robinson, *Why Nations Fail*, 453–455.

124. Easterly, *White Man's Burden*, 5, 370.

125. *Why Nations Fail*, 453–455.

126. Ernst Loevinsohn, "Making Foreign Aid More Effective," BFW Background Paper, no. 49 (March 1981); BFWI, *At the Crossroads: The Future of Foreign Aid*, May 1995, 47.

127. "Facts on International Hunger and Poverty," from Bread for the World's 2014 Offering of Letters.

128. BFWI, *2013 Hunger Report*, 58.

129. BFWI, "Reforming U.S. Food Aid," Background Paper, No. 227, (January-February 2014), 2.

130. Loevinsohn, "Making Foreign Aid More Effective," 34.

131. BFWI, "Farmers: The Key to Ending Global Hunger," *Development Works*, no. 5 (December 2012). See also BFWI, *2013 Hunger Report*, 11.

132. Timothy King, ed., *Population Policies and Economic Development*, published for the World Bank (Baltimore: Johns Hopkins University Press, 1974), 54. See also William Rich, *Smaller Families through Social and Economic Progress*, monograph, no. 7 (Washington, DC: Overseas Development Council, 1973), esp. 76.

133. Todaro and Smith, *Economic Development* (2009), 731.

134. For these statistics, see Daniel Sylvia, "Is Foreign Aid Actually Aiding?" HardHatters, June 25, 2013, accessed July 25, 2014, www.hardhatters.com/2013/06/is-foreign-aid-aiding/.

135. BFWI, *2013 Hunger Report*, 182–185.

136. Bread for the World has long urged the U.S. Agency for International Development to work more with local organizations and foster country-owned and led programs. USAID's new "Local Solutions" program is moving in this direction.

137. Gary Haugen and Victor Boutros, *The Locust Effect: Why the End of Poverty Requires the End of Violence* (Oxford University Press, 2014).

138. See Denis Goulet, *Development Ethics: A Guide to Theory and Practice*, (New York: Zed Books, 1995), 158.

139. For this section on "tied" food aid, see *Bread*, January-February, 2014 and BFWI, "Reforming U.S. Food Aid" (Background Paper no 227, January–February, 2014).

140. See further BFWI, *2011 Hunger Report*, 86–88.

141. BFWI, *The Future of Foreign Aid*, 25–33.

142. For this section, see *The Way Forward: A Reform Agenda for 2014 and Beyond* by Modernizing Foreign Assistance Network (MFAN), a broad coalition of prominent organizations including Bread for the World. http://www.modernizeaid.net/documents/MFAN_Policy_Paper_April_2014.pdf.

143. See BFWI, *2011 Hunger Report*, 88–90.

144. *The Way Forward*, 6.

145. Ibid.

146. For a list of the many development assistance programs and which government agency implements them, see Bread for the World's "What's in the 'Basket' of Poverty-Focused Development Assistance (PFDA)?," March 2014, accessed July 25, 2014, http://bread.org/what-we-do/resources/newsletter/march-2014/fyi-pfda-accounts.html. For the 2014 Act which funds many things including economic development aid and military aid, see https://beta.congress.gov/bill/113th-congress/senate-bill/1372; accessed July 25, 2014

147. Quoted in BFWI, "Farmers: The Key to Ending Global Hunger," (2012).

148. Population Action International, "Closing the Gender Gap: Educating Girls," 1993.

149. Ibid. More recent studies have supported the claim that increasing women's education reduces infant mortality. See Elsie R. Pamuk, et al, "Comparing Relative Effects of Education and Economic Resources on Infant Mortality in Developing Countries," *Population and Development Review* 37, no 4 (December 2011):637-644. Pamuk, et al, suggest that increasing men's education alongside women's has an even greater effect on lowering infant mortality.

150. *Human Development Report 2013*, 89. Used with permission, see http://hdr.undp.org/en/content/copyright-and-terms-use.

151. "U.S. Overseas Loans and Grants," USAID, accessed July 25, 2014, http://gbk.eads.usaidallnet.gov/data/fast-facts.html.

152. Simon, *Bread for the World*, 113. (The figure in Simon's text was in 1975 dollars; 2014 figure based on Consumer Price Index, calculated by Bureau of Labor Statistics, accessed August 7, 2014, http://www.bls.gov/data/inflation_calculator.htm.

153. From the highly regarded Stockholm International Peace Research Institute's "SIPRI Fact Sheet," April 2014, 2. See p. 8 for what is included.

154. For the global military expenditures figure, see "SIPRI Fact Sheet," 1; The poorest billion persons earn approximately $456 billion ($1.25 times 365 days times 1 billion people), which is nearly one fourth of $1,747 billion.

155. Quoted in Simon, *Bread for the World*, 170.

156. Arthur Simon, *The Rising of Bread for the World*, (Mahwah, NJ: Paulist Press, 2009), 158.

157. BFWI, *2013 Hunger Report*, 101.

158. See Sider, *Fixing the Moral Deficit*, 138-139.

159. See www.evangelicalsforsocialaction.org.

160. www.jubileeusa.org/ourwork; accessed July 28, 2014.

161. www.iccr.org.

Epilogue

1. Robert Bellah says that "the quality of a culture may be changed when two percent of its people have a new vision" ("Civil Religion," *Psychology Today*, January 1976, 64).

2. See my "A Case for Easter," HIS, April 1972, pp. 27–31. For a more extensive discussion, see also my "The Historian, the Miraculous and Post-Newtonian Man," *Scottish Journal of Theology* 25 (1972):309–19; "The Pauline Conception of the Resurrection Body in 1 Cor 15:35–54," *New Testament Studies* 21 (1975): 428–39; "St. Paul's Understanding of the Nature and Significance of the Resurrection in 1 Cor 15:1–19," *Novum Testamentum* 19 (1977):1–18; and "Jesus' Resurrection and the Search for Peace and Justice," *Christian Century*, 3 November 1982, pp. 1103–08. See especially the superb scholarship in N.T. Wright, *Surprised by Hope: Rethinking Heaven, the Resurrection, and the Mission of the Church* (New York: HarperOne, 2008).

INDEX

Index

danger of, 101–5
goodness of, 105–7
poverty
absolute, 5
causes of, 129–43
escape from, xv
statistics, xiii, 4–5
power, imbalance of,
138–41
private property, xiv, 74,
75, 85, 97–101
private voluntary
organizations, 227
progress in combatting
poverty's ills, 5, 14,
19–21
public transportation,
192, 252, 254
Purchasing Power
Parity (PPP), 32, 33,
35

racism, 170–71
Reagan, Ronald, 235
Reba Place Fellowship,
190, 205–6, 215–16
recycling, 252
redistribution, 232, 235,
327–35
relief organizations,
evaluation of, 193–96
renewable energy, 253,
255
righteousness and riches,
107–9
river blindness, 19–20
Rodney, Walter, 310–34
Ronsvalle, John and
Sylvia, 198–99

sabbath and our
lifestyles, 201–2
sabbatical year, 77–79
Sagan, Carl, 241
Samuel, Vinay and
Colleen, xv
sanitation, access to
improved, 15
Schneider, John, 120–22,
300–15, 17
Schuller, Robert, 39–40
Sen, Amartya, 39, 170,
225, 237, 238, 308–4
Simon, Arthur, 265
Smith, Adam, 98
Snyder, Howard A., 215
social sin, 117, 120, 122,
125–26
South Africa, 136, 170
starvation statistics, 5
structural change, 220–23
structural injustice, 71,
116–22, 145–78
stunting, 16–17
sub-Saharan Africa, 6, 7,
9, 10, 17, 18, 19, 21, 22,
23, 34, 169, 259
Sudan, 171, 172–73
supply and demand, 75,
98, 148, 151, 154, 231
sustainable development,
238
Syria, 170, 171, 172

Tanzania, 8
tariffs and non-tariff
barriers, 157–59
Taylor, John V., 29, 108
television and
consumption, 28–29,
154

terrorism, 265, 271
Third World,
redefinition of, 8
Thurow, Lester, 131,
242–43
tied aid, 261
tithing, laws on, 79
Todaro, Michael, 236
trade barriers, 149,
157–59, 245–47, 316–66
trade unions, 149,
227–28, 248
Triple Five Plan, 217–18
Tripp, Linda, 170,
319–101

UNICEF, 21, 166
United Nations, 22, 134,
168–69, 172, 252, 253
United Nations
Development
Programme, 32, 172
Uruguay Round, 228
usury (charging high
interest), 80–81, 134

Vogt, Virgil, 205

Walter, H. W., 167
war, 171–73
war on terrorism, 265
water issues, 15, 151, 155,
175, 196
wealthy elites, 134–35,
152, 168, 174, 226–27
Wesley, John, 182–83,
207
Western colonialism,
139–41
Wilberforce, William,
177

341